Free and Easy?

Free and Easy?

A Defining History of the American Film Musical Genre

Sean Griffin

WILEY Blackwell

Registered Offices
John Wiley & Sons, Inc., 111 River Street, Hoboken, NJ 07030, USA
John Wiley & Sons Ltd, The Atrium, Southern Gate, Chichester, West Sussex, PO19 8SQ, UK

Editorial Office
9600 Garsington Road, Oxford, OX4 2DQ, UK

For details of our global editorial offices, customer services, and more information about Wiley products visit us at www.wiley.com.

Wiley also publishes its books in a variety of electronic formats and by print-on-demand. Some content that appears in standard print versions of this book may not be available in other formats.

Library of Congress Cataloging-in-Publication data applied for

Hardback ISBN: 9781405194969
Paperback ISBN: 9781405194952

Cover Design: Wiley
Cover Images: (top to bottom) © George Marks/Getty Images; © kparis/Getty Images;
             © proxyminder/Getty Images, Inc.

Set in 10/12pt Warnock by SPi Global, Pondicherry, India
Printed and bound in Malaysia by Vivar Printing Sdn Bhd

10 9 8 7 6 5 4 3 2 1

Contents

Acknowledgments

This book would not have been possible without the work done by so many others in this field—particularly to the trailblazers: Rick Altman, Jane Feuer, and Richard Dyer. Their foundational work has been ably supplemented by so many others, and I have attempted to give credit to as many as possible throughout the following pages. In particular, I wish to thank Steven Cohan, Adrienne McLean, and Desirée Garcia, three people with whom I have spent much time talking about musicals and who have impacted my thinking broadly and deeply. I also wish to thank the research staff at the Cinematic Arts Library at USC, the Special Collections Library at UCLA, and the Academy of Motion Picture Arts and Sciences Margaret Herrick Library for their assistance on this project over the years. I am also grateful to Southern Methodist University for providing funding so I could travel to these institutions, and to the faculty and students of the Division of Film & Media Arts for their encouragement and support. I would also be remiss if I did not thank my longtime editor and friend, Jayne Fargnoli, who did not hesitate when I proposed tackling this project. She has guided me through so many projects, and I am indebted to her beyond measure. I am also indebted to Drew Casper, whose course on the musical genre at USC back when I was a Masters student gave me the first sense that perhaps I wanted to become a film professor. Much love to my family and friends, particularly my husband Harry, who sat me down and made certain I watched *The Apple* (1980), and to both my Mom (who dutifully went to see *All That Jazz* [1979] with me because it was rated R and I was not 17 yet!) and my Dad (who instilled my love and respect for films at a very early age). And lastly, to all those who have been involved in the creation of the films and television celebrated herein—a toast to your imagination and determination.

Introduction

"Today, there is no single definition even of what constitutes a musical, period."

—Ethan Mordden[1]

What is a musical? When I teach a course on the musical film genre, the first thing I do the first day is ask students this question. I do not bring lecture notes to this first class session, because the entire class time is spent trying to agree on a definition—and the question is left open and looms over the rest of the semester. Over the course of writing this book, I have often asked friends and acquaintances over cocktails or dinner what they think a film musical is. Although there are common concepts that carry across people's reactions, I am constantly intrigued by the range of opinions. I do not judge who is right and who is wrong, but I often like to play devil's advocate—either coming up with an example of a movie that I know they will not think fits the definition they just voiced but that they will agree *is* a musical; or, conversely, coming up with an example of a film that *does* fit their parameters, but I am pretty certain they will *not* think is a musical. The conversations often get pretty heated, but in a fun and friendly way, leaving people mulling over the boundaries of the category "musical" more than they thought was possible.

Such a question has nipped at the heels of those writing about the musical film for ages, leading to the quote by musical theatre historian Ethan Mordden that opens this introduction. Barry Keith Grant, in *The Hollywood Film Musical*, admits in *his* Introduction that "the definition of the film musical is a matter of some debate."[2] Clive Hirschorn's *The Hollywood Musical* attempts to be encyclopedic in its overview, aiming "to be as complete a record of the genre as possible, but it clearly was essential, very early on, to establish workable guidelines as to what constitutes a 'musical' ... I remain painfully aware that there will always be room for disagreement."[3] Ethan Mordden's own history of *The Hollywood Musical* includes an entire chapter called "What's a Musical?," and Richard Barrios's *A Song in the Dark: The Birth of the Musical Film* also contains a chapter entitled "Is It a Musical?"[4] A number of articles foreground

Free and Easy? A Defining History of the American Film Musical Genre, First Edition. Sean Griffin.
© 2018 Sean Griffin. Published 2018 by John Wiley & Sons Ltd.

Figure 1 Is this a musical? Trixie Friganza looks on as Buster Keaton gets crowned in the comic operetta being filmed by the characters in *Free and Easy* (1930). Snapshot taken from: Free and Easy (1930).

this conundrum, such as Richard Dyer's "Is *Car Wash* a Musical?," Andrew Caine's "Can Rock Movies Be Musicals? The Case of *This Is Spinal Tap*," and Jane Feuer eventually asking "Is *Dirty Dancing* a Musical, and Why Should It Matter?"[5] The title of this volume is taken from a 1930 MGM movie that also begs this question (Figure 1). The film contains three songs and one reprise—and the first song is not introduced until a half hour into the picture. Many would consider the picture to be a comedy, particularly due to its star, Buster Keaton.

A central tenet of this book is to explore those limits, and I am purposefully, almost tauntingly, inclusive. It is quite possible that some readers will start to get downright argumentative at certain points, such as one student who said, "If you are going to try to tell me that *8 Mile* (2002) is a musical, we are going to have to take this out into the hall." If the following chapters elicit that reaction, then I have accomplished my mission. Why? I feel that the musical genre has been hampered for generations with a limited and limiting definition, one that has led to what I feel is an erroneous conclusion: that the film musical genre is dying or dead already. Jane Feuer recognizes the prevalence of "speaking of 'the musical' as if it were a static structure, a hygienically sealed system free from the lint of changing audience tastes and of those historical transformations other forms seem to endure."[6]

On an elemental level, musical films center around and focus predominantly on the performance of music and/or dance.[7] To leave it at this seems far too broad to many, and my expansive list of possible candidates for the genre emerges from the reliance on this clear-cut condition. Rick Altman, in his landmark work *The American Film Musical*, certainly felt so, writing that "critical work on the film musical continues to depend on a definition provided largely by the film industry itself ... a film with music, that is, with music that emanates from what I will call the diegesis, the fictional world created by the film."[8] He then argues that this is an unwieldy definition, "that every conceivable film with diegetic music [must then be] accepted and treated as a musical, from *Gilda* to *Singin' in the Rain*, from *Hallelujah* to *The Lady and the Tramp* [sic], from *Paramount on Parade* to *Woodstock*, from the films of Shirley Temple to those of Elvis Presley."[9] The seeming intention of this list is to incite incredulity in the reader that all of these movies could be considered musicals, and Altman moves on to establish criteria to limit the corpus of films. Yet, if Altman rejects the self-proclaimed authority of the film industry over matters of genre, then the self-proclaimed authority of the critic must come under scrutiny as well. If someone regards any or all of the above movies as musicals, who is Altman (or myself) to tell that person she or he is wrong?

I do agree that it is possible to parse this basic statement a bit further. In centering or focusing on the performance of music, there is the expectation that the viewer will be entertained or take pleasure from that performance. Many have suggested that such pleasure comes from the sense of music and dance as a form of heightened expression—that song lifts beyond ordinary speech, that dance expands movement of the body past the everyday motions. A common canard in discussing musical theatre is that "when the emotion becomes too strong for speech, you sing; when it becomes too strong for song, you dance."[10] In a certain way, song and dance present a sense of liberation from the normal constraints of existence. We enjoy watching performers accomplish those feats of liberation (remarkable singers, gifted dancers), vicariously experiencing that liberation ourselves.

Yet, while song and dance entice as moments of emotional and/or physical release, music and choreography are highly structured art forms. Music is written to a certain rhythm and organized according to a set of particular patterns. For example, the common rhythm of an American popular song in the first half of the twentieth century was a cycle of four beats, or four beats per measure, and songs were typically set at thirty-two measures: eight measures for the first verse, eight measures for the second verse (which was very like but just slightly different than the first verse in melody), eight measures for the bridge (a new melody), and eight measures for the concluding verse (a return to original melody, but often with a unique flourish to indicate the end of the tune). Similarly, lyrics had to match the structure of the melody, usually setting up a pattern of rhyming in the first eight bars that would carry through the rest of the piece (abab followed by cdcd, for example, or aaab followed by cccb). Dancers also needed to learn how to perform certain steps, to put them into particular combinations—and to have the dance match the music being played. Such established formats give artists a foundation to build upon, and give audiences a sense of comfort in recognizing (however unconsciously) how the structure works rather than feeling confused and alienated by something strange and unknown.

Thus, the entertainment or pleasure of experiencing music and dance performance is a delicate, ongoing balance between the comfort of structure and the joy of liberation. A number of songs, dance routines, and plotlines of musical theatre and cinema hew so closely to the established patterns that they become tedious. On occasion, some do the polar opposite, trying so hard to do something new and different that it creates a sense of bewilderment in audiences. (At times, audiences find what was new and strange has become less threatening because time has helped them grow accustomed to these new structural ideas.) The largest percentage of songs, dance routines, musical theatre productions, and musical films work within the accepted parameters, but with specific planned moments that push or go beyond the usual boundaries: a singer hits an unexpected high note, a lyric piles on multiple internal rhymes at a key point in the song, the dancer accomplishes a breathtakingly new move. They bend and expand the possibilities of the format, but without breaking it—or, to put it another way, using music terminology: theme and variations. Amy Herzog, in *Dreams of Difference, Songs of the Same: The Musical Moment in Film*, focuses on "this contradiction, between the sameness of the identical repetition and a movement toward transformation, difference, and excess."[11] Intriguingly (for my purposes), she asserts at the outset that she is "not interested in establishing film distinctions between musical and nonmusical films" and that "the majority of the films [she] reference[s] ... push the boundaries of the musical canon."[12]

The need to negotiate between freedom and order runs parallel with a common issue in discussing the musical genre: the relationship between the musical number and the narrative. The requirements of the plot and the ecstasy of the musical performance need to be merged somehow seamlessly in order for the whole piece to work. Sometimes the narrative is about the struggle to successfully perform the numbers—thus the numbers are the goal of the narrative. Another strategy is to have the characters feel so deeply moved that they shift from speech to song, from walking to dancing. Another strategy pushes this last idea to its farthest point: where there is no distinction between narrative and number and the entire story is sung and danced without any spoken dialogue and/or non-choreographed movement.

Many have used the narrative/number dichotomy as an entry point for a more specific definition of the genre, with the narrative providing structure and the number providing liberation. The narrative functions as the "real world," and many musicals follow a very tried-and-true set of plot clichés (boy meets girl, the show must go on, etc.). In counterpoint, the numbers are usually outside normal logic, presenting the audience with a sense of utopia (as Richard Dyer has famously put it), liberated from constraint and want.[13] Taking from Dyer, Barry Keith Grant asserts that "film musicals typically present their song—and/or—dance numbers in an imaginary space, even if this space is ostensibly a real location, and contained within a narrative framework," and Martin Rubin defines a musical as "a film containing a significant proportion of musical numbers that are impossible—i.e., persistently contradictory in relation to the realistic discourse of the narrative."[14] Yet, exactly who gets to determine when a "real location ... contained within a narrative framework" crosses over into an "imaginary space," or how many "impossible" numbers constitutes "a significant proportion" is left unspecified.[15] Perhaps the best example of an imaginary space or an impossible number happens in what Ian Conrich and Estella Tincknell call the "musical moment": "an isolated musical presence in a non-musical film." Yet, in order "to recognise the breadth and diversity of music's role in cinema," they do not give a particular definition of where the dividing line is between a musical and a "non-musical."[16]

Rick Altman considers the "dual-focus narrative" to be a foundational element to the musical film.[17] Whatever the environment or plotline, musicals almost without exception strongly revolve around a romance (almost exclusively heterosexual even today). Altman argues that unlike the usual Hollywood film, which focuses on a central protagonist, musicals alternate between the two characters as they gradually become one couple. As such, the two usually represent diametrically opposed backgrounds or belief systems, and it is only when those larger philosophical differences are resolved that the couple can come together (in a similar vein, it is not until the couple resolves differences that the show they are putting on can become a success). One is royalty, the other is a commoner; one is intellectual, the other is a hedonist; one is a Yankee, the other hails from the deep South. By introducing the courting pair with different outlooks and goals, the dual-focus narrative pits the dreams of liberation of one character in seeming opposition to the other's. One person would find their joy and freedom at the expense of the other. So, the desire to come together (the comfort of a shared structured relationship) comes into conflict with the desire for individual freedom. Just like the basic aspect of the musical (the entertainment in how musical performance somehow expresses liberation within a structured context), the plot must figure out how each individual (and his or her supporters) must fulfill their individual dreams *and* successfully bring people together. The farmer's happiness (raising crops) comes at the cowman's expense (no room for herding cattle)—and vice versa ... but, as *Oklahoma!* asserts, "The farmer and the cowman should be friends ..."

Revolving around this dichotomy of liberation versus structure, the rights of the individual versus the needs of the community, the musical genre has similarities with the themes many have analyzed in relation to the Western genre.[18] Writers have pointed out a central negotiation between the lure of the frontier and the value of civilization. The frontier is open with possibility, unshackled by laws or social demands, but it is also dangerous, primitive, and untamed. The coming of civilization is thus welcomed, but with a certain sense of melancholy in a loss of freedom. The key figure in most Westerns is a loner figure—someone who rides in to defend the town and ensure civilization is established, but who is not considered a member of the community and usually rides off into the sunset (i.e., the frontier) once order is restored. Thus, somehow both sides are revered and respected. Both the Western and the musical balance between championing the freedom of the individual and endorsing the comfort of community ritual.

The rights of the individual and the needs of the community are also foundational tenets in the founding of the United States of America—fighting for the rights of "life, liberty, and the pursuit of happiness," but recognizing the value in bonding together as a nation to win that fight. The Western genre has been long regarded as a genre tied to American national identity. Similarly, Rick Altman's "Coda" at the conclusion to the anthology *The International Film Musical* points out "the importance of American films for both the widespread popularity and the widely accepted definition of the musical."[19] Of course, American musical theatre was, and continues to be, influenced by the cultures of other nations. Furthermore, many other countries have longstanding traditions of music-oriented filmmaking and theatre. As such, the same questions over genre crop up in Altman's "Coda." Under a subsection titled "Just What Is a Musical?," he asks, "Do fans of the Brazilian *chanchada* think of musicals in the same terms as viewers of the Mexican *comedia ranchera*? Do habitués of French realist singers or the films of René Clair employ the same definition of the musical as lovers of the films of Herbert Wilcox or 1930s stage stars? Is the Portugese *fado* defined in the same way as the Japanese *salaryman* film?"[20] These films, reflecting their own cultural concerns, might not feel as focused on the balance between freedom and structure, between the individual and the community. Yet, the global reach of American popular music and Hollywood cinema has resulted in an international familiarity with how the United States has developed a form of musical theatre and musical film—so much so that a number of films made in other countries adopt the patterns and themes of the American musical.

The balance between the individual and the group is a major issue not only on stage or on screen, but also in the making of musicals. Collaboration is key in creating a musical. Composers and lyricists must establish a compatible working relationship. The two of them work in conjunction with the author of the libretto (or book), as well as the choreographer, the director, and the producer. Performers need to meet the requirements of the production—often having to learn how to blend voices, or dance as a unit. A number of Hollywood musicals, commonly referred to as backstagers, depict the need to form a strong-knit community in order to put on a show. The obstacle to such bonding is often the ego of a particular individual. The history of the musical itself can be told as the story of people in different creative positions jockeying for dominant artistic control, asserting that they should have the freedom to express their individual creative vision, and everyone else should follow. Producers such as Florenz Ziegfeld or Walt Disney asserted that they were the leaders. Stars such as Al Jolson or Barbra Streisand claimed the spotlight around which everything else was built. Songwriters, particularly Rodgers and Hammerstein and their progeny, gained an upper hand by claiming that their scores unified projects into cohesive wholes (an argument that gained momentum when many of them became producers as well). After World War II, a number of choreographers began taking on the role of director, such as Jerome Robbins and Bob Fosse, and made arguments similar to songwriters: that *they* were the glue that pulled all of the elements together into a tightly organized piece.

The musical film represents the resolution of these two basic but seemingly contradictory tenets of the American psyche as a form of utopia. Yet, like the struggles between artists collaborating on a production, conflicts over who and what was considered American have been ongoing. The population of the country is a combination of different cultural heritages and community identities. Over the centuries, various groups were demeaned and excluded from being considered American—along with aspects of their culture (including their forms of music and dance). The dominant culture (white, European, male) worked consistently to promote its customs and artistic taste as authentically American, and those from minority communities were considered either inferior subcultures or alien. A strong counter-argument began developing during the 1800s that a uniquely American culture formed out of the blending of these various cultures. A further counter-argument developed to the celebration of the American "melting pot": that assimilation into the dominant culture only exploited and diluted the cultures of the disempowered, and oppressed communities should maintain their individual traditions. Jane Feuer has famously pointed out that "the Hollywood musical becomes a mass art which aspires to the condition of folk art," in order to mask the process of exploitation and commodification in the production of musical films.[21]

American musical entertainment has been involved in these discussions from the very beginning, coming up with different formulas in response to shifts in the population and the effects of various historical events. Musical entertainment could reinforce established patterns of belief towards racial minorities, women, and individuals who would eventually be categorized as homosexual. Yet, these same marginalized people were able to use musical entertainment for their own benefit—providing a unique opportunity to break free (however limited in time and scope) from the usual restrictions placed upon them in daily life. Their performance of new and unique types of music and dance gave them a great amount of attention from and influence on the dominant culture, thus helping shift attitudes and challenge stereotypes. In celebrating individual freedom and championing the value of a community, minoritized artists and audience found a genre that supported the concept of a community united in diversity.

As social, economic, and even technological circumstances changed, the musical genre evolved in how it defined America, defined utopia, and defined how best to combine the ecstasy of liberation with the pleasure of structural familiarity. American music and dance changed across the generations: from the folk song to ragtime to jazz to rock to rap, from the quadrille to the time-step to the Charleston to the Twist to the moonwalk. The recognized structure of live musical theatre also shifted over the decades: vaudeville to loosely structured book shows to integrated musicals to concept musicals. Yet, somehow, at a certain point, the evolution of how people defined the film musical genre stopped. Currently, historians and the average moviegoer employ a structure that became dominant right after World War II, and that definition has not been able to shift since: the integrated musical where dialogue alternates with song and dance that arises within the context of the storyline (i.e., singing when individuals should be talking, dancing when they should be walking), revealing aspects of the characters and/or advancing the plotline. I am not attempting to argue that films that fit this pattern are *not* musicals—but there are so many other ways of celebrating and focusing on musical performance that do not match this description. Many histories of the film musical describe the late 1920s and the 1930s as a sort of infancy for the genre, exploring various ways of presenting musical performance *before* the genre finally matured into its proper correct format in the mid-1940s. These histories thus report that the rejection of the integrated film musical by most audiences at the end of the 1960s resulted in the collapse of the genre as a whole. Such an assessment may explain why there has not been a new historical survey of the genre in many years: why bother writing anything if there is nothing new to report?

A central aim of this volume is to argue that there has been far too much emphasis on the comfort of the familiar structure of the integrated musical, and not enough celebration of liberation from that definition. For, whether or not critics or general audiences care to admit it, the film musical has survived ably, by evolving into new patterns and structures regardless of attempts to keep it locked in place. This book asks the reader to open him- or herself up to the potential excitement of a new regard for the film musical, to enjoy the variety of forms the genre can take rather than keeping myopically attached to one specific formula. Musicals can be integrated narratives, but they might also be concert films. Or filmed opera. Or animated cartoons. Or biographies of musicians. *The Jazz Singer* (1927) has more in common with *8 Mile* than you might imagine! *The Wizard of Oz* (1939) and *Woodstock* (1970) are kindred spirits.

Figure 2 Is this a musical? Ice Cube (O'Shea Jackson, Jr) certainly seems to be "putting on a show" in *Straight Outta Compton* (2015), a biography of the rap group N.W.A. Snapshot taken from: Straight Outta Compton (2015).

On the Town (1949) and *Straight Outta Compton* (2015) are arguably just points on a continuum rather than utterly estranged from each other (Figure 2). The farmer and the cowman should be friends, I'm just sayin'...

Notes

1 Ethan Mordden, *On Sondheim: An Opinionated Guide* (Oxford: Oxford University Press, 2016), 29.
2 Barry Keith Grant, *The Hollywood Film Musical* (Malden: Wiley-Blackwell, 2012), 1.
3 Clive Hirschorn, *The Hollywood Musical*, 2nd ed. (New York: Portland House, 1991), 9.
4 Ethan Mordden, *The Hollywood Musical* (New York: St. Martin's Press, 1981), 17–23; Richard Barrios, *A Song in the Dark: The Birth of the Musical Film* (Oxford: Oxford University Press, 1995), 309–322.
5 Richard Dyer, "Is *Car Wash* a Musical?," *In the Space of a Song: The Uses of Song in Film* (New York: Routledge, 2012), 145–155; Andrew Caine, "Can Rock Movies Be Musicals? The Case of *This Is Spinal Tap*," *The Shifting Definitions of Genre: Essays on Labeling Films, Television Shows and Media*, ed. Lincoln Geraghty and Mark Jancovich (Jefferson: McFarland & Co., 2008), 124–141; and Jane Feuer, "Is *Dirty Dancing* a Musical, and Why Should It Matter?," *The Time of Our Lives: "Dirty Dancing" and Popular Culture*, ed. Yannis Tzioumakis and Sian Lincoln (Detroit: Wayne University Press, 2013), 59–72.
6 Jane Feuer, *The Hollywood Musical*, 2nd ed. (Bloomington: Indiana University Press, 1993), 87.

7 Grant, 1, uses a similar starting definition: "films that involve the performance of song and/or dance by the main characters and also include singing and/or dancing as an important element."

8 Rick Altman, *The American Film Musical* (Bloomington: Indiana University Press, 1987), 12.

9 Altman, *American Film Musical*, 13.

10 For example, see comments by Ben Wattenberg in a discussion with a variety of musical theatre artists for his PBS program *Think Tank* (transcript can be found at http://www.pbs.org/thinktank/transcript1261.html).

11 Amy Herzog, *Dreams of Difference, Songs of the Same: The Musical Moment in Film* (Minneapolis: University of Minnesota Press, 2010), 2.

12 Herzog, 2–3.

13 Richard Dyer, "Entertainment and Utopia," *Movie* 24 (Spring 1977).

14 Martin Rubin, "Busby Berkeley and the Backstage Musical," *Hollywood Musicals, The Film Reader*, ed. Steve Cohan (London: Routledge, 2002), 57; *Grant*, 1.

15 Rubin, 57.

16 Ian Conrich and Estella Tincknell, *Film's Musical Moments* (Edinburgh: Edinburgh University Press, 2006), 2.

17 Rick Altman, *American Film Musical*, 16–58.

18 See Robert Warshow, "Movie Chronicle: The Westerner" (1954) in *Film Theory and Criticism: Introductory Readings*, 6th ed., ed. Leo Braudy and Marshall Cohen (Oxford: Oxford University Press, 2004), 703–716; Will Wright, *Six Guns and Society: A Structural Study of the Western* (Berkeley: University of California Press, 1975).

19 Rick Altman, "Coda—The Musical as International Genre: Reading Notes," *The International Film Musical*, ed. Corey Creekmur and Linda Y. Mokdad (Edinburgh: Edinburgh University Press, 2012), 258.

20 Altman, "Coda," 258.

21 Jane Feuer, *Hollywood Musical*, 3.

1

Overture: Musical Traditions before Cinema

Although the film musical celebrates a sense of liberation, the genre is itself beholden to a long heritage of music composition and performance. Thus, to start a history of the musical film with the making of *The Jazz Singer* (1927)— or even the earliest sound experiments—would be incomplete. Many writers on the film genre have examined the influence of live American theatrical entertainment.[1] Like those works, this opening chapter will survey the stage traditions that shaped what would be done on celluloid. Yet, the film musical's history requires more than acquaintance with musical theatre's history; it also necessitates some basic awareness of the history of American music at large, going back to before the United States had formed as an independent nation.

The musical film would inherit centuries of material and mindsets, laying out a number of well-established aesthetic as well as industrial and social patterns. In addition to showing how much the past would bear upon what the musical film would or could do, the history of American music is itself rife with examples of battles between freedom and control, oscillating between music as an example of individual expression and music as a type of communal bond. Various religious and political forces attempted to stifle certain forms of music and/or dance, usually over their perceived ability to liberate sexual desires. As a nation of multiple communities, various cultures mingled and sometimes clashed over each other's musical tastes. Achieving individual freedom of musical expression often came at the expense of others, most obviously in regard to racial or ethnic minority groups. As an industry formed around music, composers, performers, and publishers often struggled with each other over who was in control of the music. The musical film would not only take on many of the idioms established from earlier eras, it would also inherit these cultural negotiations and battles. Central to these interactions is the quest to define a national identity—what exactly did it mean to "be an American," and how did its music reflect this new nationality? Primary to an emergent American identity was the importance of individual liberty—but how could people come together as a national community by championing one's independence?

Free and Easy? A Defining History of the American Film Musical Genre, First Edition. Sean Griffin.
© 2018 Sean Griffin. Published 2018 by John Wiley & Sons Ltd.

Music and Dance in Early America

Rhythm, melody, and movement have been intimately tied to a sense of community and shared outlook on the world since the first instances of human civilization, and thus it is no surprise that they figured strongly within North America long before the United States declared its independence from Great Britain. Song and dance were fundamental elements to the wide variety of indigenous cultures. As with numerous other groups, music holds special importance in Native American rituals and ceremonies, vital practices that bind individuals together. Since most of these cultures relied almost exclusively on oral communication, song was also used to maintain historical memory, as well as to share tribal myths and legends. The importance of the oral tradition has remained through the centuries—and, if anything, increased as various communities were threatened (and many extinguished) with the advent of the white man. Along with the spoken word, song became a vital method literally to keep culture alive. Thus, there has grown enormous responsibility to preserve these songs and stories.

The absence of written evidence obviously requires a lot of conjecture in analyzing native cultures prior to contact with European explorers and settlers. Yet, studies tend to agree on certain patterns.[2] For example, certain figures within communities took on special roles as the keepers of the stories and of the songs. While there was pressure from within the groups to remember and repeat the tales and the structure of the songs, it was inevitable that singers and storytellers would (either intentionally or not) vary the words, the organization, and the melodies across time, and from generation to generation. Without written notation, music was thus controlled primarily by the singer. Most surviving instances of native North American music also strongly emphasize rhythm rather than melody, which allows the singer greater freedom to vary the notes from performance to performance. Lastly, when used in ceremonies or rituals, such music often went on for hours. The emphasis on rhythm over melody was tied to such uses—but also led to long and repetitive pieces. Such repetition could etch melodic patterns into community memory, but could also allow for variation as the repetitions continued.

When Europeans began settling on the east coast of North America, many regarded native tribes as primitive and animalistic, and branded their music as "heathen." Influenced by the Reformation, many early settlers attempted to forsake "sins of the flesh"—and thus as a rule regarded secular music as morally corrupt. Sacred music, on the other hand, was considered a unique method of speaking to God—and in this way, hymns paralleled music used in native rituals that helped individuals feel their interconnectedness to the rest of their community and to all of nature. Illiteracy was still incredibly common, particularly among those not of noble birth or part of the emerging bourgeoisie. Thus, as with the oral tradition in native cultures, most hymns were learned by ear. These early settlers either failed to recognize or purposefully ignored the similarities between native use of music and their own investment in music.[3]

Religious communities were not the only ones arriving on North American shores from Europe, and those settlers brought with them varied traditions of music making and dance from their homelands. The sense of rhythm, harmony, and melody structure differed from that in Native American cultures, and a history of "serious" music had also instituted a method of written notation to ensure a composition would remain the same each time it was performed. The rise of notated "classical" music increased the authority (and reputation) of the composer over the musician or vocalist, giving rise to renowned figures such as Bach, Handel, and Mozart.[4] Such attitudes would cross the Atlantic as musicians performed these works, or as composers used the same methods in creating their own works. Even churches started printing up collections of hymns for use at services. Further, the development of written notation—sheet music—would create a method to sell music, forming what would eventually become a major entertainment industry by the start of the twentieth century. Yet, the oral tradition still existed. In contrast to classical music, often commissioned and performed for nobility, folk songs among the working-class or peasant communities were shared at gatherings or at taverns, and still privileged the singer over the songwriter (so much so that the authors of these tunes are largely unknown).[5]

Another important source of musical heritage came with the arrival of Africans to the continent, most of them as slaves. The music of the African nations held much in common with that of Native American communities: rhythm-based and passed from generation to generation orally rather than in written form. Of course, captured and taken against their will, Africans transplanted to American shores were able to bring precious little but themselves and what they were able to hold in their memories. Hence, the oral tradition was practically the only option available to them in maintaining a connection to their heritage. Responding to the situation, slaves of African descendancy learned how to use music not only to hold onto their sense of self but also to survive in a hostile environment. The form of "call and response," in which a song acts as a dialogue between people, became a key method for slaves to bond with each other *and* to communicate with each other in ways their white European owners did not recognize. Call and response then was used as a method of resistance, including at times helping organize means of escape. Also, while creating a cultural bond, call and response emphasizes the talent and creativity of the individual performer involved, that each particular instance is unique and will never be sung in the exact same fashion again. It must be noted that singing among the slaves had its benefits for slave owners too. Not only did such singing provide entertainment for them, it also let owners know where slaves were even when they were out of sight.[6]

As the settlements became colonies and then states, these various forms of music encountered and interacted with each other, creating a variety of blends and influences. European styles of music dominated, since white Europeans and their progeny sat at the top of the power structure within the United States. Yet, the various cultures (and the people themselves) were bound to intermingle, no matter how hard some may have attempted to keep them separate. The Louisiana port of New Orleans serves as an apt example.[7] The mixing of European, African, and Native American blood resulted in a new identity termed Creole (although attempts to distinguish a racial hierarchy within that term still happened). Growing into a major city, New Orleans also began developing a vibrant and unique type of music, drawing from a variety of sources: French opera (since it began as a French settlement), other European popular songs courtesy of traveling sailors, plus Native American music and slave music. This type of mélange would result in styles of music unique to the United States.

Dance evolved along similar patterns. If music was potentially devil's work for religious settlers, dance definitely was too sensual and of the flesh. Hence, dancing was routinely forbidden, and one of the ways Native Americans were demonized as sinful heathens by these Christian fundamentalists was the way natives danced for hours in tribal gatherings. While European settlers tended to regard Native American dancing with curiosity and reprobation, their form of dance functioned largely the same way as did their music, as a way of maintaining and passing on ritual beliefs, myths, and history. Dance was as much a form of communication as music and, as such, did contain at least a basic structure (even if it was incomprehensible to the white explorers who witnessed it).

Of course, not all Europeans shunned dancing, and as others came to America they brought not only their music but also their styles of dance. Just as serious European music was put down on paper in order to maintain control over any performance of it, respectable social dance in Europe was highly structured, with specific steps to learn and repeat: gavottes, rounds, and so forth. Such structure helped a roomful of people dance fluidly as a group, but also helped quell the potential liberating qualities of dance that churchgoers feared. Such free joyous exhilaration could be found in many of the folk dances popular across Europe, used in village celebrations or at the local tavern. Jigs, clog dances, and the like brought people together as much as did the strict rules of a cotillion, but with less structure and more energy.[8]

Slaves from Africa attempted to preserve the style and meaning of dance in their home cultures, but often faced resistance from their masters for doing so. While owners found value in the performance of call and response among slaves, native African dancing seemed too akin to the way Native Americans danced, which was regarded as sinful, anarchic, and potentially violent. Choreographer Leni Sloan, in the documentary *Ethnic Notions* (1986), describes how African American slaves reacted to a prohibition on dancing by shuffling their feet in a manner that cunningly skirted the law's definition of dance. White viewers found amusement in such movements, seeing this shuffling as evidence of the primitive nature of people of African descent. Eventually white performers began to copy and exaggerate those movements, creating perhaps the first national dance craze, "Jump Jim Crow," in the late 1820s.[9] Thus, just as with the music, the intersection of the various forms was beginning to create a style of dance unique to the new nation, and one developed out of the power dynamic between freedom and control.

The Development of American Theatre

Various forms of presentation of song and dance to an audience had also developed in various cultures, going back at least to the days of ancient Greek theatre, with the inclusion of a chorus that commented in musical chant on the characters and action. The state of European theatre held sway over the United States as it gained independence, from high-class concerts and operas to the more bawdy entertainments aimed at the groundlings. Opera focused on epic narratives, structured around "arias" (the more lyrical melodic set pieces for the main singers) and "recitative" (sung portions that were not as memorable melodically, often involving dialogue between characters). Theatres for opera and other "legitimate" productions could be found in most major cities across the States, but more common were troupes of performers who traveled from community to community across the vast expanse of states and territories. Such companies would set up a tent or outdoor venue and put on a production for a few days before heading elsewhere.[10] The level of talent and even the type of entertainment varied wildly, and customers often could get both a Shakespearean soliloquy and a rousing off-color sing-along in the same show. Striving for cultural legitimacy, American actors, musicians, and writers followed the example of Europe—but many also strove to carve out a uniquely American style of theatre, as the entire country grappled with defining exactly what "being American" meant.

Arguably, the first particularly American form of theatrical musical entertainment came to prominence by the 1840s: minstrelsy.[11] The term derived from medieval Europe, referring to those who sang as a profession, either for the amusement of nobility or for other groups as they wandered from village to village. American minstrel shows likewise traveled from place to place, with the explicit idea of the lowly hoping to entertain their betters, for minstrel shows presented white performers doing a version of black song and dance for the delight of white customers (Figure 1.1). The popularity of white performers made up to look like black slaves singing and dancing "Jump Jim Crow" led to an entire form of theatrical entertainment. Little to no attempt was done to provide authentic representation of black culture in minstrel shows, though.

Figure 1.1 An advertisement for a minstrel show (ca. 1840), arguably the first particularly American form of theatrical musical entertainment, with white performers in blackface singing "Ethiopian melodies" or "coon songs." Snapshot taken from: Ethnic Notions (1986).

Rather, black people were impersonated as grotesque buffoons for the amusement of white audiences. The makeup style, known as blackface, was one of clownish exaggeration—as were the typical mannerisms and dialect employed by the performers. Stephen Foster and other composers developed an entire genre called "coon songs," versions of what Anglo Americans thought African Americans sang, and such songs gained popularity beyond the minstrel shows. By the 1840s, such entertainment was popular all over the country, not just the slave-holding states, and minstrel troupes traveled westward to all of the new territories being formed.

Such music was often accompanied by dance, again with white performers in blackface doing versions of what they saw being done within black communities. African Americans took the rhythmic possibilities in European clog dancing and slowly evolved it into a new form, creating more complex rhythms than before and employing more full body dexterity (traditional clog dancing tends to emphasize the feet stomping, with the upper body remaining rigid). Imitations of this new type of dance were often included in minstrel shows. Eventually, towards the end of the century, shoes replaced clogs with lighter-weight metal taps on the soles, making a cleaner sound with less effort. Tap dancing, by African Americans and others, would become one of the top forms of musical dance performance in the United States by the end of the century, long after minstrel shows had lost their audience.[12]

The format of minstrel shows exhibits a balance between control and freedom. For example, the songs, dances, and jokes were not tethered to an overarching story, but an organizational framework *did* exist. Each production began with a semicircle of male performers in rows (depending on how large the company was), all in blackface except for the man in the center, the interlocutor, who oversaw and introduced the various songs and dances done by the rest. The most prominent blackface performers were seated at either end of the stage, referred to as Mr. Tambo and Mr. Bones (after the instruments they played). Jokes arose when the interlocutor would converse with either of these two. The next act moved into various skits (called "olio"), usually farcical views of Southern plantation life, often ending with a parody (or "burlesque") of a popular play, opera, or other cultural event.

The inherent racism of minstrelsy cannot be denied, presenting incredibly stereotypical, ignorant blacks trying to act hifalutin, but still under the supervision of a white leader. The prevalence of sexual humor also reinforced common white opinion that black people were oversexualized and uncivilized, closer to animals than human beings. Further, minstrelsy also supported a notion that African Americans are naturally musical. Yet, the widespread popularity of minstrelsy also indicates the amount of fascination black culture exerted over white America. Also, one of the sources of humor in minstrel shows came from the blackface performers breaking cultural taboos or making fun of societal norms. White performers thus were able to use blackface to break free from the restrictions of what could be said or done in regular life, and white audiences could take delight in seeing someone break those rules as well. Thus, while maintaining an expected structure of performance and exerting cultural dominance over the African American community, a large aspect of the popularity of minstrel shows was their carnivalesque nature: debunking those in power, upending social propriety, and offering comedic anarchy—if only for a few hours.[13]

A sizeable percentage of minstrel performers were Irish and then Jewish immigrants who felt ostracized from WASP society. Cultural historians have described how these artists used blackface in strategic ways.[14] Firstly, donning blackface helped them argue for acceptance into white American society by demonstrating their need to "darken up" to play African American characters. At the same time, though, these ethnic groups had their own experiences with prejudice and oppression, and blackface minstrelsy gave them an outlet to express their frustrations and to rebel against the establishment in a sanctioned manner. The burlesques of high culture that occurred in the final act (such as Shakespeare or an Italian opera) lambasted the pretensions of the elite, and the lack of any narrative in the opening semicircle promoted an atmosphere of chaotic hilarity that the white interlocutor could barely contain.[15] The carnivalesque environment also encompassed issues of sexuality and gender, for these all-male troupes regularly did lowbrow female impersonations as well (also in blackface). Just as minstrel shows could employ racist caricature to challenge the powers that be, men in drag often portrayed women in incredibly sexist and misogynist ways but also made fun of and complicated gender roles and sexual desires to the delight of the audience.

Minstrel shows continued to tour throughout the rest of the nineteenth century, but lost dominance in the wake of the Civil War and the post-slavery Restoration Era. By the late 1800s, the olio structure featured within minstrelsy had become its own type of theatrical entertainment, and was eventually rechristened as "vaudeville" ("music hall" in Britain, or "variety" in the rest of Europe). Vaudeville consisted of a series of unrelated acts presented on one bill. Singers or dancers in blackface did continue to take the stage in vaudeville, but that was only one of many forms of entertainment to be found. Vaudeville emphasized its diversity, presenting comedians, singers, dancers, dog acts, jugglers, magicians, performing seals, contortionists, and more. Performers would travel all over the country from theatre to theatre, doing two or three shows a day, with the bill changing every week. As with minstrel shows, vaudeville's emphasis on spectacle and a wide range of entertainment seemed to have a liberating sense of randomness, but some form of structure did exist. Similar types of performers were not placed next to each other (so a singer was not followed by another singer), in order to accentuate the variety of talent. Also, the first on the bill was usually the lowest rung (the least popular performer), and the last was the star headliner. Lastly, because vaudeville theatres aimed at middle-class customers (offering hours of entertainment at a lower cost than serious theatre, opera, or ballet), theatre owners made certain not to hire acts that engaged in the more crude sexual humor that ran rampant during the heyday of minstrelsy.[16]

The burlesque portion of minstrelsy also became popular as its own form (and without the blackface) at end of the 1800s. Burlesque theatres initially emphasized the presentation of parodies of popular high-class entertainment or of important historical events. In tearing down the importance of these historical or cultural institutions, these burlesques often relied on sexual puns and other risqué humor, thus holding onto the ribaldry that vaudeville consciously eschewed. While minstrel shows were traditionally all male, stand-alone burlesque began including female performers rather than actors in drag. Thus, actual women became involved in the verbal and physical forms of sexual humor in burlesque. Eventually, the sexual nature of burlesque became the main attraction, with the parodies gradually replaced by comics doing brief routines or skits with a troupe of female performers who then dominated the rest of the program with their striptease routines, baring as much as they could without getting arrested (and sometimes failing in that effort).[17]

As the twentieth century began, burlesque was largely considered trash and on the margins of American culture. While the dominant reason for this attitude was the emphasis on sexual titillation, burlesque was also demeaned because it had become one of the last vestiges of what had once been a prevalent form of engagement between the performers and the audience. For centuries, in Europe long before the United States became an independent nation, theatregoing was a participatory activity. Attendees not only laughed at or cried to whatever was being performed, they also regularly voiced their reactions openly, and interacted with those on stage both negatively (heckling, booing, or throwing things) or positively (demanding an encore of a well-performed speech or song). Conversations between those on stage and audience members during a performance were also common. This type of behavior was just as common at the opera or a performance of Shakespeare as it was at a minstrel show. In the late 1800s, though, attempts grew to bring the audience under control, instructing them to remain quiet, polite, and attentive to the artists on stage. The lower the aesthetic regard, the more rowdy the audience was allowed to be. Thus, since vaudeville was lower than legitimate theatre, it still had its share of hecklers, as well as the opportunity for audience sing-alongs. Burlesque, as the lowest rung, had strippers and cheap comics continuously interacting with its customers.[18]

The burlesque queen was considered to be little more than a prostitute by mainstream society, an attitude that carried across to women in the theatrical profession by and large during the 1800s and early 1900s. Burlesque, vaudeville, and the emerging form of musical theatre regularly employed lines of "chorus girls"—skimpily clad dancers, specifically on stage to be on display, without any character names or lines of dialogue. Nonetheless, the sheer existence of women on stage challenged previous cultural gender norms, offering female customers a vision of a life outside the home.[19] By the late 1800s, all forms of theatre had become a space for women to carve out careers. As such, actresses, singers, and dancers could potentially gain a level of financial independence and security unavailable to most other women in the United States at the time. Some women gained such popularity that they were able to run their own theatrical companies, such as Eleanora Duse and Laura Keene.[20] Ironically, the roles for these powerful women were often limited to characters that upheld the value of marriage and motherhood—and characters that attempted to break free of such strictures inevitably suffered the consequences of such actions.

Women performing in legitimate theatre were more sheltered from scorn because of the association with "high art" and the continued influence of Europe, including its music. Divas such as Jenny Lind sang with a polished, trained voice that connoted respectability. While star performers mattered greatly within opera or ballet, the composers held prominence as well—unlike the composers of music for minstrel shows, vaudeville, and burlesque. In those forms, songs were taken from a variety of writers rather than one artist, and the performer was what drew audiences. Operas, on the other hand, relied on a central composer to shape a stylistically coherent, sung-through narrative. In the 1800s, a new style, dubbed "light opera" or *"opera bouffe,"* emerged in

Europe, eventually evolving into a form with the name "operetta." Such theatre employed trained voices and the lush soaring melodies found in operatic arias, but contained dialogue between such songs (replacing the recitative used in conventional opera) and tended to tell more escapist storylines. The work done by Jacques Offenbach in France and Franz Lehar in Austria also brought dance more centrally into the story than traditional opera tended to do.[21] Perhaps even more influential were the operettas written by the British team of Gilbert and Sullivan. Their light operas regularly satirize modern society, and contain not only typical operatic melodies, but also "patter songs" that are more rhythmic than melodic, in order to splay out various jokes in rapid fire, such as "I Am the Very Model of a Modern Major-General" from their 1879 production, *The Pirates of Penzance.* The dry humor of their librettos and the inclusion of patter songs began to turn operetta further away from traditional opera and into a potentially new form of musical entertainment. Many of these works were brought over from Europe and performed in the States.[22]

Where light opera turns into what we now call musical theatre is in the eye of the beholder. Many have retroactively listed *The Black Crook* as the first American musical, which premiered in New York in 1866, and toured extensively across the country through the 1870s.[23] Although theatre historians cannot definitively verify the particulars, supposedly a ballet troupe from Paris was left stranded during an American tour when the theatre where they were hired to perform burned to the ground. A theatre company agreed to wedge them into the melodramatic spectacular they were about to premiere, turning the production into something less than a light opera, but definitely more narrative-based than a minstrel show or vaudeville. Others soon attempted to copy its success, but an official recognition of a new type of entertainment called "musical theatre" would still be decades away.

Imported European operettas continued to dominate through the end of the century, leading a number of American composers to try their own hand at it. Victor Herbert began to rival his European contemporaries in popularity, writing the scores for operettas such as *Babes in Toyland* (first produced in 1903), *Naughty Marietta* (1910), and *Sweethearts* (1913). Other American composers writing for the theatre started working in a less operatic vein, bringing something of the style of music found in vaudeville and trying to input it into the narrative structure traditional to opera and operetta. Writing at the same time as Herbert was George M. Cohan, who had begun his career in vaudeville. The songs Cohan composed were jauntier than those found in operetta, and more easily sung by the average person. He also became well known for writing explicitly patriotic tunes, such as "The Yankee Doodle Boy" and "It's a Grand Old Flag," as if announcing that a uniquely American songwriter was breaking away from European influence.[24] As the 1900s began, a new sound was emerging within American culture, and its rise would be employed to create a unique form of American musical theatre as well.

The Rise of "American" Music

Just as the confluence of various racial, ethnic, and class-identified cultures began to merge into various unique forms of theatrical entertainment, so too did their interaction help a new music establish itself across the United States. Towards the end of the 1800s, march music (mostly remembered today through the work of composer John Phillip Sousa) was absorbed and transformed by African American musicians in St. Louis and other cities into what was soon referred to as "ragtime." Ragtime's emphasis on syncopated melody sat atop and energized the strong bass beat found in marches, and quickly caught fire across the country. Its evocation of vitality and confidence seemed to speak for an American sense of boisterous potential in the wake of the Industrial Revolution. Whole new worlds were opening up due to new inventions, and ragtime's brash and jaunty sound matched the feel of life moving at a faster pace.[25]

Dances were introduced to accompany the new sound: the cakewalk, the turkey trot, the Texas Tommy, and the bunny hug. Such dances did not involve complicated choreography, but did require being able to move to a different rhythm than the conventional European ballroom dances, having originated within either African American neighborhoods or working-class dance halls. They also involved dance partners holding each other, which shocked and outraged some citizens as much as the waltz had done when it was introduced to polite society across Europe in the mid-1700s.[26]

Although the foundations of ragtime are primarily from African American culture, the musical heritage of Eastern and Southern Europe (especially from Russian and German Jews) also influenced its sound. Such an amalgamation was possible because of the influx of immigrants from such parts of Europe into the working-class neighborhoods of such US urban centers as New York City, Chicago, and St. Louis. At the same time, African Americans swept up to these same cities in a "Great Migration" out of the formerly slave-holding South, in hopes of finding more economic opportunities and less discrimination. Each of these communities brought their musical heritage with them, making it possible literally to walk across the city streets and soak up a diversity of sounds.

If the movement of communities made it possible for different music traditions to find and blend into each other, it was the Industrial Revolution's transformation of music into a mass media industry that made it possible for this new music to be heard and recognized from coast to coast. In the 1700s and early 1800s, musical tastes were largely local or regional, and it took time for a new song or other piece of music or dance to reach beyond its area of origin. Touring minstrel shows, vaudeville performers, and other theatrical troupes were a major method of sharing music across the United States. Although sheet music had existed for centuries, few saw much profit potential in printed music until the second half of the 1800s. Audiences began to clamor for the latest popular tunes they had heard on stage, so that they could sing or play them at home. Soon, a host of companies specializing in mass-printing music had established themselves, mainly centered in one section of New York City that people referred to as "Tin Pan Alley," in reference to the cacophony of banged-on pianos pouring out of brownstone windows.[27]

Mass printing of music sold at low cost to the average citizen meant not just making songs available but mass producing new ones on a factory-like basis. It is no wonder Tin Pan Alley became famous for the plethora of tunes all being pounded out simultaneously. One study asserts that more popular music was churned out during the first decade of the 1900s than had *ever* been written before then, an average of about 25,000 songs per year.[28] When a particular tune caught the public's fancy, the results were staggering. To provide one particular example, the ballad "After the Ball," published in 1893, swept the country and eventually sold ten million copies over the next decade.[29] On the other side, such volume of songwriting meant a lot fell to the wayside, largely due to the sameness of the material. Publishing houses often focused on following trends, pressing songwriters to follow the patterns of other current popular tunes. "After the Ball," for example, was part of a trend towards "waltz songs" that dominated the era before ragtime.[30] Customers seemed to like songs that stood out from the crowd but were not *too* different from what they were used to hearing—unique but familiar.

The publication of sheet music became the primary method of earning a living as a composer, and remained that way largely until the middle of the twentieth century. Ideally, the publisher would give a portion of the proceeds from the sale of sheet music to the songwriter—but such was not often the case. Copyright protection for music was woefully inadequate during the 1800s. The aforementioned Stephen Foster became destitute although his songs were popular across the country because so many companies published his music and many professional entertainers used his works without his consent and without giving him compensation.[31] Although the federal government passed a new Copyright Act in 1909 that more explicitly defined copyrighted material (as opposed to music in the "public domain"), there was little enforcement in the first few years. Thus, members of the music industry took it upon themselves to create a form of protection. ASCAP (American Society of Composers, Authors and Publishers) was created in 1914 to ensure collection of license fees from people using work and distributing them to composers/lyricists as royalties. Victor Herbert was one of the founders, and most of those working in Tin Pan Alley quickly joined.

The sale of sheet music monetized the sharing of music from person to person, from community to community. To a certain extent, power was given to the publisher and (at least in intent) to the composer and lyricist, imposing upon the person who bought the sheet music to play or sing it in exactly the fashion presented on paper. Nonetheless, once someone bought the sheet music, there was nothing to keep individuals from playing or singing the song in their own fashion. The popularity of such individuation was soon evident as ragtime evolved into jazz, which consciously stresses the importance of improvisation.[32] Instrumentalists follow the basic chord structure of a song but extemporize on the "official" melodic line, including sliding into flatted (or "blue") notes. Performers often take turns riffing, performing a type of call and response among the instruments, before combining for one final reworked version of the chorus. Vocalists were added to this mix, not only contributing their own melodic spin but also abandoning the original lyrics in favor of "scat-singing" meaningless sounds ("scoot-iddly-waa" or "heidy-heidy-heidy-ho"). Sheet music publishers responded by trying to notate ragtime or jazz arrangements of songs—that is, writing down the riffs and setting in place the blue notes, thus removing anything improvisational about it.

A number of technological inventions provided more effective methods of enshrining one particular way of performing a particular piece of music during the late 1800s and early 1900s. The phonograph (and subsequent equipment devised to record music) literally carves a performance onto a tangible object so that it can be replayed and reheard in *the exact same way* over and over again. Phonograph records helped spread music farther faster. One did not need to be in New York City or New Orleans to hear a particular singer or band anymore. Audiences would also be able to hear the same performance even after the artist had passed away. While having obvious benefit, some worried that the growth of recorded music in the average home would limit amateur music making, with people no longer singing or playing for themselves.[33] While such was not fully the case, the prevalence of recorded music may have narrowed people's perception of *how* to perform music—much as sheet music attempts to authorize a "correct" way to "do" a song, people increasingly feel the need to sing or play *like* a certain performer heard on record. The ability to ship recorded music everywhere, though, meant more ability to introduce people to different types of music and to foster the type of cross-fertilization that resulted in ragtime and jazz.

The development of radio after World War I took things to a farther level of national exposure and capitalization. Most homes had radios in them by the end of the 1920s, and major national networks had formed to provide programming to listeners. A large emphasis in such programming was music—and with coast-to-coast hookups, technically the entire country could listen to the same performance *at the same time*. With radio and phonograph records making music so easily available, they helped spread jazz music quickly—to the point where many people refer to this period *as* "the Jazz Age." Just as ragtime matched shifts in post-Civil War society, jazz's speedy tempo and wild, unexpected turns in rhythm or melodic line seemed to tap into the sensibilities of the post-World War I era. In achieving victory in World War I, the United States took on a new role as global power, and jazz seemed to express that optimism. The tempo of jazz also reflected the continued modernization and urbanization of American life.[34] Yet, at the same time, the jangly nature of jazz also may have spoken to a simmering sense of trauma that many felt coming out of their experiences during World War I, where the advances of the Industrial Revolution were used to more efficiently and quickly harm or kill people.

Just as ragtime evolved into jazz, even more lively steps, such as the Black Bottom and the Charleston, replaced the popular dances of the first part of the twentieth century. The American public seemed to take to them because they felt wild, uninhibited, and liberating (and their detractors decried them for the exact same reasons). The connotations of the names given to both of these dance crazes, as well as the widespread popularity of jazz itself, indicate the continued importance of African American culture and white society's ongoing fascination with it. The result of such ongoing blending and reworking did something without anyone realizing it fully: the creation of a uniquely "American" music that brought millions together in its celebration of individual liberation.

American Musical Theatre

In the early 1900s, a number of big theatres were constructed near Times Square in New York City, many of them along Broadway.[35] Some housed vaudeville, but most were for dramas, comedies, and for plays with music. By the 1920s, Broadway was established as the theatrical center of the United States, and it was there that a unique genre known as "the musical" began to coalesce. Yet, again, exactly what constituted a musical was hard to determine because it could be argued that a number of Broadway productions of this time were just versions of earlier types of musical entertainment. For example, light opera continued in the States under the title of "operetta." While European operettas still crossed over to the United States, homegrown versions ably competed with them. The American versions used operetta to create an archly romantic fantasyland, taking place in an exotic, almost fairytale environment. In such places, it seemed allowable that characters would be so overcome with emotion that they would suddenly erupt into full-throated songs of love, sorrow, or joy. American operetta also made certain to include various comedic supporting roles, characters who sometimes poked fun at all of the fantasy and romantic passion. They also regularly got their own comic numbers, songs that sounded less like opera and more like Tin Pan Alley.[36]

The ongoing popularity of vaudeville led to a number of highly produced upscale productions on Broadway that were referred to as "revues." Revues were marketed as having nothing but "headliners" in their lists of acts, and with more money poured into the sets and costumes than was possible within

Figure 1.2 Florenz Ziegfeld, Broadway producer extraordinaire. Famous for his *Follies* revues, he also produced landmark "book shows" such as *Show Boat*, which premiered in 1927. Snapshot taken from: Author's personal collection.

typical vaudeville. The revue format was made popular by producer Florenz Ziegfeld, who aimed to put on a new revue every year (Figure 1.2). Ziegfeld not only collated the biggest stars, but also became famous for presenting a bevy of gorgeous chorus girls. Each production would include at least one or two numbers that allowed the chorus girls to appear in elaborate costumes that nonetheless seemed to show lots of skin. These numbers were called "tableaux" because the chorus girls did not exactly dance. Rather, they largely stood there to be admired by the audience.[37] Eventually, some form of motion was added by having them slowly prance across the stage or down a staircase. The success of the *Ziegfeld Follies* quickly led to other revues by other producers, such as *George White's Scandals* and *Earl Carroll's Vanities*. As with vaudeville, revues contained a variety of types of music and dance and comedy, and without a connecting storyline. Yet, certain revues would have a certain organizational through-line, largely in having a centralized theme or visual design, neither of which happened in vaudeville at all.[38]

Gradually the seed of what occurred in the creation of *The Black Crook* had taken root and blossomed into a type of theatrical entertainment that (like vaudeville or revues) used the American popular music style common to Tin Pan Alley, but within a storyline (like operetta). Some used the term "book musical" to distinguish this type of entertainment, because the songs and dances were situated within a "book" or script. Yet, most people called these shows "musical comedies" because, unlike operetta, there is greater emphasis on farce and shtick than on the high romantic dramatics typical of operetta. Furthermore, while a plot exists, most book musicals of the 1920s have just the flimsiest of plotlines. Usually, they contain a simple boy-meets-girl story filled with silly complications that are eventually easily resolved after a lot of dithering, extraneous comedy, and various numbers. Characters break into song, but usually on the slightest whim and with little to do with the plot or the characters, unlike operetta, where songs are used to reveal character or carry through major plot points. Chorus girls or boys appear out of nowhere and romp around energetically. A supporting character mentions some oddball topic like peanut butter, goes into a whole song about it, and then returns to whatever was happening in the story before the interruption. For example, in *No, No, Nanette* (which debuted on Broadway in 1925, and became one of the most popular shows of the decade), characters seem to change their motivations randomly in order to fit the needs of the song they are about to perform. One second the title character is swooning about settling down with one boy (the song "I Want to Be Happy") and in the very next number (the title song) she wants to break free and run wild. The slightness of the plot often allowed star performers to run roughshod over the book, such as when Al Jolson notoriously stopped one performance of *The Honeymoon Express* (1913), told the audience how the story ended, and turned the rest of the night into a one-man concert.[39] Thus, while having a narrative, these early book musicals still contain some of the raucous energy that occurred in vaudeville and burlesque.[40]

As the above description suggests, book musicals of the 1920s expressed the energetic optimistic abandon of the Jazz Age, the ascendancy of the United States, and faith in the opportunity for individual success. A number of the people writing songs for Broadway shows themselves personified this American Dream of "rags to riches," for a number of them came from Jewish immigrant stock.[41] The rise of musical theatre helped spur a golden age of American songwriting, and key artists in this era were fundamental in shaping the emerging "musical" genre. A number of songwriters worked in musical theatre because it helped get their songs heard and popularized, but also because it potentially gave them greater power over their work. Although tunes written by various songwriters could be interpolated into one show, the 1920s started showing a tendency for a musical's score to be authored by one person or songwriting team. Operetta was where such practice was most common, and one of the top composers of the 1920s, Sigmund Romberg, wrote the scores for a number of long-running hits, such as *The Student Prince* (debuting on Broadway in 1924), *The Desert Song* (1926), and *The New Moon* (1927).[42] On the other side of the spectrum was Irving Berlin, who began his career as a song plugger on Tin Pan Alley. A key figure in making ragtime accessible to mainstream white listeners, he became celebrated for an uncomplicated and direct manner in his lyrics, melodies, and chord patterns that matched the plain-spoken attitude that had become part of the US persona. Although he moved into musical theatre, he continued to write songs that could stand alone for potential sheet music and record sales. As such, Berlin never wrote operettas and initially seemed more comfortable writing for revues than for book musicals.[43]

In between these two musical pioneers were a number of emerging talents that focused more particularly on exploring and defining the parameters of the book musical. Granted, a number writing for them still focused on cranking out popular stand-alone tunes, enhancing the sense that the songs had little to do with the story or characters. The writing team of Lew Brown, Buddy de Sylva, and Ray Henderson were one of the most popular working on Broadway in the 1920s, putting such hit songs as "The Varsity Drag," "The Best Things in Life Are Free," and "Button Up Your Overcoat" into musical comedies like *Good News!* (which premiered on Broadway in 1927) and *Hold Everything!* (1928). But others sought to expand the possibilities. The forerunner of this particular group was composer Jerome Kern. Kern became renowned for writing extended lyrical melodies, but in a less operatic vein than Romberg and other operetta composers, and he often worked with lyricists who used more American phrasing rather than flowery operatic language. Kern contributed to a number of typically lightweight musical comedies, but he also helped propel the book musical into more serious fare. Perhaps his most important work is *Show Boat* (with lyrics by Oscar Hammerstein, debuting on Broadway in 1927), which took on American race relations and how American theatre itself was affected by such issues. As such, Kern's score contains songs fit for operetta ("Make Believe"), versions of "coon songs" ("Can't Help Lovin' Dat Man"), and a blend of both styles ("Ol' Man River").[44]

On a similar note, brothers George and Ira Gershwin wrote American popular music but regarded it as a serious form with artistic merit. Like Berlin, the Gershwins came from Jewish immigrant stock, were very much influenced by ragtime and jazz, and began writing for Tin Pan Alley before becoming involved in musical theatre. Lyricist Ira was a keen observer of American slang and pronunciation, as indicated by such song titles as "S'Wonderful" and "I Got Rhythm." Composer George was also fascinated by the uniquely American sound of jazz, but added a new ingredient to the musical "melting pot": the heritage of classical European music. George eventually expanded beyond Tin Pan Alley and Broadway theatre, into "Rhapsody in Blue," the tone poem "An American in Paris," and the operatic *Porgy and Bess* (which premiered on Broadway in 1935).[45]

Richard Rodgers and Lorenz Hart broke into musical theatre after these others had been established, but their work seems even less concerned with following European models. Composer Rodgers spoke of being influenced by Kern rather than by Europeans, for example. Lyricist Hart matches Ira Gershwin in his love of American vernacular, such as his use of the Brooklyn accent in the line "The city's clamor could never spoil/the dreams of a boy and goil" in "I'll Take Manhattan." Hart could also take American English and craft incredibly dexterous rhymes, such as in "Mountain Greenery": "Beans could get no keener re-/ception in a beanery, bless our mountain greenery home." The duo also continually sought projects that stretched the boundaries of what book musicals could cover, including writing a score for a story about Chinese eunuchs (*Chee-Chee*, first produced in 1928).[46]

The Jewish immigrant experience perhaps gave a number of these songwriters the ability to define a sense of American identity because they were "outsiders" working to assimilate into American society. Rodgers and Hart, though, came from an established Jewish middle-class background. Hart likely remained (at least in his own mind, according to biographers) an outsider due to his homosexuality. A short man who often drowned himself in alcohol, Hart's lyrics often use wit to hide deep depression. Same-sex desire had existed for millennia, but the late 1800s witnessed the growth of a sense that certain individuals were prone to certain sexual desires, creating a new category of identity. Gay male communities began to coalesce in densely populated urban areas, including New York City. Theatre was a common milieu to find gay men, perhaps due to the emphasis on role-playing (going back to the time of Shakespeare when young actors would play the female parts). Yet, homosexuality was regarded as abnormal, sinful, and criminal. While Jewish artists were gradually assimilating, homosexuals by and large had to hide themselves. Many have interpreted Hart's cynical humor as an expression of the tribulations that he and other homosexuals of the era faced.[47] Composer/lyricist Cole Porter was also gay. Porter, though, came from a Midwestern upper-middle-class Christian family, and spent much of his life living among the cognoscenti both in the States and in Europe. Like Hart, his songs contain a number of allusions to homosexuality, but perhaps less of an overarching sense of despair lurking beneath the repartee. Porter was also extremely adept at urbane humor and sophisticated rhyme, and understood well how to bring in rhythms and melodies from a variety of cultures, as in "Begin the Beguine" or a vaguely Hasidic tone that emerges at points in "My Heart Belongs to Daddy."[48]

One might notice the lack of notable female songwriters in this list. Some women did contribute, such as lyricists Dorothy Fields (who worked with Jerome Kern a number of times) and Dorothy Donnelly (who partnered with Sigmund Romberg repeatedly), but songwriting was regarded mainly as a male profession.[49] Similarly, while offering opportunities to a number of first- or second-generation European immigrants, the chances for African American composers were limited, even though the sound of Tin Pan Alley and Broadway had borrowed so heavily from African American culture. Eubie Blake perhaps succeeded the best at the time as a black composer within the Tin Pan Alley framework, most famously with "I'm Just Wild About Harry," which was part of the score he wrote for a hit Broadway revue with an all-black cast, *Shuffle Along* (1921).[50]

American music and dance had continually balanced between freedom and control because that dichotomy helped shape what it meant to be American. By the end of the 1920s, American popular music had come into its own, with a cadre of composers and lyricists and with support from a vibrant industry. Similarly, a number of methods of presenting this music as a theatrical entertainment had become available: operettas, revues, book musicals (or musical comedies). The music of Tin Pan Alley and the Broadway musical both expressed energy and excitement towards modernity. They spoke to the power and potential of the individual, and yet created something that could be shared as a nation. The sheet music and recorded music industries, and the development of national radio networks had established a strong and profitable business structure for promoting and selling music. It was at this moment, as these aesthetic and industrial patterns established, that the musical motion picture was born.

Notes

1 Gerald Mast, *Can't Help Singin': The American Musical on Stage and Screen* (Woodstock: Overlook Press, 1987); Michael B. Druxman, *The Musical from Broadway to Hollywood* (New York: Barnes, 1980); Thomas S. Hischak, *Through the Screen Door: What Happened to the Broadway Musical When It Went to Hollywood* (Lanham: Scarecrow Press, 2004).

2 Tara C. Browner, "American Indian Music and Dance," *The 1999 Grolier Multimedia Encyclopedia;* Richard Crawford, *America's Musical Life: A History* (New York: W.W. Norton, 2001), 3–14; from the perspective of a Navajo singer, see Frank Mitchell, *Navajo Blessingway Singer: The Autobiography of Frank Mitchell, 1881–1967*, ed. Charlotte J. Frisbie and David P. McAllester (Tucson: University of Arizona Press), 1978.

3 For more on the use of music by early Protestant settlers, see Robert Stevenson, *Protestant Church Music in America: A Short Survey of Men and Movements from 1564 to the Present* (New York: W.W. Norton, 1966).

4 Forms of musical notation go back to ancient Samaria (approx. 2000 BC) and ancient Greece. Today's standard European model of musical notation seems to have originated with Guido d'Arezzo, a Benedictine monk in Italy around the turn of the first millennium. See Stefano Mengozzi, *The Renaissance Reform of Medieval Music Theory: Guido of Arezzo Between Myth and History* (New York: Cambridge University Press, 2010).

5 Barbara Lambert, ed., *Colonial Music in Massachusetts, 1630–1820: A Conference Held by the Colonial Society of Massachusetts, May 17 and 18, 1973*, 2 vols. (Boston: Colonial Society of Massachusetts, 1980).

6 Dena J. Epstein, *Sinful Tunes and Spirituals: Black Folk Music to the Civil War* (Urbana: University of Illinois Press, 1977); Eileen Southern, *The Music of Black Americans: A History*, 3rd ed. (New York: W.W. Norton, 1997).

7 Henry A, Kmen, *Music in New Orleans: The Formative Years, 1791–1841* (Baton Rouge: Louisiana State University Press, 1966).

8 On dancing in European courts of the period, see Richard T. Simmons, "Branles, Gavottes, and Contredanses in the Later Seventeenth and Early Eighteenth Centuries," *Dance Research* 15:2 (Winter 1997), 35–62; on American folk dancing during this period, see Joy Van Cleef and Kate Van Winkle Keller, "Selected American Country Dance and Their English Sources," in Lambert.

9 Eric Lott, *Love and Theft: Blackface Minstrelsy and the American Working Class* (New York: Oxford University Press, 1993); see also Robert Christgau, "In Search of Jim Crow: Why Postmodern Minstrelsy Studies Matter," *The Believer* 2:1 (February 2004). http://www.believermag.com/issues/200402/?read=article_christgau

10 Susan L. Porter, *With an Air Debonair: Musical Theatre in America, 1785–1815* (Washington: Smithsonian Institution Press, 1991).

11 Robert C. Toll, *Blacking Up: The Minstrel Show in Nineteenth Century America* (New York: Oxford University Press, 1974); Lott; Dale Cockrell, *Demons of Disorder: Early Blackface Minstrels and Their World* (Cambridge: Cambridge University Press, 1997); Annemarie Bean, James V. Hatch, and Brooks McNamara, eds, *Inside the Minstrel Mask: Readings in Nineteenth-Century Blackface Minstrelsy* (Hanover: Wesleyan University Press, 1996).

12 Brian Seibert, *What the Eye Hears: A History of Tap Dancing* (New York: Farrar, Straus and Giroux, 2015).

13 On the carnivalesque potential of blackface, see Cockrell.

14 Lott; Michael Rogin, *Blackface, White Noise: Jewish Immigrants in the Hollywood Melting Pot* (Berkeley: University of California Press, 1996).

15 Lawrence W. Levine, *Highbrow/Lowbrow: The Emergence of Cultural Hierarchy in America* (Cambridge: Harvard University Press, 1988).

16 For more on the history of vaudeville, see Henry Jenkins, *What Made Pistachio Nuts? Early Sound Comedy and the Vaudeville Aesthetic* (New York: Columbia University Press, 1992), 26–95; Charles W. Stein, ed., *American Vaudeville as Seen by Its Contemporaries* (New York: Knopf, 1984); Anthony Slide, *The Vaudevillians* (Westport: Arlington House, 1981); and John E. DiMeglio, *Vaudeville USA* (Bowling Green: Bowling Green University Popular Press, 1973).

17 Robert C. Allen, *Horrible Prettiness: Burlesque and American Culture* (Chapel Hill: University of North Carolina Press, 1991).

18 Levine.

19 Allen.

20 See Helen Sheehy, *Eleanora Duse: A Biography* (New York: Alfred A. Knopf, 2003) and Jane Kathleen Curry, *Nineteenth-Century American Women Theatre Managers* (Westport: Greenwood Press, 1994).

21 For a history of operetta, see David Ewen, *European Light Opera* (New York: Holt, Rinehart & Winston, 1962); Gerald Bordman, *American Operetta: From "H.M.S. Pinafore" to "Sweeney Todd"* (New York: Oxford University Press, 1981).

22 On Gilbert and Sullivan, see Gayden Wren, *A Most Ingenious Paradox: The Art of Gilbert and Sullivan* (Oxford: Oxford University Press, 2001).

23 Raymond Knapp, *The American Musical and the Formation of National Identity* (Princeton: Princeton University Press, 2005), 20–29. Mast, 7–15; Rick Altman, *The American Film Musical* (Bloomington: Indiana University Press, 1987) writes: "It is a cliché of American Musical comedy criticism that the genre began with the 1866 Niblo's Garden performance of *The Black Crook*" (133). Julian Mates, "The Black Crook Myth," *Theatre Survey* 7:1 (May 1966), 31–43, takes exception to the hallowed place this production has received in theatre history. Martin Rubin, *Showstoppers: Busby Berkeley and the Tradition of Spectacle* (New York: Columbia University Press, 1993), 19–21, provides an evaluation of both sides of the discussion.

24 John McCabe, George M. Cohan: *The Man Who Owned Broadway* (New York: Doubleday, 1973).

25 Edward A. Berlin, *Ragtime: A Musical and Cultural History* (Berkeley: University of California Press, 1980).

26 See Linda J. Tomko, *Dancing Class: Gender, Ethnicity, and Social Divides in American Dance, 1890–1920* (Bloomington: Indiana University Press, 1999).

27 Edward B. Marks, *They All Sang: From Tony Pastor to Rudy Vallee* (New York: Viking, 1934), provides a detailed description of Tin Pan Alley, including locations of many publishing firms; David A. Jasen, *Tin Pan Alley … The Golden Age of American Popular Music from 1886 to 1956* (New York: Fine, 1988).

28 D.W. Krummel, "Counting Every Star; or Historical Statistics on Music Publishing in the United States (American Music Bibliography, IV)," *Anuario Interamerican de Investigacion Musical* 10 (1974), 186.

29 Joel Shrock, *The Gilded Age* (Westport: Greenwood Press, 2004), 190.

30 Other examples would include: "Daisy," "School Days," "In the Good Old Summertime," "Meet Me in St. Louis," and "The Band Played On."

31 In retrospect, such an end result is perhaps ironic justice for Foster's exploitation and reworking of African American music in the first place.

32 Ingrid Monson, *Saying Something: Jazz Improvisation and Interaction* (Chicago: University of Chicago Press, 1996); William Burton Peretti, *The Creation of Jazz: Music, Race, and Culture in Urban America* (Urbana: University of Illinois Press, 1992); Martin T. Williams, *The Jazz Tradition*, 2nd rev. ed. (New York: Oxford University Press, 1993); also Nat Shapiro and Nat Hentoff, eds., *Hear Me Talkin' to Ya: The Story of Jazz as Told by the Men Who Made It* (New York: Dover, 1966).

33 See Hugh Cunningham, *Leisure in the Industrial Revolution, 1780–1880* (New York: St. Martin's, 1980). Paul S. Carpenter, *Music: An Art and a Business* (Norman: University of Oklahoma Press, 1950), 13, similarly opines that phonographs "are impoverishing the musical life of our regions by pre-empting the listening ear of every town, hamlet, and farm house in the nation … convert[ing] a great many of our potential performers and

composers into passive listeners." Rick Altman concludes *The American Film Musical* with similar dire predictions that manufactured music has the potential to eliminate the pleasures of amateur music making, actually asking at one point: "Where has the harmonica gone, and the jew's harp? Who among us can still play the ukulele, the auto-harp, or the washboard? Where is the old practice of singing at the work place alive today? Does anyone still sing rounds? When did you last hear someone whistling a tune?" (351).

34 The 1920 US Census was the first to indicate that more of the country's population lived in or near big cities than in rural areas, a situation that has only increased since then.

35 On the development of Broadway and the overall emergence of modern metropolitan New York City life, see Lewis Erenberg, *Steppin' Out: New York Nightlife and the Transformation of American Culture, 1890–1930* (Chicago: University of Chicago Press, 1984).

36 On 1920s American operetta, see Ethan Mordden, *Make Believe: The Broadway Musical of the 1920s* (New York: Oxford University Press, 1997), 36–52, 161–183; and Bordman, *American Operetta*, 112–139.

37 Linda Mizejewski, *Ziegfeld Girl: Image and Icon in Culture and Cinema* (Durham: Duke University Press, 1999).

38 See Gerald Bordman, *American Musical Revue: From the Passing Show to Sugar Babies* (New York: Oxford University Press, 1985).

39 For a more detailed history of the production, see Herbert G. Goldman, *Jolson: The Legend Comes to Life* (Oxford: Oxford University Press, 1988), 73–81.

40 Mordden.

41 Kenneth Aaron Kanter, *The Jews of Tin Pan Alley: The Jewish Contribution to American Popular Music, 1830–1940* (New York: American Jewish Archives, 1982).

42 On Sigmund Romberg, see William A. Everett, *Sigmund Romberg* (New Haven: Yale University Press, 2007).

43 On Irving Berlin, see Laurence Bergreen, *As Thousands Cheer: The Life of Irving Berlin* (New York: Viking, 1990).

44 On Jerome Kern, Stephen Banfield, *Jerome Kern* (New Haven: Yale University Press, 2006).

45 On the Gershwins, Steven E. Gilbert, *The Music of Gershwin* (New Haven: Yale University Press, 1995), and Philip Furia, *Ira Gershwin: The Art of the Lyricist* (New York: Oxford University Press, 1996).

46 Richard Rodgers provides his own account of his work with Lorenz Hart in *Musical Stages* (New York: Random House, 1975). For a more complex and less idealized account of their working relationship, see Gary Marmorstein, *A Ship Without a Sail: The Life of Lorenz Hart* (New York: Simon & Schuster, 2012).

47 Marmorstein provides an analysis of the potential relationship between Hart's sexual orientation and his lyrics.

48 On Cole Porter, see Charles Schwartz, *Cole Porter: A Biography* (New York: Da Capo Press, 1977), and Joseph Morella and George Mazzei, *Genius and Lust: The Creativity and Sexuality of Cole Porter and Noel Coward* (New York: Caroll & Graf, 1995).

49 On female songwriters in musical theatre, see Sharon Guertin Shafer, "The Women of Tin Pan Alley," paper given at College Music Society Mid-Atlantic Regional Conference, George Mason University, March 20–21, 2009. (http://www.trinitydc.edu/academic-affairs/files/2010/03/Women-of-Tin-Pan-Alley.pdf)

50 On Eubie Blake, see Al Rose, *Eubie Blake* (New York: Schirmer Books, 1979). Also see Thomas L. Riis, *More than Just Minstrel Shows: The Rise of Black Musical Theatre at the Turn of the Century* (Brooklyn: Institute for Studies in American Music, 1992).

2

You Ain't Heard Nothin' Yet: The Sound Revolution

The previous chapter describes how a number of forms of business had solidified by the late 1920s, institutionalizing their patterns of industry. Similar to the establishment of the vaudeville circuit, the Broadway theatre district, Tin Pan Alley, the recorded music industry, and the radio networks was the rise of the film industry. During the first quarter of the twentieth century, motion pictures moved from a technological novelty to a multi-million-dollar concern, dominated globally in large part by a small circle of studios that centered production near the Hollywood hills in southern California. Adding sound would bring the film studios into business relations with these other industries. Almost from the invention of cinema, various people had been interested in the possibilities of film sound. Thomas Edison, for example, attempted to combine two of his patented inventions: the phonograph and the kinetoscope. Theoretically, once the engineering issues had been resolved, institutional powers simply needed to form a collaboration, employing established aesthetic formulae, to bring profits to all concerned.

Once the American film industry committed itself to sound, the shift was remarkably swift. In 1927, talking pictures were practically unheard of; by 1930, everyone in Hollywood except Charlie Chaplin had given up on silent filmmaking. Yet, the transition was anything but smooth and orderly. On multiple levels—technological, industrial, and aesthetic—various levels of chaos loomed. And it was in this volatility that some form of a film musical genre began to take shape. In terms of technology, the equipment imposed restrictions on how musical performances could be filmed and recorded. Industrially, the heads of various film studios used sound as a weapon to gain advantage over each other. At the same time, Hollywood also faced interference from outside forces, as major players in radio, theatre, and the music industries sought to expand their realms of influence. Such struggles often involved aesthetic judgments, with attempts to impose what worked on stage or on radio onto musical performance on film. As Jennifer Fleeger writes, "there was more at stake … than the economic dominance of the film industry. The goals of individual Hollywood executives, cultural associations of the specific sound

Free and Easy? A Defining History of the American Film Musical Genre, First Edition. Sean Griffin.
© 2018 Sean Griffin. Published 2018 by John Wiley & Sons Ltd.

technologies, and values of the artist and technicians affiliated with each studio all affected the conflicting representations of music and musicians during the conversion."[1]

Centuries of music and theatre heritage had laid a foundation on which the film musical could build. Even so, a clear definition of what constituted a film musical had yet to be determined. While engendering anxiety and panic for many, such a scramble to control this new medium gave others freedom to experiment. Katherine Spring, at the end of her introduction to *Saying It with Songs: Popular Music and the Coming of Sound to Hollywood Cinema*, states that "Hollywood's transition to sound from 1927–1931 ... contained a remarkably exploratory impulse around the potentialities of sound—one fostered by screenwriters, songwriters, producers, and entire institutions."[2] This developmental era for the film musical was alternately ingenious and horrendous—sometimes simultaneously!—but it was rarely boring.

Sounding Out the Competition: Technological and Industrial Influence on Filming Musical Performance

The film musical genre was not possible until the emergence of "talking pictures," and making that happen was not simple, as various parties (inventors, artists, film studios, and other large companies), each with their own interests, became involved. The strategies and negotiations that went on materially affected how the performance of music was presented. Filming song and dance proved to be trickier than many artists, engineers, and company executives had expected though. Such slipperiness sometimes provided surprising dividends. Other times, it caused headaches and failures. Slowly, though, a mutual understanding across all those concerned—including audiences—began to coalesce as to what methods succeeded most reliably in putting song and dance on camera. These gradually established stylistic patterns would function as the foundation for a more full-fledged genre called the "film musical."

Even the basic format for sound cinema was a site of contention. Audio technician Lee de Forest had developed a system for recording sound directly onto the film strip next to the frames of images (i.e., a "soundtrack"), which he named Phonofilm. Competing with de Forest was telephone giant AT&T (through its manufacturing branch Western Electric), which developed a method of recording sound to a wax disc that was then synchronized to a conventional reel of film, a process eventually christened Vitaphone. The two devices were incompatible, and thus their owners fought for primacy. As such, short test films were created both to demonstrate and to promote the rival technologies to potential customers. In large part, those short films were presentations of music and dance.

These potential customers were film producers, especially the heads of the major Hollywood studios. Most Hollywood executives, though, felt that adding sound would upset an already efficient business model. As much as possible, the studios functioned like an industrial factory, cranking out product on a smooth, regular basis and balancing cost against expected profits. Adding sound would entail a huge cost for purchasing new equipment, and possibly endanger the box-office power of certain highly paid stars who did not have "good voices." Also, with two competing incompatible sound technologies, executives did not want to bet on the wrong side. Thus, while outside forces attempted to open up new possibilities for motion pictures, the film industry acted as a community to protect their common interests.

Almost.

Two smaller studios, Warner Bros. and Fox, hoped to move up the ladder and compete with big companies such as Paramount and MGM. In the early 1920s, Warner Bros. owned no theatres, and Fox owned relatively few. Thus, both had to attract independent theatre owners to book their films. Paramount, on the other side, owned a chain of nearly 2000 theatres guaranteed to show its product. Music, and sound technology's ability to provide it, became the means by which Warners and Fox would attempt to gain greater control of the marketplace. Both embarked on a two-fold strategy: expanding their theatre holdings and offering independent theatres something the larger studios could not—sound. Even the smallest theatre could have a full orchestra accompany Warners' silent films via an exclusive agreement with Vitaphone, as well as a number of shorts showcasing some of the top stage artists of the day. Fox offered newsreels with sound to accompany its silent features, having bought up a number of patents for a sound-on-film process called Movietone.[3]

Both Vitaphone and Movietone sought to impress theatre owners and audiences with their own unique merits. For example, Movietone's equipment was more portable than Vitaphone's, and thus emphasized through its newsreels the ability to go on location to different places and events. Warner Bros., on the other hand, worked on signing up most of the top stage talent to exclusive contracts to appear in Vitaphone shorts. Both studios presented musical performers in their early short films, as did Lee de Forest in his Phonofilm tests. First and foremost, the test films highlighted technology. The focus is on the soundtrack: its acoustic range, its legibility, and its synchronization with the image. As the fellow in the parody of such a sound test says in *Singin' in the Rain* (1952), the point is to "notice how my lips and the sound issss-uing from them are synnn-chronized together in perfect oo-nison." Thus, when pianist Eubie Blake plays his "Fantasy on 'Swanee River'" for Lee de Forest in 1923, one is likely to focus on the match between his fingers on the keyboard and the music heard (or conversely, how the sound drops out on the upper notes because the recording equipment is not able to capture that high of a register) (Figure 2.1).

Figure 2.1 Eubie Blake plays his "Fantasy on 'Swanee River'" to showcase Lee de Forest's Phonofilm process in 1923, displaying not only the synchronization of sound to image, but also the limited dynamic acoustic range of the equipment. Snapshot taken from: Fantasy on "Swanee River" (1923).

In emphasizing the audio, everything else is largely secondary, including narrative. By and large, these shorts have no story lines. Rather, they are simply capturing the performance of a song or other piece of music. If the selection comes from an opera (i.e., part of a larger storyline), such context is not explained within the short film. These short films also have little to no editing. At most, they provide two angles: closer in and farther away from the performer(s) (how close and how far away differs from film to film). Cutting from one shot to another invited a slip in synchronization, and thus was kept to a minimum. No matter the proximity to the performer, the camera in these shorts is largely placed directly in front of the artist at eye level, or slightly below—as if watching them on stage from a theatre audience's perspective. As with the very first motion pictures, which also focused audience attention on their technology, the people in these early sound tests directly address the camera. Unlike narrative films, where actors are directed to never acknowledge the camera's presence, the stage-trained performers in these shorts speak or sing straight at the viewer, and at times even bow after the performance. As tests, there is also a thrill akin to live performance, in which anything might happen—and sometimes did. During one Movietone test, Scottish singer Harry Lauder stops in the middle of his rendition of "Roamin' in the Gloamin'" to announce "This is just a taste!," thus ensuring that the recording could not be used commercially. At the conclusion of another Movietone test, an unnamed

Asian American singer breathlessly comments that he's "got no more wind" upon finishing his rendition of "Yes Sir, That's My Baby!"

Such moments point out that the unforeseen was common. Performers might do anything, and the ability of the technology to keep up with them was not assured. The inability to foresee all of the consequences of adding sound quickly became apparent to Warner Bros. and its limited plans to use it simply for background music. Audiences and critics expressed more excitement over the programs of shorts than the two silent features with Vitaphone music scores that followed them (*Don Juan* [1926] and *The Better 'Ole* [1926]). Restrategizing, the studio's third Vitaphone feature included a few synchronized sound sequences. That film, *The Jazz Singer* (1927), broke box-office records, and the sound revolution was unleashed.

In the wake of the success of *The Jazz Singer*, Western Electric wielded the power that came from its parent company basically *owning* the telephone industry to make all of Hollywood its customer, not just Warner Bros.[4] The Vitaphone sound-on-disc system, though, had its problems—particularly the likelihood of sound and image to fall out of sync and run independently of each other if the record scratched or the film jumped a loop. The industry soon shifted to the sound-on-film technique, which more strongly bound the sound and image together. By 1930, even Warner Bros. had abandoned sound-on-disc. William Fox, with his Movietone system, similarly had eyes on controlling the entire film industry, and the victory of sound-on-film over sound-on-disc (and Fox's outmaneuvering of Lee de Forest's alternate sound-on-film system) made that goal seem possible.[5] His hope was that every studio would eventually have to pay him a royalty for making any sound film and, at one point, he came close to taking over MGM. MGM executive Louis B. Mayer managed to stave off this assault, ultimately leading to Fox's downfall, and almost the end of Fox Pictures.[6] Meanwhile, RCA (which had dominated early radio almost as much as AT&T did telephony) helped found an entire new studio, RKO (Radio-Keith-Orpheum), to promote its own sound technology, Photophone.[7]

The sudden rush to produce "talkies" caused untold confusion and mayhem on the set as well as the boardroom during this period, as filmmakers attempted to understand how the technology worked and how it could fit into an already established form of entertainment. The sound technician became a new job title—and the people who filled this role often ruled over the rest of the film crew during these early days, telling actors, directors, and producers what they could or could not do. Much like the early sound shorts, audio concerns trumped everything else in this era. In contrast, cameramen were literally caged into soundproofed—and non-ventilated—boxes, severely limiting the range of camera movement in early sound films. Performers crowded around the telephone or the vase of flowers where the microphone had been hidden, forbidden to move freely around the set. Orchestras were forced to situate themselves closely out of camera range in order to provide accompaniment to singers and dancers, but not drown them out. To many at the time, the coming of sound, then, had not only unleashed anarchy, but also shackled the filmmaking process (literally encasing the camera, and tethering performers to the microphone).

Eventually, solutions to these problems were discovered. Soundproofing camera motors freed cinematographers from their boxes. The inspiration of hanging microphones from overhead poles out of camera range liberated performers' ability to move. Each of these developments would be important to the fledgling musical film, allowing more camera fluidity and giving performers greater freedom and room to dance and express themselves. Of even greater impact was the development of sound playback. Instead of recording all sound simultaneously with the image, songs could be recorded ahead of time (thus ensuring the best performance and the optimal recording environment) and then played back while the camera rolled, with the performers lip-syncing and/or dancing in time to the recording.[8] Playback also helped free the camera and permitted the performer to move about, but it also hampered spontaneity: the performer had to match the recording for every take. If Harry Lauder had been performing to playback of his rendition of "Roamin' in the Gloamin,'" for example, he would not have been able to interrupt the performance (and would have been less able to keep the pre-recording from being marketed as a separate phonograph). Playback also increased the ability to replace or "dub" actors' voices—giving producers the power to literally take away someone's voice.[9] Thus, such technical solutions created greater freedom on certain levels, but created new constraints in the process.

The coming of sound also brought under control what went on in the theatres. For example, theatre owners were known to speed up projection of silent films in order to cram more shows in per day. Sync sound removed their ability to do this, as a sped-up film would also speed up the actors' voices. Silent films also did not always have the same music played with them from theatre to theatre. Huge downtown theatres would have full orchestras; small town venues may have had only a piano—or just a guitar and harmonica! Evidence indicates that some musicians radically altered the mood intended by the filmmakers, particularly jazz bands in African American neighborhood theatres.[10] Having "canned sound" wedded to the film strip eliminated that variety of moviegoing experience (and eliminated thousands of jobs for musicians as well).[11] Lastly, silent film audiences felt much freer to talk during movies (or possibly even sing along with the orchestra)—the sound era necessitated quiet from the assembled.[12]

While causing enormous stress and upheaval, the sound revolution ultimately resulted in further concentration of power for the major Hollywood studios. Many smaller film companies could not finance the conversion to sound and shuttered their doors. (Even the big studios turned to the major banks to get substantial loans to finance the conversion—which gave the banks their own leverage in exerting control over the film industry in the coming years.) The big studios also moved into other ways of making profit from music during the sound revolution. They established or bought up New York-based music publishing companies, for example. Doing so gave them full rights to a catalog of music to use in their films. Any new songs written for their films could also be published by these companies, giving them another way of making money. Warner Bros. also bought its own radio station, seeing how the music in its films, sheet music sales, and live radio performances could all act as promotion for each other.[13] Harry Warner was quoted as saying, "Who the hell wants to hear actors talk? The music—that's the big plus about this."[14] The rest of Hollywood came to agree—and the quest to determine exactly how cinema and musical performance could merge on a reliably successful basis was under way.

On with the Show: Theatrical Influence on the Film Musical

The previous section discussed how music factored into the efforts of technicians, artists, studios, and other corporations to gain leverage and control, and how musical performance sometimes exceeded the limited concepts placed upon it. Yet, the concept of a distinct classification of film *called* "the musical" had not yet coalesced during this period. The early sound tests and shorts, lacking narratives and perhaps only one song, are likely considered today more as "proto-musicals" than actual examples of the genre. Historians can look back and regard *The Jazz Singer* as a musical, but no one working on that film (or those reviewing it in 1927) referred to it as such.[15] The contours of the genre were only beginning to take shape. Granted, studios (and the banks now underwriting them) functioned as much as possible as a factory-like system with assured returns on investment, and genres provided reliable formulae. Hence, if something seemed to work in one picture, it was quickly duplicated by many others with the possibility that a codified genre might emerge. Unsurprisingly, efforts to establish successful methods of presenting musical performances in sound cinema became a major issue, almost necessitating the development of a film musical genre. The most obvious inspiration for such a development would come from the stage, as evidenced even in the short films of Lee de Forest, Vitaphone, and Movietone.

A prominent stage influence in these early sound tests is the performer him- or herself. Whatever off-camera direction existed was largely to indicate whether or not the microphones were picking up the performance, leaving the artists to do the routines they had honed to perfection on stage. Thus, while major Hollywood studio executives kept stars under contract and under their thumbs, the performers of these test films exude quite an amount of authority.

Such creative power extended to performers of color, such as the aforementioned Eubie Blake (along with his partner Noble Sissle) or the Asian American singer. Granted, one recognizes the cultural constraints placed on them, such as Blake reworking a Stephen Foster minstrel song, or the Asian American playing into the Oriental stereotype while singing "Yes Sir, That's My Baby." Yet, they are front-and-center, and both of these men use the opportunity to push a bit at the boundaries: Blake *reworks* "Swanee River" into a classical piano piece; the Asian American baldly drops the pidgin English when he announces he has "no more wind."

Blake's classical-ized rendition of "Swanee River" raises another point—the dichotomy between different forms of theatre, between "respectable" and "popular" music. Tests would alternate between upscale classical musicians and performers on one hand, and vaudeville, Tin Pan Alley, or jazz performers on the other. So, one test shows opera singer Marie Rappold; another shows novelty act Gus Vissor and His Duck warbling "Ma, He's Making Eyes at Me," with the duck loudly quacking on cue every time "Ma" shows up in the lyrics. Blake's "Fantasy" bridges the two, asserting that Foster's popular tune is worthy of consideration as serious music, but doing so by presenting a classically tinged arrangement. The ongoing cultural battles over music discussed in Chapter 1 would now play out on screen as well as elsewhere.[16]

Such a dichotomy was obvious in the two different programs of short subjects produced by Warner Bros. to accompany its first two Vitaphone features in 1926. The first set for *Don Juan* plainly meant to gain prestige and respect for Vitaphone. A speech by censorship czar Will Hays, intoning what a magnificent achievement Vitaphone is bringing to cinema—nay, humanity!—is followed by a series of opera singers and classically trained musicians. Unlike the high-class demeanor of this first program, the second set for *The Better 'Ole* presents vaudeville and musical theatre artists, including Al Jolson who was at that point inarguably the most popular entertainer in the country.

These Vitaphone programs continue almost all of the creative choices from the earlier tests. The camera is placed as if it is photographing a live theatrical performance—whether grand opera or vaudeville. Those in front of the camera perform directly outward. (At the conclusion of Jolson's segment, the film fades to black, then fades back in for Jolson to continue taking bows from what he and Warners obviously assumed would be wave upon wave of rapturous applause!) The performers also exert most of the authority (again, Jolson stands as the strongest example of this). Even the specter of influence from minority cultures infiltrates—albeit most obviously in the form of Jolson performing completely in blackface. Perhaps less apparent to today's audiences is the prevalence of Jewish and/or Yiddish culture—from violinist Ephraim Zimbalist in the first program to the schtick of Jolson and monologuist George Jessel in the second.[17]

The Jazz Singer stands as a foundational text, clearly influenced by what had gone before, but also laying out new patterns. Like the first and second programs of Vitaphone shorts, the camera still sits in the audience looking up at the stage and Jolson largely sings out at the camera. Yet, something *is* different—a feature-length narrative has devised contexts that allow such moments to believably occur. When Jolson is singing, his audience is not just us but also an audience within the film—a factor not included in the early tests or the shorts. The existence of a fictional audience justifies not only his performance, but also his performing outward towards the camera. Having Jolson play someone who *is* an entertainer by profession also helped easily explain the presence of the musical sequences. Such a strategy, as well as these other aspects, would not be lost on other filmmakers.

The script also narrativizes the cultural battles over music. Jolson's Jakey Rabinowitz yearns to sing jazz, while his father disowns him for not taking up the family tradition as cantor in the Jewish temple. The second half of the film dramatizes the turmoil as the rechristened Jack Robin tries to decide what to sing—opening night musical theatre or "Kol Nidre" in place of his dying father. While repeatedly told that he has to choose one or the other, the film eventually finds room for both—he honors his father by singing in the temple, but is back headlining on Broadway by next season. His vocal style is also described by characters as an amalgam of both sides: his jazz singing has a unique "tear in his voice," indicating the influence of the cantor tradition. Obviously, such a story emphasizes the importance of minority cultures on the landscape of American music, enacting Jewish assimilation as Jakey becomes Jack, and moves from religious music to mainstream popular songs, picking up a *shiksa* in the process (who is repeatedly in white gowns and headdresses). Part of that assimilation unfortunately comes via blackface (i.e., arguing he is closer to being white because he needs to put on black makeup). Yet, Jack first appears in blackface when he is confronted with his father's illness. Looking into the mirror at himself, his blackfaced reflection dissolves to an image of his father. Thus, while presenting a demeaning portrayal of African Americans, the blackface also indicates Jack's *own* feelings of racial/ethnic marginalization.

Most obviously like the shorts, though, is the power of the star. The film absolutely depends upon Jolson (even though Jessel had played the part on Broadway). Its famous poster shows a caricature of him in blackface on his knee with gloved hands open in supplication. There is no indication of the plot—rather, it promises the customer the complete Jolson experience, and the film delivers on that promise. After about ten minutes of basically silent film, Al Jolson finally appears on screen to a swell of orchestral music. The assembled crowd at a local bistro motions for him to sing—and suddenly, the soundtrack comes alive: it's him on stage and he's singing to the restaurant, to the camera, to *us*. The electricity is akin to Dorothy in black-and-white opening the door and walking into Technicolor. The voltage increases as he ad libs

Figure 2.2 Al Jolson launches into "Toot Toot Tootsie" in *The Jazz Singer* (1927), directly addressing the camera and asserting his eminence as a star. Snapshot taken from: The Jazz Singer (1927).

"You ain't heard nothin' yet!" (again asserting his control over the proceedings), launches into the rousing "Toot Toot Tootsie," and enters film history (Figure 2.2). Jolson's dominance is also evident in his obviously improvised conversation with Mama, with actress Eugenie Besserer giggling so nervously as she tries to keep up with Jolson's stream-of-consciousness that he blurts out, "Stop now, mama, you're getting kittenish!"

Unsurprisingly, Warners hung onto Jolson, immediately putting him into another film, *The Singing Fool* (1928). The film did turnaway business, with Jolson introducing a big hit song, "Sonny Boy." Depending on which reports are cited, *The Singing Fool* became the biggest box-office grosser in history to that point.[18] Other producers reacted by signing up all manner of stage-trained stars (as well as music idols from radio and records, such as Rudy Vallee). Various studios even opened up facilities in New York to take advantage of various Broadway talent. For example, the Marx Brothers' first film, *The Cocoanuts* (1929), an adaptation of their musical comedy hit, was filmed by Paramount at its studios in Astoria, which allowed the brothers to continue performing on stage in *Animal Crackers*. Film historian Donald Crafton has referred to the prevalence of filming renowned stage performers during this period as "virtual Broadway."[19] Star musical performers enhanced multiple possibilities of cross-promotion. In addition to connecting stage and film, the songs sung by such stars were often successfully marketed as sheet music and phonograph records, and drew audiences to radio programs on which they performed.[20]

Such film projects showcased each star's individual talents, from Fanny Brice's Yiddish comedy (and her way with a torchy ballad) in *My Man* (1928) to Sophie Tucker's randy style of saloon-singing in *Honky Tonk* (1929) to Rudy Vallee's mellow crooning through a megaphone in *The Vagabond Lover* (1929). The dominance of the star in these films was apparent even in the names of their characters. Fanny Brice plays Fanny Brand; Sophie Tucker is Sophie Leonard; Rudy Vallee is Rudy Bronson. George Jessel's character in *Lucky Boy* (1928) is simply called George Jessel. Capturing the treasured routines and songs associated with these stars often added to the running time of the film. To compensate, and keep films at regular length, scripts used audience awareness of a star's persona in place of actual scenes that explained their characters. One aspect common to all of their images was their status as entertainers. Thus, all of these films told tales of show business—watching our heroes and heroines climbing the ladder to stardom, or dealing with the perils *of* stardom. When the songs or dances happened, they occurred as part of the show in which the stars were appearing, and all still aimed squarely out at the camera. This "backstage" milieu would quite quickly dominate the budding film musical genre.

Furthering the popularity of the backstager was MGM's first major sound feature: the "all-talking, all-singing, all-dancing" *The Broadway Melody* (1929).[21] Like Jolson's films (and those of other stage-experienced stars), this film showcased the trials and tribulations of show folk. What marked it as new and different was that the lead performers (Bessie Love, Anita Page, and Charles King) were not major marquee names (Figure 2.3). Such a strategy alleviated MGM from paying huge salaries to its performers. (Many projects ended up in the red or with meager profits because of the exorbitant sums given to stars—such as Irish tenor John McCormack in *Song O'My Heart* [1930] or opera stars Lawrence Tibbett and Grace Moore in *New Moon* [1930].)[22] Nor did MGM have to deal with star egos and demands—something Warner Bros. was increasingly encountering with Jolson and others.[23] Showing that a musical backstager could work without stars restored power and control to studio executives.

Instead of relying on a key personality, *The Broadway Melody* focuses on the entire milieu—the auditions, the rehearsals, the out-of-town tryouts, and the premiere of a big Broadway revue (including a chorus girl going on in place of a featured player at the last minute and becoming a star). The film and its score (written by contract artists Arthur Freed and Nacio Herb Brown) were immediate hits with audiences and critics alike, and the film won the first Best

Figure 2.3 Anita Page, Bessie Love, and Charles King give their all performing the title number of *The Broadway Melody* (1929), helping engender an entire subgenre of backstage musicals. Snapshot taken from: The Broadway Melody (1929).

Picture Oscar ever given to a "talkie." Warner Bros.'s *Gold Diggers of Broadway* (1929), another non-star driven backstager and another huge success with audiences, confirmed the viability of the formula. For the next fifteen years, backstage plots would dominate Hollywood musicals.

With few exceptions (such as *On with the Show* [1929]), every theatrical producer in these backstagers seemed to be putting on a revue, thus allowing unrelated numbers to be presented as part of the show-within-the-show. For a while, those fictional producers were matched by their actual cinematic counterparts, as almost every studio made a musical revue during this period. Revues were another way to showcase stars but, by collecting a number of them together, each star's individual importance to the film's success is lessened, giving the producer a stronger hand. *The Hollywood Revue* (1929) led the way, establishing the power (and prestige) of MGM and its executives by showing just how many stars the studio had within its confines. Lensed in the wee hours, squeezed in between the stars' other projects, MGM used the film to give a number of its silent contract stars a chance to debut their talking and singing voices (Joan Crawford, Lionel Barrymore, Norma Shearer, John Gilbert, Buster Keaton, Marie Dressler, Laurel and Hardy, Marion Davies, and many others). That Greta Garbo and Lon Chaney are largely the only MGM stars not in the cast indicates their own unique standing at the studio at the time.[24]

The revue format also easily solves the problem of figuring out how to segue into a number: there's no narrative at all, just a bunch of unrelated skits and songs (including the new hit tune "Singin' in the Rain," again from the pens of Freed and Brown). Thus, *The Hollywood Revue* functions somewhat like one of the Vitaphone programs of shorts.

The Hollywood Revue was such a monster hit for MGM that the other studios quickly organized their own versions, including *Fox Movietone Follies* (1930), *Paramount on Parade* (1930), Universal's *King of Jazz* (1930), and Warners' *The Show of Shows* (1930). These revues often display the competition between rival studios—such as when comedienne Polly Moran does a parody of the tear-wrenching "Sonny Boy" from *The Singing Fool* in *The Hollywood Revue*. *The Show of Shows* seems to volley back by poking fun at *The Hollywood Revue*'s sentimental ballad "Your Mother and Mine," and including in the lyrics to *its* hit song, "Singin' in the Bathub," a line claiming that "singin' in the shower" is "an awful pain" because "it's like singin' in the rain."

None of these pictures approached the success of *The Hollywood Revue*, and some were complete failures. Overall, the revues were too hit-and-miss in terms of the quality of their segments, even if certain moments were entertaining (such as "Singin' in the Bathtub," the "Rhapsody in Blue" sequence of *King of Jazz*, or any of Maurice Chevalier's segments in *Paramount on Parade*). A major problem in selling these revues, though, was that no other studio had as many major stars as MGM did in 1929. Most subsequent studies of this period designate *Paramount on Parade* and *King of Jazz* as the best of the revues, indicating the importance of strong directors with clear visions—a number of top directors helmed sequences of *Paramount on Parade*, and *King of Jazz* was overseen by John Murray Anderson, a veteran of Broadway revues. Unlike the strategy practiced on Broadway to produce annual editions of revues, plans to produce further revue films were abandoned by 1930.

The revue format was not the only formula Hollywood borrowed from the stage.[25] At the same time that Warners embarked on Jolson films and projects for other Broadway luminaries, it also bought the film rights for the hit operetta *The Desert Song* (1929), which proved to be a major audience draw.[26] The subsequent box-office success of RKO's version of the stage smash *Rio Rita* (1929) ensured that a number of adaptations of Broadway musicals would follow. During the height of the transition to sound, stage-trained dialogue writers, directors, songwriters, and actors came from New York to Los Angeles *en masse*, all claiming to know better than established filmmakers what to do. As part of this expertise, they brought with them American theatre's concepts on what constituted a musical—an operetta or a musical comedy. Hollywood soon was lensing a number of operettas (such as *Song of the Flame* [1929], *Golden Dawn* [1930], and *New Moon*) and musical comedies (such as *Sally* [1930], *Good News* [1930], and *Whoopee!* [1930]). The proven popularity of these titles provided a form of box-office insurance. While some adaptations included major stars (such as the aforementioned Tibbett and Moore in *New Moon*, or Marilyn Miller, the biggest female star on Broadway at the time, recreating the title role in *Sally*), Hollywood executives used the perceived strength of the properties as another way to move beyond relying on big name performers. *Golden Dawn* and *Good News*, for example, did not have major stars in the cast.

Studios also often replaced many of the songs from these plays with original tunes written by people under contract—thus controlling all the rights (and profits) from these new compositions. For example, the 1930 film version of *Good News* retains some of the key hit songs written by Brown, DeSylva, and Henderson (such as the title song and "The Varsity Drag"). Yet, MGM had its house composers Freed and Brown add new (if ultimately unmemorable) ditties, such as "If You're Not Kissing Me" and "Football." Such a practice would be standard across Hollywood into the 1950s. Katherine Spring writes: "Sound cinema brought new commercial appeal to the film medium by introducing new songs to mass audiences, and it rivaled radio, Broadway and the vaudeville stage as the country's most important platform for popular music."[27] While studios developed new songwriters, such as Freed and Brown, they also wooed the top talents of Tin Pan Alley and Broadway to the West Coast. The Gershwins, Cole Porter, Rodgers and Hart, Jerome Kern, and many others would write a number of original songs for the movies in the ensuing years.

Theatrical musicals also provided a blueprint for original stories and scores. Thus, along with the adaptations came new examples of operettas (such as *Captain of the Guards* [1930], *Bride of the Regiment* [1930], and *The Vagabond Bride* [1930]) and of musical comedies (such as *Sunnyside Up* [1929], *Sweetie* [1929], and *Just Imagine* [1930]). In the wake of *Good News* were a number of college musicals, including the aptly titled *College Love* (1929) and *So This Is College* (1930). *Sunnyside Up*'s tale of a working-class ingénue mingling with the upper crust is not all that dissimilar to the plot of *Sally* (or the 1919 Broadway hit *Irene*).

The numbers in these filmed operettas and musical comedies (whether adaptations or originals) also betrayed the theatrical influence. Everything was directed outward at the audience (usually with the camera placing itself the equivalent of fifth-row center), and usually ended with the characters and/or chorus effectively exiting into the wings for no particular reason other than that was how it was always done on stage. The staginess is emphasized when Bessie Love and Gus Shy sing "Gee, I'd Like to Make You Happy" in *Good News*: performed in front of a blatant backdrop, the duo continually try to finish the number, but the orchestra continues with more choruses, forcing them to carry on until Bessie eventually collapses, and Gus carries her off into the wings.

Backstagers were able to justify such aspects by having an audience within the storyline watching the musical performance, but that internal audience was not present for the numbers in most operettas or musical comedies.

Musical comedies sometimes could use the excuse of a general atmosphere of zaniness, so why not have people start singing and dancing? Operettas, though, were usually deadly serious—and the singing just as intense. *The Desert Song* was a box-office success possibly because of audience interest in the first example of cinematic operetta. Customers grew increasingly unnerved and hostile to later operettas, though, as shown by *Variety's* report on the reaction to *Bride of the Regiment* in Pittsburgh: "Typical operetta flop ... how this burg hates them."[28] The resistance at this point by audiences to characters breaking into song when they are supposedly talking seemed to indicate that what worked on stage did not always translate onto celluloid. With proven stage formats not always being reliable, filmmakers boldly ventured forward with new ideas. The backstager was one such example, but many others were tried.

Beyond the Blue Horizon: Early Film Musical Experiments

With musicals already an established concept on Broadway (and Hollywood taking many properties and formats from the stage), film genre theorist Rick Altman's claim that a specific "musical" genre did not yet exist might be a bit too extreme.[29] Nonetheless, many films do show that the boundaries of the genre were still very fluid. Taking advantage of sound during this era meant almost every film being made had a song or a dance sequence in it: gangster films, westerns, you name it.[30] On the other side, some backstage narratives keep the on-stage numbers in the background, with the cast and crew of the show in the wings or dressing rooms talking over the musical performances. Other movies have music threaded throughout, but no specific start and finish to a number, sliding vaguely into and out of musical moments. Various others *do* have a clearly marked out musical performance—but just one or two, rather than the typical allotment (at least five or six became the expected norm for film musicals within the first few years). So, for example, although Gloria Swanson performed the hit song "Love, Your Spell Is Everywhere" in *The Trespasser* (1929), does that one song qualify the film as a musical?[31]

The chaos of the early talkie period helped create possibly the most openly experimental era of the genre as filmmakers and audiences both tried to figure out what was appropriate for something that could be called "a film musical."[32] Some ideas are so staggering in their bad judgment that they attain their own sense of fascination. *The Great Gabbo* (1929) serves as a good example. This backstager focuses on Erich von Stroheim (famous as a monocled martinet of a director, but starring in this picture) as a ventriloquist on the verge of a nervous breakdown, with an eerie dummy. The number "The Web of Love" adds to the oddness, with chorus girls dressed as spiders posing on a giant stylized web. Similarly jaw-dropping was director Cecil B. DeMille's *Madam Satan*

(1930), with everyone in exotic Art Deco costumes for a ball/orgy aboard a zeppelin, complete with a "Girl Auction," a bizarre "Ballet Electrique," and then a spectacular disaster sequence as the blimp crashes and everyone has to parachute to survival!

Such grand gambles were allowed because of the uncertain times. Some rolls of the dice paid off, though, discovering exciting, inventive ways to use music and rhythm in cinema. Three filmmakers who excelled in their experiments were animator Walt Disney and directors Ernst Lubitsch and Rouben Mamoulian. Paying no heed when sound technicians or other voices of authority claimed something was impossible, they went right ahead and did what they thought might be interesting to try. Critics and customers quickly shared that enthusiasm.

Disney was not the first to make an animated film with sound. Lee de Forest had already worked with the Fleischer brothers to create a number of cartoons that encouraged audiences to sing along by following lyrics on the screen in time with a bouncing ball. Yet, Disney's first sound cartoons with his new character Mickey Mouse quickly became a sensation because of the inventive ways that sound and image were put together. Music is not just dumped into Mickey's first film *Steamboat Willie* (1928); it organizes it completely.[33] The short focuses on Mickey turning a number of farm animals into musical instruments for an impromptu concert of "Turkey in the Straw," treating a goat like a grind organ and a cow's mouth like a xylophone. All the characters and objects (including the boat's smokestacks) move in tempo throughout the piece as well—as if the entire world has become musicalized.

Disney's overwhelming and immediate success led to more cartoons of Mickey performing musically. Disney also began a series of non-Mickey shorts called Silly Symphonies that, as the name implies, centered on music to help depict an environment or provide a small narrative. In each cartoon, all motion is rhythmic, and jokes are timed to the music. Using musical instruments as a form of sound effect that matches and seems to guide the movement of characters became so prevalent in Disney's shorts that the practice became known as "Mickey Mousing," even when used by others. Unlike operettas, audiences seemed to have no problem with Mickey or any other characters breaking into song—it was a cartoon, no one expected it to be realistic.

While Disney's career took off with the coming of sound, director Ernst Lubitsch had already established himself, particularly with sly romantic comedies that manage to be both risqué and charming (what critics refer to as "the Lubitsch touch"). Lubitsch does not sacrifice that "touch" in his transition to sound, the musical *The Love Parade* (1929). The film opens as a woman comes out of Maurice Chevalier's room accusing him of infidelity. Then, her husband arrives. She pulls out a pistol and shoots herself. The husband grabs the gun and shoots Chevalier. Nothing happens. It is filled with blanks. They both turn to the very alive woman. As the husband rushes to comfort her, Chevalier takes the weapon and tosses it into a desk drawer filled with similar pistols. Lubitsch plays with sound not only by the use of blanks, but by doing the whole scene in French until Chevalier unapologetically turns to the camera and speaks to the audience in English. The first song continues in this jocular vein, with Chevalier leaving town but requesting that "Paris, Stay the Same," followed by his valet also singing adieu, and then Chevalier's dog barking out a chorus to his lady poodle friends!

The opening to *The Love Parade* also exemplifies a quality lacking in many early musicals: pacing. Even in entertaining pieces such as *The Broadway Melody* or *Sunnyside Up*, slower tempos are typical. Some of this is due to problems with boxed-in cameras and the need to huddle around the hidden microphones. Even so, silent films operate at moderate rhythms, giving extra time for audiences with access only to visual information. This extra time is not needed with the addition of sound, but it took filmmakers a while to realize this. Lubitsch figured it out almost immediately. Further, as with Disney's cartoons, movement and sound effects match the rhythm of the background score. Frothy innuendo is enhanced by being spoken in tempo or sung. The title song of *One Hour with You* (1932), for example, passes from one partygoer on the dance floor to another, as they all strike up new flirtations.[34] Lastly, the emphasis on tempo helps Lubitsch's films move into and out of full-fledged numbers quite smoothly. In the early moments of *Monte Carlo* (1930), Jeanette MacDonald escapes her wedding by boarding a train. The engine and wheels create a rhythmic momentum, an orchestra slowly starts to merge with the beat of the locomotive, and suddenly MacDonald's enthusiasm for a new adventure cannot be contained as she leans out the window and trills "Beyond the Blue Horizon" (Figure 2.4). Sound effects and music combine to stir equal enthusiasm in the audience—rather than feeling disconcerted about MacDonald breaking into song, one would be disappointed if she had *not*!

Rouben Mamoulian was, like Disney, new to filmmaking but, like Lubitsch, had already made a name for himself as a director (on Broadway). Unlike a number of other New York directors, though, Mamoulian did not hope to make canned theatre. He was eager to explore how sound and film could work with each other, often overriding resistance from sound technicians and others on the set. His first film, *Applause* (1929), exemplifies one of those films that seem like a musical (a backstager about burlesque) but have very little in terms of classically constructed numbers. In order to accentuate the lurid squalor of the burlesque house, the chorus girls' singing was recorded separately and not perfectly matched to the uncoordinated bumps and grinds on screen. Mamoulian also experiments with overlapping sound, thus drawing links between events happening in two different rooms (but also talking over star Helen Morgan's rendition of "What Wouldn't I Do for That Man?"). *Applause* also contains one of the first overhead shots in a film musical—a camera angle rare for early talkies due to those soundproofed boxes, but an angle that (as will be shown) would become strongly associated with the genre by the mid-1930s.

Figure 2.4 Director Ernst Lubitsch generates such momentum through editing and the sounds of a chugging locomotive that it does not seem odd for Jeanette MacDonald to suddenly burst forth in song, singing "Beyond the Blue Horizon" in *Monte Carlo* (1930). Snapshot taken from: Monte Carlo (1930).

A few years later, Mamoulian would "out-Lubitsch" Lubitsch, by directing Chevalier and MacDonald in *Love Me Tonight* (1932). The film opens by showing the entirety of Paris waking up, revealing how the sound of footsteps, brooms, water pumps, taxi horns, and so forth create a rhythm of the city. The film goes on to use rhythmic dialogue, slow and fast motion, direct address, and split screen in delightful ways. The song "Isn't It Romantic" exemplifies such inventiveness. Sung initially by Paris tailor Maurice, the catchy tune is passed from person to person—across town, on trains, and through the countryside—until it reaches princess Jeanette in her castle. Each of the protagonists sing of romance as one person subservient to the other (him in terms of the wife taking care of home and kiddies while he has fun; she in terms of adoration by knights willing to die for her), foreshadowing their ensuing battle of the sexes—but also linking them together in song before they have even met.

By the time Mamoulian made *Love Me Tonight*, the transition to sound was complete. Unlike in the late 1920s, when almost everything was being done for the first time, filmmakers now had a history of what worked—both with the technology and with audiences. Thus, they increasingly repeated successful ideas instead of trying something new. As Chapter 3 will show, new worries faced Hollywood, ones that would mandate less experimentation and more "tried-and-true" patterns. The widespread opportunities to define what a musical was would not happen again for decades.

Other Voices: Minoritized Groups and the Emerging Film Musical Genre

This volatile era led to a search not just for new ideas, but also for unique or different voices. Granted, a number of people thought that cultured, impeccable speech was necessary (hence all the classically theatre-trained actors, as well as diction classes for silent stars), but all sorts of potential audio novelties were also hired. As such, people who spoke with pronounced accents were regularly put before the microphone and camera. Maurice Chevalier's Gallic accent added to the suave sexuality of his image. *Song O'My Heart* surrounded Irish tenor John McCormack with a variety of characters speaking with a Celtic brogue. The opening of *Sunnyside Up*, noted at the time by critics for the use of a mobile camera gliding through an urban New York neighborhood street, shows a variety of inhabitants clearly "just off the boat" from a variety of countries.[35] In *They Learned About Women* (1930), vaudeville team Gus Van and Joe Schenck perform wildly insulting novelty songs in Irish and Italian dialects ("She wants to make whoopee," Gus sings in a broad Italian accent, "I want her to make Woppies ...").

Van and Schenck's "dialect humor" was an established form of comedy—evoking laughter through the perceived oddness of how certain ethnic groups supposedly misspoke English. The most popular practitioners by the 1920s were "Dutch comics"—that is, "Deutsche," to indicate the use of exaggerated German/Jewish accents. Early musicals are littered with versions of these comics, including Benny Rubin, Sidney Franklin, Joseph Cawthorn, and the legendary vaudevillian Al Shean. Intriguingly, the most popular practitioner of dialect humor, though, was El Brendel, who appeared in a number of Fox musicals such as *Sunnyside Up*, *Just Imagine*, and *Delicious* (1931). Instead of using the typical Yiddish dialect, El Brendel employed an exaggerated Swedish accent to portray a clueless yokel.

Along with the parade of European immigrant accents came a flood of blackface. The popularity of *The Jazz Singer* and its use of the form ensured its appearance in other films. Jolson regularly put on the burnt cork. *Big Boy* (1930), an adaptation of one of his Broadway successes, had Jolson in blackface throughout, playing an African American stable hand turned jockey. *Why Bring That Up?* (1930) featured the popular blackface duo Mack and Moran. One of RKO's biggest early box-office hits was *Check and Double Check* (1930), bringing the antics of radio characters Amos n' Andy to the screen—with the white performers who played them done up in blackface. Most notoriously, all the major African native characters in the operetta *Golden Dawn* are played by white performers, and the plot centers on Dawn, an African princess whom the gods purportedly favor so much that they decide to let her be born white! (And yes, the film plays as ridiculously as it sounds.)

The most obvious aspect of such use of ethnic and racial minority culture was to amuse white audiences rather than to speak to the individual minoritized communities themselves. The supposed exotic novelty of minority cultures for white audiences also provided a pretext for musical performance. Stereotypes of blacks, Irish, or other minorities as being a bit more childlike and a bit more passionate than white folks made it believable that they were more likely to break out into music at a moment's notice (although native Africans singing operetta in *Golden Dawn* strained the credulity of most theatregoers).

At the same time, though, windows of opportunity were created by this interest in different voices. A number of minority performers got the chance to step in front the camera and speak for themselves and, at times, take some control over the proceedings. Jolson, Fanny Brice, and Eddie Cantor were stars that continually foregrounded their Jewish heritage, for example. Often these performers ad lib various Yiddishisms, usually as an under-the-breath joke about what the non-Jewish characters are doing, delighting Jewish American viewers and bewildering others.

The popularity of jazz put African American musicians in demand as well. The performances of Eubie Blake and Noble Sissle in that early sound test helped usher other African American performers in further sound shorts, including the only film of iconic blues singer Bessie Smith, performing "St. Louis Blues" in a Paramount short of the same name from 1929. She commands the screen, ripping into the song with unbridled emotion from the very start ("My man's got a heart like a rrrrRRRRRRock in the sea ...") to the final climactic chorus. The African American performers in feature-length musicals often outshone the rest of the cast. The most memorable moments of backstager *On with the Show* (1929) are the two times Ethel Waters appears, particularly when she introduces "Am I Blue?" Similarly, the otherwise lackluster *Dixiana* (1930) is at its most entertaining when legendary tap dancer Bill "Bojangles" Robinson enters to do one of his famous staircase routines. In both films, black performers perform separately from the rest of the (white) cast. This strategy would continue for decades, segregating African Americans within musicals and ostensibly lessening their importance. Yet, such segregation also gave the performers a certain authority during those moments when they took over the film from the white cast.[36]

Hollywood's interest in the musical idioms of African American culture also led to two films with all-black casts: *Hearts in Dixie* (1929) and *Hallelujah!* (1929). *Hearts in Dixie* has a skeletal plotline (a sharecropper raises his grandson after his daughter dies, working to give the child a better life than he has had), but focuses more on the entire rural community—including their use of music and movement in celebration and in sorrow. *Hallelujah!* has a stronger narrative, dealing with a young man's rocky relationship with a shady woman, leading to death (for her) and prison (for him) before he is finally reunited with his family. Yet, the fellow's emotional journey allows the film to survey many aspects associated with African American culture (the rural life, the lowdown dives, the revival meetings), much like *Hearts in Dixie*. (Both films are also further examples of threading music throughout, rather than having many easily demarcated numbers.)

Most critics favor *Hallelujah!* over *Hearts in Dixie*.[37] The former was directed by King Vidor and is more artistically inventive, such as when swamp sounds are amplified to increase the tension when the protagonist hunts down a man in the backwaters and kills him. Vidor's film also has a clearer vision of what it wants to say (creating a religious allegory of temptation and redemption), while *Hearts in Dixie* seems to wander aimlessly. Yet, the aimlessness of *Hearts in Dixie* gives the African American performers a greater sense of freedom to express themselves on their own terms. As with Bessie Smith's performance of "St. Louis Blues," the spirituals and folk songs in *Hearts in Dixie* express more open exuberance than the forced vivacity typical of numbers in other films (more on this in a moment). Even the infamous Stepin Fetchit's "lazy coon" character arguably becomes more complex—suggesting that his character consciously chooses to act slow as a form of resistance to mainstream values of hard work and assimilation (i.e., the counterpart to the main character's efforts to send his grandson off to college). Fetchit's character shows that he does have energy and ability when he decides to use it, abandoning his usual shuffling for a lively dance when he hears music he likes.[38]

While both films seem earnest in their attempts to honor the African American community, both have a patronizing attitude that comes from white filmmakers talking about black culture to white audiences (and Fetchit's presence stands as strong evidence of such an attitude). The opportunity for African Americans to present themselves *is* given, but they had to negotiate the methods in which they could do so. This dynamic is matched in many other early sound musicals. *Check and Double Check* centers around white actors in blackface playing Amos n' Andy, but includes Duke Ellington and his Orchestra introducing "Three Little Words." Groucho Marx tosses in the Yiddish term "schnorer" while singing "Hooray for Captain Spaulding" in *Animal Crackers* (1930), while brother Chico does dialect humor as a stereotypical Italian "Wop." *The Jazz Singer* itself honors Jewish culture (including a fair amount of cantoring) *and* employs blackface.

This "both-and" nature of racial/ethnic images in early film musicals at times creates an absurdly contradictory playground where stable notions of race or ethnicity start to fall apart. Eddie Cantor's first film, *Whoopee!*, has been heralded by Henry Jenkins and others as a prime example of this.[39]

The plotline centers on a "mixed-race" romance between a white girl and a Native American man—which is forbidden and thus doomed. Cantor's character, though, constantly deflates the seriousness of the situation by repeatedly taking on a variety of racial categories. He is Jewish one minute, then dressed up as an Indian the next, to be followed by a quick change into blackface. His racial identity is always seen as a costume, not something innate or ultimately important. The interchangeability of racial identity actually resolves the main conflict: it is discovered that the male romantic lead had only been *raised* by Native Americans, but was born to white parents.

While the negotiation of race and ethnicity is prominent in early musicals, opportunities for other conventionally disempowered groups also developed. Some early film musical comedies show women (who had only won the right to vote earlier in the decade) taking charge and forsaking traditional femininity. Just as Jenkins discusses the carnivalesque nature of race and ethnicity in talkies, he points to performers such as Charlotte Greenwood (starring in projects like *So Long, Letty* [1929] and *Stepping Out* [1931]) who upset conventional gender norms. Like Greenwood and her lanky limbs, stars like Fanny Brice and Sophie Tucker dominated their surroundings, despite their lack of conventional beauty.

By the end of the 1920s, growing social awareness of a homosexual subculture was also occurring. George Chauncey and others have detailed the "pansy craze" in New York nightclubs and on Broadway at this time, with straight audiences flocking to see effeminate male emcees or drag competitions much in the same way white patrons went slumming to black speakeasies in Harlem.[40] Pansies offered another form of "dialect humor" that had appeal for talkies: the high-pitched male voice with a lisp. Pansy figures show up repeatedly in early musicals, from the fey costume designer in *The Broadway Melody* to the flouncy reporter flirting with Arab men in *The Desert Song*. When El Brendel goes to Mars in *Just Imagine*, he encounters a wild tribe of aliens, including the queen and her consort Boko. Boko plainly seems to fancy El Brendel, leading the Swede to declare, "She's not the queen—*he* is!" Following the pattern of the pansy craze in New York, emcees for the studio revues evoke effeminate mannerisms as well, such as Jack Benny in *The Hollywood Revue* (particularly when he interacts with William Haines, who was as openly gay as a star could be at the time)[41] or the ironically monikered Frank Fay in *The Show of Shows*. (At one point, while Fay describes a dream, he tells of meeting his fairy godmother, followed by the sly comment, "Now don't get ahead of me ...") Just as early musicals stereotyped people of color, they also offered oversimplified, reductive images of homosexual men (albeit, though, hardly any images of lesbians), but at least their presence was acknowledged. The "let's-try-anything" environment in these early musicals thus opened opportunities for minoritized groups and potentially destabilized understandings of race, ethnicity, gender, and sexuality.

Am I Blue? US Volatility in the Late 1920s

Although the industry may have been in chaos during the sound revolution, early film musicals are usually remembered as being filled with optimism: happy-go-lucky characters singing jazzy tunes and doing the Charleston with gleeful abandon. Popular ditties verge on nursery rhymes in the simplicity of their melody lines and lyrics ("Tiptoe through the tulips"; "I was meant for you, and you were meant for me"; "Just you, just me ..."). The catchy sing-song nature of the tunes is matched by the frivolity of the dance routines that follow the singing of one chorus (usually boy and girl breaking into an unmotivated up-tempo softshoe). The typical environments further this notion of unending frolic—resorts, vacation spots, or someone's Long Island estate. Young men and women constantly run around in bathing suits and tennis or golf togs, until it is time for tuxedos and fancy evening gowns.

These properties usually tell stories of sudden unprovoked success and happiness. Comedians such as Eddie Cantor and Joe E. Brown stumble their way from schlep to hero, gaining the respect and adoration of the upper crust in the process, including a tycoon's daughter. "Shopgirl-Cinderella" stories tell of plucky working-class sweethearts finding their modern-day upper-crust Prince Charmings. Backstagers include sudden windfalls, as struggling nobodies catapult to stardom. Such stories express unbridled optimism in an environment where fortunes change at a moment's notice. The sense that neither the characters nor the audience know what might happen next contributes to the levity, and the people on screen generally have a "devil-may-care" lack of concern about such vicissitudes. There might be an abrupt downturn, but there is confidence that just as quickly an upturn will happen as well—so why worry? Let's dance ...

The presentation of such optimism at times seems a bit forced, though. What worked on stage sometimes comes off as a little too obvious or extreme when framed in close-up and then blown up on a big screen. The camera also reveals that certain performers are not as youthful as their stage reputations promoted, accentuating the artificiality of the *joie de vivre*. The feel of a "heavy sell" is furthered by what some film historians have termed "superabundance."[42] Row upon row upon row of chorus members get added to numbers. More and more elaborate sets and costumes get pulled in front of the camera. The tempo gets faster with each chorus, and the key register gets higher. By the end of certain numbers, it sometimes seems as if the population of a small country is in front of the camera, shimmying so hurriedly that either they or the camera are about to burst into flames.[43] In one notorious instance, the set *does* go ablaze: in "Turn Up the Heat" from *Sunnyside Up* (1929), Eskimo girls gyrate so wildly that their igloos melt, palm trees spring up and burst with ripe phallic bananas, and then everything catches fire, with the girls escaping perdition by jumping into nearby water!

The intent of such superabundance was to amaze and energize audiences (and to trump what was financially possible on a Broadway stage). Instead, such moments often seem one step removed from a riot set to music, more exhausting to watch than energizing. With such crowds on set singing rather than pre-recorded, it is often impossible to hear lyrics, turning the soundtrack into a big mushy cacophony. Many of these superabundant numbers were also filmed in a still unperfected two-strip Technicolor, increasing the likelihood of viewer headaches. In general, it feels like everyone is trying too hard to convince us that everything is great.

That such optimism verged on mania is reinforced by the large amount of pain and suffering also in early film musicals. While backstagers included a lot of cheery antics, they also often contained their share of extreme heartache. The concept of the backstager leant itself to this pattern: what happens *behind* the happy exterior of the show being produced. *Glorifying the American Girl* (1929) shows a young woman becoming a Ziegfeld star ... but destroying the rest of her life in the process. The inane hijinks of *Show Girl in Hollywood* are suddenly undercut by a middle-aged and washed-up female star attempting suicide (and the film includes the song "There's a Tear for Ev'ry Smile in Hollywood").[44] *Applause* is so grim about show business (ending with the lead character's death, alone and forgotten) that it is arguably cinema's first *anti*-musical (a musical that seems to hate musicals).

One can see this melodramatic trend in *The Jazz Singer*. Jolson's character Jack twists in prolonged anguish until the emotional release of his singing of "Kol Nidre." Recognizing the power of the moment, Warner Bros. put together a variation on it for Jolson's follow-up, *The Singing Fool*. In it, Jolson plays an entertainer dealing not with a dying father, but with a young son who dies suddenly. The show must go on supposedly, and Jolson's character is forced to struggle through a rendition of the ballad "Sonny Boy," valiantly fighting back tears (and, according to all reports, the large majority of the movie's customers were less successful in the battle than him). This moment made both the film and the song unmitigated hits. Jolson is reunited with Davey Lee, the kid who played Sonny Boy, in *Say It with Songs* (1929)—and this time, Jolson's character goes to prison after accidentally killing a man in a fistfight. While he's serving time, his son is run over by a truck, and only the sound of his father's voice revives him after a delicate operation. Later, in *Mammy* (1930), Jolson is also implicated in a murder—this time shooting his best friend on stage with a gun that was supposed to have blanks in it, then tearfully performing "Let Me Sing and I'm Happy" while his pal succumbs off stage. Although each of these numbers are presented as stage performances, the narratives add extra emotional heft, usually in contradiction to the cheery nature of the lyrics.

The imposing shadow of Jolson's films led to a general overly melodramatic strain in many early musical films—and not just in backstagers. Family strife led the way, with stage performers struggling with parents or children in need

(*Honky Tonk* [1929], *Lucky Boy* [1928], *Innocents of Paris* [1929], *Applause* [1929]). Selfless abasement in romantic relationships was also common (*My Man* [1928], *The Broadway Melody* [1929], *They Learned About Women* [1930], *Lord Byron of Broadway* [1930]). Illness, accidents, and child custody cases abound. At the drop of a hat, someone is falling into a coma (*It's a Great Life* [1929], *Why Bring That Up?* [1929]) or being struck blind (*Live, Love and Laugh* [1929], *Puttin' on the Ritz* [1930], *Marianne* [1930], *A Lady's Morals* [1930]).

Jolson's way with a sentimental ballad leant itself to such pathos in the plot, but other stars were not as associated with such weepiness. Maudlin was not a word associated with red-hot mama Sophie Tucker, jaunty Maurice Chevalier, cocky Harry Richman, or blackface comics Mack and Moran. Nonetheless, each of them (and many others) appeared in films that alternated between musical sequences showcasing their own unique upbeat talents and storylines of almost inconceivable suffering. In *Why Bring That Up?*, Mack actually revives Moran out of a coma by reciting lines from their vaudeville routines! That such melodramatics were not well-suited to the personalities often led to extreme and sudden swings in temperament—happy and peppy one second, and then wham! someone's at death's door.

Commentators on the musicals of the early sound era have noted this emphasis on maudlin melodrama, but not the prevalence of such manic depressive swings.[45] While the film industry was on a roller-coaster ride during the transition to sound, a sense of precariousness was emerging across the nation at the same time. Various moralists were predicting the end of civilization, due to the "loose morals" of most Americans during the Jazz Age, but the uncertainty was also tied to the evolving economic situation. Stock and land speculation had fueled extravagant economic growth during the 1920s, yet wild (but brief) dips in the Dow Jones and collapses of land schemes began happening towards the end of the decade. *The Cocoanuts* (1929) actually deals with shady land speculation in Florida—even if no one really remembers the plot! The emphasis on the haves and the have-nots in musicals indicates how much focus there was on economic matters at this time. The comics consistently try to bust into high society; the shopgirl continually yearns for her millionaire, with his wealthy parents and her female rival sneering down at her. Most Americans chose to overlook the economic indicators and stay optimistic, but suppressed anxieties may have found their expression via early musicals and the recurrent motif of wild swings of fortune.

Perhaps the epitome of such manic volatility is expressed in the Oscar-nominated performance of Bessie Love in *The Broadway Melody*. She plays Hank, the feisty, go-getting half of a sister act, only to have the shyer (but prettier) sister become a star on her own. Adding insult to injury, Hank discovers that her songwriter beau and her sister have fallen in love with each other. After gallantly wishing them well via telephone, she sits at her dressing-room table, preparing to "go on with the show." Trying valiantly to apply makeup, Hank alternates between tears and laughter at the absurdity of life. Rather than randomly being hit by a truck or going blind, as happened in other musicals, the believability of this moment, and Love's ability to balance both reactions to create an even greater emotional precariousness, increases its strength.

As the 1930s began, the nation, Hollywood, and those involved in making film musicals would have to come to terms with an economic disaster that was no longer looming but in full force. The orgy was over, the zeppelin had exploded, and everyone was grabbing for the last available parachutes ...

Notes

1 Jennifer Fleeger, *Sounding American: Hollywood, Opera, and Jazz* (Oxford: Oxford University Press, 2014), 15.
2 Katherine Spring, *Saying It with Songs: Popular Music & the Coming of Sound to Hollywood Cinema* (Oxford: Oxford University Press, 2013), 12.
3 For a more detailed history of these maneuvers, see Douglas Gomery, *The Coming of Sound: A History* (New York: Routledge, 2005), and Donald Crafton, *The Talkies: American Cinema's Transition to Sound, 1926–1931. Vol. 4: History of the American Cinema*, ed. Charles Harpole (New York: Charles Scribner's Sons, 1997).
4 Western Electric created a subsidiary called ERPI (Electrical Research Products, Inc.), which allowed other studios to deal directly with the manufacturer rather than paying Warners any time it wanted to use Vitaphone.
5 Theodore Case, the main designated patent holder, had once worked in de Forest's labs, so the lawsuit may have had some merit, but de Forest ultimately did not have the economic means to fight Fox.
6 For more history on William Fox and the days before Fox Pictures joined with 20th Century Productions in 1935, see Aubrey Solomon, *The Fox Film Corporation, 1915–1935: A History and Filmography* (Jefferson: McFarland, 2011). Fox was not alone in attempting to gobble up competitors. Warners successfully bought out First National, one of the biggest Hollywood studios of the 1920s (thus finally giving Warner Bros. a large chain of theatres).
7 Photophone became standard across Hollywood by the mid-1930s. Perhaps unsurprisingly, a number of original musicals produced by RKO in its early years (such as *Street Girl* [1929], *Jazz Heaven* [1929], *The Vagabond Lover* [1929], *Check and Double Check* [1930]) feature radio prominently either in their plots or by featuring radio stars. By that time, having accomplished its mission, RCA had already divested itself from RKO. Rather than trying to gain a stronger foothold in the motion picture industry, RCA had already been moving to build an empire in the new technology of television.

8 *The Broadway Melody* (discussed in more detail later in this chapter) has become famous for the institution of playback. In looking at rushes of one number, "The Wedding of the Painted Doll," MGM executive Irving Thalberg felt that it needed to be reshot—but that the soundtrack was fine. Since the singer was not on camera, sound technician Douglas Shearer decided to keep the already-recorded audio, playing it back on set while the number was refilmed. Among the texts where this anecdote is told are: John Douglas Eames, *The MGM Story* (New York: Crown, 1977), 49; Alexander Walker, *The Shattered Silents: How the Talkies Came to Stay* (New York: William Morrow, 1979), 138; and Crafton, 236.

9 For example, the uncredited Johnny Murray warbles for Richard Barthelmess in *Weary River* (1929).

10 Mary Carbine, "The Finest Outside the Loop: Motion Picture Exhibition in Chicago's Black Metropolis, 1905–1928," *Camera Obscura* 23 (May 1990), 8–41.

11 See Preston Hubbard, "Synchronized Sound and Movie-House Musicians, 1926–29," *American Music* 3:4 (Winter 1985), 429–441.

12 Rick Altman, *Silent Film Sound* (New York: Columbia University Press, 2004).

13 See Spring, who points out that while much work has been done analyzing media convergence in the past twenty years, little has been done to recognize such convergence in past eras, such as during the transition to sound cinema.

14 Quoted in Jack L. Warner with Dean Jennings, *My First Hundred Years in Hollywood* (New York: Random House, 1964), 168.

15 Neither *Variety's* review (October 12, 1927) nor Mordaunt Hall's review for *The New York Times* (October 7, 1927) ever use the term "musical." Hall simply refers to the film being adapted from a "play" (not a "musical"), and the closest *Variety* comes to categorizing the film is "a Jewish mother-son-religious story."

16 Fleeger, *Sounding American*, focuses directly on this issue in early sound shorts, beginning with Lee de Forest's 1923 *Opera versus Jazz*.

17 See also Charles Wolfe, "Vitaphone Shorts and *The Jazz Singer*," *Wide Angle* 22:3 (July 1990), 58–78.

18 Lon Jones, "Which Cinema Films Have Earned the Most Money Since 1914?," *The Argus* (Melbourne) (March 4, 1944), 3, lists it as the highest-grossing film until *Snow White and the Seven Dwarfs* overtook it in 1937; on the other hand, other sources, such as the webpage filmsite.org lists *The Singing Fool* second behind *The Big Parade* (1925) as the most successful film of the 1920s (http://www.filmsite.org/boxoffice2.html).

19 Crafton, 63–88.

20 See Spring, 25–29, 84–94.

21 MGM had released *White Shadows in the South Seas* (1928) and a couple of other films with musical score soundtracks prior to *The Broadway Melody*, but all of those pictures were silent films that had music added at the last moment.

22 John McCormack was reportedly paid $500,000 for appearing in *Song O' My Heart*, an enormous sum for the time, when major stars such as John Gilbert or Coleen Moore were listed as earning $500,000 *a year* ("Talkies Result in Pay Increase for Film Stars," *Tasculoosa News* [February 21, 1931], 7). Intriguingly, his pay is almost exactly the reported loss that Fox took on the film: $503,000 (Solomon, 148); Richard Barrios, *A Song in the Dark: The Birth of the Musical Film* (New York: Oxford University Press, 1995), 287, describes how the huge cost of making *New Moon* robbed the picture of what might have been a profitable release.

23 Jolson speaks to Herbert Cruikshank in "You Ain't Seen Nothin' Yet," *Motion Picture Magazine* 36:4 (November 1928), which carries the subheading "This Year I'm Tellin' the Boys Where They Get Off an' I Get On" (33). "Last year I didn't know a thing about pictures. I just said, 'Gentlemen,' I said, 'Here I am just like a lil child, do with me as you will, 'cause this is a new racket to me.' But this time I'm speaking up some" (96). This is then followed by examples of all the advice he was now giving the writers, directors, and producers of his films. Warners had encountered flak from a stage star in making *The Jazz Singer*—not Jolson, but the star of the original stage production, George Jessel. A report in *Variety* (May 25, 1927) suggests that Jessel lost his chance to be in the film when he demanded additional payment for *singing* as well as pantomime acting. Robert L. Carringer, *The Jazz Singer* (Madison: University of Wisconsin Press, 1979), 17, mentions that Jessel also demanded that Jewish actors be hired to play the role of his parents, and "balked" when Warner Oland and Eugenie Besserer (both non-Jewish) were cast.

24 While Chaney is not physically present in the film, he is paid tribute to in a number entitled "Lon Chaney's Gonna Get'cha If You Don't Watch Out," with a number of fellows in a variety of Chaney's disguises menacing nightie-clad chorus girls around the set.

25 Although the musical backstager subgenre was largely created by the Hollywood studios, a brief vogue for dramatic and comedic plays about show business occurred on Broadway in the 1920s (including *The Jazz Singer*).

26 The Internet Movie Data Base lists the film's gross as just over $3 million worldwide, a sum bettered by no other Warner Bros. film to that time except for *The Singing Fool* (http://www.imdb.com/title/tt0019813/business?ref_=tt_dt_bus).

27 Spring, 2. Katherine Spring provides an excellent depiction of what is referred now to as media convergence between the motion picture and the music industries during the late 1920s, particularly on pp. 15–65.

28 Quoted in Barrios, 329.

29 Rick Altman, *Film/Genre* (London: British Film Institute, 1979), 31–33.

30 For more on how popular music interacted with early sound cinema beyond the conventional boundaries of the emerging musical genre, see Spring.

She points out that "at least one song appeared in more than a third of the sound films produced by the major studios during the 1928–1929 season, and that this proportion increased to more than half during the 1929–1930 season" (3).

31 Spring, 6–7, also discusses the discrepancies in designating films from this period as musicals, citing reviews of various titles. "*The Desert Song,* which was based on a stage operetta ..., was labeled as an operetta, and *Fox Movietone Follies* (1929) ... was described as a 'revue in celluloid form.' In contrast, ... *Broadway Babies* (1929) was called a comedy drama in *Film Daily* but a musical comedy in ... *Variety. The Broadway Melody* ... was, for a *Film Daily* reviewer, a 'comedy drama of Broadway show life.'"

32 Altman, *Film/Genre,* and Thomas Schatz, *Hollywood Genres: Formulas, Filmmaking, and the Studio System* (New York: McGraw-Hill, 1981), 186–188, both discuss this period as a type of "formative" period, providing texts that would be retroactively considered musicals.

33 Disney had made two earlier Mickeys, *Plane Crazy* and *The Gallopin' Gaucho,* but withheld them when he decided to make *Steamboat Willie* with sound—and it became the first Mickey to actually be released, with sound eventually added onto the first two which were released later in 1928.

34 *One Hour with You* had a contentious production, with producer Lubitsch purportedly interfering so much with assigned director George Cukor (in his first full assignment to a feature film) that Cukor walked off the project—but demanded co-directing credit with Lubitsch on the final product. For more detailed (and somewhat contradictory) versions of this production history, see Scott Eyman, *Ernst Lubitsch: Laughter in Paradise* (New York: Simon & Schuster, 1993), 185–187; Gavin Lambert, *On Cukor* (New York: Putnam's, 1972), 42–44; and Patrick McGilligan, *Geroge Cukor: A Double Life* (New York: St. Martin's Press, 1991), 70–71.

35 Morduant Hall, *The New York Times* (October 4, 1929), singles out this opening sequence in order to give praise to director David Butler.

36 For more on this, see Sean Griffin, "The Gang's All Here: Generic vs. Racial Integration in the 1940s Musical," *Cinema Journal* 42:1 (Fall 2002), 21–45.

37 See, for example, Altman, *The American Film Musical* (Bloomington: Indiana University Press, 1987), 290–297, a section which begins with an extended quote from a *Photoplay* ad for *Hearts in Dixie,* but quickly asserts that *Hallelujah!* "stands out by the quality of its music, the consistency of its performances, and particularly the coherent vision imposed on it by its director, King Vidor" (291–292).

38 For more on African Americans during this period, see Ryan Jay Friedman, *Hollywood's African American Films: The Transition to Sound* (New Brunswick: Rutgers University Press, 2011).

39 Henry Jenkins, *What Made Pistachio Nuts? Early Sound Comedy and the Vaudeville Aesthetic* (New York: Columbia University Press, 1992), 153–184.

40 George Chauncey, *Gay New York: Gender, Urban Culture, and the Makings of the Gay Male World, 1890–1940* (New York: Basic Books, 1994).

41 For more on the queer connotations of Jack Benny's star persona, see Alexander Doty, *Making Things Perfectly Queer: Interpreting Mass Culture* (Minneapolis: University of Minnesota Press, 1993), 63–80; for more on Haines, see William Mann, *Wisecracker: The Life and Times of William Haines, Hollywood's First Openly Gay Star* (New York: Viking, 1998).

42 Martin Rubin, *Showstoppers: Busby Berkeley and the Tradition of Spectacle* (New York: Columbia University Press, 1993), 15, defines the term as "more than could possibly be absorbed at a single sitting by any single spectator"; Crafton, *The Talkies*, 313, uses the term to specifically talk about early sound musicals—but Rubin details the heritage of "superabundance" prior to the arrival of talking pictures, such as the development of the "three-ring" circus.

43 "Lady Luck," the final number from *Show of Shows* is just one example. The stage is decorated with girls as curtain tassels and chandeliers. While a baritone in top hat and tails sings the chorus, showgirls gambol about in a variety of gambling motif fashions (cards, horse jockeys, dice). The baritone and first line of chorus girls are followed by organdy clad girls doing high kicks, a male acrobatic dancer does something resembling choreography, then some exotic chorus girls do a combination of hula dancing and some very lewd shimmying. Then an acrobatic male–female couple toss each other around, succeeded by a female dancer with a line behind her, all doing some sort of novelty dancing *en pointe*. The organdy clad gals come back downstage at this point (everyone mentioned is still on set) to do some more high kicks, then retire upstage so another line of chorus girls can do a variety of cartwheels and splits in tights to a reprise of "Singin' in the Bathtub." Then a line of chorus boys and girls in something approaching high-class evening wear break into some high-energy steps before stepping back for a male trio who jump into even higher-energy rubber-legged motions. A light-skinned African American fan dancer with a huge feathered headdress makes her way through the crowd, takes off her skirt, and does some fast stepping. She moves aside for a line of silk-top-hatted African American males who do a lively tap routine. A black solo in an unexplained navy commander's outfit takes center stage to further go nuts before hightailing it off stage to be replaced by another black male duo in artists' togs (including berets) who do more acrobatics. The commander and the fan dancer join the artists and one of the chorus lines to finish out the "black portion" of the number and then head to the wings. The increasingly populous group moves aside for tumblers that make no pretense that they are anything but a circus routine. The original tenor somehow makes room for himself to serenade some female now parading down the staircase, supposedly embodying "Lady Luck" herself. The entire group bellows out the final repeat of the chorus, successive rows of streamers descend from the top of the frame, and finally the curtains close, after ten minutes of non-stop chaos.

44 The song was plainly based on the 1915 Tin Pan Alley hit "There's a Broken Heart for Every Light on Broadway." Adding to the power of the attempted suicide is the casting of Blanche Sweet as the washed-up actress—who had been one of D.W. Griffith's leading ladies, and was by 1929 relegated to small supporting parts ... like the one in *Showgirl in Hollywood.*

45 See Barrios, 143–160; also Altman, *American Film Musical*, 210.

3

Face the Music and Dance: The Depression

As the 1930s began, the anarchy that accompanied the changeover to sound was waning. Studios and their employees figured out how to work with the new technology, and the technology itself was becoming more refined. Unfortunately, while the film industry resolved one upheaval, the nation as a whole faced a new and greater one. The enormous economic collapse, soon christened the Great Depression, would last throughout the 1930s. At first, the major Hollywood studios hoped they would not be affected, but they too eventually faced dire prospects. Perhaps in response, production of films showcasing musical performance declined significantly, but the slump turned out to be brief. Out of that respite, a full-fledged genre seemed to re-emerge. Critics and the industry itself came to some form of understanding of what it meant to be a film musical. The genre refashioned in order to become relevant to the Depression, and audiences warmed to its offers of hope and optimism. New methods to present musical performances in a uniquely cinematic fashion further helped create a sense of abundance and liberation.

The musical genre thus helped the industry survive the Depression. A wide array of talent contributed to this renaissance. Studios lessened the sense of risk by cultivating cycles, in which stars (as well as those behind the camera) played out the same box-office-proven formula from film to film with only slight variations, helping solidify genre expectations. Nevertheless, the unique qualities of the performers' talents and personae usually made each cycle individual—thus creating perhaps the widest variety of types of musicals in the genre's history.

Blah Blah Blah: The Slump

In 1930, dozens of musicals were under production. By 1931, though, studios had released only a handful of musicals. Monetary woes led executives to roll out cost-saving strategies, and musical films tended to have larger budgets than other pictures (employing songwriters, musicians, and dance directors,

Free and Easy? A Defining History of the American Film Musical Genre, First Edition. Sean Griffin.

as well as chorus boys and girls, not to mention the expensive sets and costumes usually called for in musical entertainment). Thus, it might not be surprising that the number of musicals declined at this point. Yet, such economic measures do not explain why completed musicals (the money already spent) were trimmed to eliminate most (and in some cases, all) of the numbers, and other musicals already in production were scrapped entirely.[1] By the summer of 1930, *Billboard* magazine would feature the blunt headline "Musical Films Are Taboo."[2] Such a headline indicates that, ironically, consensus was forming as to what a film musical was by defining the elements that audiences did *not* want to see.

Historians of the genre have posited various theories for the sudden slump.[3] Firstly, the number of unpopular experiments in how to make a musical film may have soured audiences towards the genre. Extended from that hypothesis, the oversaturation of musicals during the early sound years might have created genre fatigue in audiences. The repetitive simplicity of the storylines, dance numbers, and song types most likely did not help matters, as indicated by the Gershwins' "Blah Blah Blah" in *Delicious* (1931), with El Brendel singing "Blah blah blah love/Blah blah blah croon/Blah blah blah above/Blah blah blah moon ..." "Blah Blah Blah" also vaguely indicts the sunny devil-may-care outlook of early film musicals, an attitude that no longer matched the mood of the Depression-suffering population. Watching weekends at Long Island estates, or male juveniles bounding in asking "Anyone for tennis?," most likely made many a viewer's teeth grind in irritation.

While there was a remarkable cutback, inclusion of song and dance did not stop completely, and experimentation with what a film musical could be did continue. Uncertainty about what would work with audiences gave some artists the freedom to try out new ideas. In contrast to "Blah Blah Blah," *Delicious* includes George Gershwin's "New York Rhapsody," which plays over a nightmarish pantomime as forlorn little immigrant Janet Gaynor wanders the streets (and contemplates jumping into the Hudson River!). Rodgers and Hart wrote rhymed and rhythmic dialogue that only occasionally became regular musical theatre tunes for the Depression parable *Hallelujah, I'm a Bum* (1933)—and even got Al Jolson to play a character rather than doing his usual star turn.

Songwriters were not the only ones asserting their ideas. European filmmakers, for example, suggested potential ways of including musical performance, using traditions from their own musical heritage. Obvious examples were the operettas produced in Germany, such as *The Congress Dances* (1931), *Her Highness Commands* (1932), and *The Bartered Bride* (1932), all of which were more sprightly, inventive, and risqué than typical Hollywood operetta.[4] Ernst Lubitsch, an émigré from Germany, brought similar features to his musicals, which he continued to make during the so-called slump, including *The Smiling Lieutenant* (1931) and *One Hour with You* (1932). Fox also signed Lillian Harvey, the star of *The Congress Dances* and *Her Highness Commands*, and remade *Her Highness Commands* as *Adorable* (1933), starring Janet Gaynor and Henri Garat (who had worked with Lillian Harvey in Germany).

Over in France, director René Clair made *Le Million* (1930) and *A Nous, La Liberté* (1931), critically acclaimed films with musical moments which do not fit easily into the American definition of a musical—and many tend to discuss them more as comedies. Both films have a significant amount of music, but do not have clear-cut "numbers." While there is choreographed action, neither film has any full-out dancing. Both films celebrate anarchy and individual freedom, and the random use of music and song furthers the atmosphere of delightful chaos and rebellion against convention. To take one famous example from *Le Million*, the scramble for a winning lottery ticket suddenly becomes a sort of dance sequence, as people scurry in tempo to the music (and the soundtrack includes sound effects of a crowd at a sporting event to accentuate the feel of a football match).

Hollywood as well began making "comedies with music," rather than "musical comedies."[5] Like Clair's films, these early 1930s pictures go to extremes to flout authority and power. Along with acknowledging the camera, stepping out of character, and overt circumventing of logic or physical laws of science, comedians used the absurdity of breaking into song or dance as a weapon in their raucous form of class warfare.[6] Individual films (such as *International House* [1933]) or certain stars (such as the comedy team of Wheeler and Woolsey at RKO) are included in this trend, but the most notable practitioners were the Marx Brothers and Mae West. The Marx Brothers exposed the upper crust as gangsters in *Monkey Business* (1931), attacked the hallowed halls of academia in *Horse Feathers* (1932), and decimated government as a whole in *Duck Soup* (1933). Groucho's song in *Horse Feathers*, "Whatever It Is, I'm Against It," for example, simultaneously satirizes authority (he is the new president of the university) and expresses the general rebellious nature of the films. Rather than engage in open warfare like the Marxes, Mae West asserts her authority over the blue-bloods and blue-noses through a vague sneer and some tossed off innuendo. West even refuses to "sing right," seeming to give only a modicum of effort, or to even fully memorize the lyrics. Audiences flocked to her first two films, *She Done Him Wrong* (1933) and *I'm No Angel* (1933). Just as the Marx Brothers use music to destabilize institutions of power, West wields musical performance as a weapon, commenting with contempt after her opening number "They Call Me Sister Honky-Tonk" in *I'm No Angel*, "That'll hold 'em."

Eddie Cantor also followed this pattern, playing pipsqueaks with smart mouths who resist those claiming to be in charge. In the wake of Cantor's success with the film version of *Whoopee!* (1930) just when most musicals were tanking, producer Samuel Goldwyn fashioned pictures more in the classical "musical comedy" mode than those made with West or the Marxes, including extravagant production numbers created by dance director Busby Berkeley.

Although hired by Goldwyn from Broadway for *Whoopee!*, Berkeley quickly intuited the unique opportunities of cinema, placing the camera overhead to record a posse of cowgirls waving their hats in and out of a circle.[7] Overhead shots had been used in musicals before Berkeley came to Hollywood (such as *Applause* [1929], *The Cocoanuts* [1929], and *Lord Byron of Broadway* [1930]), but the Cantor films show Berkeley expanding upon the idea in numbers such as "My Baby Said 'Yes, Yes'" in *Palmy Days* (1931) and "Keep Young and Beautiful" in *Roman Scandals* (1932), with chorus girls executing various kaleidoscopic patterns, and cameras placed in all sorts of extreme positions to make the spectacle even more eye-boggling.

The slump in musical production plainly showed that the genre needed to regroup and refashion itself, but important strides were made during this brief downturn. The carnivalesque anarchy in some "comedies with music" voiced audience frustration over the economic crisis. The creativity of Berkeley began to open up the cinematic possibilities of presenting musical performance, moving beyond the "fifth-row center" proscenium that dominated early musical films. The proper combination and use of these aspects would signal a major turning point for the genre.

A New Deal in Entertainment: Berkeley to the Rescue

Paramount (along with Goldwyn) largely kept the torch of the musical lit— producing the Chevalier–MacDonald operettas, as well as the films of the Marx Brothers and Mae West. But, by 1933, Paramount was deeply in the red and started cutting back. Extravagant operetta was an obvious target and, after *Love Me Tonight*, the studio let MacDonald go, with Chevalier departing soon as well. The economic failure of *Duck Soup* led Paramount to drop the Marxes too. While West's films were still pulling in audiences, and Paramount had put popular radio crooner Bing Crosby under contract in 1932, the studio was no longer in a position to lead the way.

Warner Bros. had also shifted strategies with the onset of the Depression. After bingeing on acquisitions and high budgets in order to announce its ascendancy up the Hollywood ladder, the studio retrenched during 1930 into much smaller-budgeted films that focused more on gutsy storytelling than high production value. Often "ripped from today's headlines," Warner Bros. became associated with gangster films and tough urban dramas. Such a shift left little room for the frivolity of musical comedy, and thus the studio that had revolutionized the industry with *The Jazz Singer* largely stopped all musical production.[8]

So, when studio executive Darryl F. Zanuck decided the time was right to revive the musical backstager, it seemed a major gamble. By having all of the major numbers bunched at the end of the film, the majority of the film did not seem like a musical (and the numbers could easily be excised if sneak preview audiences turned hostile). Doubts about the project were unfounded, and *42nd Street* (1933) became a landmark in musical history. The studio smartly linked the film's publicity to the inauguration of Franklin D. Roosevelt. Evoking FDR's "New Deal" campaign, Warners promoted the picture as a "New Deal in Entertainment," helping combat the despair of the Depression. Audiences responded in droves, making it the studio's biggest success since *Gold Diggers of Broadway* (1929).[9] Even before the film made it to theatres, the studio geared up for more and, before the end of the year, an additional two had been released: *Gold Diggers of 1933* and *Footlight Parade*. All three became box-office smashes, leading other studios to jump on the bandwagon, and the film musical was reborn.

All three pictures gave the backstager a cold shower of economic reality.[10] Show business is shown as extremely hard work. In *42nd Street*, plucky newcomer Peggy Sawyer (Ruby Keeler) faints from hunger during a marathon rehearsal. In *Gold Diggers of 1933*, when Joan Blondell's character telephones her starving roommates to tell them she has found jobs for them all, her tears of relief verge on hysteria. Putting on a show is no longer about fun and excitement—it is about staying off the breadline. This is underscored in *42nd Street* when director Julien Marsh (Warner Baxter) gives a pep talk to young Peggy just before she steps in for the injured star on opening night: "Two hundred people! Two hundred *jobs*! You're going out there a youngster, but you've *got* to come back a star." This is not just encouragement—it's desperation.

While Busby Berkeley's numbers in the Cantor films act as just another element of random lunacy in anarchic comedy, his work for this trilogy and successive musicals at Warners create an urgency for the numbers to be lavish—they've "*got* to come back a star"[11] —and his inordinate spectacles act as munificent reward for all of the suffering and strain. In each instance, the viewer is invited to enter a world of untold freedom—from want, from logic, even from concrete physicality! On a basic level, the high expense lavished on these numbers creates a dreamland of plenitude where the Depression has been completely vanquished. Excess rules these sequences: dozens of neon-framed violins in the "Shadow Waltz" number of *Gold Diggers of 1933*; millions of gallons of water rushing through the "By a Waterfall" sequence in *Footlight Parade*; an unending number of Ruby Keelers populating "I Only Have Eyes for You" in *Dames* (1934); a multitude of dancing pianos in "The Words Are in My Heart" from *Gold Diggers of 1935* (1935). While these extravaganzas are supposedly performed on stage, the numbers go far beyond what any actual theatre could accommodate.[12] The title number of *42nd Street*, for example, eventually expands to show an entire city block, complete with traffic jam, a cop on horseback, and an abused woman throwing herself from a second-story window. "By a Waterfall" sprawls across two separate massive natatoria, as well as a multi-story revolving fountain.

Berkeley's love of purely cinematic devices also breaks down organizational logic. "Invisible" cuts on motion link one space to another, even if such a connection makes no logical sense: the engraving on a hand mirror suddenly becomes a collection of chorus girls; ruffled feathers at a seamstress's table becomes an entire feathery island paradise; a singer's profile morphs into the Manhattan skyline. A variety of other camera tricks are also regularly employed, such as reverse or slow motion. At one point in the "Shadow Waltz," the camera is placed sideways to film a line of chorus girls now gliding *vertically* past a reflecting pool. At the climax of the title number of *Dames*, a shot of a tunnel of chorines revolves before suddenly turning into a still photograph that Dick Powell's head bursts through to sing the final notes. (Direct acknowledgment of the audience continues from the earliest musicals, even though Berkeley's camera is anywhere but fifth-row center.) Such audacity is liberating—anything is possible. Berkeley's signature device of overhead shots of kaleidoscopic patterns also defies what a live theatrical audience would be able to witness. These patterns move into almost pure abstraction—with the film audience practically losing sight of actual human bodies and seeing nothing but a dazzling fluid display of shapes and motion, dark and light, circles and lines. Nothing is solid or concrete (Figure 3.1).[13]

Of course, in being allowed to give his own imagination free rein, Berkeley wielded great power over those working for him, and he gained a reputation for dictatorial control on the set.[14] Enormous precision and coordination was required by the performers, the camera operators, and the lighting crew to get

Figure 3.1 A prime example of a Busby Berkeley overhead shot, turning the bodies of chorus girls into a kaleidoscopic pattern in the title number from *Dames* (1934). Snapshot taken from: Dames (1934).

a perfect take—and rehearsals and shooting often went into the early hours of the morning. Berkeley's efforts to follow his own muse also often resulted in insensitive imagery as well. Berkeley was often cavalier in his use of minority cultures, most famously in the Al Jolson production number "Goin' to Heaven on a Mule" from *Wonder Bar* (1934). Jolson in requisite blackface rapturously explores white culture's conception of a black man's heaven: pork chop trees, angels shooting dice, and overhead patterns of performers waving giant watermelon slices. Berkeley's interest in pure graphics also set black against white in "Keep Young and Beautiful" from the Goldwyn/Cantor film *Roman Scandals*, with black maids running around white bathing beauties.

Women, whatever their background, are by and large treated as playthings or props for him to maneuver—all interchangeable (Ruby Keeler notwithstanding). Shots often break the chorus girls into various body parts (faces, legs), and convert them into cogs in a kaleidoscopic machine.[15] Intriguingly, Berkeley presents treating *men* as product on a conveyor belt as reprehensible in "Remember My Forgotten Man," the stunning conclusion to *Gold Diggers of 1933*. Yet, he plainly delights in having female bodies succumb to his extravagant whims. It is perhaps not surprising that Adolf Hitler loved Berkeley's spectacles—which is borne out in the choreographed patterns in the Nazi Party's Nuremberg rallies, captured on film in *Triumph of the Will* (1934).

The sense of exhilarating acquiescence to the vision of one imagination is mirrored in the plots of *42nd Street* and *Footlight Parade*. In each, a strong-willed director (Warner Baxter in the former, James Cagney in the latter) pulls a group together and into success through sheer determination. Depression dynamics brought to the forefront the dichotomy between individual liberty and the importance of community. The selfish divas or the machinations of scheming producers are condemned (often their actions imperil the show), while working as a team is championed. Unlike the divas or producers, the director asserts his authority for the greater good, pushing himself just as hard as those around him. Everyone works in tandem, coordinating and synchronizing their movements to bring to life the director's vision.

Berkeley's shadow loomed over the resurgence of the musical, as other studios tried to copy or surpass him. MGM, for example, began spending lavish amounts to create musical spectacles. *Dancing Lady* (1933) obviously mimics the Warners backstager, particularly in its "Rhythm of the Day" finale, complete with kaleidoscopic shots of chorus girls on a stylized carousel. Similarly, "I've Got a Feelin' You're Foolin'" in *Broadway Melody of 1936* (1935) spins out in an elaborately random fashion. The studio's Oscar-winning *The Great Ziegfeld* (1936) is most remembered for its huge revolving wedding cake staircase in "A Pretty Girl Is Like a Melody," shot in three extraordinarily long and complicated takes by cinematographer Ray June. MGM was not alone in imitating Berkeley, though. The title number of RKO's *Flying Down to Rio* (1933) shows chorus girls performing on the wings of (supposedly) airborne planes, including female trapeze artists (one of them missing a catch, only to be rescued by a burly male acrobat on the wing of another plane)! In Paramount's *Big Broadcast of 1936* (1935), Ethel Merman belts out "It's the Animal in Me," while an overhead camera captures elephants cavorting in geometric patterns. The Disney cartoon short *Cock o' the Walk* (1935) shows various farm fowl erupting into a dance spectacle. Even lower-budgeted musicals felt the need to attempt a "Berkeleyesque" piece, such as Universal's *Myrt and Marge* (1933), which includes overhead shots of an odd snake-charmer production number. The emphasis on wild and inventive spectacles gave the role of dance director a heightened imprimatur, even resulting in a new Oscar category from 1935 through 1937. Following in Berkeley's footsteps, Sammy Lee, Hermes Pan, and other dance directors concocted all sorts of fantastic, cinematic excess.

The influence of the specific style of the Berkeley/Warners films ended up lasting only a short time (as will be explained shortly), but the business pattern of producing them would have a much longer impact. Warners had Berkeley work repeatedly with performers such as Ruby Keeler, Dick Powell, and Joan Blondell, songwriters Harry Warren and Al Dubin, and "book director" Lloyd Bacon.[16] Each contributed their own unique aspect to the overall re-orientation of the backstager for Depression audiences: Keeler's ingénue who makes good not so much from talent but from hard work;[17] Powell's juvenile tenor with street smarts;[18] Blondell's tough exterior hiding her sentimental side; Warren's jazzy hustling rhythms and Dubin's snappy urban slang lyrics;[19] Bacon's ability to keep the narrative moving at fast tempo. Yet, the reinvigoration of the musical by Warner Bros. was accompanied by the imposition of a formula that limited what to expect. Warners was not the first to group talent from picture to picture, but its success institutionalized the concept, and the rest of the 1930s would see others studios creating their own musical "cycles." Success began breeding confinement along with contentment.

Sweet Mysteries of Life: The Production Code

Warners backstagers also reveled in the risqué. Wisecracks run rampant, such as "As long as there are sidewalks, you've got a job!" Such innuendo was matched by Berkeley's display of the female form. Chorus girls caught in a rainstorm during "Pettin' in the Park" in *Gold Diggers of 1933* disrobe in silhouette, with a mischievous infant (Billy Barty) threatening to raise the sash and reveal everything. Inventively designed suits in *Footlight Parade*'s "By a Waterfall" create the illusion that the bathing beauties' erogenous zones are covered only by tresses of their hair. Feathered fans barely shield naked bodies in "Spin a Little Web of Dreams" from *Fashions of 1934* (1934). Much like Mae West's one-liners, such sexual hijinks were linked to the general thumbing of noses at authority in these films.[20]

Female décolletage was not the only way to challenge traditional propriety. Musicals (along with many other films) regularly showed characters flouting the prohibition of alcohol, for example. Paramount's whodunit/backstager *Murder at the Vanities* (1934) went farther, creating a production number tribute to "Sweet Marijuana"! The gay male pansy stereotype was also common, appearing in films such as *Palmy Days*, *Myrt and Marge*, and *Dancing Lady*. In *Wonder Bar*, a man interrupts another man and woman on a night club dance floor, asking if he can "cut in." The couple agrees—and the man dances off with the other fellow.[21] *Wonder Bar* also demonstrates a "situational" moral ethos rather than upholding a rigid sense of the law: when Dolores del Rio's character kills her abusive dance partner/boyfriend, Al Jolson's character stows the body in the back of a car owned by a financially ruined businessman that Jolson knows is planning suicide by driving off a cliff ... and Jolson seems to get away with the plan.

The election of Roosevelt and the onset of his New Deal shifted public opinion—instead of seeing those in power as either uncaring or actually villainous, the general population now regarded the new president as the guy who would save the country. Support for the establishment rather than resistance against it quickly became the sentiment of the day. As Warners' "New Deal" publicity campaign for *42nd Street* shows, the resurgence of the musical genre was tied to this renewed optimism: we might not be out of it yet, but we'll get there if we keep the faith and work hard. Yet, such belief in the system ran counter to the cynical, anarchic, and anti-establishment nature that many Hollywood films, including the Warners backstagers, had been espousing.

In 1933, a number of groups and communities began to loudly criticize Hollywood, regarding cinema's glorification of the gangster, its contempt for authority, and especially its growing sexual explicitness as part of the "moral failure" which supposedly caused the Depression. Calls for greater censorship and for national boycotts grew in number and stridency. Rather than have the federal government take charge, the industry announced that it would regulate itself. A "Production Code," which laid out what could and could not be shown and said in motion pictures, had been written in 1930, but had been largely disregarded by studios trying to get Depression-stricken customers into theatres. In response to this new outcry, a method of enforcing the Code was created: the Seal of Approval. All the major studios agreed to submit their films to the Production Code Administration, and agreed to pay a hefty fine if they released any film that did not get the Seal from the PCA.[22]

Musicals were an immediate target as the "Production Code Era" began. Mae West was a prime example. Consistently finding fault with scripts, costume designs, and her performances, the PCA so confined what West was allowed to do or say that it was almost impossible for Paramount to continue making films with her.[23] The PCA also got into an infamous battle over a heated romantic scene on a chaise lounge between Jeanette MacDonald and Maurice Chevalier in Ernst Lubitsch's production of *The Merry Widow* (1934). Eventually, the couple's intimacy was approved only as long as one of them managed to keep a foot on the ground (supposedly limiting the range of possible physical positioning).[24] Berkeley extravaganzas came under fire as well—with Jack Warner avoiding phone calls and letters from the PCA expressing their displeasure over *Wonder Bar*.[25] Another Berkeley opus from 1934, *Dames*, obviously derides the PCA in its story of a team of prudes trying to shut down a Broadway show celebrating the pulchritude of the titular chorus girls.

The writing was on the wall, though, and the musical genre was faced now with a new set of limitations on what was allowable. While not as immediately affected as Mae West, the Warners cycle noticeably changed. Just as Berkeley managed to get promoted from dance director to "full-out" director, the sass and sex that energized the first few films was muted. Similar to how the Code squelched the sexual independence of Mae West's characters, it generally muzzled the wisecracks of gold diggers like Joan Blondell in favor of the wide-eyed naivete of Ruby Keeler. Remarkable individual set pieces still appeared—such as "Lullaby of Broadway" in *Gold Diggers of 1935* and "All's Fair in Love and War" in *Gold Diggers of 1937* (1937)—but none of these later films seems equal to the zeal of the earlier entries. In general, libidinous energies were now mystified into a more circumspect sense of "romance": couples were transported to ethereal realms instead of the bedroom; randy lyrics were replaced with poetic courtship.

While the Warner Bros. cycle struggled to adapt to the new parameters, new cycles at other studios fit perfectly. RKO noticed the chemistry of Fred Astaire and Ginger Rogers dancing together in a short sequence of *Flying Down to Rio* (1933), and launched the couple into a highly lauded series of romantic musical comedies. The unique thrill of their partnership was how Astaire's characters courted Rogers' through dance. In the narratives, Rogers was usually annoyed with or actively antagonistic towards Astaire; but once they got out on the floor, the blend of their movements conquered all perceived difficulties. Whether a slow ballroom dance such as "Cheek to Cheek" in *Top Hat* (1935) or a snappy tap duet like "Pick Yourself Up" in *Swing Time* (1936), the two matched and complimented each other perfectly.[26]

It is perhaps unsurprising that these memorable dances have sexual overtones. "Night and Day" in *The Gay Divorcee* (1934) was their first romantic interlude. After Astaire lures a reluctant Rogers onto the floor, her body motions indicate she is giving in to the experience as the music grows in intensity, until he finally deposits her gently on a bench, leaving her breathless ... and then he asks if she'd like a cigarette. The choreography sufficiently veiled the sexual metaphor, transforming it from earthy to (as "Cheek to Cheek" put it) "heaven" (Figure 3.2). Rather than creating salacious camera moves *a la* Berkeley (such as running the camera through the legs of chorus girls), Astaire (with choreographer Hermes Pan) preferred the camera stay at a respectful

Figure 3.2 Nothing sexual happening here. Under the strictures of the Production Code, Fred Astaire and Ginger Rogers dance out their attraction to each other in "Cheek to Cheek" from *Top Hat* (1935). Snapshot taken from: Top Hat (1935).

distance to show the entire body in motion, moving only to keep the body in the center of the frame.[27] Dance sequences also tended to be performed in what RKO designer Van Nest Polglase called Big White Sets: pristine Art Deco "heavens." Further, RKO made a quite conscious decision not to show the couple ever kissing on screen, sublimating the eroticism even more.[28] Homosexuality was similarly cloaked: while quite a number of effeminate men act as comic relief in these films (played by actors such as Edward Everett Horton, Eric Blore, and Erik Rhodes), plausible deniability is provided by having these characters purportedly married, claiming to be interested in Rogers, or not seeming to have any sexual desire whatsoever. Rogers herself represents the transition into the "Code-era" musical. No longer "Anytime Annie" in *42nd Street*, Rogers' self-assertive sexuality gets coated with layers of gloss—moving from cheeky to chic. As Katharine Hepburn famously intoned about Astaire and Rogers, she gave him "sex" and he gave her "class"—or she made him seem more manly (the comic-relief sissies helped too), but he made her less crude or potentially objectionable.

A parallel remolding occurred with Jeanette MacDonald. The problems the PCA had with *The Merry Widow* indicated that her sexual frisson with Maurice

Chevalier would no longer be allowed. *The Merry Widow* was made at MGM rather than Paramount, and her move from one studio to the other resulted in a new musical cycle, with a new co-star and a new image. Rather than the sly Chevalier, MacDonald was partnered with stalwart baritone Nelson Eddy. Complimenting his blank expression and rigid body stance, MacDonald's star image turned more pure and virginal (albeit with a stubborn streak tied to the diva elements of her characters). Starting with *Naughty Marietta* (1935), which climaxed with them warbling about love as "Ah, Sweet Mystery of Life," MacDonald and Eddy were paired for the rest of the decade in loose adaptations of famous operettas. The pairing of MacDonald and Eddy was actually preceded by opera star Grace Moore's triumphant performance in *One Night of Love* (1934) at Columbia, winning both her and the film Oscar nominations. Other studios soon tried out other operatic voices: Gladys Swarthout at Paramount; Lily Pons at RKO; James Melton at—yes, even there—Warner Bros.

Championing "respectable" music helped the Hollywood studios' ongoing efforts to clean up their image. Yet, just as the magical compatibility of the bodies of Astaire and Rogers obliquely suggested copulation, so too did the intensity of the full-throated harmonies shared by MacDonald and Eddy.[29] Eddy might look stiff as a board in his Mountie uniform as he sings "Indian Love Song" with her in *Rose Marie* (1936), but the soundtrack indicates that he is avidly commingling with her—at least vocally. In much the same way as Rogers gives way to Astaire as they dance to "Night and Day," the expression on MacDonald's face as she duets with Eddy shifts from reluctant playfulness to surprise and a slight twinge of fear at the intensity of the moment, and then finally total surrender as they complete the last note and collapse into each other's arms. Only the high-class connotation of operetta made it seem as if the two never went any farther.

Over at Fox, tiny tot Shirley Temple seemed an even further step away from sexual suggestiveness, becoming the nation's number-one star in 1934 (the year the Seal of Approval began) and staying there for the next three years. Temple personified innocence, and her cheerful guileless persona was far removed from the cynicism common to many pre-Code musicals. Temple was regarded as so pure and wholesome that no major outcries of interracial impropriety occurred from her on-screen partnership with Bill Robinson in *The Little Colonel* (1935), *The Littlest Rebel* (1935), *Rebecca of Sunnybrook Farm* (1938), and *Just Around the Corner* (1938).[30] Hollywood musicals usually avoided interracial dancing, fearing the PCA's mandate against "miscegenation." Censors found no fault with Temple and Robinson, though, probably because his characters were sweet-natured and asexual (very arguably versions of the "Uncle Tom" stereotype), and his white partner was five years old.

Intriguingly, Temple's career actually mirrors that of Rogers and of MacDonald in their transitions to Code-acceptable roles. Prior to her contract at Fox, Temple had appeared in a number of shorts called *Baby Burlesks*.

Figure 3.3 Shirley Temple cuddling with one of her many on-screen "daddies," James Dunne, in *Bright Eyes* (1934). Snapshot taken from: Bright Eyes (1934).

In the *Burlesks* series, very young performers act out parodies of current Hollywood films—and thus, Temple runs around playing vamps and saloon girls cozying up to little boys in imitations of Marlene Dietrich and other screen goddesses. Just as one can still recognize libidinal energy lurking within the Astaire–Rogers and the MacDonald–Eddy films, Temple's films at Fox also arguably contain latent sexuality. Her characters are consistently charming various adult men, hoping they will "become her daddy," and quite commonly Temple's dresses were hemmed *just* below her derriere (Figure 3.3). The lyrics to "When I'm with You" in *Poor Little Rich Girl* (1936) include her singing to her father, "Marry me and let me be your wife"! British film critic Graham Greene noticed these undercurrents at the time. Fox responded by successfully suing him for libel—no one was messing with their gold mine by suggesting that something amoral might be afoot.[31]

By and large, audiences appreciated Temple as innocence personified, and soon the silver screen was littered with other talented tots expressing an unjaded outlook on life, such as Bobby Breen and Irene Dare at RKO, and Jane Withers at Fox playing in second-tier films to Temple's more high-profile projects. Hal Roach, who produced comedy shorts, began including mini-musicals within his long-running *Our Gang* series, most famously *Our Gang Follies of 1938* (1938) with "Alfalfa" Switzer yelping out "I'm the Barber of Seville! Figaro!"

The *Our Gang* shorts were distributed by MGM, which developed quite a stable of juvenile stars, including Jackie Cooper (who had been in some *Our Gang* shorts), Freddie Bartholomew, and Mickey Rooney. Cooper and Bartholomew were not associated with musicals, nor was Rooney initially.

MGM did test two female adolescent singers, but felt the need to keep only one under contract. So, after a short entitled *Every Sunday* (1936), which showcased both, MGM dropped its option on Deanna Durbin, and held onto Judy Garland. Durbin was picked up by Universal, which was in dire economic straits. The studio presented its "new discovery" in *Three Smart Girls* (1936), which became a box-office sensation and arguably rescued the company.[32] Durbin looked a bit like a slightly older Temple (round face with bright cheeks, curly light brown hair) and shared the upbeat personality. Durbin matched youthful innocence with a classically trained voice, thus marrying the respect of "serious" music with the asexuality of childhood. For the rest of the 1930s, Universal's highest-budgeted features starred Durbin. As she grew up, her characters started having teenage crushes on boys (and some older men such as Franchot Tone in *That Certain Age* [1938]), but such emotions were always chaste and charming. Finally, in 1939, the studio heavily publicized her first on-screen kiss (to Robert Stack) in *First Love*.[33]

MGM was most assuredly chagrined at Universal's success with Durbin, and worked on fashioning Garland into stardom. While Durbin's success was relatively immediate, Garland slowly built up popularity across the rest of the decade, finally becoming a bona fide star in 1939's *The Wizard of Oz*. Like Durbin, Garland was shown having school girl crushes, but either on unattainable objects (such as Clark Gable, to whom she sings a fan letter in *Broadway Melody of 1938* [1937]) or similarly innocent boys (usually Rooney).

The late 1930s, then, saw musicals developing multiple strategies for complying with the restrictions of the Code. Successful solutions were quickly copied by others, and sometimes filmmakers mixed these concepts (such as Durbin being a child star with a trained voice). What these ideas had in common was a way of diverting the energy that drove pre-Code musicals into acceptable channels—thus keeping such drives alive even if veiled. The libido of the pre-Code era might have been dampened, but it was not dead.

Out of the Red and Over the Rainbow: Surviving the Depression

In early 1934, as the revival of the musical was just under way, Fox released *Stand Up and Cheer*, a Depression fairy-tale about the federal government establishing a Department of Entertainment to keep up national morale. What followed were various musical numbers and comic set pieces—including "Baby Take a Bow," Shirley Temple's first appearance in a Fox film. The picture concludes with the ultimate happy ending for the period—a joyous celebration that the Depression has somehow ended, with the entire cast parading to the anthem "We're Out of the Red." *Stand Up and Cheer* exemplifies a common thread through musicals for the rest of the decade: lifting audience spirits during the Depression. The slump in production in the early 1930s may have been caused by a sense that musicals had no emotional connection to the economic strife of the general population, but the renaissance seems largely to have been tied to helping people believe that better times would come, or at least to forget their troubles a short while. *Stand Up and Cheer* and the Warners backstagers did both: showing a group of struggling artists achieving success through the performance of lavish musical fantasies.

Fantasy in various guises was used in musicals to help audiences escape from their day-to-day troubles. Disney animators excelled at this, creating shorts in which animals sang (*Who Killed Cock Robin?* [1935]), insects jitterbugged (*Woodland Café* [1937]), and myths and Mother Goose rhymes were told through music (*The Goddess of Spring* [1934], *Mother Goose Goes Hollywood* [1938]). Disney's first animated feature would be a musical version of the Grimms' fairy tale *Snow White and the Seven Dwarfs* (1937), which became the biggest box-office success in film history to that time. MGM would create its own musical fantasy two years later, the classic *The Wizard of Oz*. In its own way, the Astaire–Rogers cycle (with its tuxedos, designer gowns, and Big White Sets) was also a stylized fantasy far removed from the everyday lives of most moviegoers. Operettas were often associated with fairy-tale settings as well, such as *Naughty Marietta*, *The King Steps Out* (1937), and *The Great Waltz* (1938).[34]

While providing escape, thoughts of the Depression still lay beneath these musical fantasies. *The Wizard of Oz*, for example, literally transports a Dust Bowl urchin "over the rainbow" to a Technicolor neverland where she learns to be grateful for what she already has. One of Disney's most celebrated cartoons from this period, *The Three Little Pigs* (1933), taught the value of hard work rather than escapism, and introduced "Who's Afraid of the Big Bad Wolf?," a tune that quickly became a hit song across the nation, much like "We're in the Money" from *Gold Diggers of 1933*. Fred Astaire and Ginger Rogers would follow suit in *Swing Time*, with the tune "Pick Yourself Up." Even more spectacular was their climactic number in *Follow the Fleet* (1936), entitled "Face the Music and Dance." In this piece, Astaire and Rogers are in a dreamland version of Monte Carlo—but Fred has lost all of his money gambling. Just as he contemplates using a pistol on himself, he witnesses a glamorous but distraught Ginger about to fling herself off a balcony. He prevents her and the two dance each other out of their thoughts of suicide: "There may be trouble ahead, but while there's moonlight and music and love and romance, let's face the music and dance." Underneath all the gloss, the message not to give up hope is still apparent.

Child stars also functioned as symbols of hope. Temple's dimpled smile and unaffected nature proved quite the tonic to Depression audiences.[35] Temple is usually introduced as an orphan (*Curly Top* [1935], *Captain January* [1936], *Stowaway* [1937], *Little Miss Broadway* [1938]) or loses one or both of her parents as the film goes on (*Bright Eyes* [1934], *The Littlest Rebel* [1935],

Poor Little Rich Girl [1936]). Mendacious characters design against her (most startlingly in *Poor Little Rich Girl*, where a lurking man attempts to kidnap her in an obvious reference to the abduction of the Lindbergh baby). Yet, through it all, Temple's characters maintain a cheery disposition, and spend time encouraging others to "buck up"—usually through song (and a little tap dance as well). The tunes most associated with her—"On the Good Ship Lollipop" and "Animal Crackers in My Soup"—are fantasy-oriented, but she sang quite a few paeans to keeping one's chin up: "You Gotta S-M-I-L-E (to Be H-A-Double-P-Y)," "Come and Get Your Happiness," and the bluntly titled "Be Optimistic." And, of course, Temple is rewarded for her optimism at the conclusion of every picture.

Following in her tiny footsteps, other youngsters were shown brightening the outlooks of their elders. Deanna Durbin was dubbed "Miss Fix-It" because the characters she played consistently ran around manically solving adult dilemmas. The most obvious example of this pattern is her second feature, *100 Men and a Girl* (1937). The titular adults are a group of unemployed symphony musicians—including her father. On her own initiative, she uses every possible means, including her own vocal talents, to get this down-and-out troupe heard by star conductor Leopold Stokowski (playing himself). While her interfering causes all sorts of problems, she inevitably succeeds—becoming her own little public works program in the process (and getting Universal an Oscar nomination for Best Picture).

Talented tykes were not the only ones enacting such fables. Many adult stars played figurative "little guys" finding reward through hard work, virtue, and unwavering faith. Backstagers, for example, celebrated the struggling artist eventually finding success and happiness. The format of the backstager, in fact, allowed a diverse range of talents to step out of obscurity and find themselves in a major Hollywood film. "Novelty acts" proliferated in film musicals at this point, random moments where the nominal plot paused to let a juggler, oddball comic, eccentric dancer, or other unique artist take over the picture as supposedly part of the show being produced. Such a structure gave radio comics like Joe Penner or Parkyurkarkas (who did ethnic humor with a Greek accent) a chance to show themselves on camera. Others came from vaudeville—Borrah Minevitch and his Harmonica Rascals, tumblers Mitchell and Durant, Russell Patterson's Personetto puppets—all implicitly proving that anyone could make it if they tried hard enough. Most novelty acts had their one brief moment in one feature or short; some were successful enough to appear in multiple films. Olympic ice skater Sonja Henie was arguably the most successful novelty act of the decade, parlaying her gold medals and live ice show into stardom in a cycle of films at 20th Century-Fox. Henie was a shrewd businesswoman, but she usually portrayed a sweet innocent peasant girl who just happens to be a skating dynamo, becoming a star and capturing the man of her dreams (in *Thin Ice* [1937], she even manages to snag a Prince Charming, played by Tyrone Power).[36]

Henie was not alone playing nobodies achieving fame, fortune, and romance in a backstage format. At the same studio, Alice Faye played variations of a girl from a meager background struggling to make it as a vocalist. While capable of making wisecracks in the Warners backstager mode, Faye's characters were usually very self-sacrificing, helping someone else out because it was "the right thing to do" even if it caused problems and/or heartache for her. Faye's low throaty singing style lent itself to this type of character, perfect for melancholy ballads. Even though everything seemed stacked against her characters, they kept plugging away. As she counseled in the title tune from *Sing, Baby, Sing* (1936), "when troubles trouble you, sing, baby, sing!" Faye's films also encouraged people to be happy with what they had rather than wanting more, as evidenced in the title *You Can't Have Everything* (1937). By the end of each film, though, she actually does get everything. Thus, audiences were both advised to not be upset with their current life and encouraged to think that things would get better.

Filmgoers witnessed Faye's own gradual move up the ladder of success.[37] Coming from the Hell's Kitchen area of New York City, she was a singer for a band hired to appear in *George White's Scandals of 1935* (1935) starring Lillian Harvey. When Harvey abandoned the production and Fox, Faye took her place. Over the next few years, Faye moved from low-budget pictures (like *Music Is Magic* [1935]) to second-leads in bigger films (such as the Temple films *Poor Little Rich Girl* and *Stowaway*), and finally to stardom in prestige projects such as *In Old Chicago* (1937) and *Alexander's Ragtime Band* (1938).

In contrast, Eleanor Powell—who made her first on-screen appearance in *George White's Scandals of 1935*—was a full-fledged star by her second film, MGM's *Broadway Melody of 1936* (1935). She was beautiful, capable of acrobatic moves, and arguably surpassed in tap dancing virtuosity only by Fred Astaire and Bill Robinson. Her demeanor exuded confidence—not arrogance but a strong sense of self.[38] Still, she was cast repeatedly as the new girl in town trying to get her big break on the stage. Perhaps to balance the blatant obviousness of Powell's star quality, her characters often dealt with dirty tricks and mind games played by a professional and romantic rival, thus keeping her from her rightful place in the spotlight ... until the final moments of the picture. When she does finally get her chance, the resultant numbers are huge production numbers (usually with the Albertina Rasch dancing troupe), such as the blasting of battleship cannons at the climax to "Swingin' the Jinx Away" in *Born to Dance* (1936). Like Faye, Powell also succeeded in finding romance as well as fame, but her strength of personality tended to dwarf her co-stars (who were often not musically inclined—as evidenced by poor James Stewart trying to creditably rasp his way through a chorus of Cole Porter's "Easy to Love" in *Born to Dance*). Yet, Powell's characters always worked with and for others, unlike the self-centered antagonists she faced—thus displaying that she was "of the people" and not above them.

Bing Crosby in a way split the middle between Faye and Powell. By the time he graduated from Mack Sennett shorts to a Paramount contract in 1932, he had become a red hot sensation on radio and records—and many of his early films (*The Big Broadcast* [1932], *Going Hollywood* [1933], *Here Is My Heart* [1934]) cast him as already a star (sometimes playing a character *named* Bing Crosby). Yet, his relaxed crooning style of singing, his affable screen presence, and his lack of conventional matinee idol looks made him seem more like a "regular guy" than a glamorous leading man. It seems that a key loan-out to Columbia helped develop this everyman aspect, casting him as a drifter who comes to the aid of various townfolk. That film, *Pennies from Heaven* (1936) (and its famous title song), was followed by more "man on the street" roles: fellows put upon by more powerful forces, but triumphing over adversity without seeming to get too ruffled. His next project at Paramount was *Rhythm on the Range* (1936), a story about an aspiring independent ranch owner, trying to survive the machinations of big-monied competition. In *Double or Nothing* (1937), Crosby is given the opportunity to inherit an industrialist's millions, but must battle the underhanded schemes of the deceased's spoiled relatives. All through each picture, dry wit and a smooth song or a light jazzy piece indicate that he remains unperturbed. Yet, Crosby and his characters are never pushovers. His characters always rise to the challenge, and Crosby himself never got crowded out by talented co-stars (such as W.C. Fields in *Mississippi* [1935] or Ethel Merman in *Anything Goes* [1936]). And, just as with Temple, Durbin, Faye, or Powell, Crosby always ends up sitting pretty as the end titles rolled.

Musicals assured audiences that good times were around the bend, both in their narratives and in individual songs. They also celebrated the joys of "the simple life" to help viewers feel better about their current situation. Lastly, they supported a moral work ethic, rather than cynicism and rejecting the system. In this way, musicals promised plenitude and freedom by following the rules. The second half of the 1930s then sees a concerted clamping down on the musical's anarchic potential. The multitude of cycles at each studio also emphasized rules to be copied from film to film. Nevertheless, the unique qualities of the performers usually made each cycle individual—thus creating perhaps the widest variety of types of musicals in the genre's history.

Swing High, Swing Low: Blending/Competing Musical Styles

Championing the common citizen posed a bit of a problem for musicals centered around classically trained singers and their upper-class aura. A popular solution was to put these stars not in operettas but into backstagers. Grace Moore in *One Night of Love*, Lawrence Tibbett in *Metropolitan* (1935), Lily Pons in *I Dream Too Much* (1935), and MacDonald and Eddy in *Maytime*

(1937) and *Bitter Sweet* (1940) all portray newcomers struggling to make it on the operatic stage. *Love Me Forever* (1935) gets so gritty as to have Grace Moore's character move from nobody to diva through the support of an underworld figure who is in love with her.[39] How well these performers managed to play within contemporary modes varied. Grace Moore exhibits an all-American sense of determination that audiences seemed to appreciate. French-born Lily Pons, though, seems a bit lost trying to do screwball comedy in *I Dream Too Much*, only shining when she gets to sing her signature aria, the "Bell Song" from *Lakme*.

Another common strategy was to display the average public's appreciation of their talent—often by having the star open a window out onto the street, belting out an aria, and winning the general population's adulation (often with shots of scullery maids and shopkeepers stopping their work because they are so charmed by the singer's voice). A bit of folk or popular song is often tossed in as well. How much viewers enjoyed listening to MacDonald and Eddy warble "Carry Me Back to Old Virginny" in *Maytime* or Grace Moore trying to scatsing "Minnie the Moocher" in *When You're in Love* (1937), to provide only two examples, is hard to know.

The latter half of the 1930s saw an increase in such juxtapositions between classical music and American popular music, what people called "swing" rather than "jazz." The musical short *Every Sunday* shows Deanna Durbin representing classical music and Judy Garland representing swing—and then combining their styles for a big final duet. Garland would repeat this concept in "I Like Opera/I Like Swing" in *Babes in Arms*, with singer Betty Jaynes. In *Swing Time*, Fred and Ginger do a dance merger: "The Waltz in Swing Time." *Shall We Dance?* (1937) presented Astaire as a classical ballet dancer who wants to meet and dance with Ginger Rogers' musical theatre star. The Disney short *Music Land* (1935) literalizes the dichotomy, with the Isle of Symphony and the Isle of Jazz battling each other until little Prince Saxophone and little Princess Violin bring their parents to détente—and an inter-instrumental wedding. The title of the 1937 Paramount musical *Swing High, Swing Low* unintentionally expressed the dynamic: swing increasingly straddled high and low culture.

It is perhaps unsurprising that striving to boost the morale of the average citizen resulted in espousing pride in his/her music. George Gershwin led the way, as indicated by the inclusion of a snippet of "Rhapsody in Blue" among the various classical melodies performed during the epic "A Pretty Girl Is Like a Melody" in *The Great Ziegfeld*. But, Gershwin was soon not alone. The plot conceit in *Shall We Dance?* of blending ballet and tap was happening on Broadway in *On Your Toes*, with maestro George Balanchine choreographing a tap ballet for Richard Rodgers' tone poem "Slaughter on Tenth Avenue." In 1938, Benny Goodman and his Orchestra would be invited to perform their swing music at Carnegie Hall. By the end of that year, *Alexander's Ragtime Band* would fictionally dramatize that moment. Tyrone Power's Alexander, having been shunned by his rich family for pursuing ragtime rather than classical music, ascends with his band across the decades—shifting from ragtime to jazz to swing ... and eventually winning social acceptance via a Carnegie Hall concert.

The opening credits announced this film as "Irving Berlin's" *Alexander's Ragtime Band*, and the film celebrates the songwriter's catalog and his importance to American music. The strength of American songwriting during the 1930s was hard not to recognize, with such luminaries as Berlin, the Gershwins, Jerome Kern, Cole Porter, and Rodgers and Hart all continuing to work at the top of their form. The regard for American songwriting slowly started to increase the power of composers and lyricists. While all of the above worked in Hollywood during the 1930s, many were chagrined at being treated by the studios as song-plugging day labor. For example, MGM executives jettisoned the entire Gershwin score in making a film version of *Rosalie*, commissioning Cole Porter to write new songs (and forcing him to audition a number of title songs before they deemed one acceptable).[40] Rodgers and Hart eventually left the West Coast and returned to New York in order to have more creative say on their projects.[41] Berlin's centrality to the production of *Alexander's Ragtime Band* indicates an emerging shift, though. For example, composer Harold Arlen and lyricist E.Y. Harburg (supported by Arthur Freed, who had just shifted his role at MGM from house lyricist to producer) successfully challenged MGM executives who wanted to eliminate "Over the Rainbow" from *The Wizard of Oz*.[42]

Songwriters gained even more creative say when musical sequences were structurally integrated into the script. Theatrical operetta had a long-standing tradition of transitioning from dialogue into song, but increasingly the format of American popular song (and dance) also was being used in theatre and film to drive the plot or reveal character. (Ironically, the tendency in film musicals to move classical music from operettas to backstagers meant that most classical performers sung as part of a stage performance in this era.) Such "integrated" numbers were most commonly found in the fantasy musicals of the period. The fairy-tale atmosphere seemed to allow such moments, whether it be Snow White describing the power of a wishing well to a flock of doves, or the citizens of Munchkinland celebrating the death of the Wicked Witch of the East.

A large portion of the critical acclaim heaped on the Astaire–Rogers cycle came from their integration of song and dance. Almost all of the top songwriters of the period contributed to the cycle (Porter, Kern, Berlin, the Gershwins). The romantic relationship driving the story moved forward whenever the two danced. Sung conversations were also regular occurrences. For example, arguments with an underlying flirtation were common (with the beauty of the melody undercutting the bite of the lyrics), such as "I Won't Dance" in *Roberta* (1935), "A Fine Romance" in *Swing Time*, and "Let's Call the Whole Thing Off" in *Shall We Dance?* "No Strings," the opening number of *Top Hat*, encapsulates both integrated song and dance. Astaire is extolling his unattached status, stating, "In me you see a youth who's completely on the loose: no yens, no yearnings ... no strings and no connections ..." Without the audience fully realizing it, he has already spoken the first line of the song, and suddenly he's shifted into singing. His exuberance becomes dance—which wakens Rogers trying to sleep in the hotel room below. She barges upstairs to complain, they meet, and Astaire is suddenly no longer celebrating bachelorhood. He continues to dance after she leaves, but now a softshoe lullaby to help her get back to sleep, which evokes a smile from her as she rests her head on her pillow.

A number of other films toyed with integration, even minor musicals like *The Life of the Party* (1937), with Gene Raymond and Harriet Hillyard engaging in light romantic antagonism in "So You Won't Sing." Judy Garland's breakthrough in *Broadway Melody of 1938*, for example, was a sung soliloquy, "Dear Mr. Gable." Such soliloquies would become one of her trademarks in future films. "Thanks for the Memory" in *Big Broadcast of 1938* (1938) is so completely written as dialogue for Bob Hope and Shirley Ross that it is a rare instance during this era of capturing the sound on set instead of in prerecording. Paramount produced *High, Wide and Handsome* (1937), a celebration of nineteenth-century Americana with an integrated score by Jerome Kern and Oscar Hammerstein, in hopes of echoing the landmark success of the duo's *Show Boat*, which itself was adapted into film for a second time in 1936 by Universal. Two new integrated songs were written for the 1936 *Show Boat*: "I Have the Room Above Her" and "Ah Still Suits Me."

In its focus on issues of race, *Show Boat* acknowledges the importance of African American culture on this "uniquely American" music. (Furthermore, as discussed in Chapter 1, sung conversation had become part of African American culture during slavery.) The 1936 *Show Boat* often emphasizes the black point of view (possibly due to openly gay director James Whale, who had his own outsider status). On Broadway in 1935, George Gershwin (with DuBose Heyward) wrote the African American "folk opera" *Porgy and Bess*. Both properties have raised ambivalent reactions from African Americans, with non-black artists writing their version of black characters and music. Attempts in film musicals to pay tribute to African Americans were similarly problematic. Astaire's tribute to Bill Robinson in *Swing Time*, "Bojangles of Harlem," has Astaire perform in blackface. Perhaps trying again with "Slap That Bass" in *Shall We Dance?*, Astaire visits the black laborers in the engine room of a cruise ship because he appreciates their music, but the workers largely become background while he dances around the machinery (thus exposing a racial component to such Big White Sets).[43]

The above examples at least acknowledge black culture, but they do so by minimizing the actual voices and bodies of African Americans. While songwriters were getting more and more due for their craft, swing was in effect sliding African Americans out of the spotlight. *Alexander's Ragtime Band* pays tribute to ragtime, jazz, and swing as American music, as *important* music ... but completely erases the contributions of African Americans by not showing a single black performer in the entire film! Music historian Richard Crawford notes, "For many black jazz musicians, the Swing Era was a time when rewards in prestige and money fell short of the artistic influence they wielded."[44] While Duke Ellington, Count Basie, and Cab Calloway were major orchestra leaders during this period, the accolades increasingly went to the aforementioned Benny Goodman, as well as Artie Shaw and the Dorsey Brothers. Swing involved larger groups of musicians (the eponymous "big bands"), requiring a larger bankroll, to which whites were more likely to have access. Swing also ironed out the "rag" edges of earlier African American jazz, which had the effect of erasing connotations of sexual licentiousness. While still lively, swing was smooth, arguably making it more "respectable."

While the transition to sound saw the release of *Hallelujah!* (1929) and *Hearts in Dixie* (1929), only one other all-black cast feature would be made by a major studio in the 1930s: Warner Bros.'s film version of *The Green Pastures* (1936), a problematic telling of the early Bible stories using many stereotypes of African Americans.[45] When people of color did appear in film musicals, they were usually cordoned off into their own areas, as specialty acts or in production numbers (such as "Totem Tom Tom" in *Rose Marie*).[46] "Public Melody No. 1," the production number finale to *Artists and Models* (1937), is a Harlem fantasy with Louis Armstrong, and the first film sequence ever directed by Vincente Minnelli. Intriguingly, Martha Raye is also featured in the number (in blackface), but worries about censorship led to Armstrong and Raye never being in the same shot or location—and some viewers were still outraged at the proximity of white and black performers.[47] African Americans were pushed so far to the sidelines that they often ended up in short subjects rather than the main feature (such as *An All-Colored Vaudeville Show* [1935] and *The Black Network* [1936]).

African Americans nonetheless maintained some form of presence and, as during the transition to sound, used these segregated moments to assert themselves. Not tied to the plot, specialty acts had more freedom to present their own choreography or well-honed routines. (Many musical shorts offered similar opportunities, with no narrative to stand in the way.) In *A Day at the Races* (1937), Harpo Marx and the white romantic couple (Maureen O'Sullivan and Allan Jones) encounter a group of African Americans, which leads to an extraneous number titled "All God's Chillun Got Rhythm" (Figure 3.4). Quite arguably, the moment patronizes the black folk, presenting them as immature and eager to entertain their white superiors. Yet, the African Americans also crowd the main characters right off the screen, displaying awe-inspiring jitterbug acrobatics and momentarily challenging the centrality of the white-dominated plotline.

The situation for African Americans in 1930s Hollywood musicals typifies a larger trend of limiting the range of possibilities: adhering to the strictures of

Figure 3.4 Uncredited African American performers jitterbugging the Marx Brothers and the other white lead characters right off the screen in "All God's Chillun Got Rhythm" from *A Day at the Races* (1937), a number which won an Oscar for Best Dance Direction. Snapshot taken from: A Day at the Races (1937).

the Production Code; instituting a pattern of cycles. Except for the Busby Berkeley backstagers, studios created cycles around stars, thus diminishing the importance of the director. (Most musicals of this period were directed not by auteurs such as Lubitsch or Mamoulian, but by journeymen such as Norman Taurog, William A. Seiter, and Roy del Ruth.) While stars seemed to dominate over directors, they were locked nonetheless into playing the same type of role within cycles—or performing opposite the same co-stars over and over again. The heavy reliance on the backstager format also narrowed expectations.

Even so, the 1930s overcame the initial slump to provide a wealth of musical entertainment, and the sheer number of films led to a wide spectrum of possibilities. While the films within a cycle might feel interchangeable, each cycle was often recognizably different from another, usually due to the unique talent and personality of the stars. "Outlaw" hoofers like Astaire and Powell, for example, had their own singular style of dancing.[48] There was room for both classically trained voices and crooners. The space for random specialty acts in backstagers also created unexpected moments of individuality. While backstagers ruled the day, operettas still appeared, as well as comedies with music.

On rare occasions, "integrated" moments of song and dance would appear on screen. In the midst of formulas and cycles, expectations of what constituted a musical could still be hazy: *San Francisco* (1936) has Jeanette MacDonald singing up a storm, but it also has Clark Gable and Spencer Tracy doing male bonding drama, plus a spectacular earthquake … is this a musical? Thus, the 1930s musical genre offered Depression-weary audiences a cornucopia of options. As put in the opening song in one of Berkeley's final films at Warner Bros., *Hollywood Hotel* (1938): "Hooray for Hollywood."

Notes

1 John Douglas Eames, *The MGM Story* (New York: Crown, 1975), 72, describes the cancellation of a number of musicals in various stages of production at the studio in 1930, including *Great Day!*, which was to star Joan Crawford, *The March of Time*, and two musicals planned for Marion Davies, *The 5 O'Clock Girl* and *Rosalie*. (*Rosalie* was finally adapted from its Broadway origins to an MGM film starring Eleanor Powell in 1937.) Katherine Spring, *Saying It with Songs: Popular Music and the Coming of Sound to Hollywood Cinema* (Oxford: Oxford University Press, 2013), 124, also lists the shutting down of work at Fox on *New Movietone Follies of 1931*, and at RKO Radio on a version of Victor Herbert's *Babes in Toyland*. Richard Barrios, *A Song in the Dark: The Birth of the Musical Film* (Oxford: Oxford University Press, 1995), mentions RKO also canceling an original musical that was to be titled *Heart of the Rockies*. Warner Bros. pulled out all of the Cole Porter songs in its adaptation of the stage hit *Fifty Million Frenchmen* (1931).

2 "Musical Films Are Taboo," *Billboard* (August 23, 1930), 3, 91. Prior to this headline announcement: "Picture Audiences Turning 'Thumbs Down' on Revues," *Billboard* (June 30, 1930), 18; and "Producers Ponder as Small Towns Shun Musical Films," *Billboard* (August 2, 1930), 19.

3 Ethan Mordden, *The Hollywood Musical* (New York: St. Martin's Press, 1981), 43; Clive Hirschorn, *The Hollywood Musical*, 2nd ed. (New York: Portland House, 1991), 12; Barrios, 323–341.

4 German filmmakers found creative cinematic use of contemporary music as well, such as *Three from the Filling Station* (1930) or the film version of *The Threepenny Opera* (1933). For an overview of Germany's version of musical films, see Antje Ascheid, "Germany," *The International Film Musical*, ed. Corey Creekmur and Linda Y. Mokdad (Edinburgh: Edinburgh University Press, 2012), 45–58. See also Horst Claus and Anne Jackel, "*Der Kongress tanzt*: UFA's Blockbuster *Filmoperette* for the World Market," *Musicals: Hollywood and Beyond*, ed. Bill Marshall and Robynn Stilwell (Exeter: Intellect, 2000), 89–97.

5 Henry Jenkins, *What Made Pistachio Nuts? Early Sound Comedy and the Vaudeville Aesthetic* (New York: Columbia University Press, 1992), for example,

deals in depth with a number of these films, although discussing them primarily as comedies rather than as musicals. See also Steve Seidman, *Comedian Comedy: A Tradition in Hollywood Film* (Ann Arbor: UMI Research Press, 1981).

6 Jenkins.

7 During this period, Berkeley also worked on a few films besides those starring Cantor, such as MGM's *Flying High* (1931) with Bert Lahr.

8 A string of vehicles for Joe E. Brown—further examples of comedies with music—stand as the only exceptions to this case in 1931–1932.

9 Final initial gross was $2.26 million. Barrios, 378.

10 See also Andrew Bergman, *We're in the Money: Depression America and Its Films* (New York: New York University Press, 1971).

11 Martin Rubin, *Showstoppers: Busby Berkeley and the Tradition of Spectacle* (New York: Columbia University Press, 1993), 94–95, makes a similar assessment: the Cantor musicals "contain lively but still rudimentary flashes of the audacious," but Warner Bros. saw "the full flowering of the Berkeleyesque."

12 Rubin, 107, describes this as "the sustained expansion of theatrical space into spectacle space."

13 See Gerald Mast, *Can't Help Singin': The American Musical on Stage and Screen* (Woodstock: The Overlook Press, 1987), 132–133.

14 On Berkeley's dictatorial nature on the set and long workdays, see Jeffrey Spivak, *Buzz: The Life and Art of Busby Berkeley* (Lexington: University Press of Kentucky, 2010). To provide one example, Berkeley had no thought to keeping the chorus girls in the various pools used for *Footlight Parade*'s "By a Waterfall" for hours, "their fingers and toes resembling raisins. No one had the good taste to inquire if lavatory breaks were circumvented" (92).

15 The key work on Berkeley's use of women in his numbers is Lucy Fisher, "The Image of Woman as Image: The Optical Politics of *Dames*," *Film Quarterly* 30 (Fall 1976), 2–11.

16 The Warners studio was notorious for treating its contract artists as indentured servants as much as Berkeley, and most of the lawsuits from stars chafing at the power of the studios came from people working at WB (Cagney, Bette Davis, Olivia de Havilland). In 1933, all the major studios cut salaries to deal with the Depression, and Zanuck promised to restore salaries once the emergency was over. When the Warners decided not to do so, Zanuck was so enraged at having to break his word to employees that he quit the studio, creating his own company (20th Century Productions) and then merging with the ailing Fox studio in 1935.

17 Arguably her most iconic moment on film, in the title number to *42nd Street*, epitomizes this aspect: she inelegantly clogs on top of a taxicab—using wooden rather than metal taps that require a dancer to clomp harder to make a louder noise. Mordden, 46, considers Keeler to be "certainly pretty," but "her singing ... is less than passable and her dancing, though excellent in speed and power, is sometimes ungainly." Adrienne L. McLean,

on the other hand, points out that if "Keeler's movements seem heavy, her tapping a bit stolid … that was precisely the goal of the 'buck' dancer … she was performing a virtuoso turn in a mode that valued the loudness and clarity of the tap, its perfection of rhythm … If one looks closely, one can see she is wearing shoes with a split wooden sole, which help her to make the rhythm so dark-sounding; and if they look to us like shoes a comedy granny might wear—big thick lace-up oxfords—that is because of our own ignorance, not Keeler's deficiencies." Adrienne L. McLean, "Flirting with Terpsichore: Dance, Class and Entertainment in 1930s Film Musicals," *The Sound of Musicals*, ed. Steven Cohan (London: British Film Institute, 2010), 72.

18 His vocalizations of songs such as "Young and Healthy" in *42nd Street* or "Pettin' in the Park" in *Gold Diggers of 1933*, for example, express a lot of randy sexuality. Mordden, 126, agrees: "Beneath the clear-cut look and the paper-route smile lurked a hot lad with a ready kiss."

19 *42nd Street* plainly announces that the tunes of flouncy operetta are *out*. An early rehearsal of a springtime-and-rose-petals number leads director Marsh to angrily announce, "Sure, I like it … I liked it in 1905! What do you think we're putting on—a revival?!" No, this is here and now: the syncopation of "naughty, gaudy, bawdy, sporty 42nd Street!," the snappy defiance in "We're in the Money" from *Gold Diggers of 1933*: "and when we see the landlord, we can look that guy right in the eye!" The duo won a Best Song Oscar for "Lullaby of Broadway" in *Gold Diggers of 1935*, calling up the hustle of the city even as it builds up to a straightforward lullaby in its release.

20 Berkeley had been doing titillating work in the Cantor films prior to his contract at Warners. A women's gymnasium functions as the setting for the intriguingly titled "Bend Down, Sister" in *Palmy Days*; girls in a dormitory rise and bathe in the opening number of *The Kid from Spain* (1932); a female slave auction, complete with chains and whips, sets up the "No More Love" number in *Roman Scandals* (1933).

21 For more on the pansy archetype in Hollywood film during this era, see Harry M. Benshoff and Sean Griffin, *Queer Images: A History of Gay and Lesbian Film in America* (Lanham: Rowman & Littlefield, 2006), 24–28.

22 See Leonard J. Leff and Jerold L. Simmons, *Dame in the Kimono: Hollywood, Censorship, and the Production Code from the 1920s to the 1960s* (New York: Anchor Books, 1991).

23 See Leff and Simmons, 45–51.

24 See Maureen Furniss, "Handslapping in Hollywood: The Production Code's Influence on the 'Lubitsch Touch,'" *Spectator* 11:1 (Fall 1990), 52–61.

25 PCA Director Joseph I. Breen writes in a memo about his failed efforts to reach Jack Warner about *Wonder Bar*: "It is quite evident that the gentleman is giving me the run-around. He evidently thinks that this is the smart thing to do." Memo from Joseph I. Breen to Maurice McKenzie (Executive Assistant to

Will H. Hays, President of the PCA) (March 13, 1934), *Wonder Bar* PCA file (AMPAS Library).

26 The most influential study on the films of Fred Astaire and Ginger Rogers is Arlene Croce, *The Fred Astaire & Ginger Rogers Book* (New York: Galahad Books, 1972); but see also Edward Gallafent, *Astaire and Rogers* (New York: Columbia University Press, 2002); John Mueller, *Astaire Dancing: The Musical Films* (London: Hamish Hamilton, 1986); and Todd Decker, *Music Makes Me: Fred Astaire and Jazz* (Berkeley: University of California Press, 2011).

27 The RKO Astaire–Rogers films did regularly contain larger production numbers ("The Continental" in *The Gay Divorcee* [1934], "The Piccolino" in *Top Hat* [1935], "Bojangles of Harlem" in *Swing Time* [1936], the title number finale to *Shall We Dance?* [1937]) and playing with special effects occurs as well (the use of superimposition in "Bojangles of Harlem" or the slow motion in "I Used to Be Color Blind" in *Carefree* [1938]), but the focus always remained on how the two danced with each other, rather than the chorus or on the fancy effects.

28 As the series was winding down, a decision was made to finally film on-screen oscillation—and in slow motion to underline the momentous event—during "I Used to Be Color Blind" in *Carefree*.

29 For insightful queer analysis of female sexuality and the operatic voice, see Wayne Koestenbaum, *The Queen's Throat: Opera, Homosexuality, and the Mystery of Desire* (New York: Poseidon Press, 1993); on Jeanette MacDonald in particular in regard to these issues, see Edward Baron Turk, "Deriding the Voice of Jeanette MacDonald: Notes on Psychoanalysis and the American Film Musical," *Camera Obscura* 25–26 (January/May 1991), 224–249.

30 Robinson also choreographed their numbers together. See Shirley Temple Black, *Child Star* (New York: McGraw-Hill, 1988). For a discussion of how African Americans responded to this partnership, see Karen Orr Vered, "White & Black in Black & White: Management of Race and Sexuality in the Coupling of Child-Star Shirley Temple and Bill Robinson," *Velvet Light Trap* 39 (Spring 1997), 52–65.

31 See also Kristen Hatch, *Shirley Temple and the Performance of Girlhood* (New Brunswick: Rutgers University Press, 2015); Kathryn Fuller-Seely, "Shirley Temple: Making Dreams Come True," *Glamour in a Golden Age: Movie Stars of the 1930s*, ed. Adrienne L. McLean (New Brunswick: Rutgers University Press, 2011), 44–65. To read the infamous article by Graham Greene, see Graham Greene, "*Wee Willie Winkie*; *The Life of Emile Zola*," *Night and Day* (October 28, 1937), reprinted in *The Graham Greene Reader: Reviews, Essays, Interviews & Film Stories*, ed. David Parkinson (New York: Applause, 1993), 234.

32 "Deanna Durbin," *Fortune* 22 (October 1939), states "that Durbin had been keeping that underprivileged studio from bankruptcy single-handed." Thomas Schatz, *The Genius of the System: Hollywood Filmmaking in the Studio Era* (New York: Pantheon Books, 1988), 244, cites that the two films Durbin made

in 1938 "grossed $3.5 million at the box office—fully one-sixth of Universal's entire take on forty-seven releases."

33 For discussion/analysis of Durbin's work and star image see: Jennifer Fleeger, *Mismatched Women: The Siren's Song Through the Machine* (Oxford: Oxford University Press, 2014), 78–105; Jeanine Basinger, *The Star Machine* (New York: A.A. Knopf, 2007), 256–290; and, proposing that Durbin's films redirected sexual desire in ways similar to how I have suggested the films of MacDonald/Eddy, Astaire/Rogers, and Temple did: Allison McCracken, "The Musical's Masturbating Girl: Deanna Durbin and the Adolescent Musical (1936–1941)," paper presented at Society for Cinema Studies conference (May 26, 2002).

34 Rick Altman, *The American Film Musical* (Bloomington: Indiana University Press, 1989), 129–199, spends much of his chapter on the "fairy tale musical" subgenre going over the history and structure of stage and film operettas, as well as an in-depth discussion of the Astaire and Rogers films.

35 Her box-office power also cheered Fox executives and the bankers supporting them. See Charles Eckert, "Shirley Temple and the House of Rockefeller," *Jump Cut* 2 (1974), 1, 17–20.

36 For more on Sonja Henie, see Diane Negra, *Off-White Hollywood: American Culture and Ethnic Female Stardom* (London: Routledge, 2001), 84–102.

37 For more on Alice Faye, see Jane Lenz Elder, *Alice Faye: A Life Beyond the Silver Screen* (Jackson: University of Mississippi Press, 2002).

38 For more on Eleanor Powell, see Adrienne L. McLean, "Puttin' Em Down Like a Man: Eleanor Powell and the Spectacle of Competence," *Hetero: Queering Representations of Straightness*, ed. Sean Griffin (Albany: State University of New York Press, 2009), 89–110.

39 *Love Me Forever* seems strongly modeled on the career of singer Ruth Etting, but refashioning her into an aspiring opera singer, rather than a performer of popular music. Etting was still around in 1935, so an official musical biography would have to wait until *Love Me or Leave Me* (1955) with Doris Day and James Cagney. (More on this film in Chapter 6.)

40 In Gilbert Millstein, "Words Anent Music by Cole Porter," *New York Times* (February 20, 1955), Porter recounts: "I once wrote a song called 'Rosalie' for a picture called 'Rosalie.' I'd written about six of that title. I handed in the six and played it for Louis B. Mayer. 'Forget Nelson Eddy,' he said. 'Go home and write a honky-tonk tune.' It was a hit. I don't like it. The one he threw out was better."

41 For his own account of his experiences in 1930s Hollywood, see Richard Rodgers, *Musical Stages* (New York: Random House, 1975), 148–166.

42 Hugh Fordin, *The World of Entertainment: Hollywood's Greatest Musicals* (New York: Frederick Unger Publishing, 1975), 27. Granted, that same year, Freed produced *Babes in Arms*, eliminating a number of Rodgers and Hart's songs and inserting new ones (including two co-written by himself: "I Cried for You" and "Good Morning").

43 For a thorough and insightful analysis of Astaire and issues of race (particularly African Americans), see Decker.

44 Richard Crawford, *America's Musical Life: A History* (New York: W.W. Norton, 2001), 660.

45 Like *Hallelujah!* and *Hearts in Dixie, The Green Pastures* is another film that employs a lot of music, but which many people do not consider a musical.

46 See also Ana M. Lopez, "Are All Latins from Manhattan? Hollywood, Ethnography, and Cultural Colonialism," *Unspeakable Images: Ethnicity and the American Cinema*, ed. Lester D. Friedman (Urbana: University of Illinois Press, 1991), 404–424.

47 The number was cut completely when shown in Atlanta. Mrs. Alonzo Richardson, part of that city's censorship board, wrote to PCA Director Joseph I. Breen, "In the South, white women can't act with negroes themselves on the same plane" (August 31, 1937) *Artists and Models* PCA file (AMPAS Library).

48 McLean, "Flirting with Terpsichore, 67–81.

4

Singing a Song of Freedom: World War II

Just as the musical genre helped customers weather the Depression through escapism and uplift, it would bolster American audiences readying for and entering World War II. Hollywood studios produced more musicals during this period than any other era except the height of sound revolution, both distracting audiences from the war, and keeping audiences optimistic about eventual victory.[1] Creating new cycles and taking advantage of technological advances, the emotional resonance of music and the visceral thrill of spectacle whipped up patriotic fervor.

The genre's negotiation of the dichotomy between individual freedom and the importance of community also took on greater relevance during World War II, as Americans fought to protect liberty—but as a unified nation. Thus, a number of wartime musicals stress the concept of working together, and that often results in extending a wider (although negotiated) sense of welcome to previously marginalized or disparaged citizenry. In order to make room for such diversity, World War II musicals often present a cornucopia of talent in relatively unrelated moments. Yet, the zeitgeist of the era also became the breeding ground for a more coherent format that brought all performers together in a celebration of "We the People"—a format coined the "integrated musical" that would soon come to dominate how the genre would be defined.

Off to See the World: Musicals Prepare for War

As the 1940s began, a number of established and popular cycles from the 1930s were ending. Grace Moore retired from the screen after *I'll Take Romance* (1937). Busby Berkeley left Warner Bros. for MGM in 1939; Dick Powell left the studio around the same time. Astaire and Rogers parted ways at RKO after *The Story of Vernon and Irene Castle* (1939). Fox decided Shirley Temple was over the hill once she reached puberty and dropped her after *Young People* (1940). MacDonald and Eddy appeared together for the last time in *I Married an Angel* (1942).

Free and Easy? A Defining History of the American Film Musical Genre, First Edition. Sean Griffin.
© 2018 Sean Griffin. Published 2018 by John Wiley & Sons Ltd.

While each instance has its own unique reasons (such as Astaire's desire to go freelance rather than be tied to an exclusive studio contract, or Temple's adolescence), a couple of hypotheses can be ventured as to why so many cycles concluded around the same time. Firstly, the sheer repetition of formulas from picture to picture within each cycle may have started to grow tiresome to audiences. (Studio executives attempted to deal with this by varying patterns slightly—pairing Astaire with Joan Fontaine in *A Damsel in Distress* [1937], or having MacDonald and Eddy co-star with other performers, such as Eleanor Powell for him in *Rosalie* [1937] and Allan Jones for her in *The Firefly* [1937]—but audiences did not respond.) Perhaps tied to that, the established narrative patterns and character types that proved popular during the height of the Depression may have no longer matched the mood of the country.

Certainly, the Hollywood studios did not give up on the entire concept of cycles. Rather, new cycles were established as the 1940s began, and as new stars were rising in popularity. Mickey Rooney and Judy Garland, for example, triumphed at MGM in a series of adolescent backstagers, including *Babes in Arms* (1939), *Strike Up the Band* (1940), and *Babes on Broadway* (1942). Universal struck box-office gold when they put vaudeville and radio comics Bud Abbott and Lou Costello in a series of low-budget military "comedies with music": *Buck Privates* (1941), *In the Navy* (1941), and *Keep 'Em Flying* (1941). Bing Crosby and Bob Hope began a partnership as well, embarking on a series of comic adventures in foreign locales, beginning with *Road to Singapore* (1940). Fox initiated a series of extravaganzas set in Latin American resort spots (and all featuring the "Brazilian Bombshell" Carmen Miranda): *Down Argentine Way* (1940), *That Night in Rio* (1941), and *Week-end in Havana* (1941). Fox's Latin-themed cycle also distinguished itself by being filmed in three-strip Technicolor, a process that was still used only sparingly by Hollywood at this point. "South-of-the-border" environments showcased the vibrant and deeply saturated hues of the process, allowing designers to unleash a carnivalesque riot of purples, reds, greens, and yellows.[2]

Perhaps, at first glance, these new cycles do not seem vastly different from earlier musicals. Certainly, musicals in military settings were nothing new, nor were musicals in exotic locales. Yet, there is a felt difference between *Flying Down to Rio* (1933) and *That Night in Rio*, or between *Follow the Fleet* (1936) and *In the Navy*. Hollywood musicals during the 1930s celebrated the tenacity and will of the average American, focusing on the need for such gumption in surviving the national economic upheaval. Even when taking place in far-off lands, scripts would include references to domestic issues: "going on the dole" or someone being a "public enemy." In these new cycles, musicals increasingly looked outward, still championing American strength but in a global context. *Follow the Fleet* allows audiences to see what Astaire looks like in a sailor suit, but is largely unconcerned with naval operations; *In the Navy* centers on various recruits training to become an effective crew. *Flying Down to Rio* opens with a

Figure 4.1 Carmen Miranda and Don Ameche musically celebrate the "Good Neighbor Policy" in the opening number of *That Night in Rio* (1941). Snapshot taken from: That Night in Rio.

band worried about going on unemployment; *That Night in Rio* opens with Don Ameche singing references to US foreign policy (Figure 4.1).

Such a shift was occurring in the moviegoing public as well, and was spearheaded by the federal government in a strategy of "preparedness." Tensions rose in Europe during the late 1930s, as Adolf Hitler's Nazi party in Germany became more aggressive in its claims to continental territory; similar worries grew in Asia and the Pacific as imperial Japan laid claim on various south Pacific islands and portions of China. As the new decade began, Britain and France had declared war against Germany. The United States officially stood apart from such developments, but felt the impact of the global crisis nonetheless. President Roosevelt signed pacts to send equipment to Britain (thus helping lift the economy out of the Depression), instituted the country's first "peacetime" military draft, and embarked on a "Good Neighbor" policy with Latin American countries to ensure hemispheric unity in case the global crisis spread further.

These new musicals thus reflect the situation. The Fox films were often referred to as "Good Neighbor" musicals, and the *New York Post* commented that "as an advertisement for Roosevelt's good-neighbor policy, [Carmen Miranda was] worth half a hundred diplomatic negotiations."[3] Such explicit connections apply to the Abbott and Costello service comedies too: before the opening credits of

Buck Privates, a *faux* newsreel explains the new draft. Appearing with the comedy team in a number of these films were the Andrews Sisters, singing military-themed hit tunes such as the classic "Boogie Woogie Bugle Boy from Company B," "You're a Lucky Fellow, Mr. Smith," and "You're Off to See the World" (which includes the ominous lyric, "While there's still a world left to see, you're off to sea to see the world").

The Rooney–Garland backstagers, which became associated with small-town teenagers putting a show on in a barn, might seem a parochial exception to this trend. Yet, the films are awash in a patriotism not commonly seen in 1930s musicals. *Babes in Arms* ends with a celebration of America as "God's Country." *Strike Up the Band* ends with the smiling couple superimposed over the proudly waving Stars and Stripes. By *Babes on Broadway*, released in January 1942, the characters put on an amateur show with an overt global frame: a street performance to raise money for British war orphans, with Garland intoning "Chin Up, Cheerio, Carry On."[4]

Such a transition was not sudden; one can see strands emerging towards the end of the 1930s. Shirley Temple somehow finds herself in the midst of war in China at the start of *Stowaway* (1937). Busby Berkeley's concepts for "All's Fair in Love and War" in *Gold Diggers of 1937* (1937) and "The Song of the Marines" in *The Singing Marine* (1937) take on a distinctly militaristic demeanor. *Everything Happens at Night* (1939) starts out as a typical Sonja Henie ice-skating showcase, but becomes a surprisingly dark drama as she tries to get herself and her father out of Europe before war descends.

By the start of the 1940s, individual instances had amassed into a dominant trend, and the influence of "preparedness" spread even beyond the aforementioned cycles. Fox's Good Neighbor cycle helped initiate an avalanche of interest in Latin America in the States. Latin rhythms and dances (such as the samba, the conga, and the rhumba) became the latest craze, and soon other studios were joining the fiesta. Musicians such as Xavier Cugat, Desi Arnaz, and Tito Guizar were going before the cameras. Titles such as *One Night in the Tropics* (1940—Abbott and Costello's film debut), *They Met in Argentina* (1941), and *Down Mexico Way* (1941) proliferated. Rooney and Garland, under the direction of Berkeley, performed "The La Conga" in *Strike Up the Band*. Disney went down to South America, resulting eventually in two feature films: *Saludos Amigos* (1943) and *The Three Caballeros* (1945). Carmen Miranda proved such a sensation that imitations of her frequently occurred in other films. Even cartoon characters dressed up as her, including Olive Oyl (singing "Broadway Samba") in *We're on Our Way to Rio* (1942), Tom (of Tom and Jerry) in *Baby Puss* (1943), and Bugs Bunny in *What's Cookin', Doc?* (1944).

Preparedness seeped into Hollywood musicals in other ways as well. Abbott and Costello were not the only ones enlisting; so was Fred Astaire in *You'll Never Get Rich* (1941), a film that includes the memorable image of him and Rita Hayworth dancing atop a tank. In *Tin Pan Alley* (1940), Alice Faye watches her beau and his buddy march off to a world war (albeit the first one), after warbling "America, I Love You." In *Lady Be Good* (1941), Ann Sothern breaks out with the Oscar-winning eulogy to Nazi-invaded France, "The Last Time I Saw Paris." While *Everything Happens at Night* was not a box-office success, Henie's career was revived in *Sun Valley Serenade* (1941), playing a war refugee arriving in the States. Looking at these films today, it is sometimes hard to remember that the country had not entered the fight when they were produced. The country is obviously on the verge of war when even sophisticated raconteur Cole Porter writes a tune called "Shooting the Works for Uncle Sam" (for *You'll Never Get Rich*) and his tongue is only partly in his cheek.

While it can be (and was) argued that studios simply were mirroring the mood of the period, other factors led executives to consciously play up "preparedness." With Britain and France going to war against Germany in 1939, the European market was closed to exports of Hollywood films. Thus, studios began wooing Latin American markets to make up the loss of profits. That such plans supported the goals of the government reaped further potential benefits. The federal government had begun looking into possible "restraint of trade" issues in how the major studios dominated the industry, particularly in theatre exhibition. The studios responded in various ways, including hiring lawyers and doing a lot of public relations, and cozying up to the government by producing various Good Neighbor films was another strategic move. Nelson Rockefeller, who had been appointed as the Coordinator of Inter-American Affairs, was also a substantial stockholder in 20th Century-Fox—thus the office spearheading the Good Neighbor Policy helped guide that studio's burst of Good Neighbor musicals.[5] Studio executives across Hollywood also worked with the Armed Forces in producing films about military readiness, and were willing to revise projects in order to get military approval and access to their facilities and file footage.[6] Thus, behind the lunacy of Abbott and Costello and the carnivalesque revelry of Fox's Good Neighbor musicals was a government increasingly molding what exactly got included in these films in order to sway audience emotion and opinion. Now, the federal government became involved in defining what a musical could be—a trend that would only increase once the country officially entered the global conflict.

All Out for Freedom: Musicals Help Deal with the War

Everyone did not uniformly welcome the "preparedness" trend that grew in musicals and other Hollywood film production, and a Senate investigation accused the studios of actively advocating for war. That investigation ended abruptly after the Japanese attacked the Hawaiian port of Pearl Harbor on December 7, 1941. While "preparedness" pictures anticipated the possibility of intervention, the events at Pearl Harbor surprised and shocked the entire country, and any internal divisions were quickly overridden by the need to come together as a strong unified nation. Government involvement in motion picture production became even more pronounced after the declaration of war, with the establishment of the OWI (Office of War Information) to oversee (and sometimes alter or stop) film projects. In other words, the celebration of freedom and democracy was often carefully thought out in order to guide (if not outright manipulate) audience mindsets.

Musicals were a strong component of the war effort. The propaganda possibilities of the genre were immediately put to use. The emotional pull of music and dance, and the draw of spectacle, can potentially overpower the rational faculties of a viewer. Also, as Dyer and others have pointed out, the "only entertainment" escapism that has been a major appeal of the genre can effectively mask larger social messages. Musical production spiked during World War II and, if judging in terms of sheer quantity, this moment is the apex in the history of the genre. Thomas Schatz, in his overview of American film in the 1940s, points out that "twenty-five of the seventy wartime releases earning $3 million or more at the box office were musicals," including (depending on one's definition of a musical, of course) half of the top ten box-office earners.[7] Musicals repeatedly emphasized group effort and cohesion in a myriad of ways. Collective American strength was trumpeted, assuring audiences of eventual victory. Musicals also served up momentary escapes from the tensions and worries of the war. Further, musicals consoled audiences dealing with separation or loss, offering solace that as alone as they might feel, others understood. We were all in this together.

During the early months of the war (when various military setbacks made US triumph not so certain), musicals were awash with patriotic fervor. Red, white, and blue bunting swathed the screen (even if the musical was in black and white), with characters waving flags, and often singing and dancing in uniform—and sometimes the choreography consisted mainly of marching! Fred Astaire continued his military roles as an ace pilot on leave in *The Sky's the Limit* (1943). Gene Kelly made his film debut in *For Me and My Gal* (1942), playing an ambitious hoofer who learns that fighting in World War I is more important than becoming a star. Kelly became so associated with a soldier's outfit or sailor suit that he would be cast in such roles throughout his career—even after the war ended.[8] Anthems to America were endemic—including "Song of Freedom" in *Holiday Inn* (1942); "Old Glory" in *Star Spangled Rhythm* (1943); "V for Victory" in *Reveille with Beverly* (1943); "Say a Prayer for the Boys Over There" in *Hers to Hold* (1943); "God Bless America" in *This Is the Army* (1943); "All Out for Freedom" in *Up in Arms* (1944); and even "The Victory Polka" in *Jam Session* (1944).

Yankee Doodle Dandy had been in production before Pearl Harbor, and James Cagney consciously took on the project to counter rumors of Communist ties by playing the ultra-patriotic songwriter Cohan.[9] Yet, the film was exactly the type of flag-waving desired by moviegoers once war was declared, becoming the second most popular film of 1942 (beaten out only by MGM's dramatic tribute to wartime Britain, *Mrs. Miniver*), and garnering Cagney an Oscar for Best Actor.[10] Cohan's life is portrayed as the American Dream, a classic "rags-to-riches" story worthy of Horatio Alger himself. The script frames the biography by dramatizing Cohan receiving the Medal of Honor from President Roosevelt. In addition to championing the American spirit, Cohan's catalog is a treasure trove of patriotism, including the title song, the World War I hit "Over There," and "You're a Grand Old Flag." The production number for that last song is a full-out orgy of national pride (Figure 4.2). After a relatively simple once-over, Cagney/Cohan gets poetic in describing the meaning of the colors as well as the stars and stripes, which blends into a number of tableaux of national icons (the Spirit of '76; Lincoln; Teddy Roosevelt). Then, remarkably, the piece steps somewhat out of the diegesis as the chorus chants, "now that we're in it, we're going to win it." Cohan comes back out for the big finale, accompanied by his father as Uncle Sam and his mother as the Statue of Liberty. The assembled start marching in cadence towards the audience/camera as they sing the chorus, with successive curtains pulled back to show more and more

Figure 4.2 The Oscar-winning James Cagney and company pay tribute to "That Grand Old Flag" in *Yankee Doodle Dandy* (1942), a musical biography of composer George M. Cohan. Snapshot taken from: Yankee Doodle Dandy (1942).

people singing and carrying the stars and stripes—until it seems that the stage reaches from Broadway all the way back to New Rochelle. A scrim descends to project the flag waving proudly as the multitudes sing out the final notes. The audience within the film goes wild, as did likely the customers in movie houses across the nation. In case any connection to World War II had somehow escaped viewers, Warner Bros. decided to sell war bonds rather than tickets to the New York premiere of the film—and raised over $5 million.[11]

Warners followed up this success by making a film version of the blockbuster hit stage revue *This Is the Army* (1943). The stage version was cast completely with military personnel, and many of those involved in the film were also in the service, including newly commissioned Hollywood performers and filmmakers. The studio donated all profits (as well as some salaries) to the Army Emergency Relief Fund, and the film came close to doubling the box office of *Yankee Doodle Dandy*.[12] Many other wartime-related revues were made across Hollywood. Filmmakers were noticing not only the enormous success of *This Is the Army* on stage, but also the number of stars performing in USO (United Service Organizations) tours, and the establishment of "canteens" where servicemen could come for free food, non-alcoholic drink, and music served up by Broadway and Hollywood celebrities. The studios reworked the revue format as a form of USO show or "canteen." Paramount's *Star Spangled Rhythm* (1943) led the way, followed by United Artists' *Stage Door Canteen* (1943), MGM's *Thousands Cheer* (1943), Fox's *Four Jills in a Jeep* (1944), and Universal's *Follow the Boys* (1944). Warner Bros. did a number of musical revues: in addition to *This Is the Army* were *Thank Your Lucky Stars* (1943) and *Hollywood Canteen* (1944).[13]

The wartime revues were similar to the early talkie revues in showcasing stars in musical numbers, but this time largely sticking to those associated with song and dance (although Bette Davis's game rendition of "They're Either Too Young or Too Old" in *Thank Your Lucky Stars* shows that such was not always the case). The wartime revues also provided at least some form of narrative context for the various stage acts. The two *Canteen* films dramatize romances between a GI and one of the female volunteers, for example. *Four Jills in a Jeep* adapts the non-fictional adventures of Carole Landis, Martha Raye, Kay Francis, and Dixie Dunbar on a USO tour. Even *This Is the Army* fashioned a storyline to frame the individual revue sections, a backstager tale of two generations putting on military revues for two world wars (thus allowing the film to pull in some extra numbers from Irving Berlin's World War I revue *Yip Yip Yaphank*).

What connected the plots to the revue sections was the theme of group effort. In the storylines, the characters need to recognize the importance of the greater good over their own individual needs or desires. Soldiers and their gals need to put their plans on hold until victory is won; egotistic recruits have to learn how to function as part of a team; generations must overcome their differences for a shared cause. On the revue side, stars intermingle with regular

GIs, as well as showing their support by using their talents to raise money and keep up military morale. The revues (and other musicals during the war) also showcase a number of big bands. The orchestras of Kay Kyser, Glenn Miller, Harry James, Tommy Dorsey, Jimmy Dorsey, Benny Goodman, and many others appear regularly in musicals of this period. Big bands were practically a musical embodiment of a military regiment, each individual instrumentalist blending with the rest of the unit under the guidance of one leader.

Such representations were exactly what the Office of War Information desired, "a picture of a prosperous, wholesome, democratic America,"[14] but such celebrations of unity in musicals were often expressed with almost too much enthusiasm. Restraint is a rare commodity in wartime musicals. Rather, a manic, nervous energy pervades the genre during World War II. The most obvious image of such fervor can be seen in the jitterbug dancing associated with the period, and sequences in films such as *Hellzapoppin'* (1942) can still take a viewer's breath away with their breakneck acrobatics. The way one young fellow throws Bette Davis around during the aforementioned "They're Either Too Young or Too Old" in *Thank Your Lucky Stars* is almost worrisome. The whirling dervish choreography is paralleled by an increase in frantic comedy. Abbott and Costello are a prominent example, rocketing to the top of the box office in 1942. A number of high-energy comic figures run riot through musicals of this period: Betty Hutton, Red Skelton, Danny Kaye, the comedy team of Ole Olson and Chic Johnson. Hutton, Kaye, and Costello often get so wound up that they just start screaming at the top of their lungs. Disney's animated features moved from Production Code-friendly fairy-tale musicals to musical escapades with Donald Duck and pals running amok in Latin America. The scattershot nature of backstager and revues aided and abetted these types of antics, but it extended into all forms of musical comedy.

There are a variety of potential reasons for such systemic frenetics. One possible explanation for such widespread high-octane insanity is to divert audiences from their concerns about the war—and such fretting was possibly so endemic that the comedy needed to be more extreme. The "Road" series, for example, explored a variety of exotic locales removed from the actual war. Hope, Crosby, and Dorothy Lamour never acknowledge that Allied forces are fighting the Nazis in north Africa in *Road to Morocco* (1942), the most popular of the series. Rather, Hope and Crosby insistently break out of context to wink at the camera, providing escape not only from the war but even the fantasy world of the film itself. In the title song, they sing "For any villains we may meet, we haven't any fears./Paramount will protect us 'cause we're signed for five more years!" Later on, when said villains imprison the two, Hope's character recounts at length the plot to that point. When Crosby's character asserts he knows all this already, Hope explains that there might be people who came in late to the movie ... with Crosby then complaining "What?! They missed my song?!" At another point, while lost in the desert, the two sing a chorus of

"Moonlight Becomes You" with a mirage of Lamour—and the soundtrack gets mixed up so that the three start singing with each other's voices. During the climactic fight sequence, even a camel announces, "This is the screwiest picture I was ever in!"

While the "Road" pictures may have used hyperactivity to help audiences momentarily forget the global conflict, other musicals tie such manic comedy explicitly to the war, such as *The Fleet's In, Seven Days Leave* (1942), and *Seven Days Ashore* (1944).[15] The zaniness in these musicals mirrors a certain zeitgeist: to live life to the fullest while one can. Hundreds of thousands of men were suddenly being sent overseas; many others on the home front quickly relocated to industrial centers to work in factories. People married in haste before troops shipped out, and soldiers and sailors on leave often crowded as much adventure and experience as they could into a few days. Further, during much of 1942, various military setbacks made US triumph not so certain. Hence, the nervous energy in wartime musicals may be an expression of cramming everything into today, and not waiting for tomorrow.

The Gang's All Here tests the limits of excess in film musicals. Another story about a GI on leave meeting a girl at the Stage Door Canteen (this time, Alice Faye) and the complications that ensue, the plot is merely a jumping-off point for extended spectacle. (The romance is so incidental that there is not even a final romantic clinch for the couple, because the film wants to focus on the charity benefit extravaganza the characters are producing.) Under the direction of Busby Berkeley, this Fox musical includes chorus girls waving around 6 ft bananas while Carmen Miranda performs "The Lady in the Tutti Frutti Hat." Benny Goodman and his orchestra perform the number "Paducah" with Carmen Miranda as well. (Tied to the love of nonsense during this period are songs celebrating places with odd names: "Chattanooga Choo Choo," "I Dug a Ditch (in Wichita)," "I Got a Gal in Kalamazoo.") A female contortionist, an epic celebration of polka-dots, and Charlotte Greenwood's long limbs jitterbugging add to the mix. Further, the entirety is filmed in an eye-boggling array of Technicolor hues—particularly in the literally kaleidoscopic climax to the film, where viewers are hard put to find Alice Faye among the abstract prismatic patterns. The swirl of energy in this and other war-related musicals reflects the atmosphere of sudden and sweeping uncertainty, but works (extensively) to make such instability seem amusing rather than worrisome.

While asserting pride and providing diversion, wartime musicals also attempted to console the American population. Providing a form of balance to the chaotic comedy are the number of wistful songs dealing with separation, including "Mustn't Say Goodbye" from *Stage Door Canteen*, "I'll Walk Alone" from *Follow the Boys*, "There Will Never Be Another You" from *Iceland* (1942), and "Long Ago and Far Away" from *Cover Girl* (1944). Alice Faye's low throaty way with a torch song matched the attitude perfectly, singing "No Love, No Nothing" ("until my baby comes home") in *The Gang's All Here* and the

Oscar-winning "You'll Never Know" ("just how much I miss you") in *Hello 'Frisco, Hello* (1943). These love songs expressed the emotions that lingered after the pell-mell revelry ended. Some are specifically sung by women missing their fellas overseas, but overt wartime references are rare in the lyrics themselves. Perhaps direct acknowledgment that the boys might not be coming home was too much, so the songs keep things comfortably vague. Yet, missing a loved one was a common trope in ballads during this period. Few people now consider "White Christmas" (from *Holiday Inn* [1942]) as a war-related song— but it too is about being far away from home ... and Bing Crosby's rendition of it quickly became the biggest selling record of all time.[16]

"White Christmas" also emphasizes dreaming of a happier time and place, and there are quite a number of other ballads in this vein: "The Dreamer" in *Thank Your Lucky Stars*, "I Had the Craziest Dream" in *Springtime in the Rockies* (1942), "Hit the Road to Dreamland" in *Star Spangled Rhythm*, "Sweet Dreams, Sweetheart" in *Hollywood Canteen*. Fans often described Crosby and other crooners, including new heartthrob Frank Sinatra, as being "dreamy," as if to emphasize that utopian visions remained far off in the distance. Dana Polan's examination of wartime cinema points out that Hollywood movies had a uniquely hard time writing completely happy endings at this time.[17] While definitely working to keep hopes high, the war had *not yet* been won, the boys had *not yet* come home. Many musicals end with the women smiling through tears, waving as their fellas go off to battle, pledging to be there when they return (*Stage Door Canteen, This Is the Army, The Sky's the Limit, Thousands Cheer, Hers to Hold*)—promising a happy ending somewhere in the hazy future. A subplot in the Oscar-winning picture *Going My Way* (1944) also ends with a newlywed couple parting as the groom joins his regiment—but the bride at least has parish priest Bing Crosby to lean on for support. Crosby's calm demeanor seemed to console many audiences, and he topped the box office in the last years of the war, winning a Best Actor Oscar for *Going My Way*.

This lack of full confidence in the future may explain the growth of nostalgia musicals during the war—stories occurring in the past have knowledge of how things will end! In particular, a number of musicals take place during World War I, in which victory was a known quantity. The bulk of the period musicals, though, were set at the turn of the century. Audiences for such films could delight in a rosy remembrance of yesteryear that also helped solidify a sense of American national identity. Collective memory was often invoked by performing a number of old Tin Pan Alley favorites, as indicated by the number of film titles taken from such songs: *My Gal Sal* (1942), *Hello 'Frisco, Hello*, *Sweet Rosie O'Grady* (1943), *Shine On, Harvest Moon* (1944), *Irish Eyes Are Smiling* (1944), *Meet Me in St. Louis* (1944). The films helped audiences escape for a few moments from the tensions of the present moment, and bask in the glow of a supposedly more innocent age. Just as many wartime ballads never explicitly state what has caused the separation and longing, these period musicals do not necessarily explain why there is such nostalgia for this specific era. Yet, even here, the shadow of wartime concerns still lingered. The 1890s were the cusp of a society about to give way to the modern age, including the telephone, the automobile, the electric light, and cinema itself ... and technological advances in warfare as well.

The central ballad of the period musical *Shine On, Harvest Moon* (1944) is not the title tune, but a newly composed song that would strongly resonate for soldiers and sailors, and for everyone else on the home front: "Time Waits for No One." While an example of the way musicals attempted to give muted voice to wartime anxiety, the title also perfectly expresses the philosophy behind the manic energy of musical comedy during the period. Whether providing patriotism, escapism, or reassurance, musicals produced during World War II consistently "did their bit" for the war effort.

Who's a Yankee Doodle Dandy? American Diversity in the Wartime Musical

While the Office of War Information worked assiduously to emphasize the importance of national solidarity, it also recognized the need to bring as many people as possible into the war effort. This meant acknowledging and appreciating groups or individuals that had often been ignored, undervalued, or demeaned. The federal government strategized ways to show marginalized peoples that winning the war mattered to them, and that their involvement was needed and welcomed. There was also a strong effort to celebrate American democracy as a land of opportunity for all races and ethnicities, unlike the dogma of "racial purity" in Nazi Germany. Thus, while wartime propaganda regularly stressed the group over the individual, much effort was expended in recognizing and celebrating the diversity of individuals included in that group.

Musicals helped enormously in this goal, and had been doing so even before Pearl Harbor. The Good Neighbor musicals aided the attempts to strengthen the bonds with Latin American countries, to keep them from siding with the Axis powers. Musicals in Latin American settings or with Latin American performers continued to proliferate during the war. Carmen Miranda continued as the most conspicuous "south-of-the-border" representative. Prior to the war, her films were set in Latin America. During the war, her characters became residents of the United States—even appearing in a nostalgic period musical (*Greenwich Village* [1944]). She performs for a bond drive in *The Gang's All Here*, and sings for American Forces Radio in *Four Girls in a Jeep*. In *Something for the Boys* (1944), she becomes fundamental in helping lead a squadron to victory, albeit in a typically outlandish fashion: the metal in one of her dental fillings acts as a radio receiver, accessing military transmissions! Many musicals of the time also stressed how much US audiences enjoyed Latin rhythms and culture, as examples of "the melting pot" image of the country. *Springtime in the Rockies* ends with a production number entitled "Pan-American Jubilee," where "Latins like to jitterbug, like to cut a rug, like the Yankee Doodle Dandies like to do a rhumba and a samba." The opening of *The Gang's All Here* goes even further, with Carmen Miranda singing about encountering various aspects of Latin culture, but "You Discover You're in New York."

The OWI wanted the black community involved in the war effort as well—encouraging them to join the military, and to fill factory jobs vacated by individuals now in the armed services. Towards that aim, the OWI assisted a campaign spearheaded by Walter White, head of the NAACP (National Association for the Advancement of Colored People), and Wendell Willkie, chairman of the 20th Century-Fox board, to improve depictions of African Americans in Hollywood films.[18] War-related revues explicitly included black performers to showcase the cornucopia of US citizens united in preserving a free and democratic society. *This Is the Army* celebrates guys trading their zoot suits for uniforms in "What the Well Dressed Man in Harlem Will Wear." Hattie McDaniel encourages "Ice Cold Katie" to come out and marry her soldier in *Thank Your Lucky Stars*. The Delta Rhythm Boys sing "The House I Live In" in *Follow the Boys*, a hymn to American diversity ("all races, all religions, that's America to me").[19]

Black orchestras were part of the general stampede of big bands too: Count Basie's, Duke Ellington's, Louis Armstrong's, Cab Calloway's. African American specialty acts also proliferated in musicals during the war: from less notable performers such as the Berry Brothers, and Slim and Slam, to more legendary figures such as the Ink Spots, the Nicholas Brothers, the Mills Brothers, and even Ella Fitzgerald (singing her hit song "A-Tisket, A-Tasket" on a bus that Abbott and Costello happen to be taking at one point in *Ride 'Em Cowboy* [1942]). In 1942, MGM placed Lena Horne under contract, and uniquely groomed her as a glamorous star (at a time when every other black female acting in Hollywood could expect to play a servant). She sang in a number of the studio's musicals in designer gowns, with carefully done hair, makeup, and lighting—and often in glorious Technicolor. Arguably, for the first time, Hollywood was suggesting that black could be beautiful.

Such outreach to the African American population led to two all-black Hollywood musicals being produced during the war: *Cabin in the Sky* (1943) and *Stormy Weather* (1943). Other than *The Green Pastures* (1936), these were the first major studio films to be cast exclusively with African Americans since the days of the early talkies. *Stormy Weather* is more explicitly tied to the war effort. A highly fictionalized biographical tribute to Bill Robinson, the film flashes back to Robinson and his pals returning from service in World War I, and ends with a new generation of black males in uniform to do their duty for Uncle Sam. In between is an off-and-on backstage romance between Robinson and Lena Horne's character, as well as a compendium of African American music and dance. The film consciously spans the gamut—from Fats Waller's juke joint piano to Horne's rendition of the title song, from the Nicholas Brothers' gymnastic tap dancing to Katherine Dunham's modern dance troupe—displaying the breadth of artistic contributions made by African Americans. *Cabin in the Sky* is a fable rather than a backstager, but announces itself as a tribute to African American culture: "The folklore of America has origins in all lands, all races, all colors. This story of faith and devotion springs from that source and seeks to capture those values." Showing African Americans as both protagonist and antagonist, as comedic and romantic, the makers of the film aimed to give "a dignified presentation of a peace-loving and loyal people."[20]

Intriguingly, the hyperactive atmosphere of World War II musicals often resulted in suggesting that racial/ethnic categories *as a concept* were absurd. *Song of the Islands* (1942) posits the interchangeability of Irish and Hawaiian culture in the number "O'Brien Has Gone Hawaiian," complete with hula girls breaking into jigs.[21] Carmen Miranda's character in *Springtime in the Rockies* is Rosita *Murphy*, and Native Americans in full regalia are shown talking jive about their favorite big bands. Variations of slang that originated among African Americans are also regularly employed by characters of all colors in wartime musicals, such as "shoot the zoot to me," "solid, Jackson," and "get hip to the jive." The blurring of racial/ethnic categories was often for comic effect, but also provided another way to celebrate America as "melting pot." As such, the celebration of swing music that began in the late 1930s continued, and took on a more obvious patriotic demeanor. As Mickey Rooney avidly proclaimed in *Strike Up the Band*, "Look at George Gershwin. His music's as good as Beethoven or Bach. And best of all, he's American!" In the revue *Thousands Cheer*, classical pianist Jose Iturbi accompanies Judy Garland in "The Joint Is Really Jumpin' Down at Carnegie Hall." In *Best Foot Forward* (1943), June Allyson, Gloria de Haven, and Nancy Walker assist Harry James in a tribute to "The Three Bs"—not Bach, Beethoven, and Brahms, but boogie-woogie, the barrelhouse, and the blues.

While the carnivalesque humor could suggest that racial and ethnic categories were unstable, or simply costumes to try on and take off at will, such play had its downside as well. In particular, there seemed a greater opportunity for those who were considered white to try on minority identities for fun and adventure rather than the other way around. Most obvious is the continued use of blackface in many musicals during the war, such as *Dixie* (1943), *Coney Island* (1943), and *Irish Eyes Are Smiling*.[22] The "Abraham" number in *Holiday Inn* shows Bing Crosby with chorus in full grotesque blackface going all googly-eyed over Lincoln, then cuts to African American Louise Beavers singing to her two children about the man—as if both representations were interchangeable. "Abraham" also expresses a form of benevolent condescension from whites to blacks, which is common in other films too, presenting racial or ethnic minorities as happy children (with the actors having to agree to play into this conception). *Cabin in the Sky*, in its fable structure, seems metaphorically to be patting its black characters on the head with bemused appreciation. Carmen Miranda is also presented as child-like (and thus comical), even while also being somewhat sexually suggestive.

Miranda, at least, got to play actual characters in musical narratives. Such was not the case for Lena Horne. In keeping with the strategy of using minority performers as specialties, she almost always appeared as a "guest star," part of the show that the white characters were putting on, or a nightclub entertainer that the white protagonists paid to see. Consequently, Horne spent much of her career coming on, singing her song, and then exiting. Many theatres across the country were prone to cutting sequences that featured African Americans, due to the prejudices of the theatre owners or the presumed prejudices of their customers. As historian Donald Bogle explains, "because musical numbers were not integrated into the script, the scenes featuring the blacks could be cut from the films without spoiling them should local ... theatre owners feel their audiences would object to seeing a Negro."[23] Thus, the specialty act format had its pluses and minuses: it created a space for minority performers to momentarily supplant the white protagonists, but it also created a form of segregation that studios used to maintain a film's profit potential.

Musicals didn't just reflect changes in race relations. The need for people of all races and ethnicities to help with the war effort was matched by the need for women to take on roles vacated by men fighting overseas. A concerted campaign was waged to assert that women could (and should) take on traditionally masculine work—as machinists, as electricians, and so forth—immortalized in the image of "Rosie the Riveter." New opportunities arose for women in the armed services also, as women's military auxiliaries were formed, such as WAC (Women's Auxiliary Corps) and WAVES (Women Accepted for Volunteer Emergency Service). Women more than proved themselves in the workforce: productivity increased and work-related accidents decreased. With many men overseas, women also became the *de facto* heads of the household.[24]

A number of musicals reflected these new roles. Deanna Durbin's character learns how to assemble planes in *Hers to Hold*, and various musical numbers in other films celebrate women in the workforce, such as "On the Swing Shift" in *Star Spangled Rhythm* and "The Lady from Lockheed" in *Joan of Ozark* (1942). "Who's Complaining?" in *Cover Girl* (1944) has Phil Silvers encountering a constant stream of female labor, including Rita Hayworth as a taxi driver. Female characters in the military auxiliaries also appear, including Dinah Shore as a WAC in *Up in Arms*, and Betty Hutton (playing twin sisters both in uniform) in *Here Come the WAVES* (1944). These films often regard women at work or in uniform as striking (and humorous), but generally endorse the situation as necessary to American victory. The concept of more capable and powerful women began to spill beyond concrete ties to the war effort, though.

At large, women in musicals of the period exhibit more independence and even aggressive behavior. Most obvious are female comics, such as Cass Daley, Nancy Walker, or teenaged bobby-soxer Marcy McGuire. They speak their minds plainly, and often engage in brute physical action rather than traditional femininity, including actively chasing after guys.

Betty Hutton started at Paramount as another "second banana," playing best friend to Dorothy Lamour's female lead in *The Fleet's In*. In a very short time, though, she became one of the studio's top musical stars, second only to Bing Crosby. From film to film, she manically tears across the landscape, talking a mile a minute, and comically bulldozing anything in her way to get what she wants (which often was milquetoast Eddie Bracken). She was most associated with energetic novelty songs such as "Arthur Murray Taught Me Dancing in a Hurry" (*The Fleet's In*) and "Murder, He Says" (*Happy Go Lucky* [1943]). Her rendition of "I'm Doing It for Defense" in *Star Spangled Rhythm* is as astonishing as it is emblematic. While speeding around chaotically in a jeep with a number of GIs, she sings about making out with soldiers as a patriotic duty. Bouncing out onto the road, making a running leap back into the vehicle, and then being driven completely underwater and out again does not stop her from full-out vocalizing—including gargling the final notes while submerged, which makes one wonder exactly *what* she is "doing for defense."

The randy nature of "I'm Doing It for Defense" is not unique for the period. While increasingly presenting women as independent and active, musicals also quite often displayed women as sexual objects for men in the audience to enjoy. World War II saw the development of the "pin-up girl," glossy photos or pictures in magazines that guys could stick in their lockers or on the wall next to their beds. Pin-up culture was a strong component of military life, propaganda to remind men "what they were fighting for." The major Hollywood studios, with an established system for grooming and marketing talent, were a central source for pin-up material. Samuel Goldwyn, attempting to be Hollywood's answer to Florenz Ziegfeld, created The Goldwyn Girls, which he featured regularly in the musicals he made starring Danny Kaye. MGM publicized its "DuBarry Girls," models who were used for "I Love an Esquire Girl" in *DuBarry Was a Lady*, each portraying a month on the calendar. Even Disney publicized the live-action Latin lovelies that Donald Duck would chase around in *The Three Caballeros*.[25]

The two most popular pin-ups of the period were both associated with musicals: Betty Grable and Rita Hayworth. Although Grable had worked in Hollywood since *Whoopee!* (1930), she skyrocketed to fame in the early 1940s, becoming the top box-office star in the country in 1943, and the most popular female star of the war. Hayworth had also started her career in the 1930s, but did not achieve stardom until the advent of World War II, becoming Columbia's most valuable contract player. Their musicals capitalized on their beauty, with the studios obviously spending extraordinary time on their hair and makeup, as well as carefully costuming and lighting them. The American heterosexual male seemed sexually fixated on legs during the war, and dance sequences created ample opportunities to showcase those belonging to Grable and Hayworth. Grable's blonde hair and blue eyes, as well as what was then called her "peaches and cream" complexion, were perfect for the deep saturated hues of Technicolor. Smaller than Grable's studio, Fox, Columbia did not splurge on color until the end of the war—but when it did, it used it for Hayworth's pictures. Both starred in films with titles that acknowledged their status as objects of beauty: *Pin-Up Girl* (1944) for Grable and *Cover Girl* (1944) for Hayworth.

While celebrated as pin-ups, though, Grable and Hayworth also embodied the stronger image of women that developed during the war. Neither played shy, retiring creatures meekly waiting for their Prince Charmings to carry them away to happiness. Hayworth exuded an air of intelligence, indicating various levels of frustration that people were only noticing her beauty and not her other skills or capabilities. In one of the last musicals of the war, *Tonight and Every Night* (1945), Hayworth's character unites in solidarity with her fellow chorus girls to live inside a London theatre during the blitz, enduring hardships, black-outs, and bombs to keep their show running. Grable's characters often resorted to actual physical violence when men tried to exert their authority. Repeatedly, she punches, kicks, slaps, and screams and throws things at her leading men. At one point in *Coney Island*, her co-star George Montgomery resorts to handcuffing her wrists and ankles in order to quell her aggressiveness.

Grable and Hayworth were also talented dancers, and thus their films show them in action, and not just on display. This stands in marked contrast to most of Grable's leading men, who could not sing or dance. Partnered with tall, dark, and musically untalented men such as George Montgomery, Robert Young, Victor Mature, and John Payne, Grable almost literally dances rings around them. Granted, the men are often shown smiling appreciatively at Grable's performing—but the fellows are also effectively shoved to the sidelines. This is most apparent in *Pin-Up Girl*, which ends not with a lavish display of Grable and other women in skimpy outfits, but with her in military uniform drilling a group of similarly clad women in precision marching formations (Figure 4.3). Grable's voice is stern and authoritative, and the women under her command are all business. During the sequence, there are no shots of men watching the exercises—and the film fades out without a final romantic clinch between Grable and her boyfriend, played by unknown John Harvey. Instead, the final shot is a triumphant close-up of Grable alone and self-sufficient.[26]

Unlike Grable, Hayworth *did* partner with musically talented men, often the cream of the crop: Fred Astaire (*You'll Never Get Rich* [1941], *You Were Never Lovelier* [1942]) and Gene Kelly (*Cover Girl*). While Grable effectively overshadowed the men in her films, Hayworth repeatedly showed she was equal to the expertise of Astaire and Kelly, confidently keeping up with them step for step.[27] Hayworth and Astaire's *pas de deux* to "I'm Old Fashioned" in

Figure 4.3 Pin-up favorite Betty Grable becomes a member of the Women's Army Corps, leading a unit in an extended military cadence in the conclusion of *Pin-Up Girl* (1944). Snapshot taken from: Pin-Up Girl (1944).

You Were Never Lovelier is largely considered equal to his best romantic dances with Ginger Rogers—and she shows equal capability matching him in the jaunty tap number "The Shorty George" later in the same film. The narratives of these films give her a sense of power that creates problems for her suitors. In *You'll Never Get Rich*, Hayworth consistently rebuffs Astaire, and he resorts to numerous ruses in attempts to curry her favor. In *You Were Never Lovelier*, Astaire again has to create an elaborate scheme to break through the wry skepticism of Hayworth. *Cover Girl* is perhaps even more overt in demonstrating Hayworth's power. Rather than remaining a chorus girl under the command of boyfriend Gene Kelly in a Brooklyn nightclub, she becomes the toast of the town as a magazine model (working with magazine editor Eve Arden—the epitome of no-nonsense), and eventually stars on Broadway. The title number is a classic example of the wartime pin-up tableaux—various models posing for the covers of a variety of actual journals. Yet, the final cover is of women in uniform for *Liberty* magazine—and is followed by Hayworth descending from a multi-story ramp, as if from Mt Olympus, to dance with a line of chorus boys before running back up to the heavens.

The upheaval in gender roles due to the war affected men as well as women. Two dance solos, one by Fred Astaire and one by Gene Kelly, both indicate the anxiety and frustration that at least some men may have been feeling in the shakeup of gendered expectations. Astaire's dance to "One More for the Road" in *The Sky's the Limit* is a drunken tantrum by a man who has been rebuffed by a strong-willed female photographer (played by Joan Leslie). Gene Kelly's dance with his alter ego in *Cover Girl* similarly shows him grappling with his insecurities in the face of a woman surpassing him in fame and success. (Many who have written about Kelly's career point to this particular number as the one that helped him break through to full stardom.[28]) Both numbers climax with the dancer angrily heaving a large object through glass and then shuffling off in despair.

While these two sequences point out the anxiety that strong, independent women may have caused men, musicals were more likely to treat male gender instability with humor. Nowhere is this more obvious than in the prevalence of female impersonation in musicals of this period. One of biggest hits of the original Broadway production of *This Is the Army* was "Ladies of the Chorus," with an entire stage of soldiers performing in drag—a number that was scrupulously duplicated in the film adaptation. Such a moment reflected the prevalence of cross-dressing in the armed services during the war. Soldiers and sailors entertained themselves overseas by creating amateur shows and, without any women, men regularly donned female garb. Consequently, many musicals during this period have men in women's clothing. In the "Road" movies, for example, there are constant references to Hope's characters wearing girdles or snoods, and in *Road to Morocco*, Hope plays his character's aunt. Mickey Rooney dresses up as Carmen Miranda at one point in *Babes on Broadway*. (Indications are that servicemen often impersonated Carmen Miranda in amateur endeavors.)[29] In a clear imitation of "Ladies of the Chorus," a chorus line of men in drag prance through the "Bessie in a Bustle" number in *Irish Eyes Are Smiling*. Men in women's clothing is at times linked to the growth of women in men's roles. The drag chorus in "Bessie in a Bustle" surrounds star performer June Haver, who is dressed in a man's suit and has her hair pinned up underneath a boater. *Bathing Beauty* (1944) showcases the athletic prowess of MGM's new star champion swimmer Esther Williams *and* displays Red Skelton attending a dance class in a pink tutu. *Here Come the WAVES* includes a comedy routine called "If WAVES Acted Like Sailors," with Betty Hutton and her gal pal as wolves on the prowl during shore leave, and Bing Crosby and Sonny Tufts worrying about what outfits to wear on their dates.[30]

Also, male couples appear repeatedly in films of this era. The two men usually are not absolutely or overtly homosexual, but definitely share an intense bond (a version of what American popular culture in the 2000s began referring to as "bromances"). Abbott and Costello are a prominent example, as are Hope and Crosby. They are not alone though—others include William Holden and

Eddie Bracken in *The Fleet's In*, Gene Kelly and Frank Sinatra in *Anchors Aweigh* (1945), and Danny Kaye and Dana Andrews in *Up in Arms* (1944). Usually, the men seem more closely connected to each other than to any of the women they encounter. Abbott and Costello are almost always paired with each other at the end of their films, not with women. (In *In the Navy*, Costello re-enacts the joke from *Wonder Bar* [1934] by breaking in on a couple on the dance floor, and then dancing off with the man.) Hope and Crosby consistently double-cross each other in their efforts to woo Dorothy Lamour in their "Road" movies, but they spend more time with each other than either spends with her. In *Road to Morocco*, during the reprise of "Moonlight Becomes You," Hope and Crosby lean in to kiss the mirage of Lamour, but end up kissing each other as the mirage disappears (Figure 4.4).[31] In *Anchors Aweigh*, Kelly is so committed to helping his pal that he agrees to pretend to be a girl so that Sinatra can practice asking one out.[32]

The emphasis on strong male friendships, or "buddies," was fostered by the military. The buddy system was a strategy to help new recruits deal with the upheaval and major physical and psychological strain placed on them. Men created major emotional attachments with each other: a buddy had been in the trenches too and knew better than anyone else the turmoil a fellow had

Figure 4.4 A representative moment of the comedic anarchy and the queer implications of buddies in World War II musicals. Bing Crosby and Bob Hope, leaning in to kiss a vanished mirage of Dorothy Lamour prepare to lip-lock each other in *Road to Morocco* (1942). Snapshot taken from: Road to Morocco (1942).

encountered. Evidence suggests that some buddies did evolve into actual same-sex relationships, and in the earliest part of America's involvement in the war, the military "looked the other way" and accepted gay men into the ranks because of the need for manpower. It would not be surprising then if some of those dressing up as Carmen Miranda to entertain the rest of the guys in the unit were using the situation as a chance to more openly express their sexual orientation. (Similarly, women's auxiliary units created—albeit briefly—a more comfortable environment for lesbians.)[33]

The influence of gay men in the musical genre became perhaps a bit more overt during the war as well, and not just through drag numbers and jokes about buddies. Musicals easily lent themselves to camp, a reading strategy developed within the gay male community that reveled in anything overly artificial or heavily stylized. During wartime, the sometime lurid use of Technicolor and the sweeping movements of boom cameras created a sense of over-exaggeration that was matched by the manic behavior of certain performers. A number of designers, songwriters, and other behind-the-camera talent were homosexual men, and thus some of the camp elements in these musicals may have been put there intentionally. Musical scholar Steve Cohan argues that straight audiences most likely enjoyed these camp aspects, even if they did not know the term "camp" or its association with gay male culture.[34] Camp often revels in a sense that gender is also artificial: one is performing whether in drag or "passing for straight," for example. Just as musicals created a carnivalesque space that could suggest that racial or ethnic categories were just masks to don and discard, the genre also indicated such could be the case for gender roles.

Yet again, as with attitudes about race and ethnicity, such an attitude was double-edged. Often there was the indication that such gender instability was "just for the moment." Once the war was over, women would take off those overalls and go back to their "natural" roles—and men would come home, leaving behind their buddies and returning to girlfriends and wives. Hayworth comes back to Kelly and his ramshackle nightclub at the end of *Cover Girl*. Grable is manhandled and handcuffed in order to learn who knows best in *Coney Island*. *Lady in the Dark* (1944) presents Ginger Rogers as a strong-willed editor of a fashion magazine ... who subconsciously desires to be dominated by a man. On the other side, buddy musicals often show the more traditionally masculine pal successfully teaching the other, weaker one how to "become a man."

Danny Kaye's first feature, *Up in Arms*, encapsulates much of the dynamics just discussed. Kaye plays a hypochondriac living with buddy Dana Andrews, and together they are drafted into the Army. Kaye is feminized not only via his character's "unmanly" hypochondria, but also through the film's visual style. Another Technicolor musical, Kaye's natural reddish hair has been turned blonde. The curled golden tresses combined with subtle yet perceptible eyeliner may have been done to lessen his Jewishness, but they also make him seem like another Goldwyn Girl![35] The feminization continues when Kaye lip-syncs to a song sung by Dinah Shore. At another point, Kaye and buddy Andrews meet up with WACs Dinah Shore and Constance Dowling on leave in (perhaps amusingly) San Francisco. Catching a cable car, the men end up sitting with each other on one side and the women together on the other side. The ensuing conversation between them alarms the rest of the passengers as it sounds like Andrews prefers Kaye "with a blue ribbon in your hair" rather than in a uniform, that Dowling has bought Shore a box of cigars, and that Kaye entered Andrews' picture in a beauty contest at camp—and he came in third!

Throughout the film, Kaye also gets a chance to take on different personae, including a variety of ethnic accents: Scotch, German, and—in the climactic sequence—Japanese. In this last moment, Kaye somehow manages through his impersonation to capture an entire troop of Japanese soldiers. Thus, while his manic sensibility potentially upends the social order on multiple levels, he ultimately proves himself a man (and war hero) through the use of racial stereotyping. Wartime musicals may have thrown everything "up in arms," but there was the hope that all would be caught and put back right with Allied victory.

The problem, though, is that the prevalent "aggregate" structure in Hollywood musicals (and much of Broadway during the war too) often seems to give only vague support to such a return to normalcy. The emphasis on random specialty acts, chaotic comedy, and spectacular excess generally overwhelms whatever is going on in the plot—and it is often hard to figuratively put the lid back on the pot by the end of the film. The first number in *Up in Arms* has Kaye doing a one-man encapsulation of the chaos of a typical film musical at the time, complete with a singing cowboy (whose horse "is a baritone too"), a tap-dancing coloratura soprano, and some sort of convoluted spy intrigue that ends with the ingénue tapping out Morse code ... and climaxing with a number by "Carmelita Pepita, the Bolivian Bombshell."[36] *Up in Arms* does not deviate from this pattern. Along the lines of *The Gang's All Here*, *Pin-Up Girl*, and other musicals of the time, the film ends somewhat abruptly, seemingly recognizing the importance of spectacle over narrative in this instance by randomly replaying the conclusion of the film's biggest production number.

In juxtaposition to this carnivalesque atmosphere were musicals that "integrated" narrative, number, and visual style into a cohesive, interrelated whole. While various examples of integrated musicals had existed on film and stage before the war (as described in previous chapters), they were relatively small in number. In 1943, though, a momentous shift began. The huge success of songwriters Rodgers and Hammerstein's integrated *Oklahoma!* heralded "a beautiful mornin'" for musicals in which song and dance *supported* the narrative rather than deviated from it. A year later, MGM's Christmas release of the integrated *Meet Me in St. Louis*, became the biggest hit in that studio's history.[37] Both *Oklahoma!* and *Meet Me in St. Louis* celebrate the American past—and do so by suggesting that America is such a glorious place that its inhabitants are prone to breaking out into song. Instead of celebrating American democracy via a cornucopia of diverse entertainments, these two musicals presented a unified and committed family/community/nation. Audiences were enthralled, and as the war ended, more and more integrated musicals were being produced.

Integrated musicals have little use for specialty acts or anarchic comedy. Thus, the opportunities that women, queer artists, and performers of color often found within musicals during the war were about to be compromised. For example, *Oklahoma!* and *Meet Me in St. Louis* both create their nostalgic Americana by erasing the existence of people of color.[38] Thus, perhaps ironically, these integrated musicals presented a space where its characters felt free to burst into song and dance by limiting who got to do so.[39] Such an attitude matched the reactions of many people to the attempts to open up opportunities for women, homosexuals, and racial/ethnic minorities. At the same time that "Rosie the Riveter" became an icon, the image of the femme fatale in film *noir* also grew in popularity. After initially "looking the other way" as lesbians and gay men entered military service, the government began actively weeding them out and giving them dishonorable discharges.[40] A number of race riots broke out in cities across the nation in reaction to attempts to racially integrate factory lines—including a not-so-nostalgic St. Louis.[41] The Zoot Suit riots in Los Angeles in 1943 showed that not every white American considered Latinos to be "Good Neighbors." (And, of course, while supposedly celebrating America's "melting pot," the US government felt no compunction in incarcerating much of the Japanese American population during the war.) As World War II ended, America and the musical genre were entering what many considered to be a glorious era: the United States as undisputed leader of the world, and the golden age of the integrated musical. While many hoped to further the social reforms begun during the war, many were working to get that lid back on that pot. Musicals had helped audiences weather the war, just as they had helped them weather the Depression. As integration became a more defining element, the genre would have to negotiate how to help audiences weather peacetime.

Notes

1 To offer one basic measure, Clive Hirshchorn, *The Hollywood Musical*, rev. ed. (New York: Portland House, 1991), lists 42 musicals for 1940, 56 for 1941, 52 for 1942, 75 for both 1943 and 1944, and 53 for 1945. No other year after 1945 reaches 50 or more. The only year to surpass 1943 and 1944 in number of films listed is 1930, with 76.

2 While creating a strong sense of carnival and joyous abandon, the decision by Fox (and any other studio) to use Technicolor cameras meant also hiring a color consultant from Technicolor—someone who advised on (and possibly vetoed)

design ideas, much as sound technicians gained greater say over entire productions in the early days of sound. See Scott Higgins, *Harnessing the Technicolor Rainbow: Color Design in the 1930s* (Austin: University of Texas Press, 2007).

3 Wilella Waldorf, "'The Streets of Paris' Opens at the Broadhurst Theatre," *New York Post* (June 20, 1939), Carmen Miranda Production Files, Academy of Motion Picture Arts and Sciences, Margaret Herrick Library.

4 For more on Rooney and Garland's films together, see Sean Griffin, "Mickey Rooney and Judy Garland: Babes and Beyond," *What Dreams Were Made Of: Movie Stars of the 1940s*, ed. Sean Griffin, (New Brunswick: Rutgers University Press, 2011).

5 For information on Rockefeller's financial interests in Fox, see F.D. Klingender and Stuart Legg, *Money behind the Screen: A Report Prepared on Behalf of the Film Council* (London: Lawrence and Wishart, 1937).

6 For example, not only was *In the Navy*'s script rewritten to gain consent from the Navy, the completed picture was put back into production (albeit very briefly) to appease the Navy, turning a climactic sequence (in which Lou Costello's character creates mayhem during maneuvers and potentially destroys the fleet) into a dream sequence. See *In the Navy* production file, Universal collection (USC).

7 Thomas Schatz, *Boom and Bust: The American Cinema in the 1940s* (New York: Charles Scribner's Sons, 1997), 225. He claims three of the top ten were musicals, with the caveat that *Going My Way* (1944) and *The Bells of St. Mary's* (1945) are two others in the top ten on the borderline of being considered musicals.

8 Such films would include *Thousands Cheer* (1942), *Anchors Aweigh* (1945—which earned him an Oscar nomination for Best Actor), *Living in a Big Way* (1946), *On the Town* (1949), and *It's Always Fair Weather* (1955).

9 "Hollywood Stars Accused as Reds Before Grand Jury," *New York Times* (August 14, 1940), 1. See also Patrick McGilligan, *Cagney: The Actor as Auteur* (San Diego: A.S. Barnes & Company, 1982), 145–148, on these accusations and the production of *Yankee Doodle Dandy*.

10 "All-Time Grossers," *Variety* (January 8, 1964), 69.

11 "$5,750,000 'Gate' All in War Bonds for New Picture," *St. Petersburg Evening Independent* (May 30, 1942), 12.

12 "Berlin's 'This Is the Army' Film to Have Big Premiere," *Pittsburgh Press* (August 1, 1943), 30; also Laurence Bergreen, "Irving Berlin: This Is the Army," *Prologue* 28:2 (Summer 1996), 95–105.

13 See Steven Cohan, "Star Spangled Shows: History and Utopia in the Wartime Canteen Musical," *The Sound of Musicals*, 82–92.

14 Clayton C. Koppes and Gregory D. Black, *Hollywood Goes to War: How Politics, Profits and Propaganda Shaped World War II Movies* (Berkeley: University of California Press, 1990), 43.

15 On Broadway, the same was happening. Composer Leonard Bernstein's collaboration with choreographer Jerome Robbins on a dance piece titled *Fancy Free* focused on the three sailors and the girls they meet on leave in New York City. This formed the basis for the musical comedy *On the Town*, written with Betty Comden and Adolph Green. More on this film adaptation of this property is in Chapter 5.

16 *Guinness Book of Records*, 2009 edition, ed. Craig Glenday (London: Guinness World Records Limited, 2008), 14–15, lists the single as having sold at least 50 million copies. Elton John's version of "Candle in the Wind," re-recorded in 1997 in commemoration of the death of Princess Diana of Wales, is listed as coming in second with 33 million copies sold.

17 Dana B. Polan, *Power and Paranoia: History, Narrative, and the American Cinema, 1940–1950* (New York: Columbia University Press, 1986), 101–157.

18 Clayton R. Koppes and Gregory D. Black, "Blacks, Loyalty, and Motion-Picture Propaganda in World War II," *Journal of American History* 73 (September 1986), 383–406; Thomas Cripps, *Slow Fade to Black: The Negro in American Film (1900–1942)* (New York: Oxford University Press, 1977), 349, also details this campaign.

19 RKO would make a musical short out of this song a year later starring Frank Sinatra, which would win an Oscar.

20 Hugh Fordin, *The World of Entertainment! Hollywood's Greatest Musicals* (New York: Frederick Ungar, 1975), 72–73, contains a quote from an interview given by Freed to an unidentified "Negro paper."

21 Representations of Irish American assimilation were prevalent in wartime musicals. See Sean Griffin, "The Wearing of the Green: Performing Irishness in the Fox Wartime Musical," *The Irish in Us: Irishness, Performativity, and Popular Culture*, ed. Diane Negra (Durham: Duke University Press, 2006), 64–83.

22 While *Dixie* uses traditional blackface in its fabricated history of the development of the minstrel show, *Coney Island* and *Irish Eyes Are Smiling* respectively present Betty Grable and June Haver in a lighter "café-au-lait" makeup—possibly reflecting the impact of Lena Horne's stardom.

23 Donald Bogle, *Toms, Coons, Mulattoes, Mammies, and Bucks: An Interpretive History of Blacks in American Films* (New York: Viking, 1977), 121.

24 See Michael Renov, *Hollywood's Wartime Women: Representation and Ideology* (Ann Arbor: UMI Research Press, 1988).

25 Eric Smoodin, *Animating Culture: Hollywood Cartoons from the Sound Era* (New Brunswick: Rutgers University Press, 1993), 112–113, reproduces and analyzes Disney marketing of *The Three Caballeros* by promoting the inclusion of live-action bathing beauties.

26 See Adrienne L. McLean, "Betty Grable and Rita Hayworth: Pinned Up," *What Dreams Were Made Of: Movie Stars of the 1940s*, ed. Sean Griffin (New Brunswick: Rutgers University Press, 2011), 166–191. For analysis of *Pin-Up Girl*, see specifically 173–178.

27 See Adrienne L. McLean, *Being Rita Hayworth: Labor, Identity, and Hollywood Stardom* (New Brunswick: Rutgers University Press, 2004).

28 As early as "'Cover Girl': Hayworth and Kelly Play Hoofers," *Life* (Feb. 21, 1944), 74, it was felt that "if *Cover Girl* does nothing else, it may serve to establish lean, glossy-haired Gene Kelly as the logical heir to the cinematic dancing throne which is now occupied by Fred Astaire." Among those seconding that opinion, see Jeanine Basinger, *Gene Kelly* (New York: Pyramid Publications, 1976), 40; Tony Thomas, *The Films of Gene Kelly: Song and Dance Man* (Secaucus: The Citadel Press, 1974), 53; James Robert Parish and Michael R. Pitts, *The Great Hollywood Musical Pictures* (Metuchen: Scarecrow Press, 1992), 125.

29 Allan Bérube, *Coming Out Under Fire: The History of Gay Men and Women in World War Two* (New York: Plume, 1990), 89–90, details the number of amateur GI shows that included impersonations of Carmen Miranda. See also Shari Roberts, "The Lady in the Tutti-Frutti Hat: Carmen Miranda, a Spectacle of Ethnicity," *Cinema Journal* 32:3 (Spring 1993), 3–23.

30 This sequence seems to be a conscious variation on a comedy sequence in *Star Spangled Rhythm*, also produced by Paramount, entitled "If Men Played Cards Like Women." Vito Russo, *The Celluloid Closet: Homosexuality in the Movies*, rev. ed. (New York: Harper and Row, 1987), 68–69, was the first to write about this sequence from *Star Spangled Rhythm* as a not-very-subtle skit about male homosexuality.

31 For a more thorough examination, see Steven Cohan, "Queering the Deal: On the Road with Hope and Crosby," *Out Takes: Essays on Queer Theory and Film*, ed. Ellis Hanson (Durham: Duke University Press, 1999), 23–45.

32 Steven Cohan, *Incongruous Entertainment: Camp, Cultural Value, and the MGM Musical* (Durham: Duke University Press, 2005), 149–199, focuses on the camp value of Kelly's star persona.

33 Bérube.

34 Cohan, *Incongruous Entertainment.*

35 The use of makeup and hair styling to mute ethnic otherness in Kaye also parallels the extensive makeover done to "whiten" Rita Hayworth (originally Marguerita Cansino), including lightening her hair and doing extensive electrolysis to rid her of "widow's peak."

36 As inane as the fictional musical described in this number sounds, *I Dood It* (1943) *does* climax with Eleanor Powell tapping out Morse Code to thwart an Axis plot and capture a ring of spies.

37 Not all of the numbers in *Meet Me in St. Louis* specifically drive the plot forward—and, to a degree, the film has little actual narrative momentum until the end of the "second act," when Father announces the family is moving to New York. Yet, the careful choice of songs that the family members sing combine with the detail in the visual design and the seemingly minor activities

played out in the script to subtly craft a cohesive atmosphere—one that is suddenly threatened by the announcement of the move to New York.

38 *Oklahoma!* does include peddler Ali Hakim—supposedly a Persian émigré, but originally played on Broadway by well-known Jewish comedian Joseph Buloff ... and eventually portrayed on screen by very WASP Eddie Albert.

39 This is the central thesis of Richard Dyer, "The Colour of Entertainment," *Musicals: Hollywood and Beyond*, ed. Bill Marshall and Robynn Stilwell (Exeter: Intellect, 2000), 23–30.

40 Bérube, 201–254, details the history of the dishonorable discharge given to gay men and women in the later half of the war.

41 For an overview of the summer of race riots in 1943 across the nation, see Gerhard Falk, *The American Criminal Justice System: How It Works, How It Doesn't, and How to Fix It* (Santa Barbara: Praeger, 2010), 8.

5

There's Beauty Everywhere:
MGM and the Freed Unit

As described in the past three chapters, all of the major Hollywood studios contributed to the evolution of the film musical genre. Each crafted its own unique cycles and stars, yet each also noticed and borrowed ideas from what was being done elsewhere. Paramount, MGM, Warner Bros., 20th Century-Fox, RKO, Columbia, and Universal all made innovations and all influenced each other (as did, on occasion, artists and films outside the major studios). This balance would shift markedly just as World War II ended. Various factors resulted in MGM taking a commanding lead within the musical genre, both critically and at the box office. MGM, and in particular the musicals produced by Arthur Freed, would come to dominate the Hollywood musical throughout the rest of the 1940s and into the 1950s. According to film historian Thomas Schatz, "only 4 percent of all Hollywood releases [from 1946 to 1955] ... were musicals, yet over 25 percent of MGM's total output—81 of 316 productions—were musicals. Indeed, MGM produced over half the musicals made in Hollywood [during this period]."[1]

While World War II was arguably the apex of the genre in terms of sheer quantity, many have come to regard the postwar MGM musical as the aesthetic summit of the cinematic musical—that is, the definition of what a film musical can or should be.

This chapter discusses those aspects of the MGM musical that are so lauded and were so influential on filmmakers at other studios. Doing so requires not only examining the creative choices in the films themselves, but also the particular historical and industrial circumstances that fostered such creativity. As such, the first part of this chapter will step slightly out of this book's chronological progression to analyze the mechanics of the classical studio system, with special focus on the development of the "production unit." Discussing the Freed Unit as only one (albeit extremely lauded) example of a larger business strategy also feeds into the genre's ongoing dichotomy between freedom and control, and between individual autonomy and the needs of the community.

Free and Easy? A Defining History of the American Film Musical Genre, First Edition. Sean Griffin.
© 2018 Sean Griffin. Published 2018 by John Wiley & Sons Ltd.

Musicals under the Classical Hollywood Studio System

The structure of the motion picture industry in the United States from the 1930s through the mid-1950s was in many ways ideal for the fostering and development of the film musical genre. The major Hollywood studios dominated the industry, placing artists under long-term contracts (usually seven years). Thus, coteries of performers, writers, directors, and others could be assembled at each studio to work together consistently—forming something akin to theatrical repertory companies. Such circumstances at worst were stifling, with certain talented people feeling chained creatively and churning out product rather than art. On the other hand, the studio system could also function as a conservatory: artists working as a team to nurture and/or inspire each other in a relatively stable environment. Talent could be groomed, having time to grow and show their potential—both in front of and behind the camera. Performers could move from bit parts to bigger supporting roles to stardom. Esther Williams, for example, was cast in an MGM short, then was put into a small role in one of the studio's "Andy Hardy" pictures opposite Mickey Rooney and, from there, starred in *Bathing Beauty* (1944). Directors might also start out doing shorts before being given their first feature film. Mark Sandrich's success directing the RKO musical short *So This Is Harris* (1933) (winning an Oscar nomination for Best Live Action Short) led to the minor feature *Melody Cruise* (1933), and then shepherding Astaire and Rogers in *The Gay Divorcee* (1934) and *Top Hat* (1935).

Many historians of classical Hollywood talk about the concept of "house style": that each studio had its own unique look, feel, and personality. Such "branding" (to use today's terminology) emerged largely because the people that worked at these studios expressed or embodied these attitudes—and once such a brand had developed, successful artists figured out how to fit into that studio's personality. The average moviegoer most likely associated a "house style" with the people on camera—if Bing Crosby was in a film, it was most likely a Paramount picture; if Shirley Temple appeared, almost assuredly it was a Fox film. As such, the most overt expression of "house style" in Hollywood musicals is in the development of cycles centered around stars, often with the plot varying only slightly from film to film. Audiences might not have fully recognized the number of people behind the camera who also shaped the unique feel of a studio's product. The most obvious exception is choreographer Busby Berkeley. Although many at other studios attempted to match or surpass Berkeley, his audacious vision was unique and easily individuated Warner Bros. films in the mid-1930s. Other contract artists made more subtle contributions that helped distinguish the flavor of musicals made at different studios. The orchestrations for many a Warner Bros./Berkeley opus include a chorus led by the flute section, for example. Later, after World War II, music arranger

Ray Heindorf's bright, optimistic use of the brass section in orchestrations for Warner Bros. musicals sounds distinct from the greater emphasis on strings at Metro. Watch enough Columbia Technicolor musicals and one might notice the prevalence of rooms painted in either a subtle pale rose color or a sea foam green. The New York street on MGM's backlot (particularly its "department store window display" façade) shows up repeatedly in musicals. Universal's opera house set (built way back in 1925 for the silent version of *Phantom of the Opera*) appears with regularity in that studio's musicals, and Fox's plantation exterior (constructed for Temple's *The Little Colonel* [1935]) is similarly recognizable from musical to musical.[2]

The ability to develop and maintain a strong "house style" was possible because of other aspects of the classical studio system's business strategies. Namely, studios instituted methods of discipline and efficiency, thus minimizing expenditures and risk, and maximizing profit. This meant regulating film production as much as possible in order to establish a consistent flow of output and a consistent level of quality. Studios set up yearly schedules that determined how many films would be made, established an overall budget for annual production, and then distributed those funds across the various projects, depending on each project's potential return on investment. Such concentration created a security net: with risk spread across multiple films, the profits from one film could help mitigate the losses from another. This security net setup made it more possible to produce musicals, which often demanded larger budgets (higher production values, more talent involved). The drive for business efficiency also meant dominating the distribution and exhibition of films, and the "Big 5" (Paramount, Warner Bros., 20th Century-Fox, RKO, and MGM) all owned their own chain of theatres. This ensured that there would always be theatres willing to show every film produced—so a studio's worst musical still would play *somewhere*.

Leo C. Rosten, writing in 1941 about Hollywood's studio system, argued that "in the final analysis, the sum total of a studio's personality, the aggregate pattern of its choices and its tastes, may be traced to its producers."[3] In the early days of filmmaking, artists wore many hats—possibly working simultaneously as director, cameraman, writer, producer ... and possibly even acting as well. Eventually, certain people began specializing in certain areas, but with a still loose and ever-shifting chain of command. Sometimes the director was the driving force of a production; other times, the star might be the one in charge. As the studio system emerged in the 1920s, centralized production shifted "responsibility to orchestrate the entire filmmaking process from conception and story development through editing to release ... to the producer."[4] The executives were the ones that set the schedules, set the budgets, and the ones that oversaw the long-term contracts.

The figure most recognized for helping conceptualize the classical Hollywood system—and for putting it into practice—was Irving Thalberg. Thalberg was able to only make a tentative start on his ideas at Universal, where he began his career in the early 1920s. Upon transferring to the newly formed Metro-Goldwyn-Mayer as Vice President and General Manager, he quickly established the dominance of the producers who managed and supervised everyone else's work. From constant story conferences to extensive editing room sessions, Thalberg (and a very small group of assistants) kept a never-wavering eye on everything that had the MGM logo on it. Success for MGM and Thalberg's system was quick: by the end of the silent era, the studio was second in revenues only to Paramount. During the 1930s, Metro was the only studio to always have a yearly profit, at a time when some studios had to dig themselves out of various forms of bankruptcy.

While one of the central aims of the studio system was to rein in costs, Thalberg recognized that the large scope of a major studio created the capacity to judiciously spend a bit more on certain projects (with the thought that the extra budget would result in even higher profits). Thus, MGM swiftly became known for its gloss and sheen, and was often referred to as "the Tiffany's of studios." Metro's lower-budgeted films often looked more expensive than "prestige" pictures from smaller studios. The importance, though, was on *judicious* spending—and the lavishness was not simply to make something seem expensive but "tasteful." Whereas 20th Century-Fox's studio look was also lavish, its studio style seemed louder (and perhaps more vulgar?) than MGM's. On the other hand, Metro felt less like "old world money" and more Americanized than Paramount. (This may be due to European trained directors with stronger artistic signatures working at Paramount, such as Ernst Lubitsch and Josef von Sternberg.) MGM also quickly became known for its concentration of stars, with a larger "stable" of screen idols than any other studio. At one point, the studio marketed itself as having "More Stars Than There Are in the Heavens."

With MGM carving out this sort of identity for itself, it is perhaps unsurprising then that the studio would be so strongly associated with musicals. In their emphasis on style and star performers, the genre matched perfectly with Metro. The studio's preference for high-key lighting (so audiences could better see all of the beautiful sets, costumes, and people assembled before the camera) also lent itself well to the bright, cheery nature of musical comedy. And, because so many hands were always needed for a musical, it was a genre in which the producer seemed more necessary as the one in control of coordinating everything. Remember that MGM's first musical, the Oscar-winning *The Broadway Melody* (1928), had no marquee-name stars trying to dominate the production, and the picture's songwriting team of Arthur Freed and Nacio Herb Brown were "house composers" (Figure 5.1). Perhaps it is also unsurprising that the next MGM musical to win a Best Picture Oscar, *The Great Ziegfeld* (1936), is a biographical tribute to a producer.

From 1924 to 1932, Thalberg somehow oversaw every production coming out of MGM. While such an accomplishment might be due to his youthful zeal

Figure 5.1 The songwriting team of Arthur Freed (standing) and Nacio Herb Brown (at the piano) in *The Songwriters Revue* (1929), before Freed became a producer of some of the most well-remembered film musicals of all time. Snapshot taken from: The Songwriters Revue (1929).

(he was in his mid-twenties when MGM was founded), it is perhaps not surprising that Thalberg eventually collapsed from exhaustion. When he returned, the studio had created a new system of middle-management: instead of one central producer (Thalberg) supervising every single film, the studio's yearly output was broken up and given to a small group of executives to produce. While each producer worked separately, they all answered to President L.B. Mayer, and had to negotiate with each other for their share of the annual production budget and the talent under contract. Thalberg took on a smaller load in being one of these producers, and with his death in 1936, what was termed the "unit system of production" remained in force—not just at MGM, but across Hollywood. Under this revised system, Metro would have three units devoted exclusively to musical production by the mid-1940s, and the most prestigious of these units was helmed by Arthur Freed.

Freed in the Classical Hollywood Studio System

As described in Chapter 2, Arthur Freed began his career at Metro with a long-term contract as a lyricist. Under the terms of the contract, any and all songs written by him (whether with his regular composer Nacio Herb Brown or with someone else) were the property of the studio. Freed was paid a weekly salary, not receiving any percentages from sheet music sales, recordings, or license agreements to use his work. While Freed might have expressed interest in working on certain individual projects, ultimately he was assigned films whether he cared for them or not—and there were no guarantees that any of the songs he helped write would end up being used. Nonetheless, being a house artist meant a stable income and continual work, rather than living from inspiration to inspiration. Songs by Arthur Freed can be found in quite a number of 1930s MGM musicals.[5]

Perhaps realizing that the power to be independently creative lay in the hands of the producers, Freed seemed to waste no time venturing beyond the music department and making connections around the lot. His first promotion came with *Broadway Melody of 1936* (1935), for which he not only wrote the song score but acted as Music Supervisor. His interest in moving over to management was abetted by developing a close bond with studio chief Mayer himself. Thomas Schatz writes that "over the years Freed ... had become Louis Mayer's chief confidant and troubleshooter."[6] Mayer purportedly bought the film rights to *The Wizard of Oz* (1939) based on Freed's recommendation. Freed took on the responsibility of organizing nine months of pre-production for this film, for which he would not get screen credit. Rather, he used the project to demonstrate his potential as a budding producer. While *Oz* was still being filmed, Freed earned his first official credit as producer on another film: *Babes in Arms* (1939), the start of the Rooney–Garland backstager cycle. Although *Oz* was the bigger film, and ultimately became one of the most enduring of Hollywood classics, its high budget kept it from turning a profit in its initial release—while the smaller-budgeted *Babes in Arms* brought in very hefty immediate profits.[7]

Even before becoming a producer, Freed showed his strengths in pulling together a unit of people to work with him. In 1934, he noticed a talented pianist and vocal arranger named Roger Edens, and got MGM to put the man under contract. Edens became a go-to person when special orchestrations or extra scoring were needed for a picture—or even if there was a last-minute need for an extra song—and he and Freed quickly established a strong working relationship. One of Edens' most important roles in the late 1930s was helping groom and refine young Judy Garland's singing voice. With Edens already working as Freed's assistant, and Garland under Edens' tutelage, the threesome were already functioning somewhat as a unit by the time *Babes in Arms* was green lit. If this was not a strong enough foundation, Freed also managed to convince Berkeley to leave Warner Bros. for MGM—and to take "a sizable pay cut for the job."[8] Berkeley would direct most of the Garland–Rooney cycle.

Perhaps unsurprisingly, the studio initially kept Freed to the formula that proved so successful the first time—a common Hollywood strategy that resulted in so many cycles across Hollywood during the 1930s and 1940s.

Yet, Freed managed to widen his productions beyond the *Babes* films. At first, he stuck with Garland, but put her in vehicles without Mickey Rooney: *Little Nellie Kelly* (1940) and *For Me and My Gal* (1942), both directed by Berkeley. Berkeley also supervised the musical numbers for Freed's first non-Garland production, *Lady Be Good* (1941). And Edens contributed to each film on multiple levels.

During this period, the Freed Unit continued to grow. As a close friend of Edens, singer and vocal coach Kay Thompson often helped Garland and others. *For Me and My Gal* was the first film appearance of Gene Kelly. According to Kelly himself, Freed had hoped to get MGM to put the up-and-coming Broadway star under contract, but miscommunications led to Kelly signing with independent producer David Selznick instead.[9] Freed persevered, though, and Selznick agreed to transfer Kelly's contract to MGM when he realized he had no projects in which to put the performer. Freed also got the studio to put theatrical designer/director Vincente Minnelli under contract, and Minnelli's career at MGM is a strong testament to the benefits of the studio system. The scope of the studio was such that Freed was able to let Minnelli basically wander around the lot for a time and learn how everything functioned, slowly preparing him to move into the director's chair—grooming him much like a potential star performer. Minnelli's first contribution was to a portion of one number in *Strike Up the Band* (1940), and then devising individual numbers in various musicals. Perhaps echoing the one screen credit he had before coming to Metro (the Harlem fantasy number "Public Melody No. 1" in Paramount's *Artists and Models* [1937], described in Chapter 3), Minnelli was regularly put in charge of developing sequences for Lena Horne.

Having Berkeley working with the Freed Unit likely helped Minnelli think about making musicals cinematically rather than theatrically, particularly in using the camera. Yet, while Minnelli was given time and opportunities for his directorial talents to blossom, Berkeley's time at MGM showed the other side of working in the classic studio system. Berkeley most likely jumped over to MGM because he recognized that Metro was more committed to ongoing musical production than Warners was by the late 1930s. While this was true, working at his new studio meant submitting to the power structure. In his heyday at Warners, Berkeley had a sizable amount of control over his projects; at MGM, he had less free rein for his elaborate fantasies, and the person in charge of keeping him in check was his producer Arthur Freed. While Berkeley would continue working throughout the 1940s and into the early 1950s, his association with the Freed Unit lessened, and his marketability waned considerably.

Nothing succeeds like success, and the profitability of the Garland–Rooney films and his other forays gave Freed greater and greater cache as a producer. His studio superiors, trusting his ideas and opinions, increasingly approved bigger budgets. During the war years, Freed acquired the film rights to a number of Broadway musicals, such as *Panama Hattie* (1942), *DuBarry Was a Lady*

(1943), and *Best Foot Forward* (1943). He also had MGM buy the rights to the stage hit *Girl Crazy* from RKO (who had filmed it in 1932), and refashioned it into the last of the Garland–Rooney films. As a further sign of Freed's growing importance, he convinced the studio to invest in a Broadway show, getting the option for the screen rights in the process. That show was *Cabin in the Sky*, which is not the typical legs-and-laughs show then popular on Broadway (*Hattie* and *DuBarry* are more in that vein). As mentioned in Chapter 4, this is an all-black cast in a relatively integrated book musical. Thus, producing the show—and making a movie of it—was a bit of a risk, but one that Freed was able to get the studio to take.

Cabin in the Sky (1943) is also the first feature film directed by Minnelli (and perhaps all of his work devising numbers for Horne was seen as good preparation). The relative success of this film led immediately to Freed assigning him to direct the Unit's next production: *Meet Me in St. Louis* (1944). Freed stretched himself and his Unit again—the film was a major musical *not* based on an already successful Broadway property. Freed also supported Minnelli's desire to build a whole new street on the MGM backlot to create a full-scale Victorian neighborhood, and got the studio to increase the budget by over $200,000. Garland was reticent to play another teenaged character, but Minnelli quickly impressed her (so much so that they were married soon after the production wrapped). Edens helped with orchestrations and contributed some songs. That work went uncredited, but *St. Louis* marked the beginning of Edens being listed as "Associate Producer," a role he largely already had been fulfilling for five years. Even Freed himself contributed as a performer—dubbing the singing voice of actor Leon Ames as the father.[10]

St. Louis was quickly heralded by critics and audiences as something special—and soon became the biggest box-office success that Metro had ever had at that point in its history.[11] From that point on, Arthur Freed and his colleagues were without argument the most powerful musical unit on the lot, and what many historians refer to as the Golden Age of the Hollywood musical was under way. Throughout the rest of the 1940s and into the 1950s, the Freed Unit not only dominated MGM but all of Hollywood musical production, as others saw its successes and tried to adapt. Thus, in order to understand the evolution of the musical genre after World War II, one needs to recognize what exactly the Freed Unit was doing in its films.

The Freed Unit Style

Perhaps the most striking aspect of the Freed Unit's style is, ironically, its relative *lack* of a coherent style in comparison to other musical units at MGM or elsewhere. Most units centered on cycles in which each film was a variation of the others in plot, look, and sound, such as the Warner Bros. backstagers of the

1930s or Fox's "Good Neighbor" musicals in the early 1940s. While Freed began his career as producer with the popular cycle of Rooney–Garland back-stagers, he was determined not to keep repeating himself. *Meet Me in St. Louis* was a huge hit, but his next project, *Ziegfeld Follies* (1946), was something completely different. *The Harvey Girls* (1946) was a musical Western; *Good News* (1947) was a remake of the iconic 1920s college musical; *The Pirate* (1948) was a Caribbean fantasy; *Easter Parade* (1948) was a period backstager; *On the Town* (1949) happened in modern-day Manhattan, and so on.

What *did* link Freed's films—and what most people consider the most influential aspect of them—was their philosophy: integration. *Meet Me in St. Louis* was not only *not* a backstager, but its use of musical numbers helped define the characters and their environment, and sometimes narrative was propelled during the numbers. For example, early on in the film, teenage Esther Smith (Garland) gazes longingly out her living-room window at young John Pruitt, who has just moved in next door. Leaning against the window frame, Esther indicates her feelings to the audience by breaking into a sung monologue, "The Boy Next Door" (Figure 5.2). Later, as the family spends what may be their last Christmas in St. Louis before moving to New York, Esther tries to cheer up her little sister, Tootie (Margaret O'Brien) in the number "Have Yourself a Merry Little Christmas." Perfectly encapsulating how the integrated

Figure 5.2 Judy Garland sits at a window and laments musically about "The Boy Next Door" in *Meet Me in St. Louis* (1944), helping shift the musical genre to a focus on integrating song, dance, and narrative. Snapshot taken from: Meet Me in St. Louis (1944).

number can express narrative and character complexity, the song obliquely points out Esther's own melancholy even while she tries to paint an optimistic picture for her little sister.

While song integrated into dialogue, the ideas in the music also integrated with the visual design and the camerawork. Everything worked in tandem, each element supporting the others, creating a unified concept. The amount of detail in the Smith house, for example, and the way the camera weaves through it works with the conviviality of the music to draw the audience more intimately into this home and its inhabitants—so that when the father announces they are moving to New York, the audience shares the trauma the rest of the family feels. This pattern would continue in Freed's subsequent films—each project might be different in story and feel but the drive was always to create a vision that cohered in all areas, with numbers working in conjunction with the other creative aspects rather than standing independently.

That said, the sense that every number in a Freed musical happened with characters singing when they should be talking or dancing when they should be walking is patently untrue. *Ziegfeld Follies*, as the name indicates, is a big-scale musical revue. The Freed Unit would also continually return to the back-stage milieu—whether with biographies of songwriters (Jerome Kern in *Till the Clouds Roll By* [1946]; Rodgers and Hart in *Words and Music* [1948]), or with stories about making it big on Broadway (*Easter Parade, The Barkleys of Broadway* [1949], *The Band Wagon* [1953]). *Singin' in the Rain* (1952) is a back-stager taking place in Hollywood during the transition to sound (using many of the songs Freed himself wrote during that period). As backstagers, these films inevitably contain numbers that occur as stage performances. Yet, in all of these, there are also moments where integrated numbers happen as well. Even the biopics are about songwriters who were early champions of integrated shows, and Freed includes examples of such work: *Till the Clouds Roll By* starts with an encapsulated performance of *Show Boat*; the climactic set piece of *Words and Music* is the extended "Slaughter on 10th Avenue" story in dance.

The emphasis on integration also led to another difference from most other musical units, in that the Freed Unit was not dependent upon a single star performer. For units working at certain studios, there was no other choice than to focus on one star, because that individual was the extent of headliner musical talent under contract. Paramount's reliance on Bing Crosby comes to mind, although Betty Hutton also rose to stardom at that studio in the mid-1940s. Joseph Pasternak's unit at Universal in the 1930s focused exclusively on Deanna Durbin. MGM, on the other hand, held a general strategy of garnering or developing stars, and thus built up a large and diverse list of musical talent. By the late 1940s, the Metro contract list would include Judy Garland, Gene Kelly, Frank Sinatra, Lena Horne, Kathryn Grayson, Jane Powell, June Allyson, Esther Williams, Van Johnson, Red Skelton, Ann Miller, Virginia O'Brien, Oscar Levant, and Xavier Cugat (with his orchestra). In 1950, Howard Keel and

Figure 5.3 Frank Sinatra, Betty Garrett, Jules Munshin, Ann Miller, Gene Kelly, and Vera-Ellen joyously prepare to go "On the Town" in *On the Town* (1949), an example of the number of musical performers under contract at MGM during this period, and of the importance of the group dynamic in Freed Unit musicals. Snapshot taken from: On the Town (1949).

Debbie Reynolds would join the list. It is the classical studio system that made it possible to congregate so much talent under one roof (Figure 5.3).

Still, having such a deep talent pool to draw from did not keep some producers from centering their units around one or two key performers. Pasternak moved from Universal to MGM in the early 1940s, becoming second in importance after Freed in producing musicals.[12] He generally stuck to the pattern he developed at Universal with Deanna Durbin by grooming young soprano Kathryn Grayson, and then classically trained juvenile Jane Powell (even remaking some of the films he had produced with Durbin into vehicles for Powell).[13] Similarly, Freed had strong ties with Garland and Kelly. But, Freed took much more advantage of Metro's wide range of talent than did Pasternak. Once the Garland–Rooney cycle ended, Freed took care to vary Garland's co-stars, and would do the same with Kelly. Major Freed musicals such as *Good News*, his remake of *Show Boat* (1951), *Kismet* (1955), and *Gigi* (1958) are without either Garland or Kelly.[14] In films such as *Ziegfeld Follies*, *Till the Clouds Roll By*, and *Words and Music*, he created all-star showcases to parade the cornucopia the studio had to offer.

Even in the number of films starring either Garland or Kelly, Freed's musicals are consistently "group efforts." Whereas Crosby or Durbin often shouldered the lion's share of the musical responsibilities for their films, Freed musicals concertedly spread numbers out across the cast of characters. *Meet Me in St. Louis* begins this way, with the title song being passed from family member to family member. While Garland is obviously the star of the picture, almost everyone in the family gets a chance to perform at some point. The family bond is enhanced by having little Tootie (Margaret O'Brien) perform "Under the Bamboo Tree" with her older sister Esther (Garland), and by having Mother and Father (Mary Astor, Leon Ames) duet to "You and I," instead of having Esther sing everything. Similarly, the Oscar-winning song "On the Atchison, Topeka, and the Santa Fe" from *The Harvey Girls* (1946) runs through an entire narrative sequence, as the titular females arrive by train to a small frontier town. As the number rolls out, the men express their anticipation, and each of the women explains her own hopes and desires in coming out West. While the sequence lays out that the cowboys are rough-and-tumble and the women represent the arrival of civilization, it also shows them all harmonizing vocally and choreographically—thus indicating that these two opposite sides will be able to blend successfully into one community by the end of the film.

The panoply of performers also worked perfectly for the Freed Unit's emphasis on integration. The "Lucky in Love" number in Freed's remake of *Good News* provides an apt example, turning what had been a conventional (if highly popular) "book musical" with tangential tunes into an integrated piece. Additional lyrics were written for "Lucky in Love," creating separate choruses for the various characters at a sorority social to describe the current status of their romantic lives: the co-ed dating one guy while flirting with another, the sweet girl bemoaning her lack of a love life (while washing party dishes), the vamp's attempting to land the wealthiest boy, and the football captain trying to land the vamp (and getting publicly refused at the climax of the number). With stories no longer confined to "putting on a show," the entire world could erupt into music and come together in perfect rhythm. Thus, the integration championed by the Freed Unit helped create a new sense of freedom in the genre: song and dance could emerge out of any situation and any person, bringing everyone together into a community. As the climactic number in *Ziegfeld Follies* exclaimed, "There's Beauty Everywhere."

At the same time, though, integration worked against another form of freedom that had been prevalent in musicals. Backstagers and comedies with music may have been formulaic in their plotlines, but they created a framework that allowed a wide variety of musical entertainment. Anyone could come out and do anything as part of "the show" being put on within the film or as part of the anarchy that accompanied the scattershot comedy. In contrast, integrated musicals continually broke narrative formulas, but the songs and dances had to *fit into* the story and environment. An apt example would be Freed's use of

Esther Williams in the more integrated structure of *Take Me Out to the Ball Game* (1949). There is no easy justification for the aquatic musical spectacle typical of her films in a story about baseball in the 1890s, and thus there is only one small moment with her in a pool. For Williams to be included in the musical community of the film, she must integrate herself rather than being free to display her own unique talents.[15]

The other major aspect of the Freed Unit's style was its emphasis on dance. As mentioned, the Pasternak Unit distinguished itself in its emphasis on trained voices. In addition to Kathryn Grayson and Jane Powell, Pasternak's films are littered with classical bit parts or guest stars, such as pianist Jose Iturbi and operatic baritone Lauritz Melchior. Freed was not adverse to trained voices, and the singing of Garland was prominent in his films, but his unit focused on dance almost from the outset. His first produced films were directed by Berkeley, and the addition of Kelly further strengthened the accent on choreography. By the end of World War II, Kelly was considered second only to Astaire as Hollywood's top male dancer—and Astaire signed a multiple-picture deal with Metro in 1945 as well.

Across the next decade, some of the most memorable dance sequences on film would be done by MGM, as the Freed Unit experimented with and refined how to choreograph for the camera. The influence of Berkeley was apparent in the broad, fluid cinematography, making it seem as if the camera was dancing too. Yet, the moves were carefully modulated for specific effect rather than the spectacular stunts common to Berkeley's oeuvre. When the camera did a sudden leap and circle into the air, such as at one magnificent point in the title number to *Singin' in the Rain*, it matched the joyous energy of Kelly's character. At other times, the camera might move more subtly, slowly drawing the viewer more intimately into the scene, such as when Astaire reunites with Ginger Rogers to "They Can't Take That Away from Me" in *The Barkleys of Broadway*. Another important difference in the emerging Freed Unit style was that the camera was dancing around actual dancers instead of the chorus girl "cogs in a machine" that Berkeley preferred. Astaire and Kelly (and others) were also fascinated with aspects unique to cinema in creating dance—and to a certain extent, one can see almost a competition as to who can come up with the more creative idea. Kelly's star-making moment in *Cover Girl* (1944) involved him dancing with a superimposition of himself. The following year in *Anchors Aweigh* (1945)—produced by Pasternak—Kelly famously danced with the cartoon mouse Jerry. Astaire would dance in slow motion in *Easter Parade*, with a cadre of shoes come to life in *The Barkleys of Broadway*, and on the ceiling in *Royal Wedding* (1951) (Figure 5.4).

Both also helped lead the Freed Unit into long-form dance numbers. Astaire's two big sequences in *Ziegfeld Follies* were stories in dance. "This Heart of Mine" shows him as a gentleman thief romancing a young woman in order to lift her jewels—only to discover that she's willing to give them to him in return

Figure 5.4 Fred Astaire dancing in slow motion to "Steppin' Out with My Baby" in *Easter Parade* (1948). The Freed Unit placed great emphasis on exploring uniquely cinematic methods of presenting dance. Snapshot taken from: Easter Parade (1948).

for the affection. In "Limehouse Blues," he plays a Chinese man yearning for a beautiful woman but, through various circumstances, dying without her ever even noticing him. Astaire's next film for Freed was *Yolanda and the Thief* (1946), which centered around an extremely Daliesque dream ballet. The concept of a "dream ballet" had become popular via choreographer Agnes de Mille's work for *Oklahoma!* and *Carousel* on Broadway. The lengthy ballet sequence in the British film *The Red Shoes* (1948), which was a major box-office success in the United States, further influenced this trend. Kelly in particular became interested in this form in the wake of *The Red Shoes*, and performed long-form dance sequences in *The Pirate, Words and Music*, and *On the Town* (which itself started off as a ballet piece called "Fancy Free"). The apex of this exploration occurred with *An American in Paris* (1951). The climactic number is an eighteen-minute ballet set to the Gershwin tone poem, as Kelly and Leslie Caron dance through the works of various painters (Dufy, Utrillo, Renoir, Van Gogh, Toulouse-Lautrec). The critical and popular reaction to this film was immense (and will be discussed further in Chapter 6).

During the late 1940s and early 1950s, Metro put more and more dancers under contract: Vera-Ellen, Ann Miller, Leslie Caron, Cyd Charisse, Tommy Rall, Bobby Van, Bob Fosse, and the dancing team of Marge and Gower Champion. The community dynamic that pulled everyone together in song also functioned in terms of movement—a sense of bonding was visualized by showing everyone and everything moving in sync with each other. Those who were not trained dancers still could be pulled into rhythmic movement, and numbers that consisted largely of walking in tempo became common in Freed Unit musicals.[16] Even props moved gracefully: umbrellas twirled perfectly in the air, coatracks acted like living dance partners, police cars and automobiles chasing a speeding cab wove in and around each other in choreographed pursuit.

Yet, just as integration worked against stand-alone specialty acts, integrated dance also meant that the choreography had to blend in with the rest of the elements.[17] There was little room for flash acts such as the Nicholas Brothers, who had to tone down their abilities in order to integrate with Kelly in the "Be a Clown" number in their only MGM musical, *The Pirate*. Eccentric dancing, such as that done by Ray Bolger, could only be admitted if it fit the situation (such as being a clumsy Scarecrow in *The Wizard of Oz*). Astaire and Kelly had their own individual dance personalities—the sophisticated Astaire who made every step seem easy and graceful, the energetic Kelly who made every step seem an amazing feat of athleticism. Yet, even they adapted their styles for the sake of integration. Astaire in Freed musicals, for example, regularly played characters who learned to become part of a team instead of being his own (amazing) talent. In *Easter Parade*, he starts by trying to mold Garland to his own designs, but ends up learning the joys of working as equal partners, even shedding his top hat and tails for a hobo's outfit in "A Couple of Swells." In *The Band Wagon*, he sings one solo chorus of "By Myself" at the start of the film, and learns the value of being part of a community through the rest of the film. He never does a solo dance, even doing his usual top hat number (in this film, "I Guess I'll Have to Change My Plans") as a duet with George Buchanan. Everything and everyone needed to work together.

The community *esprit d'corps* celebrated on screen functioned within the Unit as well. Unlike certain other major Hollywood producers like Samuel Goldwyn or David Selznick, Freed did not call undue attention to himself nor claim to be the strongest creative voice in his films. While a songwriter, he did not try to equate his work to that of Berlin, Porter, Kern, the Gershwins, or Rodgers and Hart. Irving Berlin assessed that Freed's "greatest talent was to know talent, to recognize talent, and to surround himself with it."[18] The strength of his Unit came from the combination of talents—the whole being greater than the sum of its parts.[19] Rather than situating himself as the controlling imagination in the top-down power structure of the classic studio setup, Freed is generally lauded for creating an environment that fostered the imagination of others. Freed could use MGM's deep pockets to put the best talent in all departments under contract—and they liked working for Freed, because he trusted them to know what they were doing, so gave them room to experiment and be creative. In the other direction, his consistent box-office success gave him the power to shelter the talent in his Unit from business executives and numbers crunchers—even in the face of occasional failure with moviegoers (such as with *Yolanda and the Thief, The Pirate*, and *Summer Holiday* [1948]).

In addition to the onscreen talent was the cream of the crop behind the camera. Irene Sharaff was a consistent costume designer for Freed's films—and Freed extended her creativity to the set design of the "Limehouse Blues" segment in *Ziegfeld Follies*. Composers and music arrangers such as Kay Thompson, Lennie Hayton, Alan Jay Lerner, and the songwriting team of Hugh Martin and Ralph Blane also congregated around Freed. Much as Freed recognized that Sharaff's design ideas for *Ziegfeld Follies* extended beyond wardrobe, he worked with Lerner not only in songwriting but in writing scripts. Lerner wrote both the book and lyrics for *Royal Wedding, Brigadoon* (1954), and *Gigi*, as well as the script for *An American in Paris* (1951) and the Mickey Spillane-style narration for the "Girl Hunt Ballet" in *The Band Wagon*. The most lauded writing team in the Freed Unit, though, were Betty Comden and Adolph Green, who adapted their own Broadway hits *On the Town* and *Bells Are Ringing* (1960), and did the books for *Good News, Singin' in the Rain, The Band Wagon*, and *It's Always Fair Weather* (1955).

In stressing dance, choreographers such as Robert Alton and Jack Cole were important figures in the Freed Unit as well. A number of choreographers moved into becoming directors under Freed—thus giving whole films, not just the numbers, a sort of choreographed feel. These director auteurs would marshal the various talents—pulling together sets, costumes, lighting, camera, performance—into one coherent "integrated" vision. Again, Berkeley blazed this trail, coming to MGM as both choreographer and director. Metro's structure gave other choreographers a mentorship period, allowing them to grow and develop before being seated in the director's chair.

Charles Walters worked on the choreography for *St. Louis*, and some of the sequences in *Ziegfeld Follies* before directing his first film, *Good News*. The success of that film moved him into working with bigger stars: Garland and Astaire in *Easter Parade*, and a reunited Astaire and Rogers in *The Barkleys of Broadway*. By the 1950s, Walters branched out beyond the Freed Unit, directing such notable non-Freed MGM musicals as *Lili* (1953), which won him an Oscar nomination, and *High Society* (1956). Walters' films constantly emphasize getting along, and show empathy for all. Usually even the antagonists are reclaimed back into the group and find happiness by the end of his films. The worst thing to be accused of in a Walters film is being selfish or self-centered. Such emphasis on the group, of course, extends to the musical numbers, with everyone contributing. Although *Dangerous When Wet* (1953) is a typical Esther Williams showcase, the picture fits in moments for all of her family and friends to perform, including the long-limbed Charlotte Greenwood as her mother. *High Society* has the high-powered talents of both Bing Crosby and Frank Sinatra, but Grace Kelly gets to sing too (creating a top-selling recording of "True Love" with Crosby). *Lili* is arguably his masterwork, a story of two emotionally isolated people who come to depend on each other, but are unable to recognize or admit their feelings. In many ways, the film is harsh—the girl contemplates suicide at one point, the fellow slaps her in frustration at another point—but Walters creates enormous sympathy for both, and their union at the very end of the film is beautiful and gratifying.

Like Walters, Stanley Donen moved his way up the ladder during the 1940s. Being a friend and professional colleague of Kelly brought him to MGM, often helping to devise and choreograph numbers in Kelly's films. The two became a co-directing team with *On the Town*, then *Singin' in the Rain*, and *It's Always Fair Weather*. Freed gave Donen his first solo credit with *Royal Wedding*. Like Walters, Donen would eventually work outside the Freed Unit, directing such major hits as *Seven Brides for Seven Brothers* (1954) and *Funny Face* (1957). Donen's films also stress the group dynamic—particularly with trios of friends, as in *On the Town, Singin' in the Rain, It's Always Fair Weather*, and *Funny Face*. Yet, they do not have the humanist outlook common to musicals directed by Walters. Rather, individuals are often punished for their egotism in very physical, albeit humorous, fashion. Fistfights and all-out brawls are not uncommon (*Royal Wedding, Singin' in the Rain, It's Always Fair Weather, Funny Face*), and the massive donnybrook that erupts in *Seven Brides for Seven Brothers* is as choreographed as any more traditional dance number. In a certain way, everyone in a Donen musical realizes they are equal once they all have black eyes and bruises![20]

While Walters and Donen became notable, Vincente Minnelli was always considered the most important director in the Freed Unit, and thus the most important director of musicals at MGM. A designer rather than a choreographer, Minnelli's films always displayed a unity of vision, and his signature outlook dealt with characters similar to himself—people trying to get the actual world to match the ideals in their heads. Minnelli's protagonists tend to be artists in some fashion—from painters and performers to con men and courtesans—and the stories show them in the act of creation. Dream sequences are thus very common in Minnelli musicals (*Cabin in the Sky, Ziegfeld Follies, Yolanda and the Thief, The Pirate, An American in Paris*). The group dynamic motif in Minnelli musicals occurs as the artist either finds others who share that vision, or the artist is inspired to revise that vision when encountering the dreams and desires of other individuals. Tragedy occurs only when the individual remains alone in his or her quest. *Brigadoon* is a good example, with one citizen of the magical village feeling trapped rather than blessed—and he is killed as he tries to escape.[21]

Perhaps the most important collaborator behind the scenes in the Freed Unit, though, was Freed's associate Roger Edens, who functioned as a creative jack-of-all-trades: acting as vocal coach, orchestrator, and (when an extra tune was suddenly needed) composer. For example, Kelly credits Edens with suggesting the "doo-de-doo-doo" intro to Kelly's version of "Singin' in the Rain," a small but vital detail of that number. Edens often helped draw others into Freed's circle. While Edens had strong ties with a number of women (Garland and Thompson in particular), he also had a special bond with many of the other men in the Unit. Recent scholars have pointed out the profusion of homosexual men within the Freed Unit, including (but not limited to) Edens, Walters, and Cole Porter. The Unit's reputation for gay men was so well known within the industry that they were often referred to as "Freed's Fairies."[22]

Steven Cohan argues that a critical aspect of the MGM musical is a camp aesthetic, and that the number of gay men working on MGM musicals resulted in a style *intended* to be enjoyed from a camp perspective: "As the genre developed at Metro to serve as its signature product ..., the studio's musicals all conformed in one way or another to a distinctive studio look, highly polished but excessively stylized and overblown, at least in the numbers."[23] Cohan further argues that such intentional camp was part of the appeal even to straight audiences, even if they had never heard of the term or its connection to the gay subculture.

As Chapter 4 discussed, the musical genre as a whole is well suited to a camp aesthetic. Many films at studios other than MGM have a high camp value, and queer artists were not working solely for Freed or at Metro. Yet, the camp inflections in Freed's films are often different than in other musicals, even others at MGM. A central example is the "refined vulgarity" of Judy Garland in "The Great Lady Has an Interview" from *Ziegfeld Follies*, with her parodic performance of a cinematic diva, the "paradoxically spare and yet overwrought" décor, and the flock of young male reporters who can be read as a group of gay men.[24] While the set piece is joyously flamboyant, the filmmakers seem to be indicating that they *know* it's vulgar and they are actually better than this. The other most commonly cited example of camp in the Freed canon is *The Pirate*, with Kelly and Garland seemingly trying to out-ham each other, and Minnelli running riot with a baroque Caribbean visual design.[25] Most writers now suggest that its failure at the box office was due to it being *too* overtly camp, instead of the more refined camp usually on display in Freed musicals.

This high-class version of camp in Freed musicals stands in contrast to camp found in other MGM musicals (such as the trio of female contortionists in *Broadway Rhythm* [1944] or any Esther Williams water spectacle).[26] It is perhaps this interest in being "above it all" that worked against MGM director George Sidney ever fully becoming part of the Freed cohort. Sidney did work for Freed on some major projects: *The Harvey Girls, Annie Get Your Gun, Show Boat*. Yet, his predilection for over-the-top random silliness (such as in *Bathing Beauty, Anchors Aweigh*, or *Holiday in Mexico* [1946]) did not mesh well with the Freed aesthetic, either in terms of integration or in terms of hifalutin' camp.

The notion of high-class or "tasteful" camp matched Metro's efforts to be regarded as the "Tiffany" of studios. It also bolstered the growing opinion that musicals could be art rather than simple schmaltz or just "leg shows." And this is perhaps the lasting impact of the Freed Unit's style. In its emphasis on creating integrated unified works rather than "hodgepodges," in its push towards dance sequences called "ballets," the Freed Unit—along with the integrated work on Broadway being led by Rodgers and Hammerstein—made critics and audiences take the musical genre more seriously. In addition to knowing talent, Freed recognized what was of "artistic" importance—moving towards integration, experimenting with long-form dance, bringing Astaire and Rogers back together, remaking *Show Boat*. And as a result, Freed became the most lauded of musical producers in Hollywood—ultimately winning two Oscars for Best Picture (*An American in Paris* and *Gigi*), as well as the Academy's prestigious Irving Thalberg Award for ongoing artistic success as a producer. Freed's career stands as a testament to the strengths of the classical Hollywood system, and how that system created the perfect environment for the musical genre to grow and thrive.

Notes

1 Thomas Schatz, *The Genius of the System: Hollywood Filmmaking in the Studio Era* (New York: Pantheon Books, 1988), 447.

2 Universal was still using the opera house set in *Thoroughly Modern Millie* (1967) with Julie Andrews; Fox's plantation façade shows up as late as *High Time* (1960) with Bing Crosby.

3 Leo C. Rosten, *Hollywood: The Movie Colony, The Movie Makers* (New York: Harcourt, Brace, and Co., 1941), 242–243.

4 Schatz, 36.

5 For example, the scores to *Going Hollywood* (1933) and *Broadway Melody of 1936* (1935), as well as individual tunes such as "Alone" in *A Night at the Opera* (1935) and "Would You" in *San Francisco* (1936).

6 Schatz, 263.

7 Hugh Fordin, *The World of Entertainment! Hollywood's Greatest Musicals* (New York: Frederick Ungar, 1975), 29, lists the final cost of *The Wizard of Oz* as $2,777,000, and grossing $3,017,000 in its initial release, while *Babes in Arms* cost $465,000 and grossed $3,335,000 in its initial release. See also Aljean Harmetz, *The Making of 'The Wizard of Oz'*, updated ed. (Chicago: Chicago Review Press, 2013).

8 Schatz, 265.

9 Fordin, 60–63.

10 On production of *Meet Me in St. Louis*, see Fordin, 90–118.

11 Fordin, 118, lists the film's initial release grossing $7,566,000.

12 By the 1940s, "the two most active and successful producers at Metro were Freed and Pasternak. They were responsible for one-quarter of the twenty-eight productions on MGM's schedule for 1945." Schatz, 379.

13 Durbin's star-making film *Three Smart Girls* (1936) was remade with Jane Powell as *Three Daring Daughters* (1946); Durbin's *It's a Date* (1940) was turned into Powell's *Nancy Goes to Rio* (1950).

14 One could technically add *Annie Get Your Gun* (1950) to that list, but that was not by design, since Garland was initially cast in the lead role but dropped out in the middle of production and was replaced by Betty Hutton on loan from Paramount.

15 Freed would produce a more conventional Williams aquacade, *Pagan Love Song* (1950), which is possibly the film least identifiable as his.

16 One can see the first instance of the "walking number" in Freed's first film as producer, the title number of *Babes in Arms*. Other examples include "Three Men on a Date" in *Best Foot Forward*, "Be a Ladies Man" in *Good News*, "A Weekend in the Country" in *The Barkleys of Broadway*, the conclusion of the title number of *On the Town*, and arguably Garland and Astaire's classic rendition of "A Couple of Swells" in *Easter Parade*.

17 Adrienne L. McLean, "Flirting with Terpsichore: Dance, Class and Entertainment in 1930s Film Musicals," *The Sound of Musicals*, ed. Steven Cohan (London: British Film Institute, 2010), 67–81, argues that one can see this move to streamline all screen dance into two dominant modes (tap and ballet) in the 1930s. I would argue that the move towards integration in the musical furthered this trend.

18 Schatz, 448.

19 Donald Knox, *The Magic Factory: How MGM Made 'An American in Paris'* (New York: Praeger, 1973), uses interviews with a number of people from the Freed Unit describing the filming of the ballet in *An American in Paris* as an example of the collaborative work done in the classical studio system.

20 For more on Donen, see Stephen M. Silverman, *Dancing on the Ceiling: Stanley Donen and His Movies* (New York: Knopf, 1996); and Joseph Andrew Casper, *Stanley Donen* (Metuchen: Scarecrow Press, 1983).

21 The downside of the artist/dreamer tends to happen more in the melodramas Minnelli would direct than in his musicals (*Madame Bovary* [1949], *The Bad and the Beautiful* [1952], *Lust for Life* [1956]). For more on Minnelli, see Vincente Minnelli, *I Remember It Well* (London: Angus and Robertson, 1975); Stephen Harvey, *Directed by Vincente Minnelli* (New York: Harper & Row, 1989); Robert Lang, *American Film Melodrama: Griffith, Vidor, Minnelli* (Princeton: Princeton University Press, 1989); *Vincente Minnelli: The Art of Entertainment*, ed. Joe McElhaney (Detroit: Wayne State University Press, 2009).

22 Steven Cohan, *Incongruous Entertainment: Camp, Cultural Value, and the MGM Musical* (Durham: Duke University Press, 2005), 47; William J. Mann, *Behind the Screen: How Gays and Lesbians Shaped Hollywood, 1910–1969* (New York: Viking, 2001), 270; David Ehrenstein, *Open Secret: Gay Hollywood: 1928–1998* (New York: William Morrow and Co., 1998), 82; Matthew

Tinkcom, *Working Like a Homosexual: Camp, Capital, and Cinema* (Durham: Duke University Press, 2002).

23 Cohan, *Incongruous Entertainment*, 60.

24 Tinkcom, 59.

25 For example, see Cohan, *Incongruous Entertaiment*, 76–83; and Brett Farmer, *Spectacular Passions: Cinema, Fantasy, Gay Male Spectatorships* (Durham: Duke University Press, 2000), 99–109.

26 That said, the opening number in Freed's *Ziegfeld Follies* is the exception that proves the rule. Its extreme pink color design, the excess of pseudo-ballerinas, an overwrought carousel, and particularly animal tamer Lucille Ball cracking her whip to rein in a coterie of cat-women, holds no claims to refined taste at all. Cohan features this sequence on the cover of *Incongruous Entertainment*.

6

Something's Gotta Give: The Postwar Musical

The postwar period in the Hollywood musical is often fondly remembered as the apex of the genre. The success of integrated musicals spread beyond Rodgers and Hammerstein on Broadway and MGM's Freed Unit in Hollywood. On stage, integrated scores supplanted the looser structure of earlier book musicals, and revues practically disappeared. On screen, other studios (and producers other than Freed at MGM) tried to figure out how to create their own integrated musicals, often quite successfully. In the process, the musical gained in critical regard—no longer seen as a simple mélange of escapist trivialities but as a uniquely American art form, creating what many regard as a Golden Age for the American film musical. The blossoming of integration paralleled the rise of the United States itself as a global "superpower." America congratulated itself as the apex of human civilization: a haven of opportunity and freedom that resulted in continually high scientific, cultural, and moral achievement.

Yet, troubling aspects brewed in the midst of such glorification of both the integrated musical and postwar American society. While integrated musicals opened up a wealth of narrative possibilities for the genre, the concept of integration also began to constrict what was defined as a musical film, thus forcing filmmakers to fit into those confines. As a result, integration quelled much of the anarchic potential traditional to musicals before and during World War II. In many ways, this matched social trends in American society after the war. While promoting itself as "the land of the free," postwar America was a major period of social retrenchment, resulting in strong efforts to keep people within tight guidelines of thought and action. Attempts were made to reverse the small gains in equality that people of color, women, and homosexuals had made during the war. Postwar musicals paint a utopian picture of American life, but as the 1950s progressed the strain on those happy faces slowly became more apparent.

Free and Easy? A Defining History of the American Film Musical Genre, First Edition. Sean Griffin.
© 2018 Sean Griffin. Published 2018 by John Wiley & Sons Ltd.

Jumping on the Band Wagon: The Ascendancy of Integration

Why *The Band Wagon* (1953) is *titled* "The Band Wagon" is never explicitly explained by the film: there is no dialogue reference to the title, and no song with that name performed. Musical historians recognize the connection: the film uses the catalog of songwriting team Howard Dietz and Arthur Schwartz, who were most famous for their score for the 1930s Broadway revue *The Band Wagon* (which, like the film, starred Fred Astaire). Yet, for audiences unschooled in theatre lore, a more likely explanation for the title lies within the narrative: a backstager plot in which the group trying to put on a show feel pressured into "jumping on the band wagon" of creating an integrated musical (in this case, a musicalized update of *Faust*).

Certainly, from Broadway to Hollywood, integration had become the clarion call for the genre. The critical acclaim of the work of Rodgers and Hammerstein continued to grow after the war. Soon, established songwriters were trying their hand at writing integrated pieces, such as Cole Porter (with *Kiss Me, Kate*, *Silk Stockings*, and *Can-Can*) and Irving Berlin (with *Annie Get Your Gun*, which was produced by Rodgers and Hammerstein). Upcoming talents were judged by their success at integrated projects, such as the teams of Alan Jay Lerner and Frederick Loewe (*Brigadoon, My Fair Lady, Camelot*) or Richard Adler and Jerry Ross (*The Pajama Game, Damn Yankees*). On the West Coast, MGM's Freed Unit soon was not alone in investing in integration. For example, Disney abandoned the type of grab-bag animated anthology films it had been making through most of the 1940s (*Saludos Amigos* [1943], *The Three Caballeros* [1945], *Make Mine Music* [1946], *Melody Time* [1948]), and returned to animated fairy tales with integrated musical scores (*Cinderella* [1950], *Alice in Wonderland* [1951], *Peter Pan* [1953], *Sleeping Beauty* [1959]). Other studios were soon "jumping on the band wagon" as well.

Integration proved popular with general audiences, and it also helped grow the musical genre's artistic stature, giving it an increased air of legitimacy (as alluded to in the fictional attempt to do a musical version of *Faust* in *The Band Wagon*). Rodgers and Hammerstein would win a Pulitzer Prize for drama for *South Pacific* in 1949 (only the second musical to have done so at the time).[1] The same regard was extended to integrated work in Hollywood, with the Freed Unit eventually picking up two Best Picture Oscars for *An American in Paris* (1951) and *Gigi* (1958). It is perhaps unsurprising then that, all over Hollywood, filmmakers were concocting their own integrated musicals.

Other studios often looked to the ideas of the Freed Unit and of Rodgers and Hammerstein to figure out how to create a successful integrated musical. The most immediate and obvious effect was the surge of integrated musicals reveling in nostalgic Americana, after the success of *Meet Me in St. Louis* (1944) and the mammoth popularity on Broadway of *Oklahoma!* and *Carousel* (which transplants the French story *Liliom* to early 1900s New England). One could see the rise of integrated Americana in Broadway musicals such as *Bloomer Girl*, *Up in Central Park*, and *Annie Get Your Gun*. Unsurprisingly, a number of these Broadway projects were adapted to the screen. *Up in Central Park* (1948) was turned into a Deanna Durbin vehicle; Freed himself produced *Annie Get Your Gun* (1950) (*Bloomer Girl* was not adapted to the screen—its subject matter of early feminism, slavery, and the Civil War might have been too edgy for Hollywood producers at the time.)

A number of original cinematic properties taking place in the Wild West also seem influenced by the success of *Oklahoma!* In addition to Freed's own original western musical, *The Harvey Girls* (1946), was Universal's *Can't Help Singing* (1944) (with Deanna Durbin and cast singing "Californ-Ai-Ay" with much the same gusto as "Oklahoma!"), Warner Bros.' *Calamity Jane* (1953), Paramount's *Red Garters* (1954), *Seven Brides for Seven Brothers* (1954) (made at MGM by producer Jack Cummings), and Universal's *They Learned About Women* (1955).[2]

During the war, Fox specialized in turn-of-the-century backstagers starring Alice Faye or Betty Grable. After the war, the studio continued producing nostalgic musicals, but doing so in an integrated format. Its first effort was to hire Rodgers and Hammerstein themselves to write the book and score for a musical version of Fox's 1933 film *State Fair* (1945). While not a period piece, the film's laconic narrative of a middle-class family participating in a fair definitely echoes *Meet Me in St. Louis*. The staging of the Oscar-winning "It Might as Well Be Spring" is almost identical to *St. Louis's* "The Boy Next Door"—lead female sits by a window longing for romance—and comes at about the same point in each film's running time (Figure 6.1). Fox's *Centennial Summer* (1946) was even more obviously imitative of *St. Louis*: a middle-class family excited to attend the 1876 Centennial Exposition in Philadelphia. *State Fair* was very successful; *Centennial Summer* less so.[3] Other examples of integrated Americana at Fox showed similar mixed results: *Three Little Girls in Blue* (1946) seemed to charm audiences; Betty Grable's first integrated musical, *The Shocking Miss Pilgrim* (1947), was one of her least popular pictures.[4]

While Fox's imitations of *St. Louis* occurred quickly, copies from Warner Bros. did not appear until the early 1950s. Most likely this was because the studio did not have a strong musical cohort as World War II ended to match the Freed Unit at MGM. Fortunes changed with the arrival of Doris Day in 1948, who quickly became the central musical performer on the lot. In 1952, Day starred in *By the Light of the Silvery Moon* (1952), a light family musical comedy set in the late 1910s and sprinkled with episodic anecdotes rather than a strongly plotted through-line. The success of the film led to the further adventures of the family, *On Moonlight Bay* (1953).

The conviviality expressed in such family-oriented pieces, and the move towards integration in general, meant spreading the musicality around.

Figure 6.1 The influence of the MGM Freed Unit musical is plain to see here, as Jeanne Crain performs "It Might as Well Be Spring" in 20th Century-Fox's *State Fair* (1945). Compare this shot to Figure 5.2. Snapshot taken from: State Fair (1945).

While Rodgers and Hammerstein (and those following in their wake) worked with major Broadway stars (such as Mary Martin and Gertrude Lawrence), they did not write "star vehicles." Earlier book musicals usually were designed to showcase a specific marquee name, with the character tailored to the star. In contrast, integrated musicals focus on the story—thus performers need to fit the characters, rather than the other way around. While studios still had their star players, the postwar years saw fewer and fewer musicals in which only one person dominated all of the songs and/or dances. As discussed in Chapter 5, the Freed Unit musicals strongly emphasize the importance of communal bonding, with multiple performers gathered into each production.

Other producers of musicals at MGM had perhaps an easier time following in Freed's footsteps in this area than those at rival studios. Although Joseph Pasternak was often content with only one star (say, Jane Powell), he could take advantage of the wealth of talent under contract (such as *The Duchess of Idaho* [1950] starring Esther Williams, but with cameos by Lena Horne and, in her last film appearance, Eleanor Powell). In the 1950s, MGM producer Jack Cummings began rivaling Freed in success by pulling together multiple stars to create integrated musicals. Cummings had been at MGM almost since its inception, working as an office boy when he was seventeen. Being Louis B. Mayer's nephew may have helped him move up to being a producer there long before either Freed or Pasternak, overseeing many of Eleanor Powell's extravaganzas in the 1930s and producing a number of Esther Williams' aquacade films in the 1940s. Nonetheless, one can see the impact of the Freed Unit's move toward integration on musicals produced by Cummings as the 1950s began. *Two Weeks with Love* (1950) has a touch of *St. Louis* in its family-oriented period atmosphere. Leading lady Jane Powell works with newcomers Debbie Reynolds and Carlton Carpenter, and is arguably upstaged by their duet to "Aba Daba Honeymoon." *Three Little Words* (1950) stars Fred Astaire and Red Skelton as the songwriting team of Harry Ruby and Fred Kalmar—and has Vera-Ellen, Gloria de Haven, and Debbie Reynolds as well. Cummings then got the rights to remake *Roberta* from RKO, retitled it *Lovely to Look At* (1952), gathered an array of talent (Howard Keel, Kathryn Grayson, Red Skelton, Ann Miller, and Marge and Gower Champion), and even got an uncredited Vincente Minnelli to direct the big fashion show finale. Cummings followed this success with an adaptation of Cole Porter's integrated Broadway smash, *Kiss Me, Kate* (1953), with Keel, Grayson, and Miller as well as new upcoming dance talents Bob Fosse, Bobby Van, and Tommy Rall. *Give a Girl a Break* (1953) showcased Marge and Gower Champion, Debbie Reynolds, and Bob Fosse, and was directed by Stanley Donen. In 1954, Cummings would outshine Freed. Freed's big-budget *Brigadoon* combined the talents of Gene Kelly, Cyd Charisse, and Vincente Minnelli, with a score by Alan Jay Lerner and Frederick Loewe. While that picture did only middling business, Cummings' much smaller-budgeted musical, *Seven Brides for Seven Brothers*, with Donen directing Keel, Jane Powell, Tommy Rall, and a raft of talented dancers, became one of the biggest hits of the year, winning an Academy Award nomination for Best Picture and earning a special Oscar for choreographer Michael Kidd.

While Cummings (and Pasternak) had the same contract list as Freed to keep up with his group-oriented outlook, producers working outside of MGM increased their roster of talent in order to compete. Warner Bros. quickly worked to surround its new star Doris Day with strong supporting talent. At first, all they had on hand were Jack Carson (who specialized in hammy comedic acting) and Irish tenor Dennis Morgan (whom the studio had been trying to promote to stardom throughout much of the 1940s to little success). As the 1950s began, they were replaced in Day's pictures with a more vivacious (and younger) cadre of players, including baritone Gordon MacRae, athletic dancer Gene Nelson, and sexy Virginia Mayo (who had started as a Goldwyn Girl during World War II). The strength of the contract list grew so that Warners ventured into musicals without Day, such as *She's Working Her Way Through College* (1952) with Mayo and Nelson, and *About Face* (1953) with MacRae, Nelson, and newcomer Joel Grey as army cadets.

The most obvious shift happened in the musicals made at Paramount starring Bing Crosby. Prior to this period, it sometimes seems as if a Crosby musical entails nothing more than Bing singing three or four songs on his own. This is not necessarily true—a number of other major talents appear in Crosby films: Ethel Merman in *Anything Goes* (1936), Fred Astaire in *Holiday Inn* (1942) and *Blue Skies* (1946), and of course Bob Hope and Dorothy Lamour in the *Road* pictures. Crosby's romantic co-stars from film to film, though, were invariably unmusical: Carole Lombard, Constance Bennett, Ida Lupino. (Ingrid Bergman could also be added, although she is not technically Crosby's *romantic* co-star in *The Bells of St. Mary's* [1945].) Every once in a while, he got paired with singers like Kitty Karlisle or Mary Martin, but they were the exceptions rather than the norm. Such casting creates a lopsided atmosphere, with him crooning his emotions and the heroine merely looking on adoringly. The growing emphasis on the group began to change this dynamic in Crosby musicals by the early 1950s. Jane Wyman can musically hold her own with him in a pair of films, *Here Comes the Groom* (1951) and *Just for You* (1952). *White Christmas* (1954) puts Crosby with recording star Rosemary Clooney, as well as Danny Kaye and Vera-Ellen. This was followed up by a loose remake of *Anything Goes* (1956), where Crosby shares the screen with Mitzi Gaynor, French ballerina Jeanmaire, and Donald O'Connor.

The remake of *Anything Goes* exemplifies another strong MGM influence—the growing importance of dance in postwar screen musicals. Crosby could fake a few steps if need be, but he was first and foremost a singer, whereas all of his co-stars in this film are dancers. Over at Warners, Gene Nelson was often trotted out to give Doris Day the opportunity to show she had dance training, even though she was mostly known as a vocalist. The athletic solo dance numbers devised for Nelson, such as the "gymnastics tap" sequence in *She's Working Her Way Through College*, also seem modeled on the type of routines Gene Kelly was doing for MGM. The quotient of dance in Betty Grable's films at Fox also increased after the war. Grable was an extremely capable dancer—and early 1940s Grable films usually included at least one dance sequence to show off her famous legs. Yet, paralleling the situation for Crosby, she was rarely paired with a co-star who could dance. This situation changed when Fox partnered her with fellow hoofer Dan Dailey in a number of films. Her first with him, *Mother Wore Tights* (1947), became one of her most popular pictures ever (and manages to be both a typical Fox period backstager *and* an example of family-oriented Americana). The two would work together three more times, in *When My Baby Smiles at Me* (1948), *My Blue Heaven* (1950), and *Call Me Mister* (1951).

Across the studios, the *style* of dancing also starts to become similar to the choreography common to the Freed Unit—"integrated" dancing that reveals character emotion instead of a straightforward spectacle of technical proficiency. Just as novelty and eccentric dancing or flash acts fell out of favor in the Freed Unit, so too did they gradually disappear from musicals at other studios across the 1950s. Uniformity across dancers became more and more expected, a direct effect of the rise in importance of the choreographer. Agnes de Mille's lauded work for Rodgers and Hammerstein led to the notion of choreographers as auteurs—with everyone in the ensemble adhering to her or his vision of body movement. "Outlaw" dancers such as Astaire and Eleanor Powell were being supplanted with dancers who could take direction. The tensions caused by this shift sometimes found expression in the films themselves—Astaire and Charisse desperately trying to keep in step as smoke bombs explode around them during "the damnation sequence" in *The Band Wagon*, or Danny Kaye musically griping in *White Christmas* that "chaps who did taps aren't tapping anymore, they're doing 'choreography.'"

This move to "choreography" further enhanced the claims of artistic merit. The acclaim given to the "dream ballets" in *Oklahoma!* and *Carousel* on stage, and in *An American in Paris* on screen, resulted in a number of subsequent film musicals having extended "ballet" sequences. Unsurprisingly, MGM itself led the way. Since it was Gene Kelly's next musical after *An American in Paris*, the studio felt it incumbent to put a thirteen-minute "Broadway Ballet" into *Singin' in the Rain* (1952). Similarly, since Leslie Caron was introduced to American audiences in *An American in Paris*, her film *Lili* (1953) includes two lengthy dream dance sequences (even though the film contains only one actual song). *The Band Wagon* (1953) contains a climactic "Girl Hunt Ballet," giving Fred Astaire the opportunity to dance through a Mickey Spillane-influenced narrative.[5] Perhaps the apex of MGM's investment in long-form dance was that Arthur Freed produced *Invitation to the Dance*, a collection of three half-hour choreographed vignettes starring and directed by Kelly, which was released in 1956.[6]

Non-MGM films also began including long-form ballet. Samuel Goldwyn's musical biopic of *Hans Christian Andersen* (1952) came a year after *An American in Paris*. While the film stars Danny Kaye as Andersen singing a score written by Frank Loesser, both Kaye and Loesser are pushed to the sidelines during an extended "Little Mermaid" ballet—adapting melodies from Tchaikowsky and danced by Jeanmaire (Figure 6.2). Goldwyn's decision to do so was likely influenced not only by MGM: the enormously successful British ballet film *The Red Shoes* (1948) had been based on one of Andersen's tales. Ballet sequences at other studios, though, are obviously more beholden to *An American in Paris*. Paramount's aforementioned remake of *Anything Goes* shows Jeanmaire in a dream ballet of a Parisian in America (complete with her in a tutu dancing with sailors and hepcat teenagers in a stylized Times Square). Fox's *Daddy Long Legs* (1955) goes further, showing Leslie Caron dreaming about being a French girl dancing through Rio and Hong Kong.

The sweeping influence of the structure of integrated dance and song was immense and, in many ways, changed the average person's definition of what a musical was. These musicals proclaimed that everyone had music and rhythm in their soul, and all it took was the right combination of factors to bring it out. You did not need to be a professional performer to feel a song in your heart. Musicals now told stories about cowboys, Siamese kings, low-life New York

Figure 6.2 Danny Kaye, as the famed storyteller in *Hans Christian Andersen* (1952), prepares the audience for the type of extended ballet sequence found in a number of musicals after the success of MGM's *An American in Paris* (1951). Snapshot taken from: Hans Christian Andersen (1952).

gamblers, or British phonetics professors and Cockney flower sellers. Many musicals even suggested that the lyricism inside someone could come bubbling up without them realizing it. A repeated setup in musicals in this era has people breaking into song while trying to deny they are in love, or disavowing their feelings by discussing love in the third person. The words say "no," but the music says "yes." On Broadway, Rodgers and Hammerstein were experts at this ("People Will Say We're in Love" in *Oklahoma!*, "If I Loved You" in *Carousel*). Other examples would include "They Say It's Wonderful" in *Annie Get Your Gun*, "I'll Know" in *Guys and Dolls*, and "I'm Not at All in Love" in *The Pajama Game*.

The sense that "being a musical" meant breaking out into song or dance outside of a performance context may have liberated the characters in such integrated pieces, but it simultaneously began to limit what films were accepted as "musicals." Including integrated moments became so *de riguer* that some films without them were no longer regarded as musicals even though they contain multiple numbers performed by a star associated with the genre. Rita Hayworth's most famous solo number on film is "Put the Blame on Mame," but very few consider the movie it is in—*Gilda* (1946)—to be a musical, even though she performs this song twice and does another ("Amado Mio") as well.[7] Comedian-centered musicals had been part of Hollywood's production slate almost from the start of talking pictures—Goldwyn's films with Eddie Cantor in the early 1930s or with Danny Kaye during World War II; the Marx Brothers at Paramount and at MGM; Abbott and Costello interspersing their routines with appearances by the Andrews Sisters or other musical acts. Such a dynamic ebbed after the war. Abbott and Costello began blending comedy with horror rather than music, beginning with the huge hit *Abbott and Costello Meet Frankenstein* (1948). Bob Hope starred in a few movies that could be regarded as musicals (*Son of Paleface* [1952], *Here Come the Girls* [1953]), but by the end of this period was doing straightforward comedy. The last major examples of blending comedian-centered comedy with music were the pictures made at Paramount with the team of Dean Martin and Jerry Lewis: one brought the voice, the other brought the clowning. The break-up of their partnership in the mid-1950s in a way symbolizes the end of this type of musical entertainment on screen.

Even the backstager began adapting to expectations of integrated numbers. Backstagers did not disappear during the postwar period—but they lost their pre-eminence. To stay current, a number of backstagers began including one or two integrated numbers along with the musical performances taking place on stage. This was unsurprisingly most prevalent in MGM Freed Unit backstagers (*Royal Wedding* [1951], *Singin' in the Rain* [1952], *The Band Wagon* [1953]), but integration happened in backstagers at other studios too. Compare two Doris Day backstagers made only a few years apart: *Tea for Two* (1950) and *Lucky Me* (1954). Both have plucky and optimistic Day working with her friends to get a show produced. Yet, every number in *Tea for Two* is a potential part of the show being rehearsed, while *Lucky Me* starts off with an integrated number, introducing Day's character singing about her belief in superstitions (black cats, ladders, four-leaf clovers) as she walks to the theatre where she works.

In following trends set by Rodgers and Hammerstein and by MGM, definitions of the genre shifted in a major way. Musicals now could tell any kind of story, but they had to tell it in a specific (i.e., integrated) way—thus sacrificing certain pleasures (random anarchic comedy, specialty acts, spectacle for the sake of spectacle) in order to achieve others (expressing a character's surge of emotion through song or dance). The importance of fitting in with the group, of cohering to the overall property, overrode the value of individual expression. Ironically, then, it is possible to read *The Band Wagon* as a *mea culpa* from the Freed Unit. The plot shows the strained efforts to create a pompous self-important integrated musical, before finding happiness and success in deciding to make a light-hearted revue instead (i.e., what the original Broadway *Band Wagon* was back in the 1930s). The film ends with a reprise of the show business anthem "That's Entertainment"—but increasingly, the boundaries of what was accepted as entertainment within the musical genre were being tightened.

"And then I wrote …": Enshrining the "American Songbook"

The postwar period also saw a narrowing of what type of music was supposed to be used in a musical. Prior to this era, the songs in film musicals covered a wide range: hillbilly, jazz, opera, Latin American (and sometimes all in the same picture!). Furthermore, American popular music and musical theatre tunes were one and the same. With the rise of the integrated musical, though, audiences began to regard the songs in musicals to be their own unique category of music: the showtune. In the late 1940s, the recording industry introduced the long-playing record (running at 33 1/3 rpm), which held just about twenty minutes or so of music on each side. This was perfect for recording an entire score of a musical, and cast albums and soundtracks to musicals quickly became best sellers, furthering the regard of "showtunes" as their own category of music.[8]

At about the same time, the output of composers from the 1920s to the 1940s began being referred to as the "great American songbook." Frank Sinatra, Ella Fitzgerald, and the like began re-recording older songs, establishing a canon of standards in the process. Recognition of "the songbook" may have also begun because the figurative well was drying up. New compositions in the "songbook" style increasingly had a hard time measuring up to the old stuff. Hit pop tunes such as "How Much Is That Doggie in the Window?" or "The Music Goes Round and Round" seemed like infantile nursery rhymes in comparison to "Night and Day" or "Thou Swell." Yet, new trends in music were disquieting to many, such as the shift from big bands to more experimental jazz (or "be-bop"), although on a certain level postwar jazz helped define the great America songbook, as quartets or other small combos improvised on certain tunes. The growing popularity of rhythm-and-blues, a trend that would help foster the emergence of rock music, also worried certain sections of the country.

These shifting attitudes about music may help explain the one noticeable trend in the postwar musical that was not related to the shift towards integration: the musical biography. These films were a variation on the backstager, in that the lead character was a historical figure—although the storylines often have little to do with the actual facts of their lives. Certain examples occurred in the first decade of the film musical—most notably with MGM's *The Great Ziegfeld* (1936). During World War II, musical biographies tapped into the call for nostalgia. Warners' *Yankee Doodle Dandy* (1942) and its salute to songwriter George M. Cohan led to other biographies of composers and lyricists, such as *My Gal Sal* (1942, about Paul Dresser) and *Irish Eyes Are Smiling* (1944, about Ernest Ball). The number of biographies, though, increased *after* the war. Tributes were made to George Gershwin (*Rhapsody in Blue* [1945]), Cole Porter (*Night and Day* [1946]), Jerome Kern (*Till the Clouds Roll By* [1946]), and Richard Rodgers and Lorenz Hart (*Words and Music*

[1948]). Soon even Tin Pan Alley tunesmiths with little name recognition from the general public were getting the same treatment (*I Wonder Who's Kissing Her Now* [1947], *My Wild Irish Rose* [1947], *Oh, You Beautiful Doll* [1949], *Three Little Words* [1950], *I'll See You in My Dreams* [1951]). The pattern had become so standardized by 1950 that Warner Bros. animators could do a musical biopic parody of Bugs Bunny in *What's Up Doc?*.

Few women songwriters had managed to build notable careers in Tin Pan Alley or on Broadway, so female musical stars appeared in biographies of renowned performers. Examples during the war included Ann Sheridan as Nora Bayes in *Shine On, Harvest Moon* (1944) and Betty Hutton as Texas Guinan in *Incendiary Blonde* (1945). Men followed suit after the war, particularly when *The Jolson Story* (1946) (with Larry Parks lip-syncing to new recordings by Al Jolson himself) became Columbia's biggest box-office success to that point in its history. (The film did so well that it became one of the rare times that a musical spawned a sequel: *Jolson Sings Again* [1949].) Other musical performer biographies included those of opera legend Enrico Caruso (*The Great Caruso* [1951]), Civil War songstress Lotte Crabtree (*Golden Girl* [1951]), radio favorite Jane Froman (*With a Song in My Heart* [1952]), and torch singers Ruth Etting (*Love Me or Leave Me* [1955]) and Helen Morgan (*The Helen Morgan Story* [1957]). In the mid-1950s, musical biopics began focusing on popular band leaders. Although the Dorsey brothers had played themselves in an early entry, *The Fabulous Dorseys* (1947), it was Universal's success with *The Glenn Miller Story* (1954) that led to such imaginatively named productions as *The Benny Goodman Story* (1955), *The Eddy Duchin Story* (1957), *The Gene Krupa Story* (1957), and *The Five Pennies* (1959, about Red Nichols and his band).

Musical biographies further helped establish a catalog of standards, showing that these songs could still be relevant for a new age by offering new orchestrations. With *The Jolson Story* providing contemporary arrangements, for example, Al Jolson experienced a renewed fandom. Young audiences rediscovered Jolson largely because he offered a vibrance and emotion often not found with postwar "hit parade" singers where the emphasis was on being smooth—and being dreamy began to slip into being comatose. Singers such as Perry Como or Mel Torme were often parodied for being almost too relaxed in their crooning style, for example.

Musical biographies often try to negate any sense of blandness and being out of date by portraying their protagonists as energetic with new ideas. Following the typical narrative pattern of the backstager, the main characters are nobodies struggling to make it in showbiz, and facing resistance when they try to do something different. It is usually precisely that uniqueness (Jolson's belting style, Cole Porter's smart lyrics, Glenn Miller's deft orchestrations) that eventually lead them to fame and fortune. Yet, by being set in the past, what is new and vaguely threatening to other characters in the film is already well known and comfortable to the movie-going audience—as are the well-trod clichés of the backstager plotline. Often the lives of various figures are deeply contorted or wholly fictionalized in order to get them to fit the iron-clad structure of the backstager, perhaps the most extreme being transforming upper-class gay Cole Porter into a struggling song plugger in a conventional heterosexual romance.[9]

While working to market old tunes to new audiences, musical biographies nonetheless vaguely indicate that the best times are behind, and even many non-biographical musicals began relying heavily on the already-written rather than creating new scores. The lauded Freed Unit created a string of films that emphasized songwriters' catalogs rather than new tunes—*Easter Parade* (1948) with a number of classic Irving Berlin songs; *An American in Paris* employing the work of the Gershwin brothers; *Singin' in the Rain* using mainly songs written by Arthur Freed himself with Nacio Herb Brown; and *The Band Wagon* recycling the compositions of Howard Dietz and Arthur Schwartz. Other films at MGM or elsewhere interpolate one or two older melodies into otherwise new scores—but it is the chestnut that stands out: "They Can't Take That Away from Me" in *The Barkleys of Broadway* (1949), the title song in *April in Paris* (1952), "I've Got a Crush on You" in *Three for the Show* (1955), "My Funny Valentine" in *Gentlemen Marry Brunettes* (1955).

Warners' *Young at Heart* (1955) unintentionally exposes the growing problem. Doris Day's character embodies life and optimism, and she tries to rescue Frank Sinatra's character from his gloomy (and eventually suicidal) tendencies. The musical program accentuates this dichotomy by having Day sing nothing but newly composed upbeat songs, while giving Sinatra melancholy older tunes—until the end when Sinatra indicates his new outlook by singing a new melody with Day. The problem is that none of Day's new ditties can compare with Sinatra's gorgeous renditions of "Just One of Those Things" or "One for My Baby." (Oddly, the one stand-out new composition—the title song—is sung by Sinatra over the credits but not in the film itself.) Thus, the music accidentally works opposite of intention: the audience wants to wallow in the past with Sinatra rather than look to the future with Day.[10]

Such reactionary tendencies may also explain the revival of the classical music musical—including a number of musical biopics. Along with *The Great Caruso* are films about Grace Moore (*So This Is Love* [1953]), opera impresario Sol Hurok (*Tonight We Sing* [1953]), and diva Marjorie Lawrence (*Interrupted Melody* [1955]). As mentioned in Chapter 5, MGM's Pasternak Unit focused on trained voices such as Kathryn Grayson and Jane Powell, so it is perhaps not surprising that Pasternak groomed the most prominent classical-oriented star of the postwar period: Mario Lanza. Lanza's booming delivery and wide vocal register were displayed in a series of films at MGM, debuting in *That Midnight Kiss* (1949) and finishing with (ironically) *For the First Time* (1959). His popularity grew so large that MGM's most successful musical of 1951 was not any of the films produced by Arthur Freed (*Royal Wedding, Show Boat*, or the

Figure 6.3 Mario Lanza performs "Vesti la Giubba" from *Pagliacci* in *The Great Caruso* (1951), one of the most successful of the musical biopics that proliferated after World War II. Snapshot taken from: The Great Caruso (1951).

Oscar-winning *An American in Paris*) but Lanza's portrayal of *The Great Caruso* (which also resulted in a hit song, "The Loveliest Night of the Year") (Figure 6.3).[11]

Operetta also surged back into prominence in the 1950s, offering film versions of a number of classics from the 1920s: *The Desert Song* (1953), *The Student Prince* (1954), *Rose Marie* (1954), *The Vagabond King* (1956). Operetta composer extraordinaire Sigmund Romberg got his own all-star musical biopic, *Deep in Your Heart* (1954), with Roger Edens producing for the first time after years as Freed's assistant. The resurgence of filmed operetta was likely tied to the growing interest in integration, since operettas had characters singing as part of conversation rather than on stage. (Furthermore, Oscar Hammerstein had been the lyricist for many of these 1920s operettas.) Yet, the ultimately short-lived revival of cinematic operetta, along with the number of musical biographies and the growing reliance on recycled song catalogs, seems to indicate a strong desire to hold onto the past, and a vague concern about an uncontrollable future.

It's Always Fair Weather? Postwar Anxieties

The manner in which integration simultaneously opened up and closed down options for the musical genre mirrored in certain ways what was happening within American culture as a whole after World War II: celebrating a land of freedom, opportunity and success—but also pressuring its citizens to conform to certain behaviors and attitudes. Perhaps unsurprisingly, postwar musicals reflect this zeitgeist. The rules of integrated musicals often attempted to limit the range of how race, gender, and sexuality could be represented within the genre. Yet, such efforts arguably only highlighted and exacerbated tensions over such issues. Yet, as Susan Smith has written, "while the musical's utopian vision has often been expressed in ways that seem designed to serve the dominant needs of white patriarchal society, there are areas of the Hollywood musical that demonstrate a much more progressive attitude towards race and gender."[12]

At the time, many considered the victories of World War II to herald a new "American century," and the nation's economy soared as it helped rebuild Europe, Japan, and other areas around the globe. After the hardships of the Depression and the war, many citizens were now flush with cash, and the market was bursting with new materials to purchase— new suburban homes, new cars, new push-button appliances (including televisions, which will be discussed in Chapter 7). It seemed that democracy and American "can-do" energy and optimism had resulted in just the sort of communal utopian abundance promised in musicals. Alongside such elation, though, lurked fears and anxieties. American superiority was due in part to the development of atomic weaponry. That humanity now had such destructive capabilities worried many; when the Communist-controlled Soviet Union announced that it, too, had successfully acquired such technology, the United States was thrown into an even greater panic.

A common reaction was that someone within the US must be secretly working for the USSR, and paranoia about "internal subversion" became rampant. Such a climate of suspicion touched Hollywood directly when Congress decided to investigate allegations of Communist propaganda being placed secretly into motion pictures. Larry Parks, after rising to stardom in *The Jolson Story*, had his career crushed by allegations of Communist sympathy. Those who tried to defend accused artists by joining the Committee for the First Amendment, such as Gene Kelly, Lena Horne, and Danny Kaye, soon discovered the dangers of doing so, having to quickly do damage control or find their own careers imperiled.[13]

Across the United States, anyone who seemed to deviate from the accepted social norm was deemed suspicious. One odd comment or offbeat attitude, particularly if it somehow suggested that America was not perfect, could make someone a possible Communist sympathizer. Ironically, then, while criticizing Communist societies as dogmatic and oppressive to the individual, America in the 1950s strongly pressured people to follow a carefully monitored existence. Everyone was supposed to be happily wallowing in all of their new homes and gadgets, but for many the flashy cars and fancy wardrobes were small recompense for how constricted they felt.

Musicals had worked effectively as propaganda during World War II, championing America as a utopia, so it stood to reason that they could do the same in the face of this new Cold War between the United States and its Communist rivals. If anything, the rise of integrated musicals could increase audience delight in presenting America as a place so glorious that song and dance erupted unrehearsed and unfettered among its citizens. Certainly, many film musicals glorified the benefits of capitalist materialism—parading gaudy colorful settings and costumes for the delight of the viewer. If anything, musicals became gaudier after the war—with more spangles, more color, larger sets, larger groups of dancers. Such use of American musicals as Cold War fodder became explicit when Soviet Premier Nikita Khrushchev was invited to visit the set of *Can-Can* (1960). To the undoubted glee of many, he was scandalized and incensed by the excess and explicitness of the can-can sequence being filmed.[14]

Certain films were more overt in their linking of money and consumerism to utopia. *The Pajama Game* is centrally about labor problems at a factory, with the main couple (Doris Day and John Raitt) at odds because he is management and she is organized labor. Yet, instead of becoming a paean to the proletariat, the union members plainly desire a life of material ease, as they sing about all the gadgets they will be able to buy with their "7½ Cents" raise—and the tension is resolved when management discovers on its own the one bad apple that is holding up the raise. A number of postwar musicals emphasize Americans bringing their energy and money to Europe, such as *Lovely to Look At* (1952), *April in Paris* (1952), *Call Me Madame* (1953), and *The Seven Hills of Rome* (1957). Such plots mimic the American government's Marshall Plan, which gave massive loans to help Europe rebuild after the war (and also to keep them from shifting towards socialism). *Daddy Long Legs* follows a similar pattern, as millionaire Astaire adopts a French gamin (Leslie Caron), finances her enrollment at an American college, and takes her on a whirlwind trip across Manhattan.

During this period, Fred Astaire regularly played the carefree American inviting his potential paramour to partake of the advantages of capitalism, with music and excessive cinematic stylization demonstrating the lure of materialist pleasure. In *Funny Face* (1957), fashion photographer Astaire introduces bohemian intellectual Audrey Hepburn to the sublime beauty of designer gowns and high living. An extended sequence has Astaire's character taking Hepburn's on a photo shoot around Paris, as she increasingly gives herself over to the extravagance of the clothes and settings. Even more overtly, in *Silk Stockings* (1957), movie producer Astaire seduces Soviet official Cyd Charisse (as well as a number of others in her cohort) away from Communism and into capitalist luxury. A dance to the title song of *Silk Stockings* shows Charisse's cold distant comrade shedding her dowdy garments in order to revel in earrings, petticoats, and the titular stockings, which she has hidden around her hotel room.[15]

As these two films and *The Pajama Game* demonstrate, the common device of having each partner in a romance represent an opposing side of a larger issue was employed to discuss capitalism and its potential detractors. Usually, musicals showed both sides learning from the other. *Funny Face* and *Silk Stockings* make some attempt to show Astaire's character bending—but, in general, capitalism is strongly upheld and his partner relents more than he does.

By and large, Hollywood musicals kept such discussion of capitalism light, frothy, and humorous. Sometimes, though, the pressure of keeping everyone happy and together is acknowledged, exposing the effort needed to keep the figurative lid on a pot of simmering dissatisfaction. *Daddy Long Legs*, while attempting to remain sweet and airy, carries a tinge of melancholy that is hard to dispel. Giving Caron's orphan an anonymous economic boost does not solve her loneliness—rather it exacerbates her isolation. *It's Always Fair Weather* (1955) similarly threatens to expose that many Americans were living lives of quiet desperation. Obviously invoking the trio of sailors from *On the Town* (1949), the film shows three Army buddies reuniting ten years after the war, but realizing how disappointed they are with themselves at what they have become. A key motif of the film is a dollar bill torn into three pieces—indicating the centrality of money, but also the alienation of the old pals. Crucial to this discussion, Dan Dailey's character has devolved from a painter to an advertising executive in an unhappy marriage. His solo number, "Situation-Wise," happens not when he has become overcome with joy or love, but when he becomes fall-down drunk, and suggests that he is on the verge of a nervous breakdown. Typical of a film (co-)directed by Stanley Donen, the musical climaxes in a brawl that brings the threesome back together—but the film actually ends on an elegiac note, with the sense that the buddies most likely will never see each other again.

In their bid for greater artistic reputation, integrated musicals not only added "ballet" sequences: they also became increasingly dramatic instead of comedic. Many musical biographies and backstagers began to emphasize intense suffering, in a return to the melodramatic plot points of many early talkies. Topics like alcoholism, polio, spousal abuse, and suicide become featured in many musicals of the period.[16] A number of musicals after the war show a tinge of the stylistics associated with film *noir*, including *noir*'s typical exposure of the underside of the American Dream.[17] Thus, while musicals still proclaimed that it was possible to enjoy individual freedom and be part of a community, they increasingly indicated how hard it was to do so. Singing and dancing became less about actual happiness and fulfillment and more about trying to convince one's self (and others) that you *were* happy and fulfilled—and perhaps getting a bit neurotic about it in the process.

Worries about the slightest bit of subversive behavior resulted in increased pressures placed on women and various minority groups after World War II, and efforts were made to roll back opportunities that had been advanced during the war. Postwar musicals initially seem to endorse this conservative turn—returning to the old ways, whether it be tried-and-true tunes or traditional social attitudes. At the same time, though, the genre continued to rely heavily on the talents of women, people of color, and gay men. Thus, postwar musicals often seem unable to submerge growing tensions occurring among various communities—and subtly suggesting that perhaps these groups are not capable of (and not even interested in) uniting into one utopian harmony.

In its own manner, the term "integration" became as important after World War II for Americans of color as it was for the musical genre. Racial integration became a key goal for many in the late 1940s and 1950s. Various industries became racially mixed (including professional baseball when the Brooklyn Dodgers hired Jackie Robinson), and President Truman integrated the armed forces in 1947. The Supreme Court's 1954 decision in *Brown v. Board of Education* decreed the integration of public schools. During the war, American culture tried to distance itself from the overt racism of Nazi Germany by celebrating the diversity of the country's population. Overcoming (or denying) racial prejudice was regarded as important during the Cold War too: how could the United States claim social superiority if such racial oppression was clearly occurring? Yet, friction over such efforts to end unequal treatment grew across the period. Many African Americans (and other racial/ethnic minorities) began demanding their civil rights rather than meekly accepting what few crumbs might be given to them. By the late 1950s, an energized movement was in place, organizing boycotts and marches. On the opposite side, many white citizens (including politicians and police) actively resisted such advances, including barring the doors of schools and keeping minority families from moving into certain neighborhoods.

Musical integration posed problems for performers of color as well. Where could one logically fit in a black specialty act in *Hans Christian Andersen* or *The Student Prince*? Consequently, moments when people of color appear are often quick and in the margins. Fred Astaire dances with an uncredited shoe shiner in "Shine on My Shoes" in *The Band Wagon*.[18] Judy Garland does the same with two (also uncredited) African American kids in "Lose That Long Face" in *A Star Is Born* (1954). If one looks carefully, two Algerian boys join the crowd watching Marilyn Monroe and Jane Russell perform "When Love Goes Wrong" in *Gentlemen Prefer Blondes* (1953). Their presence was literally to provide some color for the musical numbers, but not be part of the storyline. As Louis Armstrong succinctly puts it after he performs the somewhat extraneous opening song of *High Society* (1956): "End of number, beginning of story!" The postwar period *did* see the end of straightforward blackface in musical films (other than for strictly historical reference—such as Larry Parks as Al Jolson). Intriguingly, images of Native Americans in musicals rose slightly during this era, including *Annie Get Your Gun* and the remake of *Rose Marie*, and there was much more likelihood to use broad caricatures—as in the

"Big Chief Hole-in-the-Ground" number in *Two Tickets to Broadway* or "What Makes the Red Man Red?" in Disney's version of *Peter Pan* (1953). On the other hand, the vogue for Latin American culture abated after the war, so "south-of-the-border" musicals (and the Latin Americans that performed in them) largely disappeared during the 1950s.[19]

Richard Dyer has argued that "bursting from the confines of life by singing your heart out and dancing when you feel like it—this is the joy of the musical. Where the musical most disturbingly constructs a vision of race is in the fact that it is whites' privilege to do this."[20] As the above examples indicate, such a dynamic certainly seemed to apply to postwar integrated musicals. When racial or ethnic minorities *did* begin to find a way to gain more attention in postwar musicals, it was to reflect precisely the difficulties of racial integration. Rather than non-integrated carnivalesque celebrations of racial inclusion that were typical in previous eras, the genre's use of integration to expand beyond comedy and into drama resulted in the advent of "social problem" musicals dealing with racial prejudice. *Show Boat* laid down this pattern back on Broadway in 1927. Julie, the mixed-race chanteuse who tries to pass as white, is left broken and discarded by the end. The MGM film version in 1951 brings her back for the finale, but she stands on the dock while the showboat sails away, taking its white leads off to a happy future that she will not enjoy. And, as if to accentuate this separation, MGM employed two white performers to create the part rather than Lena Horne, who was still under contract at the studio: Ava Gardner in dusky makeup, with her singing voice dubbed by Annette Warren.[21] (Lena Horne left the studio while this remake was in production to focus on her career on records and in nightclubs.) Dramatizations of racial disharmony would continue in musicals from the mid-1950s onward—but almost exclusively told from a white perspective (more on this in Chapter 7).

Opportunities for women (whether white or of color) diminished after the war within the musical and across the country in general. In order to find positions for returning soldiers, female workers were summarily let go from jobs and strongly encouraged to return to hearth and home. Postwar culture stressed that a woman could not find any greater happiness than as a wife and mother (especially in her new suburban palace). At the same time, the ascendancy of the integrated musical led to a wealth of folksy Americana, and the roles for women in such tales were usually limited to mothers or sweet young things longing for romance. With integration picturing such environments as utopian, the postwar musical regularly became yet another instrument to drum into the minds of women notions of dependency on men and of contentment via domesticity.

Female waifs become a recurrent motif in postwar musicals, including performers such as June Haver, Debbie Reynolds, Leslie Caron, and Audrey Hepburn. Films consistently emphasize their immaturity and their tiny physical stature to argue that they need the protection and care of an older and wiser male.

Their youthfulness was also emphasized by often pairing them romantically with much older men—particularly Fred Astaire, who had thirty years on these co-stars. Often the characters these young female stars played would be a bit feisty, but eventually learning the bliss of letting a man (or, at least, the *right* man) take charge. On the other hand, there is a sense that the male lead characters are turning toward such young things because they feel intimidated by women their own age. (It was not uncommon for the man in these musicals to forsake an older, more sophisticated female for the waif.) And if audiences did not get the message in other films, Maurice Chevalier would baldly state it in the opening number to *Gigi*: "Thank Heaven for Little Girls."

Arguably the biggest new female star of the postwar musical was Doris Day. While Day did play ingénue roles, being just slightly older than Reynolds and the other waifs made audiences accept her playing a wife or mother too. Her image of an ever-optimistic girl-next-door (which complimented the bright, clear tone of her singing voice) seemed perfectly suited for idealizing suburban domestic femininity. Repeatedly in her musicals, her characters come to realize the rewards of being a sweet, pretty bride or housewife. *I'll See You in My Dreams* is a musical biography of lyricist Gus Kahn, played by Danny Thomas, with Day as the "woman behind the man," subsuming her own talents in order to support and bolster *his* career.[22] Day also regularly played tomboys who discover the bliss of womanhood—such as the baseball-playing, car-repair whiz in *On Moonlight Bay* and *By the Light of the Silvery Moon*, or the buckskin-wearing, pistol-toting title character in *Calamity Jane*. Love with the right man awakens femininity, and by the end of the films she is in makeup and a beautiful frock, arm in arm with her fella.

Older female musical stars posed a greater problem, particularly since many of them had risen to fame playing talented, driven, and energetic women. World War II had championed strong, assertive personalities in women, but such traits were problematic to the postwar mindset—and many major talents retired from the big screen by the end of the 1940s: Alice Faye, Deanna Durbin, Sonja Henie, Jeanette MacDonald. Fox tried repositioning Betty Grable as wife and mother, showing her characters trying to balance being a homemaker and being a performer in films such as *Mother Wore Tights* (1947) and *My Blue Heaven* (1950). Betty Hutton would star in the film version of *Annie Get Your Gun*, in which Annie Oakley realizes she needs to subsume her sharpshooting expertise in order to find happiness with a man. (Warner Bros. would rework this lesson for Doris Day in *Calamity Jane*.) Judy Garland's Hollywood star Vicki Lester must suffer endlessly in Warners' *A Star Is Born* because her career skyrockets just as her husband's falls apart.

At times, the felt need to put strong female performers back in their place led to actual physical incapacitation. As one of *The Dolly Sisters* (1946), Betty Grable wallows in drink after choosing her career over her beau—and drives her car off a cliff in Monte Carlo. Playing swimming pioneer Annette Kellerman, dynamo Esther Williams is also horribly injured chasing career instead of romance in *Million Dollar Mermaid* (1952), allowing Victor Mature to return and coach her back to health. In much the same manner, manic Betty Hutton's fictional version of Pearl White in *The Perils of Pauline* (1947) has to be crippled by a daring stunt in order to make her viable for her male suitor at the end of the film. (By the mid-1950s, all three of these women would also stop making films.) Perhaps the high (or low) point of such physical assault occurs in *Seven Brides for Seven Brothers*, which metaphorically endorses rape by showing that the brides ultimately like that the brothers kidnapped them in order to force them into marriage.

The overarching lesson is that women need to know their place—and that happiness and fulfillment come through following and supporting your husband. While Grace Kelly was not a musical performer, the two musicals she made in the 1950s reiterate this lesson. In *The Country Girl* (1954), Kelly is married to alcoholic singer Bing Crosby, forcing her to be the strong half of the marriage, and this "unnatural" dynamic turns her from her typical glossy chic persona into a pinched frumpy hausfrau (the performance won Kelly an Oscar). Two years later, the two would co-star again in *High Society* (1956), where he and others lecture her about being too superior to the men in her life (and they eventually manage to pull her down from her pedestal). As overt as Chevalier's paean to little girls is, the song "Without Love" in *Silk Stockings* has the converted female Soviet official croon that "a woman to a man is just a woman, but a man to a woman is her life." Yet, possibly the ultimate example is the final line of *A Star Is Born*. Judy Garland's character introduces herself to the world not as movie star Vicki Lester—nor even as Esther Blodgett, her birth name: she is "Mrs. Norman Maine."

The mammoth stardom of Marilyn Monroe might seem initially to stand in opposition to this argument. Her breakout film, *Gentlemen Prefer Blondes*, surrounds her with weak males, such as geriatric Charles Coburn, eight-year-old George Winslow, and wimpy Tommy Noonan. The following year, she largely overwhelms Donald O'Connor in *There's No Business Like Show Business* (1954). While her star image is not reconcilable with the typical postwar housewife, her breathless baby doll voice, wide-eyed looks, and often naive behavior do manage to tap into the predilection for little girls. Her last full-out musical, *Let's Make Love* (1960), includes her singing Cole Porter's "My Heart Belongs to Daddy." Thus, her sexual allure is made less threatening by her childishness, emphasized by the fact that schlubs like Tommy Noonan or Donald O'Connor are able to win her.[23]

Nonetheless, Monroe's musical performances certainly expressed more overt sexual energy than had been seen in Hollywood to that time. The opening number *Gentlemen Prefer Blondes*, "Two Little Girls from Little Rock" (note the "little girls"), showcases Monroe and co-star Jane Russell in costumes that emphasized their breasts, with choreography that consists mainly of shimmies, hunched over shoulders, and slightly toned-down bumps and grinds. In *There's No Business Like Show Business*, her outfit for "After You Get What You Want, You Don't Want It" is flesh toned with white beading that creates starbursts at her nipples, and her ensemble and dance moves for "Heat Wave" daringly draw attention to her crotch. Musicals had always paraded girls in various stages of undress for the pleasure of the straight male viewer, but the postwar period saw an increased explicitness. Part of the appeal of Cyd Charisse's dances, for example, is their eroticism—whether the seduction of Gene Kelly in the "Broadway Ballet" in *Singin' in the Rain*, the slinking around Fred Astaire in the "Girl Hunt" ballet in *The Band Wagon*, or the highly charged Arabian fantasy with James Mitchell to "One Alone" in *Deep in My Heart*. Even Doris Day walks on wearing nothing but John Raitt's pajama top at the conclusion of *The Pajama Game*.

For even as the postwar period worked to push back most of what had been unleashed during World War II, such freedoms were not easily erased, and greater discussion of sex and sexuality continued—even if it was simply to condemn it. While celebrating the woman as homemaker, American culture also saw the premiere issue of *Playboy* magazine (with Monroe on the cover). Challenges to the Production Code began to pile up during the 1950s, leading to a revision of the Code in 1955 and another in 1961 in order to allow latitude in discussing previously taboo topics (under the admonition that it be done with "taste and restraint"). *Seven Brides for Seven Brothers* ends with all seven maidens declaring that they have had a child out of wedlock. *Gigi* is pretty baldly about training a girl to be a kept woman.

Those last two examples display once again the dominance of integration—sexual titillation folded into the plot rather than the random trotting out of showgirls common to musicals prior to this period. Women were still on display, but such objectification had to be narratively motivated—watching the Soviet official succumb to the pleasure of wearing lingerie and silk stockings; watching Doris Day move from tomboy to debutante; watching beatnik ugly duckling Audrey Hepburn blossom into a *haute mode* swan. Such motivation, though, encourages the viewer to identify with the female in question—something one never did with a Busby Berkeley chorine or a Goldwyn Girl. In lecturing women to forsake careers and independence, these postwar musicals also often dramatize the pain and heartache caused by social pressure to adopt the frilly dependent feminine role. For example, Doris Day's character in *I'll See You in My Dreams* has obviously more drive and intelligence than her songwriter husband, but is castigated by him for "interfering" when she tries to help push his career along, including at one point receiving a smack across the face from him.[24] In a number of Day's other films, she (and potentially the female viewer) is convinced to leave her tomboy ways behind, but scenes are included that show her characters, alone and quiet, crying in bitter frustration because of the calumny heaped on her (Figure 6.4). Thus, unwittingly, the viewer can

Figure 6.4 Tomboy Doris Day on the verge of tears as the title character in *Calamity Jane* (1953), demonstrating the pain caused by the pressures to conform to postwar gender expectations. Snapshot taken from: Calamity Jane (1953).

feel that an injustice is being done to her and to many other female characters. Prior to this period, musicals had often been referred to as "the businessman's delight" because of the expected uncomplicated spectacle of female pulchritude. With the move to integration, though, straight men seemed to grow less attached to the genre.

Integration affected images of men as well. When backstagers dominated the genre, male stars who sang and danced often presented their talents as a form of sexual prowess. Bing Crosby crooned and the ladies swooned; Fred Astaire danced and Ginger Rogers succumbed. Male characters in integrated musicals, though, were supposedly singing and/or dancing without realizing it. Thus, the music was not a performance but an open display of their emotions—a behavior not typically associated with masculinity. Perhaps in response to this dilemma, men in postwar musicals (and the stars that played them) seem at pains to stress their masculinity. In contrast to Astaire's tuxedo-clad grace, Gene Kelly's characters were "regular Joes" and his dancing emphasized its athleticism.[25] (Even Astaire gets gruff as a Spillane-like detective in the big "Girl Hunt" number in *The Band Wagon*.)

Another strong example would be the renovation of Frank Sinatra's star persona in the 1950s—from spindly and naive to worn-down and cynical. The Sinatra of *Anchors Aweigh* (1945) and *On the Town* (1949) is too shy to talk to girls; the Sinatra of *Meet Danny Wilson* (1952) and *Young at Heart* is too world-weary to care about broads. Rita Hayworth would have been "too much woman" for wartime Sinatra to handle, but he effectively romances her in

Figure 6.5 Frank Sinatra demonstrates his disdain while singing "The Lady Is a Tramp" at a seated Rita Hayworth in *Pal Joey* (1957). Snapshot taken from: Pal Joey (1957).

1957's *Pal Joey* by singing "The Lady Is a Tramp" not to her so much as *at* her (Figure 6.5). This film adaptation of the 1940 Broadway musical epitomizes much of the gender politics going on in *postwar* musicals. Rita Hayworth, in her last musical film, insisted that she get top billing over Sinatra. She plays the older, wiser, richer woman attracted to Sinatra's charming cad, and the two spar over who has the upper hand in the relationship. In the end, he walks off into the sunset with the innocent, younger chorus girl played by Kim Novak (a divergence from the stage play, which ends with him alone).

While such "tough guy" behavior was definitely a way to assert authority over women, another possible reason also exists for such accentuated posturing. If breaking out into song or dance to express emotion potentially feminizes male performers, then it could also create an aura of homosexuality. Postwar America was in many ways extremely oppressive to homosexuals. They were given dishonorable discharges from the military, hounded by police, regarded as pederasts, institutionalized as mentally ill, and considered susceptible to Communist influence. Just as women were pressured to leave the workforce, lesbians and gay men were strong-armed into the closet. Homosexuals were no longer seen as silly; now they were scary. Yet, ironically, the outspoken condemnations meant that homosexuality was increasingly being discussed, making more and more people aware that such individuals existed.

Men running around in drag, a common occurrence in World War II musicals, rarely happens in musicals after the war—as if such actions were no longer regarded as humorous.[26] What postwar musicals did have, though, were quite a number of chorus boys, perhaps even more than chorus *girls*. Male dancers usually appear in support of a female performer—but the fellows do not often seem to be expressing sexual interest in the woman they surround. Rather, they seem to adore her panache and sense of style—or, if anything, they vaguely seem to be more interested in each other than her! Examples include (but are not limited to) "Get Happy" in *Summer Stock* (1950), "A Lady Loves" in *I Love Melvin* (1952), "Love, You Didn't Do Right by Me" in *White Christmas*, and "Thanks a Lot, But No Thanks" in *It's Always Fair Weather*. The classic example of this trend is "Ain't There Anyone Here for Love?" from *Gentlemen Prefer Blondes*, in which busty Jane Russell tries in vain to get the attention of a troupe of male Olympic athletes who are more focused on their own bodies than hers.

Male backup singers and dancers had been used in many earlier musicals, but "Ain't There Anyone Here for Love?" exemplifies a new trend: using bodybuilders in numbers. Musclemen on display in their own version of tableaux appear in a number of postwar musicals, including *Meet Me After the Show* (1951), *Athena* (1954), *Jupiter's Darling* (1955), and *Li'l Abner* (1959). The display of male bodybuilders in musicals had obvious appeal to gay men. The interaction between chorus boys and their female divas had a high camp quotient as well: a denial of love in the lyrics, a tendency in the choreography to have the chorus boys extend their derrieres, and certain lines that could easily be read as "gay code," such as "I've got a guy who's Marlon Brando and Clifton Webb combined!" in "Thanks a Lot, But No Thanks."[27] Furthermore, many gay men adored various postwar female musical stars, identifying with the sense of oppression such women were receiving for their uniqueness and talent.

There were moments for lesbians to decode as well, such as Lauren Bacall excitedly asking a young woman to return after the rest of the party has left in *Young Man with a Horn* (1950), or Doris Day and Allyn McLerie extolling the expertise of "A Woman's Touch" while moving in together in *Calamity Jane*. *Calamity Jane*'s Oscar-winning ballad, "Secret Love," was a mainstay in jukeboxes at lesbian and gay bars for many years.[28] Russell and Monroe also seem much more attached to each other than to either of the men they end up marrying at the end of *Gentlemen Prefer Blondes*.[29]

While multiple types of customers enjoyed musicals during the war years, a number of population segments began to show signs of disinterest after the war. For example, growing awareness of the concept of camp beyond gay subculture, and the increased use of the term "musical" to infer that someone was gay, led more and more straight men to dissociate from the genre. Efforts in musicals to present a cohesive group were starting to look exactly like "efforts." Pictures such as *Young Man with a Horn*, *A Star Is Born*, and *It's Always Fair Weather* were getting increasingly neurotic. The dominance of integration was turning the structure of musicals into an immovable object, and the pressure cooker of growing social discontent was becoming an unstoppable force. As Fred Astaire sings in *Daddy Long Legs*, "Something's gotta give."

Notes

1 The first was the political satire *Of Thee I Sing* in 1931, with a book by George S. Kaufman and Morrie Ryskind and a score by George and Ira Gershwin.

2 While all emerging in the wake of *Oklahoma!*, some of these productions were so successful in their own right that a chain effect sometimes resulted. *Annie Get Your Gun*'s focus on a famous female sharpshooter would find echoes in *Calamity Jane*, for example. *Seven Brides for Seven Brothers* was a Western reworking of a tale of the Roman Empire, "The Rape of the Sabine Women"— which was followed by *They Learned About Women*, which situated the Greek play *Lysistrata* in the American West.

3 Darryl F. Zanuck himself asserted that "*State Fair* is the most popular musical we have had in years and the business nationwide is just sensational." Story Conference Notes on Temporary Script for *Carnival in Costa Rica* from September 27, 1945 (October 1, 1945), quoted in *Memo from Darryl F. Zanuck: The Golden Years at Twentieth Century-Fox*, ed. Rudy Behlmer (New York: Grove Press, 1993), 92. Aubrey Solomon, *Twentieth Century-Fox: A Corporate and Financial History* (Lanham: Scarecrow Press, 2002), provides the following statistics: *State Fair*, cost: $2,075,000 (242), domestic rentals: $4,000,000 (221); *Centennial Summer*, cost: $2,275,000 (243), domestic rentals: $3,000,000 (221).

4 Aubrey Solomon, *Twentieth Century-Fox: A Corporate and Financial History* (Lanham: Scarecrow Press, 2002), provides the following statistics: *Three Little Girls in Blue*, cost: $2,335,000 (243), domestic rentals: $3,000,000 (221); *The Shocking Miss Pilgrim*: cost: $2,595,000 (243), domestic rentals: $2,250,000 (222)—thus, losing money, the first film starring Grable to do so.

5 Astaire had almost played the lead on Broadway for *On Your Toes*, which climaxed with Richard Rodgers' tone poem "Slaughter on 10th Avenue," choreographed by George Balanchine. He eventually opted out—and it seems that Rodgers never forgave him. Note that in all of Astaire's long career, Rodgers *never* worked with him. See Richard Rodgers, *Musical Stages: An Autobiography* (New York: Random House, 1975), 170–171.

6 The film was actually shot in 1952, but Freed and the studio recognized the difficulty in trying to market this film to a general audience, so kept it on the shelf for over three years. See Hugh Fordin, *The World of Entertainment! Hollywood's Greatest Musicals* (New York: Frederick Ungar, 1975), 371–396, for an overview of the history of this troubled production.

7 *Gilda* is more commonly regarded as a classic *noir* thriller. *Noir*, though, commonly engages in musical performance, with shady dames singing torch songs in smoky nightclubs acting as a recurrent motif from film to film. A classic example of genre amorphousness would be *Christmas Holiday* (1944), with Deanna Durbin and Gene Kelly, which certainly sounds like it should be a

musical, but is generally regarded as a *noir* thriller (largely because Kelly plays a sociopath with mother issues, and thus doesn't dance). As will be discussed later in this chapter, the association of musicals with darker moods was another postwar development.

8 For more on the evolution of the recorded music industry after World War II, and its effect on music styles including the rise of the "showtune," see Tim J. Anderson, *Making Easy Listening: Material Culture and Postwar American Recording* (Minneapolis: University of Minnesota Press, 2006).

9 Richard Barrios, *Screened Out: Playing Gay in Hollywood from Edison to Stonewall* (New York: Routledge, 2003), 176–177, recounts the effort taken to wedge Porter's life into a conventional musical biopic narrative. The contortions for *Night and Day* are acknowledged in the later attempt to do a musical biopic of Porter, *De-Lovely* (2004), with Kevin Kline as Porter despairing after watching the film (not that *De-Lovely* is without its own problems). As indicated, Porter was not alone. Lorenz Hart's homosexuality was also incapable of being mentioned (due to the Code) in *Words and Music*.

10 The second section of Ian Garwood, "The Pop Song in Film," *Close-Up* 1 (London: Wallflower Press, 2006), 107–133, does an insightful comparative analysis of *Young at Heart* and *Pal Joey*.

11 At a cost of $2,724,000, *An American in Paris* grossed in excess of $8,005,000 (Fordin, 328, 331); *Show Boat* cost $2,295,000 and grossed over $8,650,000 (Fordin, 344); the relatively modest *Royal Wedding* cost $1,591,000 and grossed about $3,925,000 (Fordin, 303); at $1,853,000, *The Great Caruso* cost just slightly more than *Royal Wedding*, but grossed $9,269,000 (*The Eddie Mannix Ledger*, Margaret Herrick Library, Academy of Motion Picture Arts and Sciences).

12 Susan Smith, *The Musical: Race, Gender and Performance* (London: Wallflower Press, 2005), 117.

13 Peter Wollen, *Singin' in the Rain* (London: BFI Classics, 1992), 44–52, discusses Gene Kelly's involvement in the Committee for the First Amendment, and its impact on his career.

14 See Peter Carlson, "Nikita Khrushchev Goes to Hollywood," *Smithsonian* (July 2009). The Soviet Union and its Eastern bloc neighbors saw possibilities for the musical genre themselves—particularly how the celebration of community could reinforce socialist philosophies. A whole cycle of "tractor musicals" were made in Soviet Russia in the 1930s, for example, with farmhands joyously singing while they all did their bit for the latest of Stalin's five-year plans.

15 Robin Wood, "Art and Ideology: Notes on 'Silk Stockings," *Film Comment* (May/June 1975), 28–31, argues that *Silk Stockings'* use of music ultimately provides a better argument for the lure of capitalism than *Ninotchka* (1939), the Greta Garbo comedy on which the musical is based.

16 Alcoholism shows up in *When My Baby Smiles at Me* (1948)—giving Dan Dailey an Oscar nomination for Best Actor; *A Star Is Born* (1954)—giving Judy

Garland an Oscar nomination for Best Actress; and *I'll Cry Tomorrow* (1955)—giving Susan Hayward an Oscar nomination for Best Actress; polio strikes opera star Marjorie Lawrence in *Interrupted Melody*—giving Eleanor Parker an Oscar nomination for Best Actress; spousal abuse is intimated in *A Star Is Born, Love Me or Leave Me,* and *Carousel* (1956); and suicide (or an attempt thereof) is featured in *A Star Is Born, Interrupted Melody,* and *Young at Heart.*

17 Such titles would include *Lady on a Train* (1948), *Young Man with a Horn* (1950), *Meet Danny Wilson* (1952), and *The Helen Morgan Story* (1957). Intriguingly, MGM producer Joe Pasternak, who is usually associated with schmaltz and operatic voices, dabbled quite a lot in *noir* musicals: *The Strip* (1951), *Love Me or Leave Me* (1955), and *This Could Be the Night* (1957).

18 The bootblack, LeRoy Daniels, was an actual bootblack "found in downtown Los Angeles, at the corner of Sixth and Main" (Fordin, 405).

19 The most obvious indication of US fatigue with Latin American rhythms appeared in one of the few successful postwar Broadway revues, *Call Me Mister*: a song entitled "South America, Take It Away." Intriguingly, Murray Forman, *One Night on TV is Worth Weeks at the Paramount: Popular Music on Early Television* (Durham: Duke University Press, 2012), 273–319, argues that Latin American music was quite prevalent on American television during this period. The success of Cuban bandleader Desi Arnaz stands as possibly the prime indicator, and it should also be noted that Carmen Miranda's last performance was on television, on *The Jimmy Durante Show* in 1955.

20 Richard Dyer, "The Colour of Entertainment," in *Musicals: Hollywood and Beyond*, ed. Bill Marshall and Robynn Stilwell (Exeter: Intellect Books, 2000), 25.

21 Horne did get to vaguely play Julie in a ten-minute truncated version of the piece at the start of *Till the Clouds Roll By* (1946).

22 Although talking about 1950s films in general rather than musicals in particular, see also Nowak and Miller, *The Fifties: The Way We Really Were* (Garden City: Doubleday, 1977), 328–330.

23 Also, the sense that Monroe was just the latest Fox blonde to come off the studio conveyor belt further heightened the sense of domination over her— particularly when she began fighting back in the mid-1950s for greater say over her parts. Her death in 1962 worked to enshrine her image as a victim of studio (and male) manipulation. Much has been written on Monroe, including Barbara Leaming, *Marilyn Monroe* (New York: Crown Publishers, 1998); Matthew Solomon, "Reflexivity and Metaperformance: Marilyn Monroe, Jayne Mansfield, and Kim Novak," *Larger Than Life: Movie Stars of the 1950s*, ed. R. Barton Palmer (New Brunswick: Rutgers University Press, 2010), 107–129; and Lois W. Banner, *Marilyn: The Passion and the Paradox* (New York: Bloomsbury, 2012).

24 Granted, the script presents the smack as accidental rather than intentional.

25 Steven Cohan, *Incongruous Entertainment: Camp, Cultural Value, and the MGM Musical* (Durham: Duke University Press, 2005), 149–199.

26 Two examples: Gene Kelly, Frank Sinatra, and Jules Munshin masquerading as harem girls to avoid the cops in *On the Town*; and Bing Crosby and Danny Kaye lip-syncing to a recording of Rosemary Clooney and the voice double of Vera-Ellen singing "Sisters" in *White Christmas*.

27 Rumors about Brando being bisexual had circulated within gay male circles, and Clifton Webb had improbably risen to Hollywood stardom in the postwar years playing variations of prissy snobs that epitomized the stereotype of the gay male pansy, earning two Oscar nominations, for the *noir* classic *Laura* (1944) and for the domestic comedy *Sitting Pretty* (1948).

28 *Calamity Jane* is ripe with queer notions of gender and sexuality. See Eric Savoy, "'That Ain't *All* She Ain't': Doris Day and Queer Performativity," *Out Takes: Essays on Queer Theory and Film*, ed. Ellis Hanson (Durham: Duke University Press, 1999), 151–182.

29 Although not emphasizing a lesbian connotative meaning, Lucie Arbuthnot and Gail Seneca, "Pre-Text and Text in *Gentlemen Prefer Blondes*," *Film Reader* (1982), 13–23, present a similar reading, emphasizing the female bond between the two female leads.

7

Bustin' Out All Over: The Rise of the Musical Blockbuster

The previous chapter described how musical films after World War II started to show some strain behind the ever-glowing smiles of the characters, and suggested that such tensions mirrored various struggles occurring within the rest of American society. This chapter examines how industrial pressures may also explain the increasingly neurotic nature of the postwar film musical. A number of developments severely undercut the smooth and confident efficiency of the Hollywood studio system, including the Paramount Decision, the "baby boom," and the explosive growth of television.

All of Hollywood had to deal with the upheaval caused by a dismantling of the business structure and suddenly dwindling audiences. Thus, the nervousness that subtly pervades many postwar musicals may be an unintended influence of the jitters felt by the people making them. A number of Hollywood executives turned to the musical genre as a strategy to draw customers back to the box office. This chapter will examine the impact of these challenges on the film musical, including the musical entertainment being provided by the new television industry and the birth of the blockbuster musical motion picture.

Love Me or Leave Me: The Breakup of the Studio System

Musical production was severely impacted by a number of legal decisions during the 1940s that found aspects of the classical Hollywood studio system unlawful. The first of these occurred in 1943, when actress Olivia de Havilland successfully sued Warner Bros. over the way studio executives interpreted long-term exclusive contracts. This practice *de facto* extended studio control over artists' careers indefinitely. As a result of the judgment, all of the studios were forced to relax their iron-clad grip over talent, and soon many stars and big-name directors became independent artists.[1]

As described in Chapter 5, a studio's ability to maintain a coterie of talent under long-term contract helped develop a type of repertory company for

Free and Easy? A Defining History of the American Film Musical Genre, First Edition. Sean Griffin.
© 2018 Sean Griffin. Published 2018 by John Wiley & Sons Ltd.

producing musicals. Such a system also allowed studios to nurture and develop talent. Keeping talent under contract also meant trying to keep them busy with projects in order to justify their weekly salaries. Thus, studios regularly loaned out artists to other studios rather than paying them while they idled away—and the studio typically received more money from the loan out than it was actually paying the employee. Such practices aided studios attempting to match the look and feel of MGM musicals: they simply got MGM to loan out their talent. Ann Miller and Gloria de Haven were loaned to RKO for *Two Tickets to Broadway* (1951). Warner Bros. borrowed Howard Keel for *Calamity Jane* (1953), Kathryn Grayson for *The Desert Song* (1953) and *So This Is Love* (1953), and Jane Powell for *Three Girls and a Sailor* (1953). Bob Fosse and Tommy Rall went over to Columbia for *My Sister Eileen* (1955). Leslie Caron was loaned to Fox for *Daddy Long Legs* (1955). Such a strategy extended behind the scenes as well. MGM choreographer Robert Alton went to Fox to stage the numbers for its adaptation of the Irving Berlin stage hit *Call Me Madame* (1953), and to Paramount to direct the dance sequences in *White Christmas* (1954). Although the film adaptation of *Oklahoma!* (1955) was an independent production, most of the interiors were built and shot on MGM soundstages, and Adolph Deutsch and Johnny Green were loaned to the production from Metro's music department.[2] *Funny Face* (1957) was an MGM production in everything but name. The project had been developed there, with the hopes of having Paramount loan them Audrey Hepburn. When Paramount refused, Metro sold the whole package to Paramount, attaching all of the talent involved: producer Roger Edens, director Stanley Donen, and co-star Fred Astaire.[3]

Such production patterns seem to parallel the dynamics celebrated within the musical genre itself: individuals banding together in a glorious expression of community that gives everyone a sense of freedom and fulfillment. Certainly, those who ran the studios promoted the image of being a big, happy family. Such was not always the case, as competition and personal enmity often existed within studio workforces. A number of contract employees also chafed at the control that the studio executives had over them. In fact, the studios faced major strikes by workers after the war (resulting in riots outside the gates of the Warner Bros. studio, complete with lead pipes and fire hoses). The music industry was not immune to these tensions: the American Federation of Musicians went on strike twice over compensation for recorded music. The first strike lasted for two years (1942–1943); a second strike occurred in 1948. (The record labels and the radio networks were the hardest hit by these strikes. The Hollywood studios reached an agreement quickly in order to keep music in their motion pictures.)[4]

Production of Hollywood musicals often exemplified growing labor tensions after the war. Mario Lanza's ego (and weight gains) became a growing problem for producer Joseph Pasternak and the MGM brass. At the height of such struggles, the studio replaced Lanza in the title role of *The Student Prince* (1954) with

Edmund Purdom, with Purdom lip-syncing to recordings Lanza had made before being jettisoned. Betty Hutton was initially overjoyed to be loaned by Paramount to MGM for the lead role in Arthur Freed's production of *Annie Get Your Gun* (1950), but "cold shoulder" treatment by MGM employees led her to bouts of extreme depression.[5] The snubbing of Hutton was likely due to internal tensions happening within the Freed Unit itself at this time involving Judy Garland (whom Hutton replaced). In the late 1940s, Garland became increasingly combative: complaining of being overworked, missing rehearsals or days of shooting, and going through major mood swings (possibly tied to a growing drug dependency). While she remained a box-office favorite after the war, the amount of time and money spent dealing with her waywardness became a growing liability, and she was replaced by other leading ladies on a number of projects (not just Hutton in *Annie Get Your Gun* [1950], but also Ginger Rogers in *The Barkleys of Broadway* [1949] and Jane Powell in *Royal Wedding* [1951]). Eventually, Freed and the MGM front office reached their limit. Garland was fired—and the next day, headlines blared that she had made some form of suicide attempt.[6]

Many artists, on screen and off, successfully freed themselves from exclusive studio contracts as the 1950s progressed, thus giving them the opportunity to explore new projects and new partnerships. Astaire had led the way, going independent in 1940 after finishing up his contract at RKO, and signing non-exclusive multiple picture deals with various studios. This included MGM, meaning that he signed his own deal with Fox to star in *Daddy Long Legs* rather than being loaned out like Caron. Some artists were able to use their independence to advance their careers—Donald O'Connor had languished through the 1940s at Universal, but blossomed in the 1950s as he moved to bigger and better pictures at MGM, Fox, and Paramount. Mitzi Gaynor similarly had a hard time breaking through when put under contract at Fox in the early 1950s, but moved into lead roles as an independent at MGM and Paramount, eventually returning to Fox in the plum role of Nellie Forbush in Rodgers and Hammerstein's *South Pacific* (1958).

Although studios loaned out their contract artists during the 1930s and 1940s, it was relatively easy during that era to guess which studio made which musical simply by looking at the performers. It grew harder to do so in the 1950s. Doris Day and James Cagney, both icons from Warner Bros., would star in *Love Me or Leave Me* (1955), a musical biopic with gangster elements (also a genre staple of Warners)—but the film was made at MGM. Bing Crosby finally left Paramount in 1956, moving on to *High Society* (1956) at Metro. Stanley Donen left MGM in 1957, directing film adaptations of *The Pajama Game* (1957) and *Damn Yankees* (1958) at Warners.

Another court case had even more dire effects on the major Hollywood studios. Central to the classic Hollywood system was its own business version of integration: each major studio owning a stake in all aspects of the industry—production, distribution, and exhibition. This *vertical* integration ensured the profitability of an ongoing stream of films—including a steady diet of musicals. In 1948, the Supreme Court sided with the Department of Justice in a lawsuit claiming that the major Hollywood studios had engaged in unfair restraint of trade, that their business system of vertical integration helped maintain an oligopoly. The Paramount Decision, as it was called (after the first studio listed in the lawsuit), decreed that the studios had to divest themselves of one arm of their holdings. All of the studios involved complied by dropping their owner-ship of theatres, thus removing the security net that had ensured that any and all films produced by a studio would get exhibited.

In reaction to the Paramount Decision, studios cut back on production, and consequently also slashed the number of people they kept on contract. Many people in front of and behind the camera were let go, in effect *forcing* talent to become independent whether they wanted to or not. For example, after the box-office failure of MGM's *Jupiter's Darling* (1955), the studio said goodbye to most of the top talent involved: Esther Williams, Howard Keel, Marge and Gower Champion, and director George Sidney. House composers (such as Ray Evans and Jay Livingston at Paramount, or Sammy Fain and Paul Francis Webster at Warner Bros.) were set free as well—another reason postwar musicals often relied so heavily on old standards rather than new tunes. Such actions inevitably disrupted the ability to hold onto the conservatory environ-ment that ensured a consistent line of musical production. The Unit system of production came to an end and from this point on, by and large, the people working on a musical would have to be culled one by one for each project—with no guarantee that the individual talents would work well together.

Musicals had blossomed under the classical Hollywood system, balancing the risk of big-budget musicals with the guarantee of returns from smaller films. It is perhaps unsurprising then that the number of musicals produced in Hollywood decreased after the Paramount Decision, as the studios began com-plying with its dictates. It is also perhaps unsurprising that the one exception to this reduction in musicals was MGM. The Decision gave the studios ten years to fully shed their theatre holdings. Paramount was one of the first to comply; MGM (which was where the system had been perfected) was the last. It waited until the very final moment: 1958, the year Freed produced *Gigi*. Thus, although Freed would continue to produce films for a few years after-ward (including one more musical—*Bells Are Ringing* [1960], directed by Minnelli), *Gigi* is often regarded as the climax of the Freed Unit, and the end of the Golden Era of the original Hollywood musical.

In My Own Little Corner: The Arrival of Television

While the Paramount Decision was creating havoc with the structure of the Hollywood studio business model, an even more obvious challenge to the musical genre (and motion pictures in general) emerged after the war: the exponential growth of television. Television had debuted as a technology back in 1939, but the growth of broadcasting had been delayed by the needs of World War II. Once the war was won, though, the new technology spread quickly across the country. The motion picture industry felt the impact almost immediately, as attendance dropped in a calamitous fashion during the late 1940s and into the 1950s. While a number of factors contributed to such a drop (population shifts to the suburbs away from urban movie theatres; the "baby boom" keeping adults at home with their offspring), the film industry regarded television as the main culprit. Now people could stay home and be entertained for free (once they finished paying for the television set itself) rather than go out and pay for a ticket.

Television seemed to pose a particular threat to the film musical. The first breakout nationwide hit program was *Texaco Star Theater*, starring Milton Berle in what amounted to a televised hour of vaudeville comedy and music. While Berle dominated the proceedings with his anarchic clowning, the show featured a quartet of singing gas station jockeys, a number of chorus girls for miscellaneous routines, and various musical guest stars. The "variety show" quickly emerged as a staple of TV programming. Early examples include *Arthur Godfrey and His Friends* (1949–1957), *The Colgate Comedy Hour* (1950–1955), and *All-Star Revue* (1951–1953). By the late 1950s, variety hours included *The Perry Como Show* (1955–1959), *The Tennessee Ernie Ford Show* (1956–1961), *The Dinah Shore Show* (1957–1962), and *The Garry Moore Show* (1958–1964).

Hollywood executives were soon commanding their star talent not to appear on television—if audiences wanted to see them, they would have to pay for theatre tickets and not watch them in the comfort of their living rooms. Unfortunately, as described above, more and more stars were becoming independent performers. Consequently, stars such as Tony Martin, Dean Martin and Jerry Lewis, Donald O'Connor, Jimmy Durante, and Martha Raye appeared regularly on these programs. While many established musical performers did cross over from motion pictures to television, perhaps an even greater problem was television's ability to put new talent in front of the camera faster than filmmakers could. Whereas film producers would need at least six months to hire the latest singing sensation, shoot the picture, finish post-production and get it out to theatres, a television program could hire that same talent and have him or her on the air by next week. Television soon showed its ability to create new stars, such as teen heartthrob Ricky Nelson (appearing with his parents Ozzie and Harriet Nelson on their show) and crooner Tony Bennett (who was introduced to the nation by Arthur Godfrey). In this way, television stepped in for the crumbling studio system, acting as a training ground and grooming performers for possible transition from the small screen to the big screen. Dance couple Marge and Gower Champion moved from television appearances to MGM musicals, for example, and singer Pat Boone's success on Arthur Godfrey's program led to his film debut in *Bernadine* (1956). Walt Disney very specifically transitioned Annette Funicello from a member of TV's *Mickey Mouse Club* (1955–1959) to a star of musicals on the big screen.

Although they were filled with song and dance, television variety shows did not meet what was becoming the dominant definition of a musical after World War II: integration. Other programming did present narratives of ongoing characters who at times broke into song and dance. As mentioned, the family series *Ozzie and Harriet* acted as a platform to launch the music career of Ricky Nelson. Playing nightclub owner Ricky Ricardo gave Desi Arnaz plenty of opportunities to sing and play the conga drum on *I Love Lucy* (1951–1957). Danny Thomas also sang regularly on his show *Make Room for Daddy* (1953–1965). Yet, such on-stage performances happened only sporadically, and these shows have been regarded almost always as exemplars of the situation comedy genre instead of as musical comedies.

The major networks *did* start producing full-scale book musicals, particularly an explosion of TV versions of hit Broadway musicals. Some titles had already been turned into motion pictures. Ann Sothern starred in a 1954 broadcast of *Lady in the Dark*, Janet Blair performed in a version of *One Touch of Venus* (1955), and TV audiences were able to watch original cast members Alfred Drake and Patricia Morison recreate their roles in *Kiss Me, Kate* (1958). *Colgate Comedy Hour* presented condensed versions of *Anything Goes* (in 1954, with original cast member Ethel Merman, as well as Bert Lahr and Frank Sinatra) and *Roberta* (in 1955, with Gordon MacRae). Others, though, had not been adapted to film, such as *Wonderful Town* (with its original star, Rosalind Russell, in 1958), *Bloomer Girl*, and *Peter Pan* (both on *Producers Showcase* in 1955). *Peter Pan* was so successful that NBC had its star Mary Martin reprise her performance in 1960 for a color broadcast.

Television had access to Broadway stars such as Ethel Merman and Mary Martin because the main television networks had broadcast operations in New York, an advantage that the networks could play up to rival Hollywood motion pictures. The connections between television and theatre were further enhanced by the emphasis on live broadcast. Videotape would not be invented until 1956.[7] The immediacy of live performance is often credited with creating a special charge between cast and audience, in which anything could happen. Even with tiny black-and-white screens making it seem as if one was watching through bad opera glasses from the second balcony, television was able to approximate that spontaneity in a manner that motion pictures could not.

Thus, shows such as *Tonight on Broadway* (1948–1949), *Admiral Broadway Revue* (1949), and *Broadway Open House* (1950–1952) allowed audiences far away from the Great White Way a chance to sample the latest musical theatre sensations. *Colgate Comedy Hour* presented "Highlights of Broadway" in 1955, with scenes from that season's hit integrated musicals *Damn Yankees*, *Fanny*, and *House of Flowers*. As the king of variety show hosts, Ed Sullivan on CBS regularly introduced major Broadway figures. His opening show in 1948 included an appearance from Rodgers and Hammerstein themselves. The duo visited Sullivan again in 1951, with Gertrude Lawrence in costume as the star of their latest hit, *The King and I.* In 1954, General Foods presented a ninety-minute *Tribute to Rodgers and Hammerstein*, with members from the original casts of their collaborations performing classic numbers. The program was considered so monumental that it was carried on all of the networks simultaneously.[8]

Perhaps expectedly, with such resources at the networks' disposal and an appreciative audience for televised musical theatre, new integrated musicals created specifically for television began debuting. In 1952, the first opera written for television was aired: a Christmas story about the Magi entitled *Amahl and the Night Visitors*. In the late 1950s, titles came tumbling out with regularity: *Pinocchio* (1957) with Mickey Rooney; *The Gift of the Magi* (1958) with Gordon MacRae; *Aladdin* (1958) with Cole Porter's last score. A musicalized rendition of *Our Town* (in 1955, for *Producers' Showcase* again) starred Frank Sinatra as the House Manager, giving him the hit song "Love and Marriage."[9] In 1956, a musical entitled *High Tor* starred Bing Crosby and a British newcomer named Julie Andrews, days before she was about to become the toast of Broadway in *My Fair Lady*. The following year, Andrews would star in *Cinderella*, a musical written for television by Rodgers and Hammerstein. An audience of 107 million watched the live CBS broadcast, as she sang "In My Own Little Corner," magically experienced "A Lovely Night" at the ball, and eventually lived happily ever after with her Prince (Figure 7.1).[10]

Figure 7.1 Julie Andrews mirrors the television audience, enjoying the pleasures that come from sitting at home "In My Own Little Corner" in Rodgers and Hammerstein's version of *Cinderella* (1957). Snapshot taken from: Cinderella (1957).

Television was obviously thriving. By 1960, almost 90 percent of American households had a TV set.[11] The desire to see the newest Broadway luminaries and to watch the latest singing stars—for free—kept people at home rather than going out and paying to see a musical film. Producers of motion picture musicals had to come up with new strategies to lure customers to the box office.

To Get the Public to Attend a Picture Show: Competing with Television

Movie musicals, like all American cinema of the postwar period, strove to find some way of convincing audiences to leave their television sets. An initial gambit was to promote films as being of higher artistic quality than television. Such genre developments as the integrated musical, long-form ballet sequences, and a growing emphasis on more serious subject matter certainly lent themselves towards considering the musical more as art than frivolity. Yet, while the notion that TV is "kitsch" and "cinema" is "art" continues to hold sway with some even today, early television programs countered by asserting their association with live theatre.

A more concerted effort by the film industry then was to provide something that audiences could not get on television. The edict forbidding television appearances by stars under contract to the studios was one aspect of this plan. Group-oriented musicals increased during the 1950s not only because of the rise of integration—they also provided audiences with a conglomeration of star talent that TV arguably could not afford. The *Colgate Comedy Hour* might be able to show Ethel Merman with Frank Sinatra and Bert Lahr in a version of *Anything Goes*, but (in the same year) Fox's *There's No Business Like Show Business* (1954) brings Merman together with Dan Dailey, Donald O'Connor, Mitzi Gaynor, new singing heartthrob Johnnie Ray, *and* Marilyn Monroe. Bing Crosby stars in TV's *High Tor*, but with then-relative-unknown Julie Andrews, while in *White Christmas* he performs with Danny Kaye, Vera-Ellen, and recording star Rosemary Clooney.

Early television programs were also limited in what they could provide in terms of the scale and scope of production. Most television programs had only one or two standing sets, and usually the production design was extremely low scale. Furthermore, the smallness of console screens meant an emphasis on close-ups that precluded a need for intensive production design. As a consequence, Hollywood motion pictures began emphasizing their lavishness: huge sets, extravagant costumes. After World War II, Hollywood producers increasingly left the confines of the studio backlot to film pictures on location as well. The Freed Unit's *On the Town* (1949) begins at an actual New York City dock to show the sailors played by Gene Kelly, Frank Sinatra, and Jules Munshin excitedly rushing off their ship for a day's leave. The ensuing number, "New York, New York," is an energetic montage of the trio running literally all over the city, with footage of them at such locations as the Statue of Liberty, Central Park, and Rockefeller Center. *Funny Face* includes a similar musical tour of Paris (culminating at the Eiffel Tower) in "Bonjour, Paris!" Major portions of *Gigi* were also filmed on location in Paris. Even less acclaimed musicals went out on location, such as the self-explanatory titles of *Meet Me in Las Vegas* (1956) and *The Seven Hills of Rome* (1957).

Motion pictures also tried to trump TV through technology. Not only were early TV screens small, the programs were in black-and-white and in mono-aural sound. Color filmmaking had increased during the 1940s, particularly in musicals. (For example, the last black-and-white musical Arthur Freed produced was *Girl Crazy* [1943].) However, color really gained momentum in the 1950s, specifically to give audiences something they could not have watching television. By the early 1950s, almost all musicals made by the Hollywood studios were shot in color.[12] Producers were able to afford to make more films in color with the debut of newer and cheaper color film stocks in the 1950s. Musicals in the early 1940s tended to use color specifically for spectacle, reveling in almost riotous combinations of oversaturated hues. Many musicals continued this trend into the 1950s—for example, the lurid reds, greens, and purples in the "Mandy" number in *White Christmas*, or the lime greens and neon pinks in the "Now Baby Now" number in *The Opposite Sex* (1956). Certain others, though, showed more careful consideration of the use of color. For example, as Ruth Etting in *Love Me or Leave Me*, Doris Day starts the film wearing light-colored outfits, but as she becomes more and more beholden to the gangster who promotes her career, she moves to darker and darker colors. When she is most completely under his control, while singing "Ten Cents a Dance," she is completely in black. Color could also function as part of a musical's integration. Vincente Minnelli's start as a scenic designer ensured that the color design blended with the overall attitude of each musical—whether using soft nostalgic pastels in *Meet Me in St. Louis* (1944) or recreating the palettes of different Impressionist painters in the dream ballet of *An American in Paris* (1951).

Color was only the start. Soon, producers of musicals (and others across Hollywood) were searching for additional technological advances to increase the divide between film and television. A flurry of films in 3-D debuted in 1953 and early 1954, for example. Most were hurriedly made and exploitative, with characters throwing or thrusting something out towards the camera/audience at the slightest justification. The manner in which Howard Hughes promoted his musical production *The French Line* (1953), for example, seems to indicate the sole objective was to see Jane Russell's breasts jutting outward.[13] A few projects, though, attempted to use 3-D more creatively. While some might not regard *Miss Sadie Thompson* (1953) as a musical (based on a famous non-musical play, *Rain*, by Somerset Maugham), a voice-dubbed Rita Hayworth as the title character performs a few songs—including one that takes advantage of the illusion of depth by having her sing amid the smoke of a barroom. MGM's adaptation of *Kiss Me, Kate* (1953) was undeniably a musical. While including the requisite props tossed at the camera (a garter, a banana, a tankard), the picture also uses depth to emphasize how Kathryn Grayson's temperamental diva is being held captive within the theatre by filming her down long hallways or inside doorways. While all of these films were shot in 3-D, interest waned quickly, and most audiences saw only the 2-D "flat" versions.

Kiss Me, Kate featured another technological change: it was MGM's first film to feature stereo sound. The quality of sound recording for motion pictures had steadily improved across the decades, increasing the level of fidelity and the dynamic range, and lessening the hiss of the recording apparatus. While the soundtrack to the 1926 Phonofilm test of Eubie Blake often crackles with extraneous noise and is incapable of capturing the higher octaves of the piano, the soundtrack to *Naughty Marietta* (1935) is noticeably cleaner and easily captures the high notes of Jeanette MacDonald and the low notes of Nelson Eddy. By the end of the 1930s, Hollywood studios had begun using at least two microphones in pre-recording musical sequences to better control the mixing of sound. Leopold Stokowski recorded his orchestra with nine tracks for their appearance in the Deanna Durbin picture *100 Men and a Girl* (1937). Stokowski's involvement with Disney's *Fantasia* (1940) resulted in not only recording with six tracks of audio but releasing it to certain theatres in multi-channel sound.[14] While this was an isolated experiment, stereophonic sound was possible, and needed only a desire by the industry to make the shift. Competition from television was just the stimulus required. Early use of stereo was a bit simplistic, throwing voices either extreme left or extreme right to emphasize directionality (such as when Howard Keel and Kathryn Grayson waltz from dressing room to dressing room while singing "Wunderbar" in *Kiss Me, Kate*). Filmmakers soon developed a more nuanced approach, using the breadth of stereo to offer lusher orchestrations in which the individual instruments of the orchestra could be heard more clearly. (Ironically, the debut of stereo records on the American market did not take hold until the very end of the 1950s.)[15]

Widescreen filmmaking literally tried to expand the difference between movies and TV, juxtaposing the smallness of the video screen with large rectangular theatre screens. Fox's first forays with CinemaScope were not musicals: the Biblical epic *The Robe* (1953) and the sex comedy *How to Marry a Millionaire* (1954). Nonetheless, filmmakers seemed to recognize how the musical could use the widescreen. *This Is Cinerama* (1952), while rarely regarded as belonging to the musical genre, contains some music performances. *How to Marry a Millionaire* opens with a lengthy unmotivated prologue of house score composer Alfred Newman conducting an orchestral performance of his tone poem *Street Scene*. By 1954, musicals in CinemaScope proliferated. In addition to Fox's *There's No Business Like Show Business* was Warner Bros.' *A Star Is Born* and *Lucky Me*, and MGM's *The Student Prince*, *Brigadoon*, and *Seven Brides for Seven Brothers*. Disney decided to refashion *Lady and the Tramp* (1955), which had already begun production in the traditional square-like Academy ratio, so that audiences could watch two canines smooch while eating spaghetti in CinemaScope. Rather than pay a fee to Fox to use CinemaScope, Paramount invested in its own widescreen process—and the studio's first production in VistaVision was the Bing Crosby musical *White Christmas*.

As with color, 3-D, and stereo, the musical genre's emphasis on lavish production values lent itself towards the "bigness" of widescreen technology, allowing audiences to revel all the more in ornate settings and spectacular costumes. The widescreen was also advantageous to the genre's increase in location shooting and multiple star performers. With a rectangular screen, one could show a panoramic view of Paris in *Funny Face* or *Gigi*, for example, or fit all six of the leads of *There's No Business Like Show Business* on screen at the same time (Figure 7.2). With a screen this large, one could now show all seven brides and seven brothers! Backstager musicals often use the widescreen to give audiences a sense of seeing the entire stage during a number—somewhat of a return to the "fifth-row-center" framing of early talkie musicals.[16] There is also an emphasis on the horizontal in these rectangular productions—the eruption of slide trombones around Judy Garland as she warbles about "The Man That Got Away" in *A Star Is Born*, or the reclining legs of Cyd Charisse while putting on the titular *Silk Stockings*. Perhaps most inventive is the

Figure 7.2 Johnnie Ray, Mitzi Gaynor, Dan Dailey, Ethel Merman, Donald O'Connor, and Marilyn Monroe (along with a bevy of chorus girls) fill up the CinemaScope frame in the finale of *There's No Business Like Show Business* (1954). Snapshot taken from: *There's No Business Like Show Business* (1954).

dollar-bill motif used in *It's Always Fair Weather*, equating the CinemaScope dimensions to the shape of US currency.

Hollywood's new emphasis on technology was so prevalent that Cole Porter wrote a song about the situation for *Silk Stockings*. Fred Astaire and Janis Paige sing that "to get the public to attend a picture show," movies now had to have "glorious Technicolor, breathtaking CinemaScope, and stereophonic sound."[17] Hollywood musicals seemed to be getting bigger and bigger, more and more epic (and more and more expensive), in order to garner attention. This trend fed into the felt need to celebrate American opulence in the middle of the Cold War. Yet, this move also helped generate the neurotic tinge in postwar musicals, working harder and harder to convince viewers (and filmmakers themselves) that everything was just fine. The move towards "legitimacy" through integration, the turn towards technological advances, and the general enlargement of musical production would culminate in the emergence of musical blockbuster filmmaking by the middle of the 1950s.

High as an Elephant's Eye: The Epic Broadway Adaptation

Oklahoma! is regarded as a major landmark in the history of American musical theatre. The play's importance lies in how it ushered in the dominance of the integrated format. The movie's importance lies more in how it ushered in a new industry model for the musical: the blockbuster. When the picture premiered in 1955, it enlisted almost all of the competitive strategies discussed above. The opening images announce that exteriors were shot on location (albeit Arizona rather than the actual Oklahoma) with cowboy Curly riding past corn that actually is "as high as an elephant's eye." The film was shot in color, was recorded in stereo to capture the lush orchestrations of Rodgers' lovely melodies, and debuted a new widescreen technology named Todd-AO (Figure 7.3). Added to these strategies, *Oklahoma!* was distributed on a "roadshow" basis—playing only in certain theatres in major cities where customers had to buy advance seating as if they were going to see a stage play. (Audiences not near such theatres had to wait a year for the film to go into general release.) Furthermore, glossy souvenir programs were sold, an overture preceded the actual picture, and each screening included an intermission—necessary because the running time of the film was 145 minutes.

Oklahoma! was not the first film to get a roadshow release. Hollywood in general began turning to epic blockbuster moviemaking in the 1950s, turning a film release into an awe-inspiring event that would theoretically blast TV viewers out of their couches and into theatres. Although studios made fewer films each year, they invested enormous funds in a few mammoth productions. Biblical-era spectacles led the charge, including *The Robe*, *The Ten Commandments* (1956),

Figure 7.3 Shirley Jones listens to Gordon MacRae extol the virtues of "The Surrey with the Fringe on Top" in *Oklahoma!* (1955), with the Todd-AO widescreen process seeming to take in half the western United States in the background. Snapshot taken from: Oklahoma! (1955).

Ben-Hur (1959), and *Spartacus* (1960). Yet, other genres caught the blockbuster bug as well: westerns (*The Alamo* [1960], *How the West Was Won* [1962]), costume dramas (*War and Peace* [1957]), war films (*The Longest Day* [1962]), and comedies (*It's a Mad, Mad, Mad, Mad World* [1963], *The Great Race* [1965]). Such a strategy had its advantages and disadvantages. Traditionally, when blockbuster movies do well, they do phenomenally well; but when blockbuster movies do not find an audience, they can imperil the financial health of the entire company. Hence, every blockbuster was a gigantic risk that could result in monumental failure.

Oklahoma! mitigated that risk. It had proven itself as wildly popular in its theatrical debut on Broadway and through a decade-long national stage tour. With motion pictures having to compete with television *and* to stand on their own merit now that the studios had to divest their theatre holdings, many film producers began relying on tried-and-tested subject matter. Thus, the 1950s saw a rise in pictures based on best-selling novels or hit plays. This proved an obvious option for the musical genre with the explosion of musical theatre successes on Broadway in the postwar period. Audiences had not only thronged to these stage productions, they also had turned original cast albums (available with the advent of the long-playing record) into top sellers.

Oklahoma!'s pre-sold reputation proved correct: it made $7.1 million when it finished its roadshow and regular release in the United States and Canada.[18] *Oklahoma!* was independently produced (more on this in a moment), but almost every studio contributed to its making. MGM donated members of its music department, as well as its soundstages. Male leads Gordon MacRae and Gene Nelson were loaned from Warner Bros. RKO handled the distribution of the 70 mm Todd-AO roadshow prints, and Fox was brought in to film and distribute a second version of the picture in 35 mm CinemaScope for the eventual wide release. Thus, the production of *Oklahoma!* acted as a sort of training ground for the major studios on how to make a blockbuster musical adaptation. If any studio executives were reticent, Samuel Goldwyn's profitable release of the lavish and long film version of the Broadway musical *Guys and Dolls* (1955), (released within a month of *Oklahoma!*'s roadshow premiere) ended any doubts about big-budget musical adaptations.[19] The other Rodgers and Hammerstein successes were obvious candidates for the blockbuster strategy: *Carousel* (1956), *The King and I* (1956), *South Pacific* (1958), *Flower Drum Song* (1961)— even a grandiose remake of *State Fair* (1962). Along with them came big-budget versions of *Porgy and Bess* (1959), *Can-Can* (1960), *West Side Story* (1961), *Gypsy* (1962), *The Music Man* (1962), *The Unsinkable Molly Brown* (1964), and *My Fair Lady* (1964). In order to keep up with this trend, Disney put together a large-scale adaptation of the Victor Herbert chestnut *Babes in Toyland* (1961).

Of these, only *South Pacific, Porgy and Bess, Can-Can,* and *My Fair Lady* were specifically given roadshow releases, but the others can be termed blockbusters in comparison to other musicals produced at the time, with longer running times, bigger casts, and larger scales of production. It went without saying that all of these pictures would be shot in color, in widescreen, and presented in stereo. For example, *Carousel* debuted Fox's new CinemaScope55 technology. The studio's insistence on this resulted in Frank Sinatra walking off the picture, because each shot needed to be filmed twice (once with the new cameras for the roadshow, and a second time with regular 35 mm cameras for the general theatre release) and he felt he should be paid twice. (Sinatra was quickly replaced with Gordon MacRae.)[20] In addition, most of these films went out on location. *Carousel* filmed sequences in and around Boothbay Harbor, Maine. Most of *South Pacific* was shot on the Hawaiian island of Kaua'i. The opening moments of *West Side Story* emphasize the use of actual New York City streets. When Harve Presnell sings about "Colorado, My Colorado" in *The Unsinkable Molly Brown*, the film makes certain that the audience can see what appears to be most of the Rocky Mountains in the background of every shot. When not indulging in grandiose vistas, these films rolled out expansive sets and costumes, such as the ornate Thai royal palace in *The King and I* or the soundstage recreation of London's Covent Garden in *My Fair Lady*.

The lavish expenditure on these adaptations was culturally justified because American musical theatre during the era became regarded as a serious art form. Composer and conductor Leonard Bernstein told a national television audience in 1956 that "for the last fifteen years, we have been enjoying the greatest period our musical theater has ever known."[21] Perhaps unsurprisingly, many of these adaptations included long-form dance sequences: the dream ballet in *Oklahoma!*; "Louise's Ballet" in *Carousel*; "The Small House of Uncle Thomas" in *The King and I*; another dream ballet in *Flower Drum Song*; and the landmark choreography in *West Side Story*. Unlike such journeymen directors of old like Norman Taurog, Norman Z. MacLeod, and H. Bruce Humberstone, "important" award-winning directors helmed these films. Fred Zinnemann shepherded *Oklahoma!*, fresh from directing the western *High Noon* (1952) and the military drama *From Here to Eternity* (1953). Four-time Oscar-winning writer/director Joseph Mankiewicz brought *Guys and Dolls* to the screen. Robert Wise and Broadway director/choreographer Jerome Robbins would share the Academy Award for Best Director for their work on *West Side Story* (1961), and longtime director George Cukor would finally win an Oscar for his adaptation of *My Fair Lady*.

Similarly, there was a growth of "serious" actors appearing in these adaptations, people not necessarily associated with the musical genre. In *Oklahoma!*, Gloria Grahame (largely known for playing tough dames in films *noir*) was cast as the comic second lead Ado Annie, and urban tough guy Rod Steiger (who had just been in *On the Waterfront* [1954]) was chosen for the villainous Jud. Marlon Brando and Jean Simmons play the main romantic leads in *Guys and Dolls*. Deborah Kerr portrays the governess Anna in *The King and I*. *West Side Story* stars Natalie Wood—who would also play the title role in *Gypsy* alongside Rosalind Russell. As integrated musicals, these properties fashioned unique and complex characters that extended beyond the demands of a typical ingénue or vaudeville comedian. Increasingly, actors in musicals were getting Oscar nominations. The Academy would present Oscars for Best Actor to Yul Brynner for *The King and I* and to Rex Harrison for *My Fair Lady*. *West Side Story* would win Oscars for Best Supporting Actor (George Chakiris) and Best Supporting Actress (Rita Moreno).

The serious subject matter of a number of these musicals also earned them greater respect. In particular, issues of racial prejudice are recurrent in the blockbuster adaptations of this period. The stage version of *South Pacific* won the Pulitzer Prize for Drama in 1949 for its depiction of interracial romance between white characters and Pacific islanders.[22] *West Side Story* refashions Shakespeare's *Romeo and Juliet* into a contemporary gang war between the white Jets and the Puerto Rican Sharks (Figure 7.4). *Flower Drum Song* offers a lighter comedic outlook, but focuses on Chinese emigrants attempting to build new lives in the United States. The attraction between English governess Anna and the King of Siam is so forbidden that it is never acknowledged outright in *The King and I*. Their emotion for each other can only find expression in his ever-so-slow grasping of her waist while her chest heaves in response as he prepares to polka her like she has never been polkaed before. Such a topic was considered too problematic and downbeat for earlier musicals to handle (*Show Boat* being notable in its exception). These musicals take on the challenge and present the tragic results of such prejudice: the interracial romances all end in death.

Figure 7.4 Puerto Rican Bernardo (George Chakiris, far left) faces off against the Jets, a white gang, in *West Side Story* (1961). The film's musical portrayal of gang violence and racial tension won multiple Academy Awards, including Supporting Actor for Chakiris. Snapshot taken from: West Side Story (1961).

The felt need to honor the seriousness and artistic credibility of these musicals at times conveys a sense of reverence toward the material in adapting it to the screen. Such respect substantially differs from how filmmakers tended to regard Broadway shows *before* the mid-1950s, when studios usually tinkered with the property to greater or lesser degree. On one side, for example, RKO's version of *Roberta* (1935) follows the original play relatively closely—with Jerome Kern and Dorothy Fields adding two songs for the film, "Lovely to Look At" and "I Won't Dance." The reworking of *Sweethearts* (1938), though, is more extensive, becoming a screwball backstager about a married show-business couple (Jeanette MacDonald and Nelson Eddy) putting on the original Victor Herbert operetta. In an extreme case, the Judy Garland–Mickey Rooney version of *Strike Up the Band* (1940) tosses out the entire political satire of the original play in order to use the title song for a story about high school students and swing bands.

Hollywood adaptations during the 1930s and 1940s also tended to replace much of the original score with new tunes. The film version of *The Gay Divorce* may have added an extra "e" to the title (making it *The Gay Divorcee* [1934]), but it also removed every Cole Porter song except "Night and Day." The entire Gershwin score for *Rosalie* was replaced with new Cole Porter compositions for the MGM film in 1937. The pieces written by Leonard Bernstein with Betty Comden and Adolph Green for *On the Town* (1949) survived in somewhat better shape, but some still were cut and replaced with new tunes composed by Roger Edens. To a degree, such decisions came about as part of making a stage property more "filmic." Broadway musicals were usually three-hour performances with an intermission but the usual Hollywood movie came in under two hours, so time considerations led to eliminating some of the numbers. Original properties were also often resculpted to fit the personae or talent skills of the stars under contract. Yet, money considerations also led studios to commission new tunes—ones to which they would hold the rights and from which they would potentially be able to reap more profit from sheet music sales and performance licensing.

The era of integrated musicals, as well as the debut of the original cast album, began to challenge these practices. It was easy to drop, replace, or change numbers in earlier book musicals because their connection to the narratives was usually minimal. The storylines themselves tended to be loose and insubstantial, and thus also easily rewritten. Such was not the case for integrated musicals—the storylines were much more unique and tightly woven, and the songs arose out of the narrative, either explaining character motivation or actually moving the plot forward during the number. Cast recordings point out this feature—listeners can generally follow the plot just by listening to the songs. Furthermore, the popularity of cast albums helped create a new phenomenon: rather than a musical producing one or two hit tunes, integrated musicals seemed to result in the entire score becoming popular. Thus, customers expected to hear *all* of the songs from the Broadway show when they paid to see the movie version. During the 1950s, movie versions of Broadway hits become increasingly faithful to the original property. The Freed Unit's adaptations of *Annie Get Your Gun* (1950), *Brigadoon* (1954), and *Kismet* (1955) have no interpolated tunes. Even "non-blockbuster" adaptations made in the wake of *Oklahoma!* maintain a fidelity to the stage work. *The Pajama Game* (1957), *Damn Yankees* (1958), *Li'l Abner* (1959), and *Bye Bye Birdie* (1963) not only retain most of the original score, they also contain members of the original Broadway cast recreating their roles.

The increasingly sacrosanct nature of the integrated score granted songwriters greater control, a very different situation than when Richard Rodgers first came to Hollywood in the early 1930s. Rodgers and his then-partner Lorenz Hart shared the frustrations of other studio contract artists described earlier in this chapter, becoming so disgruntled at being treated like day labor by executives that they decamped back to Broadway. When it came time to make a film version of *Oklahoma!*, though, Rodgers and his new partner Oscar Hammerstein did not have just the power of integration on their side: they had also become the producers. Via the independent company Magna, the duo ensured that any deviations from the original stage property to the screen had to be approved by them. Thus, *Oklahoma!* is a very faithful adaptation—missing only two songs and adding only one new sequence (a runaway buggy ride in order to play up the spectacle of the new Todd-AO widescreen).[23] While Rodgers and Hammerstein did a more conventional sale of the movie rights of *Carousel* and *The King and I* to 20th Century-Fox, the studio worked hard to keep the team happy—and the duo would once again hold the reins of power for the film version of *South Pacific*, producing independently and releasing through Fox. The best proof of their importance is in the absence of the traditional Fox drumroll and fanfare over its logo in *Oklahoma!*, *South Pacific*, or *The Sound of Music* (1965—to be discussed at length in Chapter 9): Rodgers did not write that snippet of music, and thus he did not want it included.

In addition to the dominance of Rodgers and Hammerstein over their projects, other songwriters angled for greater creative control. Some of them (such as Alan Jay Lerner and Jule Styne) had worked in Hollywood before, and thus knew how the dynamics in the industry worked. The use of high-name directors may have given these adaptations cultural cache, but their relative lack of experience in directing musicals gave greater authorial control back to the songwriter/producer. The casting of actors not tied to the genre had a similar effect, lessening the power that musical stars often wielded. *Oklahoma!* was not going to be reworked for Fred Astaire, so to speak, and *West Side Story* was not going to be tweaked to fit Doris Day. By the end of the 1950s, a number of artists who had become musical stars began moving beyond the genre to find projects. Day moved into a number of highly successful sex comedies, for example. Astaire and Judy Garland both appeared in dramatic roles (the nuclear holocaust film *On the Beach* [1959] for him, the World War II Holocaust film *Judgment at Nuremberg* [1961] for her). A number, including Astaire, Garland, Gene Kelly, and Danny Kaye, also shifted into weekly programs or specials on television.

The films usually work around the issue of casting actors with limited musicality by hiring others to replace their singing voices. Voice doubling in musicals had been occurring in Hollywood almost since the introduction of sound (as memorialized expertly in *Singin' in the Rain*). As mentioned earlier, some musical biographies used the actual singing voices of their subjects for the performances in the film, and the opening credits of *The Student Prince* (1954) gave credit to Mario Lanza's singing voice emerging out of actor Edmund Purdom's mouth. A number of female dancing stars (Eleanor Powell, Rita Hayworth, Vera-Ellen, Cyd Charisse, Leslie Caron) had voice doubles handle the singing chores. Yet, there is a measurable growth in voice doubling in the age of the Broadway blockbuster. Most of the cast of both *South Pacific* and *West Side Story* are dubbed in their singing, and voice double Georgio Tozzi is given screen credit for replacing Rosanno Brazzi's singing at the start of the first film. Although uncredited, Marni Nixon started becoming famous for her voice doubling: for Deborah Kerr in *The King and I*, for Natalie Wood in *West Side Story*, and for Audrey Hepburn in *My Fair Lady*. This felt need to mold and combine bodies and voices adds another level to the sense of enshrinement in these blockbusters.

The prevalence of voice doubling in these blockbusters factors into the attempt to control female stars and women's roles in postwar musicals overall, as discussed in Chapter 6. Overseen by male producers/directors/sound technicians, dubbing actresses can be described quite literally as robbing a woman of her own voice. Leslie Caron was denied her request to sing her own songs for *Gigi* (1958) and Rosalind Russell unsuccessfully voice auditioned for her numbers in *Gypsy*. Even some actresses with capable singing voices were dubbed because the men in charge felt that they did not have the "right kind" of voice: Dorothy Dandridge in *Carmen Jones* (1954) and *Porgy and Bess*;[24] Juanita Hall (who had originated the part of Bloody Mary on Broadway!) in *South Pacific*; Nancy Kwan in *Flower Drum Song*; Rita Moreno in *West Side Story*. While Audrey Hepburn unsuccessfully lobbied to do her own singing in *My Fair Lady*, Rex Harrison was allowed to sing/speak his numbers—and even do an on-set recording of his rendition of "I've Grown Accustomed to Her Face" rather than the more typical practice of pre-recording.[25] The plot of *My Fair Lady* mirrors this imbalance, as a male professor of dialect teaches a woman how to speak. Hepburn's body is constrained as well. Even though she trained as a dancer, she gets to do little more than some soft shoeing in "Wouldn't It Be Loverly" and a brief pirouette on a staircase during "I Could Have Danced All Night."[26]

All of these musicals were also written, produced, and directed by white artists—and predominantly with white audiences in mind.[27] Thus, the stories of racial prejudice are usually from the perspective of the white characters. The leads of the two narrative strands in *South Pacific*, for example, are the American nurse Nellie Forbush (Mitzi Gaynor) and Lt Cable (John Kerr). Cable's Tokinese love interest Liat (Frances Nguyen) has no lines of dialogue at all, and the half-Tonkinese children of Nellie's beau Emile (Rosanno Brazzi) only trot on screen to sing the ditty "Dites Moi."[28] While these musicals attempt to overcome racism and discrimination, many audiences of color have found images such as the character of Bloody Mary in *South Pacific*, or the entire cast of *Flower Drum Song* singing "Chop Suey," insulting and stereotypical in their own right.

Voice doubling impacted many performers of color as well, male and female, including Harry Belafonte, someone with a bigger career as a singer than as an actor, for his role in *Carmen Jones*! Dorothy Dandridge was dubbed in *Carmen Jones*, by white singer Marilyn Horne, and in *Porgy and Bess*. Dandridge's co-star in *Porgy and Bess*, Sidney Poitier, was also dubbed.[29] Otto Preminger directed both films, and many stories of his cruel, abusive behavior towards Dandridge on the set have been told over the years.[30] This was a long way from when she had partnered with the Nicholas Brothers in their specialty act performance of "Chattanooga Choo Choo" in *Sun Valley Serenade* (1941). Now, Dandridge was playing lead roles in big-budget artistically lauded musicals—but for her (and other performers of color) to do so, they had to agree to blend (or *integrate*) into the overarching ideas of white imaginations. Integrated musicals had no room for specialty effluvia, or the relative freedom they allowed minority performers.

Thus, the sense of reverence that pervades the emergence of the blockbuster Broadway musical adaptation begins to limit the ability of characters and artists to express themselves freely. The enormous expense and the extended running times of these projects similarly weighs on them. Many modern-day audiences have a hard time understanding why *Oklahoma!* is so important: basically it is just about a farm girl figuring out which boy she will let take her to the social. The original stage production was a small intimate thing—but mid-1950s Hollywood demanded something blown up into mammoth scale. Encased and enshrined almost as museum pieces, audiences were in effect invited to "pay homage" rather than "simply be entertained." (Intriguingly, a visual motif of being "fenced off" occurs in all the cyclone fencing and fire escapes in *West Side Story* and in the numerous iron fences, doorways, and cages in *My Fair Lady*.)

Doing so seemed to succeed at the box office, nonetheless. Although *Carousel* and *Gypsy* did not do the business expected, most of the others appeared to do quite well with both audiences and critics. *The King and I* and *The Music Man* would be nominated for Best Picture, and *My Fair Lady* would win that award. *West Side Story* would sweep the Oscars for 1961, winning a total of ten, including Best Picture. Yet, a number of consumers were turning away from these films and the music contained within them. The African American community was singing, playing, and dancing to a completely other type of music, and American youth of all races, colors, and creeds were beginning to join them. The film version of *Oklahoma!* was released in 1955; that same year, "Rock Around the Clock" became the number one song in the nation.

Notes

1 Many of these stars and directors were further encouraged to set themselves up as independent corporations in order to evade new federal income tax laws.

2 MGM Survey for *South Pacific* by Arthur Gameral (to Sid Rogell, January 2, 1957) (*South Pacific* FX-P files, UCLA) 1st Box. In this memo, 20th Century-Fox was researching MGM's contract arrangements with Rodgers and Hammerstein on *Oklahoma!* in preparation for making similar arrangements for the film adaptation of *South Pacific* (1958).

3 See Stephen M. Silverman, *Dancing on the Ceiling: Stanley Donen and His Movies* (New York: Alfred A. Knopf, 1996), 228–230, on MGM selling *Funny Face* package to Paramount.

4 Tim J. Anderson, *Making Easy Listening: Material Culture and Postwar American Recording* (Minneapolis: University of Minnesota Press, 2006), 3–47, gives an excellent history of these strikes. See 19–20 on the major studios and the AFM.

5 Hutton describes her despair in an interview with Robert Osborne for the Turner Classic Movies program *Private Screenings* (2000).

6 See Sean Griffin, "Judy Garland and Mickey Rooney: Babes and Beyond," *What Dreams Were Made Of: Movie Stars of the 1940s* (New Brunswick: Rutgers University Press, 2011), specifically 138–141.

7 Filmed programming did exist—and would increase as the 1950s rolled onward. Somewhat expectantly, most filmed shows were done in Los Angeles.

8 In 1954, in addition to NBC, CBS, and ABC, Dumont existed as a major network, and it too carried the show. Such shared programming had occurred the year before when CBS and NBC jointly broadcast a celebration of Ford's fiftieth anniversary, with a memorable fifteen minutes of Ethel Merman and Mary Martin partnering a medley of the history of American popular song.

9 The production also starred Eva Marie Saint, fresh from her Oscar-winning performance in *On the Waterfront* (1954), and a still relatively unknown Paul Newman.

10 "Ratings," *Broadcast-Telecasting* (May 6, 1957), 51.

11 Winthrop Jordan, *The Americans* (Boston: McDougal Littell, 1996), 798.

12 1951 seems to have been the last year to see a steady stream of black-and-white musicals released by the major studios such as Paramount's *Here Comes the Groom* with Bing Crosby; MGM's *The Strip* with Mickey Rooney and Louis Armstrong; and the Warner Bros. biopic *I'll See You in My Dreams* with Doris Day. From 1952 onward, the number is minuscule—Universal's *Meet Danny Wilson* (1952) and *The Benny Goodman Story* (1956); Warner Bros.' *The Helen Morgan Story* (1957); and MGM's *This Could Be the Night* (1957). (This does not count the various musicals made or released by the major studios featuring the new music of rock and roll—a topic to be discussed in Chapter 8.)

13 The posters advertising the film used the tagline "J.R. in 3D—Need we say more?," accompanied by an image of Russell in an extremely low-cut outfit, elbows back, knees bent, head up, and bosom prominent.

14 Mark Kerins, *Beyond Dolby (Stereo): Cinema in the Digital Sound Age* (Bloomington: Indiana University Press, 2011), 20–28, describes the development of multi-channel sound (including a discussion of *Fantasia*) as foundation for his larger focus on contemporary digital sound systems.

15 See Russell and David Sanjek, *Pennies from Heaven: The American Popular Music Business in the Twentieth Century* (New York: Da Capo, 1996), 358–363, on the recording industry's transition to stereo. Also Anderson, 105–178.

16 See, for example, the opening moments of Doris Day singing "Shakin' the Blues Away" in *Love Me or Leave Me* (1955) or either "The Black Bottom" or "Birth of the Blues" in *The Best Things in Life Are Free* (1956).

17 The song also equates the reaching out to new technology with the growing desire to impress audiences with a musical's "high art" status. Another section of the number opines that it is no longer enough "to see a dancer at his ease"—now

a movie has to have "glorious Russian ballet or modern ballet or English ballet or Chinese ballet or Hindu ballet or Bali ballet or *any* ballet!"

18 "All Time Domestic Champs," *Variety* (January 6, 1960), 34.

19 Both stand in contrast to *A Star Is Born* (1954), a big budget musical with an intermission which was released a year before—but not an adaptation of a Broadway success. Warner Bros. quickly grew nervous over the film's box-office prospects, pulled the film, and almost a half hour was cut out of it. See Ronald Haver, *A Star Is Born: The Making of the 1954 Movie and Its 1983 Restoration* (New York: Alfred A. Knopf, 1988).

20 Henry Ephron, *We Thought We Could Do Anything: The Life of Screenwriters Phoebe and Henry Ephron* (New York: Norton, 1977), 162–165.

21 Leonard Bernstein, *The Joy of Music* (New York: Simon and Schuster, 1959), 174. For a comparable assessment, see also Lehman Engel, *The American Musical Theater: A Consideration* (New York: Macmillan, 1967).

22 Technically, the key non-white characters are Tonkinese (i.e., Vietnamese).

23 The two eliminated songs are "Lonely Room" (which was sung by Jud, the villain of the piece) and "It's a Scandal! It's an Outrage!" (sung by Ali Hakim, which was performed in front of the stage curtain so that the sets could be changed—an issue that the film did not have to worry about).

24 *Carmen Jones* predates the release of *Oklahoma!* by a year, but is an adaptation of a Broadway show with lyrics by Oscar Hammerstein, so I am including it as part of this cycle of films.

25 Her versions of "Wouldn't It Be Loverly" and "Show Me" are contained in the extra features on the DVD release of the film.

26 Although Hepburn does get to dance during the Embassy Ball, it is not presented as a specific musical number, and "The Rain in Spain" is downright embarrassing in its overly rehearsed impromptu.

27 See Sean Griffin, "The Gang's All Here: Generic vs. Racial Integration in the 1940s Musical," *Cinema Journal* 42:1 (Fall 2002).

28 See Sean Griffin, "Bloody Mary is the Girl I Love: U.S. White Liberalism vs. Pacific Islander Subjectivity in *South Pacific*," *The Sound of Musicals*, ed. Steven Cohan (London: BFI/Palgrave, 2010).

29 Unlike Dandridge and Poitier, Sammy Davis Jr does perform with his own voice as the character Sportin' Life. Intriguingly, Davis does not appear on the soundtrack album. Because he already had a recording contract with Decca, his voice could not be used in the soundtrack album produced by Columbia. Cab Calloway was hired as a substitute.

30 See Donald Bogle, *Dorothy Dandridge* (New York: Amistad Press, 1997), 412–423.

8

In a Minor Key: The B Musical and Beyond

On March 5, 1955, the MGM film *The Blackboard Jungle* premiered. The picture was a "social problem" film rather than a musical, but the opening credits featured a song by Bill Haley and the Comets called "Rock Around the Clock." The film strongly equates the new, loud, and aggressive rhythm of the song with juvenile delinquency, thus encouraging theatregoers to be shocked and appalled at such music.[1] All reports, though, indicate that most teenagers in the audience reacted in a completely opposite manner, with some dancing in the aisles while the song played.[2] Although the song had been recorded many months before, the release of *The Blackboard Jungle* revitalized it, and "Rock Around the Clock" became the top-selling single of 1955. A year later, almost to the day (March 21, 1956), *Rock Around the Clock* was released to theatres— this time a musical *celebrating* this new type of music called "rock and roll." Importantly, although Columbia acted as the distributor, *Rock Around the Clock* was not actually made by one of the major studios. It was produced at a relatively unknown company called Clover Productions that had begun operations only a year earlier. Perhaps almost as important are the economic statistics for both films. *The Blackboard Jungle* cost estimatedly $1.16 million to make, and took in a little over $5 million at the box office in the United States.[3] *Rock Around the Clock* brought in less in domestic receipts—$1.2 million, but it only cost approximately $300,000.[4]

To fully comprehend how the musical genre dealt with the arrival of rock means stepping beyond what was being done within the big Hollywood studios. Even though the major film companies aimed at dominating the industry, they were not the only ones making movies in the United States. Within Hollywood, there existed a whole substratum referred to as "Poverty Row" studios, turning out low-budget films commonly referred to as "B movies." Also, around the country there were a variety of motion pictures aimed exclusively at ethnic or racial minority audiences. In all of these examples, musical performances occurred regularly. This chapter focuses on these often overlooked musicals, examining how they functioned within the overall motion picture industry. The reliance on marginalized groups and their tastes in music would lead these

Free and Easy? A Defining History of the American Film Musical Genre, First Edition. Sean Griffin.
© 2018 Sean Griffin. Published 2018 by John Wiley & Sons Ltd.

shoestring-budget filmmakers into the production of rock and roll films. Going where the major studios feared to tread would have enormous impact on the entire film musical genre.

Don't Fence Me In: B Musicals of the 1930s and 1940s

B filmmaking was a specific business development within the American film industry, and came the closest (at least in intent) to creating the equivalent of factory mass production. B films were intentionally low-budget features with quick shooting schedules and short running times meant to maximize the use of facilities and talent (rather than paying to let both stand idle). B films also guaranteed a steady (if unspectacular) stream of income to the studios—as long as they kept within a certain budget, the flat rental fees charged to theatres would ensure a very predictable level of profit. Although Rick Jewell argues that some form of B film production was in place during the silent era, B film-making became more institutionalized during the early 1930s.[5] Theatres, scrambling for ways to entice Depression-era customers, began advertising double-features: two movies (plus short subjects) for the price of one ticket. B films became the "bottom half" of these programs. The demand for B films to fill double-feature bills led to a number of companies forming specifically to churn out nothing but low-budget "programmers." Many such companies opened and folded quickly, but two lasted for decades: Republic and Monogram.

The major Hollywood studios often used their own B films either to test out and groom new talent (both in front of and behind the camera), or to phase out contract artists who had fallen in popularity. B films, though, by the nature of their budget constraints, could not hire big stars. Therefore, B films often relied on the popularity of certain genres in order to attract audiences: horror films, gangster films, detective mysteries, and musicals. Initially, musicals might seem antithetical to the tenets of B filmmaking. Previous chapters have described the centrality of the star performer, as well as the wealth of extra talent required (musicians, songwriters, choreographers, backup singers and dancers), and the emphasis on spectacle. B musicals negotiated these expectations in a number of ways. Firstly, there was a wealth of second-tier performers to be grabbed from vaudeville, burlesque, or nightclub shows, and a number of lesser-known big bands. Secondly, these artists used already-established routines, which required no extra help from a choreographer or chorus line. Lastly, the production design of these films was kept minimal—with musical numbers often taking place simply in front of a stage curtain.

Such creative choices meant that B musicals relied heavily (almost exclusively) on the backstager format. The formula was popular and easy to duplicate, and made it simple to insert musical performances as part of the show being produced. Two wartime B musicals from Columbia serve as typical examples: *Reveille with Beverly* (1943) and *Jam Session* (1944). Both feature Ann Miller, before MGM signed her and started putting her into A musicals. In each, her character attempts to make it in show business. The first shows her success as a disc jockey playing records for the boys at the nearby army camp. In the second, she gets a job as a screenwriter's assistant on a film called "Jam Session." Each scenario provides ample opportunity to pause the narrative and showcase various performers: in the first, the Mills Brothers, Ella Mae Morse, and various big bands; in the second, the orchestras of Charlie Barnet, Alvino Rey, and Louis Armstrong (among others). At the end of each, Miller finally gets her big break, with a modest production number finale to showcase her tap-dancing skills.

Having limited time schedules and often lesser imaginations at work, B movies often simply copy what worked in A productions. Of course, all the studios copied each other's successes, but the lack of budget (as well as the talent that could be gathered with a low budget) inevitably makes efforts to do B versions of A-formula musicals look exactly like the shabby knock-offs they are. Vera Hruba Ralston's ice-skating musicals at Republic provide a good case in point. Republic's owner Herbert J. Yates attempted to fashion her as competition for Fox's skating star Sonja Henie (an effort no doubt enhanced when he married her). Unfortunately, spectacular ice ballets require imagination and high production value—something that Republic just could not accomplish. Ralston herself is capable enough on ice, but projects very little of Henie's on-camera charisma. Further down the chain was ice skater Belita at Monogram, who was given even less budget to work with than Ralston.[6]

While B films as a concept were consciously designed to be little more than fodder, many film historians champion B filmmaking as a vestige of independence and rebellion. Studio executives cared little about the content, as long as the films came in on (or under) budget and had some marketable hook for advertising purposes. Thus, screenwriters, directors, or other artists, "liberated from such burdens as having to recoup a large investment" could take advantage of less supervision and "experiment with inventive new ideas."[7] In particular, enthusiasts have championed how B versions of film *noir* are often bleaker and more cynical than A *noir*—and that the small budgets make such films grittier and moodier (using lots of shadows to hide the lack of actual set design).

B musicals have not received the same level of plaudits as B *noir*. Yet, they too offered opportunities for greater freedom of expression. The slapdash, breakneck shooting schedules of B musicals often create a chaotic carnivalesque atmosphere. Such a production setup, plus the lack of carefully crafted integrated numbers, gives performers in B musical backstagers more creative authority. It is in these moments when B musicals can transcend their imposed limitations and become thrilling—watching jitterbugging dancers explode with an energy not seen in typical A musicals; seeing specialty acts in a more "raw," unpolished manner. Furthermore, using artists who could be paid less than the major A-list stars meant including a number of performers of color—as in *Reveille with Beverly* and *Jam Session*.

The most interesting B musicals are those that go their own way rather than providing pale imitations of A musicals. B studios reaped the benefits of developing their own types of low-budget musicals, particularly when they aimed at marginalized communities overlooked by the major studios.[8] Republic, for example, consciously marketed to moviegoers in small towns and rural areas by creating musicals emphasizing what the recording industry referred to as "hillbilly" music.[9] From the 1920s through the 1940s, the bulk of "hillbilly" music was recorded on minor independent labels, and most radio programs devoted to this form of music were broadcast from local stations.[10] One can see Republic's focus just by looking at the names of a number of their musicals: *Western Jamboree* (1938), *Village Barn Dance* (1940), *Grand Ole Opry* (1940), *Barnyard Follies* (1940), *Country Fair* (1941), and *Hoosier Holiday* (1943).

Republic found greater success making a star out of hillbilly comedienne Judy Canova and her backwoods yodeling than it did with Vera Hruba Ralston. She regularly played "rubes" who manage through energy and plain-spokenness to impress and triumph over big city folk. In *Sis Hopkins* (1941), when a number of high society women attend a recital of "authentic American folk songs," Canova's "plain folks" version of "Wait for the Wagon" interrupts and overwhelms the well-dressed baritone. Later in the film, in the song "That Ain't Hay," Canova proclaims "Hooray hooray hooray for the little guy! He's what this country is living by—he's more of a hero than you and I sing about!" Canova's avowed lack of class also upended traditional notions of accepted feminine behavior. In *Sleepy Lagoon* (1943), for example, Canova plays the mayor of a small town (who clearly dominates her boyfriend, played by tenor Dennis Day), and brings a bunch of racketeers to justice by rallying the other women in the town into battle!

Republic found its greatest success with its "singing cowboys": Gene Autry (who began working at Republic in 1934) and Roy Rogers (hired in 1938) (Figure 8.1). Autry's movies of the 1930s in particular spoke to a rural America dealing with the Depression and the huge dust storms that ravaged the countryside.[11] Inevitably, Autry meets simple folk who are in danger of losing their homes, or have had their life savings erased. Reflecting how real-life farmers were losing their homes and land to bankers, lawyers, and businessmen, big-city slickers are often the villains in these films, cheating honest, hardworking people. Autry brings the culprits to justice in the end, though, usually after a high-speed chase and fisticuffs. This plot structure worked so well and so consistently that when Rogers started making films for Republic in the late 1930s, his pictures followed the same outline. His first starring role in *Under Western Skies* (1938) has Rogers elected to Congress in order to fight for those made destitute by the Dust Bowl. He also sings the Oscar-nominated song "Dust."

Figure 8.1 Gene Autry, Republic's top star of the 1930s, singing "Moon of Manana" in *South of the Border* (1939). Autry's popularity spurred a slew of other "singing cowboys," even at some of the major Hollywood studios. Snapshot taken from: South of the Border (1939).

While addressing serious concerns facing rural America, the singing cowboy movies always had plenty of lowbrow comedy as well, usually via the cowboy's sidekick, such as Smiley Burnette (for many of Autry's films) and George "Gabby" Hayes (for many of Rogers'). The heroes vanquished the city folk through physical and legal force; the sidekicks did so by undermining and making fun of upper-class propriety. While Edward Buscombe describes how Herbert J. Yates actively encouraged Republic's singing cowboys to cultivate a clean-living and morally upright image, their comic counterparts were given more leeway to engage in transgressive outrageousness.[12] It was not beyond Burnette's characters to engage in female impersonation or get into blackface, for example. Even Burnette's singing broke convention. He was often called "Frog" in his films with Autry because he had a surprising habit of switching into and out of a growly, raspy "frog voice" in the middle of a song.

In catering to a unique audience with a different style of music, Republic's "singing cowboys" eventually rivaled the popularity of stars from the majors. In 1940, Autry came in fourth in the movie exhibitor's annual top-ten list, and stayed in the list until he began military duty in late 1942. Roy Rogers would make it onto this top-ten list in 1945 and 1946. Most Poverty Row studios, and even a number of majors, invested in their own singing cowboys as a result. Monogram starred Tex Ritter in a number of films, and then Jimmy Wakely.

Producers Releasing Corporation (PRC) hired a fellow named Eddie Dean. Warner Bros. cast Dick Foran in a number of singing cowboy B movies in the late 1930s. In 1937, Universal hired Bob Baker (after passing on Roy Rogers!) to compete with Autry. RKO's B westerns starred non-singing Tim Holt, but with troubadour Ray Whitley as his companion. Even some A musicals acknowledged the popularity of the singing cowboy. Fox's *Stand Up and Cheer* (1934) includes a big production number called "Broadway's Gone Hillbilly." Bing Crosby croons "I'm an Old Cowhand" in Paramount's *Rhythm on the Range* (1936). Republic would occasionally loan Roy Rogers out to major studios, which gave him the chance to sing "Don't Fence Me In" in Warner Bros.' *Hollywood Canteen* (1944).

While Republic aimed at "the sticks," Monogram specialized in product appealing to low-income urban neighborhoods. Although Monogram tried its hand at singing cowboy films, it was more committed to gangster and mystery films, as well as a number of horror films. Because Monogram's budgets were even more threadbare than Republic's, they did not invest in musicals as often. Yet, after finding success with a series of films featuring the comic antics of the East Side Kids (beginning in 1940), the studio began to focus on modern American youth. In the early 1940s, the studio produced a string of college-situated musicals, such as *Let's Go Collegiate* (1941) and *Campus Rhythm* (1943). Directly after the war, Monogram created the "Teen Agers Series," beginning with *Junior Prom* (1946).

Definitely, Monogram was not alone in this area. America's top box-office star from 1939 to 1941 was MGM's Mickey Rooney, and one can see these B musicals as imitations of Arthur Freed's backstagers with Rooney and Judy Garland. In fact, June Preisser, who appeared in the Rooney–Garland films, was also in the "Teen Agers" films. Yet, these films do not feel much like the MGM pictures. Unlike the wholesome characters Metro had Rooney and Garland play, Monogram's youth are scrappier and more likely to be figuring out a way to outfox their professors or parents. MGM aimed its Rooney–Garland pictures at a general audience, whereas these Monogram musicals seem to be for teenagers themselves—particularly in championing "their" musical tastes for a more wild, frenetic type of swing and jazz.[13] Calling the latter series "The Teen Agers" (separating the term into two words) indicates that the concept of teenagers as an identity category was still forming in American culture. During World War II, a generation of kids roamed relatively free and unsupervised because Dad was overseas and Mom was in the factory. Monogram seemed to sense the potential in aiming at them at a time when the concept of target marketing was not widely used.

Intriguing evidence of how these films draw battle lines between young adults and their elders occurs in *Let's Go Collegiate*. As in a number of B films, this youth musical contains its share of racist humor. Mantan Moreland appears in this and a number of other Monogram films playing variations on the shiftless, low-intellect Negro stereotype. Chinese American actor Keye Luke is also in the cast, as one of the members of the fraternity. The film seems to encourage viewers to laugh at the "politically incorrect" jokes said by Luke's white frat brothers (i.e., the lead characters), but such humor is regarded as off-limits for adults. When a blustering alumnus asks "What tong do you belong to?," Luke's character stares evenly at the fellow and then walks away without dignifying a response—suddenly *now* racial insensitivity is insulting.

Just as other studios latched onto Republic's success with singing cowboys, others began to notice Monogram's momentum in exploiting youth culture. In the late 1940s, Columbia lured away the man who produced the "East End Kids" and the "Teen Agers" to make B films for them: Sam Katzman. One of his first pictures with Columbia was prescient. Granted, the title of *I Surrender, Dear* (1948) is from a song written in 1931 and popularized by Bing Crosby. The film, though, delves into teenagers' growing fascination with radio disc jockeys and the consternation this causes their parents. Although the film features big bands and vocal ballads typical to most 1940s musicals, white teenagers in real life were beginning to seek out radio DJs showcasing a different kind of music, a style that *Billboard* would christen "rhythm and blues" in 1949. Around the same time, the music industry shifted from the term "hillbilly music" to "country-and-western." Music that had been marginalized was gaining greater presence, and B musicals were where to go to find it.

Don't Let Them Turn Our Love Song Turn Into a Blues: Marginalized Communities and Film Industries

Other filmmakers made pictures with even smaller budgets than Republic and Monogram used, and aimed these movies at even less well-served audiences. These motion pictures never expected or even aimed for mainstream success. Rather, they were produced specifically for a select group of potential customers. These marginalized groups often strengthened their sense of a communal bond through a shared musical heritage. Thus, music in these various alternative forms of filmmaking reached out to those communities and reinforced those cultural connections.

Perhaps the most extreme examples of filmmaking "in the shadows" were the various stag films and burlesque shorts produced across the United States during the first half of the twentieth century. A number of these films were silent, and distributed through underground channels for individuals to purchase and run in the privacy of their own homes. Yet, shorts with sound were also made, capturing the acts of various striptease artists—complete with music and (let us say) a diverse range of choreographic movement. These striptease shorts are typically just the "number," but some often include the briefest of backstager narratives. By the 1950s, a few feature-length films such as *Striporama* (1953) and *Varietease* (1954) were being distributed. These films made explicit the sexuality that Hollywood musicals (and "legitimate" Broadway shows) had to sublimate (particularly for studios during the Production Code era). In presenting women bumping-and-grinding through various forms of undress, these movies simultaneously exploit the female body *and* express rebellion against and liberation from societal restraint. Such films had their place in heterosexual male ritual gatherings (at bachelor parties or lodge meetings), thus helping forge bonds between men. Film historian Eric Schaefer points out, though, that some of these films (like *Varietease*) push the carnivalesque nature of musical performance past heterosexual male comfort levels when certain ecdysiasts are revealed to be men in drag.[14]

Other forms of filmmaking were more "above board" yet similarly beyond the view of mainstream moviegoers. A number of motion pictures were made in the United States for various emigrant populations in languages other than English, for example. A musical called *Ljubav I Strast* (*Love and Passion*) (1932), the first sound film in Serbo-Croatian, was created in New York. *Arshin Mal Alan* (*The Peddler Lover*) (1937), a "Persian operetta" sung and spoken in Armenian, was also shot in New York. At least two musicals in Ukrainian were shot in New Jersey: *The Girl from Poltavka* (1936) and *Marusia* (1938).[15]

Even more notable were the number of films made in Yiddish.[16] Yiddish cinema was a transnational phenomenon, happening not only in the United States, but also in such countries as Poland, the Soviet Union, and Austria. Such films reaffirmed Jewish cultural identity in the face of increased global anti-Semitism. Yiddish cinema in the United States was also made as "entertainment to the lonely and homesick immigrants."[17] A certain number of theatres in the Jewish neighborhood of New York City would show these films, but outside of that area, Yiddish cinema in the United States could only find room at local Jewish community spaces.

Various historians agree that some form of silent Yiddish cinema existed, but the transition to sound created a more specific Yiddish film culture. Like the examples of Ukranian, Armenian, and Serbo-Croatian-language cinema made in the United States, Yiddish films regularly included music. An entire genre called the "cantorial" focused on the importance of religious music within the community. Cantor Moishe Oysher starred in some of the best regarded US Yiddish films, including *Dem Khazans Zundl* (*The Cantor's Son*) (1937), *Der Lebediker Yusem* (*The Singing Blacksmith*) (1938), and *Der Vilner Balebesl* (*Overture to Glory*) (1940). Many films also adapted plays from Yiddish theatre, a form of entertainment dating to the 1870s which regularly used music and dance. Many of the performers, songwriters, and musicians who started in Yiddish theatre subsequently appeared in Yiddish cinema. Actress Molly Picon excelled at musical comedy, and went to Poland to star in that country's most popular Yiddish film, *Yidl mitn Fidl* (*Yiddle with a Fiddle*) (1936). In the film, she disguises herself as a man in a roving European musical troupe. Leo Fuchs, who starred in the short American film *Ich Vil Zeyn a Boarder* (*I Want to Be a Boarder*) (1937) and the musical feature *Amerikaner Shadkhn* (*American Matchmaker*) (1940), was often regarded as the "Yiddish Fred Astaire" because he was a dancer with a cosmopolitan demeanor, but also as the "Yiddish Ray Bolger" because his dancing style was often comically eccentric.

More prolific than Yiddish-language film production was the industry making "race movies" about and for African Americans. These low-budget films, with African Americans as the lead characters rather than bit players or specialty acts, were shown almost exclusively in theatres in black neighborhoods. During the silent era, many of these movies were also produced, written, and directed by African Americans, giving them opportunities behind the camera not available in Hollywood. In many ways, then, these pictures created a space for African Americans to speak for themselves, and *to* themselves, about their lives and concerns. With the coming of sound, race movies showcased black contributions to American music no matter the genre—including westerns presenting Herb Jeffries as an African American singing cowboy.[18] Not having the budgets to do pre-recording of numbers, the musical performances in race movies retain a sense of immediacy and intensity not typical in mainstream musicals.

Whichever the minoritized group, these parallel cinemas regularly use music as an attempt to hold their diasporic populations together. Yiddish-language cinema maintained a romanticized version of the "old country" for emigrants to America. Race movies helped African Americans deal with the transition from rural life to modern industrial life that occurred during the Great Migration, when many moved from southern states to northern urban areas in search of (supposed) greater opportunity and less oppression. These films celebrate tradition and family, and look critically upon modernity and the encroachments of assimilation (somewhat ironically using a modern form of industrialized entertainment to do so). Music often factors into such negotiations.[19]

Unlike *The Jazz Singer* (1927), in which Al Jolson's character somehow manages to honor his Jewish heritage *and* to become a big star on Broadway, Yiddish cinema consistently saw nothing but suffering and tragedy resulting from any attempt to break away from the old ways. In both *The Cantor's Son* and *Overture to Glory*, Moishe Oysher plays cantors who must learn the value of staying true to their roots rather than chasing after fame and fortune. Film historian J. Hoberman refers to *The Cantor's Son* as "the anti-Jazz Singer" with the main character deciding to go back to his shtetl and marry a village girl. *Overture to Glory* ends with the cantor returning to his community to sing "Kol Nidre"—then collapsing dead from his wanton ways.

Eli Eli (1940) is another example of how music was typically employed. The title refers to the Biblical phrase "My God, My God, Why hast Thou forsaken me?," and was also the name of a popular Yiddish song about a mother lamenting the behavior of her children. The film stars Esther Field, who gained some fame singing on radio as "The Yiddishe Mama." In the film, she and her husband, living on a farm in upstate New York, learn their home is about to be taken back by the bank. Their adult son and daughter refuse to contribute money to save the farm, and instead decide that Mama should live with the son in New York, and Papa should live with the daughter in Philadelphia. After being forcibly separated from each other, both endure the indignity of being ignored and/or castigated by their children and their spouses for being too old and set in their ways. After further indignities, fortune finally steps in via an old friend dying and giving his farm to the two of them in his will. All is magically restored at the end, and they are visited at the farm by their repentant offspring.

There are four musical sequences in the picture. The first happens as Mama and Papa say their tearful goodbye to each other. The second is Field's heart-wringing rendition of the title song. The third is an upbeat number for the comic relief: two relatives from the old country who are also having a hard time adjusting, but find camaraderie (and romance) with each other. The final number concludes the film, as Mama celebrates the return of her family around a bountiful harvest at their new home. Importantly, after Mama sings a chorus, the rest of the family join in—the first (and only) time her children and their spouses sing. Song is used to support the traditional ways, and is not associated with modern living.

Such nostalgia for the rural life and its sense of community is common in race movies as well. Although most take place in the big cities, urban life is pictured as fraught with temptation and danger, and the upstanding characters often have maintained their connection to the church and the "old ways." This attitude is overt in *The Blood of Jesus* (1941), one of the most successful race movies ever made. In a rural community, a church-going woman is accidentally shot by her wastrel husband. In the afterlife, she is lured by Satan to the unscrupulous existence of urban life (sex, alcohol, and eventually more violence), but eventually escapes his clutches by running back to the country (with the help of the Lord). The film leaves viewers to decide whether all of this was a dream, or if she has miraculously come back to life—with her husband repenting his own ways in the process. Unlike *Eli Eli*, this picture *does* connect music to both the rural and the urban—a gospel choir seems to be singing constantly in the backwoods community, while her urban experience centers around various honky tonks. Nonetheless, the film plainly sides with the rural gospel music over jazz—and the success of the picture with African American audiences indicates its message strongly connected with people.

Immigrants from Mexico felt similar senses of displacement and nostalgia. The Mexican film industry's development of the *comedia ranchera* genre presented a nostalgic rural culture (complete with music and dance), "but tellingly placed it in contemporary Mexico."[20] *Alla en el Rancho Grande* (*Over on the Big Ranch*, 1936) is often cited as the start of this film genre, and did major business in the United States, which led to a renewed (albeit short-lived) interest in producing Spanish-language films in the States. Tito Guizar, the lead performer in *Alla en el Rancho Grande*, for example, starred in *Papa Soltero* (1938), an American-produced film about a Mexican migrant to Los Angeles who finds success as a singer and nightclub owner—but by hanging onto and valorizing his ranchero heritage.[21]

As part of the overall romanticized notion of rural life, *Papa Soltero* shows its characters breaking into song outside of an on-stage performance. *Papa Soltero* was not unique in this respect: so do *The Blood of Jesus* and various Yiddish and other non-English films made in the States. B movies made in Hollywood (whether at major studios or by Poverty Row companies) are often disparaged for their overreliance on the backstager formula to justify the musical performances easily. In contrast, the songs in a number of these movies for racial/ethnic minorities arise naturally out of the situation, and are intentionally positioned as something shared by the group. Desirée Garcia argues that these films presage and influence the development of such integrated folk musicals as *Oklahoma!* and *Meet Me in St. Louis*.[22]

Yet, while Yiddish language films and race movies employ musical performance regularly, they do not always conform to the structure developed within the typical Hollywood studio musical. A film may only have a couple of musical sequences. There may be no musical performances at all for the first two-thirds of the film. The first song in *Eli Eli*, for example, is not sung until about twenty minutes into the film, and the next song does not happen until about a half hour after the first. Most historians of race movies do not discuss *The Blood of Jesus* as a musical, even though sung music threads through the entire film. Rather than conforming to the dominant definition and structure of the musical genre, these films (and the communities they served) used music in their own ways, with their own traditions and expectations.[23]

Nonetheless, these film cultures were not completely separate from the Hollywood film industry—or from each other. Although produced by an independent company, *Papa Soltero* was distributed by Paramount. Child performer Jerry Rosenberg, who appeared in the Yiddish film *Der Lebediker Yusem (The Living Orphan)* (1937), would change his professional name to Jerry Ross and write the scores for *The Pajama Game* (1957) and *Damn Yankees* (1958). Composer Nicholas Brodzsky would move from Yiddish films to an MGM contract, writing songs for Mario Lanza as well as "Hi-Lili Hi-Lo" for *Lili* (1953). Editor Jack Kemp worked on both Yiddish films and on race movies; key Yiddish film producer (and director) Joseph Seiden also directed the race movie *Paradise in Harlem* (1939). Edgar G. Ulmer stands as the most notable, having directed Yiddish films, race movies, and working in Hollywood on major projects (the Universal horror film *The Black Cat* [1934] and the United Artists musical *Carnegie Hall* [1947]) and on B films (including his most famous film, the *noir* masterpiece *Detour* [1945]). Garcia's contention that the emphasis on community and music in these marginalized cinemas influenced the rise of the integrated folk musical on Broadway and in Hollywood is potentially supported by the number of artists that made the move from the margins to the major studios and the Great White Way.

Some historians (and perhaps some audiences) regard such cross-influence as a threat to the "purity" of independent filmmaking. For example, when most black film companies were unable to finance conversion to sound production and folded, white entrepreneurs stepped into what they saw as a potentially lucrative market. As long as budgets were kept small, a potential profit could be made exploiting the desires of the African American moviegoer. Many critics have pointed out that race movies during the sound era tend to fall back on white stereotypes of African American culture. The sound era also sees an increase in "escapist" genres rather than "serious" dramas tackling social issues important to the African American community.[24]

Yet, many genre theorists have argued that films providing "only entertainment" still have social and ideological import—and often are more effective because they are less coercive than overt dramatic narratives.[25] One can find discussion of social uplift and other matters vital to the African American community within certain race movie musicals. An apt example would be *Swing!* (1938), written and directed by Oscar Micheaux, considered by historians as one of the most important makers of race movies—and one of the very few to move from silent films to sound. In order to finance the shift, Micheaux entered into an arrangement with white theatrical manager Frank Schiffman and Leo Brecher. Thus, according to historian Mark A. Reid, the Micheaux Film Corporation was "controlled by two whites."[26] Nonetheless, *Swing!* still exhibits Micheaux's penchant for juggling multiple narratives and for including significant ellipses in time. The film also typically presents an upstanding hardworking individual who has migrated to the northern cities as its protagonist—in this case, Mandy (Cora Green) who has moved from Birmingham to New York City. In contrast to other Micheaux protagonists trying to make better lives for themselves as teachers, doctors, or lawyers, Mandy and other characters in *Swing!* strive for success on the stage—and the film gives opportunity for a number of black performers to shine. Granted, one moment does feel more exploitative than expected in a Micheaux film: one woman dances an energetic burlesque routine and has to adjust her falling bra strap. Yet, the film also overtly acknowledges issues concerning white financing of black entertainment. A white producer agrees to bankroll the show the characters are trying to put on—but he will take it to Broadway only if the show is called "Ah Lub's Dat Man."

In contrast to *Swing!* is *The Duke Is Tops* (1938), another race musical largely financed and overseen by white producers. This backstager follows an African American theatrical producer who sacrifices his relationship with a promising singer (Lena Horne), thinking she will go farther without him.

Figure 8.2 Lena Horne performs in the "race movie" short *Boogie Woogie Dream*, which was filmed in 1941 but released in 1944 after she had become a star at MGM. Snapshot taken from: Boogie Woogie Dream 1944.

Neither do well apart from each other, and only reuniting brings them success and happiness. The film gives audiences better production values than *Swing!* but less social awareness. For example, the film uses stereotypes of a lazy, shady con man and his dim-witted customers for comic relief. The film also expresses doubts about chances for social advancement. This is most apparent when Lena Horne's character is judged as not talented enough for mainstream (i.e., white) audiences, with her new white producers exclaiming "That girl's a specialty—not a star!" (On the contrary: when Horne became a star at MGM in 1943, the film was re-issued under the title *The Bronze Venus*, as was an earlier short featuring her *Boogie-Woogie Dream* [1941] [Figure 8.2].) Horne's ballad in *The Duke Is Tops* is "Don't Let Them Turn Our Love Song into a Blues." Yet, arguably, in exploiting what had been a cinema by, for, and about African Americans, the producers of *The Duke Is Tops* and other race movies like it *were* attempting to accomplish that sort of transformation.

Race movies and Yiddish-language films existed because of the absence of minority figures as protagonists in Hollywood films, but they also worked to shore up the traditions and attitudes of their respective subcultures. Both race movies and Yiddish-language films died out in the years after World War II in large part due to increasing assimilation. A new generation of Jewish Americans felt less tied to Yiddish and the importance of the farm; a younger generation of African Americans who had been born and raised in big cities had little nostalgia for rural life.[27] Hollywood also started developing its first African American stars, such as Sidney Poitier and Dorothy Dandridge. Yet, in at least one development, certain marginalized groups were not feeling forced to assimilate into dominant white culture. Rather, the dominant white culture (including the major Hollywood studios) found itself being pressured to do the assimilating. Rock and roll was about to raise a serious challenge to mainstream American culture and the American musical, and small record labels and small film companies would lead the way.

Don't Knock the Rock: Exploitation Musicals in the 1950s

The development of rock and roll brought together a number of the population segments discussed in this chapter. With a more intense driving rhythm than jazz or swing and pared-down orchestrations that emphasized hard-strummed guitars (plus bass and perhaps saxophone), rock and roll combined elements of "race music" and "hillbilly songs" into something loud, vibrant, and raw. Although the music industry in the 1920s and 1930s framed "race music" and "hillbilly music" as two separate styles, they both shared heritage from blues and from gospel music.[28] Rock and roll subverted this divide, reuniting musicians and listeners. *Time* magazine, disdaining this new trend, described rock as based on "Negro blues" but with "a moronic lyric in hillbilly idiom."[29] Along with black rock artists, a number of rockabilly bands rose to prominence.

Both rhythm-and-blues and country-and-western records had been largely regarded as marginal to mainstream tastes. Most of the major labels did not pursue these types of music (except for perhaps one or two major stars), and ASCAP (the American Society of Composers and Producers) also showed little interest in acquiring licensing rights for the songs written in these styles. Such attitudes largely continued within the top record companies and at ASCAP as rock and roll began. Performed almost exclusively by new and unknown artists, their only outlets were a number of small and regional record labels. Thus, rock and roll might have been just another marginalized form of music. What brought rock into mainstream consciousness was another sector of the population mentioned earlier: teenagers.

The postwar period has often been called the "Baby Boom" era, as the birth rate in the United States exploded. Many of the white middle-class kids growing up in the postwar years considered suburban life to be stifling in its conformity— and thus they increasingly refused to follow the patterns laid out by their parents. Adult concern about juvenile delinquency and a "generation gap" began to circulate. Rock and roll music was rough-edged and rebellious. It also originated outside the white suburban enclaves. Teenagers ate it up—and parents forbidding their kids to listen to rock only made it more enticing.

Various developments in the music industry helped white teenagers gain access to rock music. BMI (Broadcast Music Inc.), a rival to ASCAP, was formed in 1939 and grew in importance in the ensuing decade by reaching out to a variety of forms of music ASCAP refused to consider. "The work of many country and black musicians to whom ASCAP had refused admission regardless of prior publication ... provided a fertile field for BMI exploitation."[30] Thus, while ASCAP seemed unwelcoming to rock and roll music, BMI offered an alternative resource. New disc formats also aided in the dissemination of rock and roll. As mentioned in Chapter 6, the debut of the LP (long-playing record) by Columbia Records was perfect for releasing original cast or soundtrack albums of musicals.[31] In response to the LP, RCA unveiled the 45 rpm record— which was capable of holding one song per side. The 45 format was not a good match for musical scores, but it was perfect for new rock and roll artists who might not have an LP's worth of material. Furthermore, 45s cost less to produce—so bands or vocalists just starting out could more easily afford to record a 45 than an LP (and a number of small labels which focused on producing 45s rather than LPs proliferated).[32] Also, 45s were priced lower than LPs—and therefore teenagers could more easily afford them.[33] Thus, teenagers quickly got exposed to rock and roll (while their parents were more likely to purchase LPs of musicals). Lastly, as networks such as CBS and NBC abandoned radio for television, radio stations were strapped for programming—and began to rely more and more on "disc jockeys" playing records. These DJs increasingly relied on 45s rather than LPs (again, due to cost)—and a number of them began broadcasting rock and roll on a regular basis.

Rock and roll's initial audience base—rural white audiences, African American urban audiences, and teenagers of all colors and geographical points—were the same consumers catered to by B studios and other marginalized film companies. Thus, it is perhaps unsurprising that almost all of the first musicals to include rock music came from outside the major Hollywood studios. Although the Paramount Decision described in Chapter 7 ended B filmmaking within the major Hollywood studios, low-budget filmmaking still existed beyond the confines of the big studios. Taking the reins from earlier B studios such as Republic and Monogram, postwar "exploitation" filmmakers continued to recognize the potential in serving under-addressed audiences, using new research concepts in target marketing.[34] By keeping budgets low and aiming films at a particular group, filmmakers could reap substantial profits. In particular, exploitation films recognized the growth of teenagers as a burgeoning consumer group. They also noticed a new venue for reaching teenagers in the 1950s: drive-ins. Initially promoted after World War II as a place where the entire suburban family could enjoy an evening's entertainment, drive-ins quickly gained a reputation as "passion-pits" for teenagers and college students eager to escape home and the supervision of their parents.

Among the first to capitalize on teenage audiences was producer Sam Katzman, "the task master of the 'fad-pic'" (as *Variety* called exploitation films) and an independent producer by the 1950s.[35] After producing arguably the first rock musical film, the aforementioned *Rock Around the Clock*, Katzman followed up with *Don't Knock the Rock* (1957) and *Jukebox Rhythm* (1959). Another studio founded precisely on making films for teenagers at drive-ins was AIP (American International Pictures). Co-founder Samuel Z. Arkoff aimed at teenagers by making movies that presented "pure escapism, a never-never land without parents, without adults, without authorities."[36] AIP produced more than 130 low-budget feature films from its start-up in 1945 to 1967, grossing around $250 million.[37] In the late 1950s, a number of AIP pictures emphasized rock and roll, including *Rock All Night* (1957), *Carnival Rock* (1957), and *Daddy-O* (1959). They were not alone. In short order, a plethora of low-budget films swept the country, cashing in on the rock phenomenon. The titles might not have been imaginative, but there was no denying what they were about: *Rock Rock Rock* (1956), *Shake, Rattle and Rock* (1956), *Rockin' the Blues* (1956), *Rockabilly Baby* (1957), *Disc Jockey Jamboree* (1957), *Mr. Rock and Roll* (1957), *Go, Johnny, Go!* (1958), *Let's Rock* (1958), and *The Big Beat* (1958).

Katzman, AIP, and others turned to rock and roll because it perfectly fit into the patterns that exploitation producers with limited budgets relied on to draw in potential customers. One method was promoting a unique but inexpensive gimmick not available in other movies. Rock and roll performers were not high-priced talent. Most had cut records for small regional labels, and many had just gotten started in show business. Exploitation filmmakers could hire them at low cost, but feature them prominently in advertising as something that audiences would not see in major studio films (more on this in a moment). With performers going for cheap, producers often scooped up a number of them for a motion picture—thus, promising customers an abundance of talent. Exploitation rock musicals thus inherited a tendency from their B musical forebears: relying on the backstager as a formula to shoehorn in various artists. Such aggregation of rock and roll acts also mirrored the growth of live theatrical "rock and roll shows" put on around the country, as well as the use of rock performers as guests on television variety shows.

Another common exploitation strategy was promising more violence or sex than could be found in mainstream movies (the key word being "promising"—but usually not fully delivering). The term "rock and roll" itself was a euphemism for sex, and the hard driving beat seemed to indicate aggressive passion rather than polite romance. Dancing to rock and roll involved the entire body shaking, thrusting, and grinding with abandon in a manner that left little to the imagination. Exploitation rock musicals took full advantage of this, displaying women gyrating to the rhythm in a manner not too dissimilar from burlesque films. (Realize that independent film companies had not signed onto the Production Code.) *Don't Knock the Rock* (1957), for example, shows a line of chorus girls rehearsing to Bill Haley and the Comets performing "Hot Dog Buddy Buddy." The women are in leotards and high heels, and the camera eagerly closes in on their behinds bumping to and fro with the beat. Voluptuous Mamie Van Doren graced a number of exploitation rock musicals, sometimes even performing a few songs—such as her bump-and-grind to "Baby" in *Sex Kittens Go to College* (1960).

As evidenced by MGM's use of "Rock Around the Clock" in their social problem exposé *The Blackboard Jungle*, rock was also associated with gangs and juvenile delinquency. Exploitation films also often included motorcyclists, rebellious youth, and some sort of threat of violence or lawlessness in their plots. Rock and roll's raw energy often spilled off the screen, out of the speakers, and into the aisles. There were continual reports of teenage moviegoers at these movies refusing to sit still. Rather, they regularly shouted with excitement over their favorite performers, and often got up out of their seats and started dancing. Alarmed theatre managers often attempted to restrain them physically or eject them from the movie house, and at times enlisted the local police for assistance.

Such cultural battles between teenagers and adults over rock and roll became an increasingly explosive issue—thus falling in line with a third strategy for exploitation filmmakers. Having short production schedules, exploitation films could take advantage of a hot button issue in the forefront of people's minds, and get a film about the topic out to theatres before the major studios. Attempts to censor rock and roll spread across the country. In certain areas, rock and roll records were banned from radio airwaves. Angry letters poured in to television stations showing rock and roll performers (leading Ed Sullivan's CBS show to carefully keep the camera above Elvis Presley's hips when he appeared). In various places, actual record burnings were held. Calling in the police because teenagers were "rioting" in the aisles of movie theatres showing rock musicals further fanned the flames (and provided quite a lot of free publicity). What may have started as simple enjoyment of the music did at times become more violent in response to the exaggerated response by the establishment. Newspapers reports circulated of customers tearing out theatre seats and slashing cushions in retaliation for not being allowed to dance during screenings of rock musicals.[38]

While parents claimed that rock was immoral because of its raw sexuality, and because it was associated with "violent elements," an underlying source of discomfort was that it brought white middle-class youth into contact with African Americans. Although rock and roll had its "hillbilly" elements, black performers were certainly prominent: Chuck Berry, Little Richard, Fats Domino. Parents who had relocated to the suburbs at least in part to get away from the racial minorities in urban areas (a practice termed "white flight") were no doubt alarmed to see their children being thrown into untold frenzies of excitement from watching black rock artists. At its most extreme, "Asa E. Carter, self-appointed leader of the White Citizens Councils of Alabama, charged rock music was a plot inspired by the National Association for the Advancement of Colored People."[39]

White teens were usually the main characters but, just as in the 1930s and 1940s, the backstager format created a structure for performers of color to

Figure 8.3 Chuck Berry doesn't need elaborate production design to mesmerize an audience as he performs "You Can't Catch Me" in *Rock Rock Rock* (1956). Snapshot taken from: Rock Rock Rock (1957).

perform ... and to dominate. The entire point of these low-budget films was to showcase these musicians. Posters for these films list the "guest stars" prominently, and audiences poured into the theatres not to watch whatever threadbare (and often badly acted) plotline had been concocted but to get to the performances. For example, the story for *Rock Rock Rock* is practically nonexistent (a young girl wants a new dress to go to a rock and roll party), but when Chuck Berry shows up to perform "You Can't Catch Me," the film catches fire (Figure 8.3). Alone against a completely barren cyclorama, Berry commands the screen with his singing, guitar playing, and unique dance moves. White teenage audiences had likely never seen anything like it before. Furthermore, unlike integrated musicals in the same period that dealt with race (*South Pacific* [1958] or *West Side Story* [1961], for example), these films showed people of color performing their *own* music rather than music written by white songwriters.

Suburban parents were not alone in their alarm and outrage. The music establishment found the growing popularity of rock and roll aggravating as well. Echoing a common disparagement that rock and roll was asinine and more noise than music, a number of noted musical theatre composers complained that rock and roll was destroying American popular music. Lyricist Otto Harbach (then president of Song Writers Protective Association) protested radio DJs playing so much rock and roll, asking "Would 'Smoke Gets in Your Eyes' be allowed by broadcasters to be heard instead of 'Be-Bop-A-Lula?' Could 'Indian Love Call' penetrate the airways which are flooded with 'Hound Dog?'"[40] Similarly, Oscar Hammerstein "objected that 'unworthy' music was crowding his material off the airwaves."[41] In support of this assertion that rock was a step backward in music, many claimed that rock and roll could not fit into the format of integrated musicals—it was too simplistic and too primitive for the sophisticated and artistic aims of integration. Although exploitation rock musicals employed the backstager formula simply because it was easier than trying to create an integrated musical, critics used this to argue that rock music and integration were fundamentally unable to mix. Therefore, following this train of thought, the critical elite largely excluded rock and roll films from the musical genre.[42]

The major film companies were largely focusing on integrated musicals by the late 1950s. Also, unlike independent or exploitation filmmakers, the majors still aimed their films at a general audience, and rock music seemed to divide audiences rather than unite them. Thus, while low-budget exploitation rock musicals abounded, the Hollywood studios held back. At times, when they stuck their proverbial toes in the water, the results were misguided. Writing for MGM, Cole Porter tried a couple of times to work rock and roll into songs, but inevitably came up short. In *High Society* (1956), Bing Crosby sings Porter's "Now You Has Jazz" with Louis Armstrong—and in one line refers to rock and roll as just a new form of jazz. This tune was followed up by a new song for the film version of *Silk Stockings* (1957), in which Fred Astaire introduces "The Ritz Roll and Rock." While Porter gets the basics (the meter and chord patterns) correct, associating rock and roll with upper-class white adults (even in jest) still displays a disconnect as to how this new type of music worked.

"The Ritz Roll and Rock" exemplifies how rock and roll resisted a time-tested pattern of smoothing out a new type of music for mainstream (i.e., white, middle-class adult) sensibilities. Not that the recording industry did not try. Major record companies routinely would take a hit tune recorded by an African American performer on a small label, and hire a white singer to do a cover version that smoothed out the edges (and often cleaned up the lyrics). One of the major cover artists was Pat Boone. Perhaps unsurprisingly, 20th Century-Fox put Boone under contract, and promoted him as the wholesome youth alternative to what parents considered caterwauling. Boone's first contribution to a motion picture was singing the theme song to *Friendly Persuasion* (1956), a film about Quakers during the Civil War. His first onscreen role was in Fox's musical *Bernadine* (1956). Boone claimed that he consciously modeled his performance on Bing Crosby's relaxed demeanor. The picture is so careful to make him unthreatening that he is given no romantic interest at all. His next film, *April Love* (1957), has him playing a supposedly rebellious teen, but Boone himself took such precautions about his image that he refused to perform an onscreen kiss with his co-star Shirley Jones.

Certain exploitation films also tried to mitigate the furor over rock music. Commotion during the screening of rock musicals made for good publicity, but a growing trend of banning these films from playing in certain cities was a threat to their profits. Thus, a recurring storyline in early rock musicals has parents or other adult authorities learning to accept rock and roll as energetic but ultimately wholesome fun. *Don't Knock the Rock* is about intergenerational struggles over rock in a small town—the adults banning concerts, and some teenagers thinking about breaking the law in response. The tensions are quelled when the teens put on a skit for their parents, pointing out how the music their elders listened to and danced to when *they* were young—jazz and the Charleston!—was decried by *their* parents. A similar tactic happens in *Shake, Rattle and Rock*: when a DJ is brought to trial for supposedly inciting a riot by playing rock at a stage benefit, the jury is shown a film of teenagers in the 1920s doing the Black Bottom—with one of the local blue noses as a young man dancing madly in said footage. In *Mr. Rock and Roll*, DJ Alan Freed (playing himself) defends rock and roll against a blistering editorial by a magazine editor by rallying rock fans to contribute to the editor's favorite charity. The outpouring of donations softens the editor's opinion.

Some exploitation filmmakers also agreed with the mainstream music industry's predictions (and hopes!) that rock and roll would burn fast and die quickly.[43] Thus, a number of films in 1957 jumped on what might have been the "next big thing": calypso music. Low-budget movies like *Calypso Heat Wave* (1957), *Bop Girl Goes Calypso* (1957), and *Calypso Joe* (1958) were released, and various other movies included calypso numbers, such as Mamie van Doren's "Go, Go Calypso" in *Untamed Youth* (1957) and "My Calypso Baby" in *Rockabilly Baby* (1957). Calypso was "exotic" but less raucous than rock and roll. (The social protest aspect of calypso in its home country of Jamaica was largely eliminated in the transition to the US market.) Calypso was mild enough for even Pat Boone to try it out, singing a tune called "Technique" in *Bernadine*.

Although calypso made singer Harry Belafonte an international star, it ultimately did not eclipse rock and roll. Rock was more resilient than initially imagined, and its fans resisted efforts to smooth it out and make it acceptable. Consumers increasingly by-passed the white cover versions of rock tunes in favor of the originals by African American artists. Rock and roll reached out on record and in film to white artists and audiences, but it *expanded* its community rather than *replaced* African American performers with white ones. The rebellious nature of rock and roll was also not easily eliminated. While *Untamed Youth* samples the possibilities of calypso, this tale about a youth correctional facility also includes white teenage rock idol Eddie Cochran singing a rhythm-and-blues tune *a capella* in defiance of working in the prison fields: "No, you ain't gonna make a cotton picker out of me."

If rock and its adherents refused to be co-opted, then the next strategy by establishment critics was to claim that a corrupt cohort within the music industry was manipulating and brainwashing the youth of America to buy rock music. Such accusations asserted that no one could actually *like* this music—it had to be a plot! ASCAP used this argument to fight against the growing strength of its rival BMI, saying that rock n' roll was "foisted upon adolescents by the broadcasters who 'profited' from BMI."[44] In order to support this viewpoint, Vance Packard, author of the best-selling *Hidden Persuaders* (1957) (which claimed that advertisers were putting subtle mind-control elements into their campaigns to sway consumers), was brought in as a consultant. Packard "made headlines by accusing BMI and broadcasters of foisting rock music on 'passive' teenagers."[45]

Accusations were made that organized crime was infiltrating the music industry, forcing rock music into jukeboxes and bribing DJs into playing rock and roll on the radio (such payments were referred to as "payola"). One can see the effect of such accusations in early rock musicals. Musical backstagers prior to the rock era often focused on unknowns trying desperately to get the notice of theatre producers or agents, who are incredibly hard to see but generally honorable, well-respected businessmen. With the arrival of rock and roll, agents and managers are now shown as corrupt figures who regularly manipulate and exploit young talent—finding someone who can "fit the suit," forcing them to work endlessly, and to sing what they are told to sing.[46] Such machinations are present right from the start in Katzman's *Rock Around the Clock*. In that film, an unscrupulous talent agent concocts a variety of plans to either blackball or manipulate rock performers trying to break into show business. Similarly, the machinations of a talent agent in *Disc Jockey Jamboree* break up a boy–girl singing team, and threaten each of their potential solo careers. *Sing, Boy, Sing* (1958), based on a teleplay, *The Singin' Idol* (1957), ratchets up the melodrama as a ruthless manager controls a country boy's singing career, even trying to keep the young man from learning his grandfather is on his deathbed. Even though *Go, Johnny, Go!* presents DJ Alan Freed (playing himself) favorably, the film nonetheless shows Freed consciously seeking out a young talent that he will wedge into a pre-formed image named "Johnny Melody."

Such storylines seemed to appeal to the mindsets of both disapproving adults and enthusiastic teenagers. For adults, this type of narrative reinforced their notion that rock and roll was a huge swindle being foisted onto impressionable young minds by disreputable people. For teenagers, these plots seemed to represent the struggle against such oppression and (ironically) exploitation from authority figures trying to control the music, its performers, and its fans. The connection to both sides of the debate made this type of plot something that the major Hollywood studios felt they could use to negotiate their way into producing rock musicals. The view of the music business as corrupt and unethical is a common thread in the musical films the big studios made starring rock idol Elvis Presley.

While some people at this time seemed to consider Presley the anti-Christ, Hollywood executives could not ignore his phenomenal popularity, or the

Figure 8.4 Elvis Presley gets the MGM treatment: a production number surrounds him as he sings the title number in *Jailhouse Rock* (1957). Snapshot taken from: Jailhouse Rock (1957).

huge audience that tuned in to watch him perform on *The Ed Sullivan Show*. Presley made major films in the late 1950s at Fox, Paramount, and MGM. The first, *Love Me Tender* (1956), is a western with a few song opportunities for Presley in what is basically a supporting part. The next three were star vehicles, and each told of the dirty tricks and shady maneuvers associated with his characters' attempts to become a professional singer. Since Presley himself actually had a strong-willed, hands-on manager, Colonel Tom Parker, these pictures turn towards villains other than corrupt agents and managers. In *Loving You* (1956), a campaign manager for a politician sweet talks a naive Presley into singing at election rallies in order to lure voters. In *King Creole* (1958), a New Orleans crime boss threatens Presley and his loved ones if the young man refuses to sing exclusively at the mobster's nightclub. *Jailhouse Rock* (1957), arguably Presley's best film, makes *him* the conniver, using and discarding a number of people in his ruthless climb to stardom (Figure 8.4).

Each of these films associates Presley with the threat of violence as well— how he stands to start singing is not far removed from how he crouches in preparation to sock someone. Yet, by the end of the films, all has been set right. Justice comes to the gangsters in *King Creole*. The campaign manager in *Loving You* repents her callous treatment of the young singer. Presley's ne'er-do-well in *Jailhouse Rock* comes to realize how much he owes the people he has used, when a number of them come to his side after he injures his voice. Accompanying such transformations are studio-mandated tender love ballads meant to widen Presley's appeal—and to show that his characters eventually learn to sing "good" music. *Love Me Tender* and *Loving You* are the titles of the films *and* the romantic tunes. *Jailhouse Rock* ends not with the famous title tune, but with Elvis softly crooning "Young and Beautiful"—ostensibly testing out his injured singing voice, but also implicitly apologizing to the woman he has been treating like dirt throughout the movie. Presley's final song in *King Creole*, "As Long as I Have You," is as much a song of love to his father in the audience as it is to his girl. While recognizing the appeal of Presley's rebel image, the studios nevertheless felt compelled to iron out some of the rough edges. As the first major white rock star, he already served a certain function in making rock music more mainstream.

None of Presley's pictures holds claim as the most full-out, no-holds-barred celebration of rock and roll by a major studio. That honor goes to Fox's *The Girl Can't Help It* (1956). In it, director Frank Tashlin depicts an America that is itself energetic, loud, brash, and vulgar—and thus, rock and roll reflects the national identity! Towards that end, the picture is the first rock musical shot in full Technicolor and CinemaScope.[47] The narrative fully accepts the unsavory elements of the music industry: a gangster hires a washed-up talent agent (Tom Ewell) to turn his voluptuous but tone-deaf female protégé (Jayne Mansfield) into a singing star. The resulting inane novelty record (with the woman's singing two high-pitched screeches) spurs an underworld battle over the jukebox racket—until the gangster stumbles into becoming a teen idol himself (with his hit record, "Rockin' Round the Rockpile"). Scattered in between the cartoonish storyline are a plethora of the hottest names in rock music at the time, including major black artists Fats Domino, the Platters, and Little Richard. Richard sings the title song over the opening credits, drowning out Tom Ewell's introductory speech and indicating what is more important here. Richard's performances of "The Girl Can't Help It," "She's Got It," and "Ready Teddy" are unapologetic in their sexual intensity, and emphasize the flagrant display of Mansfield's awe-inspiring chassis. Rather than trying to rein in rock and roll, *The Girl Can't Help It* lets it run gloriously and hilariously rampant, indicating what the big studios could do if they really tried to engage with rock music.

But the major companies did not follow up on this indication. As the 1950s came to a close, there were some signals that rock and roll was fading. After making *King Creole*, Elvis was inducted into the Army. Although graft had been part of all areas of the music industry, Congressional investigations focused largely on those using payola to promote rock music. As a result, a number of DJs who championed rock and roll (including Alan Freed) saw their careers ruined. The large studios maintained their focus on prestigious integrated musicals, leaving rock and roll to the little guys. B studios and other marginalized filmmaking had laid out a foundation for small film companies to take advantage of the majors' reticence. The 1960s would see independent filmmaking—and rock—become stronger and more important. The cultural battles that began in the 1950s would become more strident, and the musical genre would be caught in the crosshairs.

Notes

1 A radio spot described in a letter from Scott Meredith to Evan Hunter (the writer of the original book *The Blackboard Jungle*) from March, 16, 1955, featured the song while an announcer intoned that the "violent" music fit the "explosive screenplay." Quoted in Adam Golub, "They Turned a School Into a Jungle! How *The Blackboard Jungle* Redefined the Education Crisis in Postwar America," *Film & History* (Spring 2009), 39:1, 25.

2 Dick Hebdige, "Posing ... Threats, Striking ... Poses: Youth, Surveillance, and Display," in *The Subcultures Reader*, ed. Ken Gelder and Sarah Thornton (London: Routledge, 1997), 401.

3 Budget for *The Blackboard Jungle* from Turner Classic Movies Database, citing then-MGM vice-president Dore Schary (http://www.tcm.com/tcmdb/title/1206/Blackboard-Jungle/notes.html). Box-office figure for *The Blackboard Jungle* from "The Top Box-Office Hits of 1955," *Variety Weekly*, January 25, 1956.

4 Budget and box-office figures for *Rock Around the Clock* come from R. Serge Denisoff and William D. Romanowski, *Risky Business: Rock in Film* (New Brunswick: Transaction Publishers, 1991), 42.

5 Richard B. Jewell, *The Golden Age of Cinema: Hollywood 1929–1945*, (Malden: Blackwell Publishing, 2007), 70.

6 For an overview of the various female figure-skating stars in Hollywood history, see Jane Feuer, "Nancy and Tony and Sonja: The Figure of the Figure Skater in American Entertainment," *Women on Ice: Feminist Essays on the Tonya Harding/Nancy Kerrigan Spectacle*, ed. Cynthia Baughman (New York: Routledge, 1995), 3–21. Another example would be Republic echoing the practice of MGM and Paramount in creating a string of semi-annual musical showcases. MGM had its *Broadway Melody of 1936* (1935), *of 1938* (1937), and *of 1940* (1940). Paramount did its *Big Broadcast of 1936* (1936), *of 1937* (1937), and *of 1938* (1938). Republic made *The Hit Parade* (1937), then *Hit Parade of 1941* (1940), *of 1943* (1943), and *of 1947* (1947).

7 Manny Farber, "Blame the Audience," *Commonweal* (December 19, 1952), reprinted in *Kings of the Bs: Working within the Hollywood System*, ed. Todd McCarthy and Charles Flynn (New York: E.P. Dutton and Co., 1975), 45.

8 While hoping to get bookings in movie houses all across the United States, B studios knew their best chances were with theatres not owned by the major companies in the era of vertical integration. The big studios concentrated their holdings in the upscale downtown areas of major cities, leaving independent exhibitors to own cinemas in other parts of the country.

9 Archie Green, "Hillbilly Music: Source and Symbol," *The Journal of American Folklore* 78 (1965), describes the industry category of "hillbilly music" "as a rubric covering a kaleidoscope variety of sub forms: old time, familiar tunes, Dixie, mountain, sacred, gospel, country, cowboy, western, country-western, hill and range, western swing, Nashville, rockabilly, bluegrass" (205).

10 See Ryan Carlson Bernard, *The Rise and Fall of the Hillbilly Music Genre: A History, 1922–1939*, unpublished MA thesis (East Tennessee State University, 2006); and Russell and David Sanjek, *Pennies from Heaven: The American Popular Music Business in the Twentieth Century* (New York: Da Capo, 1996), 64–65.

11 See Peter Stanfield, *Horse Opera: The Strange History of the 1930s Singing Cowboy* (Urbana: University of Illinois Press, 2002).

12 Edward Buscombe, "Gene Autry and Roy Rogers: The Light of Western Stars," in *What Dreams Were Made Of: Movie Stars of the 1940s*, ed. Sean Griffin (New Brunswick: Rutgers University Press, 2011), 45.

13 Perhaps the best evidence that these B musicals were intended specifically for the youth market occurs not in a Monogram film but in Republic's *Youth on Parade* (1942). When the college kids in the film complain that sitting in classes seems pointless when others their age are enlisting, a professor chastises them—and looks directly at the camera when he intones that staying in school is vital for helping beat the enemy. In the middle of an otherwise innocuous musical comedy, this speech is *deadly* serious and is obviously intended to reach the younger moviegoer directly.

14 Eric Schafer, *"Bold! Daring! Shocking! True!" A History of Exploitation Films, 1919–1959* (Durham: Duke University Press, 1999), 303–324.

15 J. Hoberman, *Bridge of Light: Yiddish Film between Two Worlds*, 2nd ed. (Hanover: Dartmouth College Press, 2010), 182, 246–247.

16 Yiddish is "the vernacular of the Ashkenazin (German Jewish community), and like English, a fusion tongue. An amalgam of High Middle German, Hebrew, Aramaic, and various Slavic languages … that evolved during the Middle Ages." Hoberman, 11 (n.1).

17 Judith N. Goldberg, *Laughter through Tears: The Yiddish Cinema* (Rutherford: Fairleigh Dickinson University Press, 1983), 24.

18 Jeffries starred in *Harlem on the Prairie* (1937), *Two-Gun Man from Harlem* (1938), *The Bronze Buckaroo* (1939), and *Harlem Rides the Range* (1939). Jeffries' actual racial identity has been the source of speculation over the years (see, for example, "Herb Jeffries Lists Self 'White,' *Jet* [June 11, 1959], 48–49).

19 The centrality of issues tied to migration and modernism in the musical film is the focus of Desirée J. Garcia, *The Migration of Musical Film: From Ethnic Margins to American Mainstream* (New Brunswick: Rutgers University Press, 2014).

20 Carl J. Mora, *Mexican Cinema: Reflections of a Society, 1896–1980* (Berkeley: University of California Press, 1982), 47.

21 See Garcia, 72–98.

22 Garcia.

23 Richard Dyer makes a similar assertion using a much later film in his essay "Is *Car Wash* a Musical?," *In the Space of a Song: The Uses of Song in Film* (New York: Routledge, 2012), 145–155. Oddly, Robin R. Means Coleman,

Horror Noire: Blacks in American Horror Films from the 1890s to Present (New York: Routledge, 2011), 75–78, argues *The Blood of Jesus* is a horror film.

24 See for example, Anna Everett, *Returning the Gaze: A Geneology of Black Film Criticism, 1909–1949* (Durham: Duke University Press, 2001); Mark A. Reid, *Redefining Black Film* (Berkeley: University of California Press, 1993). Such assessments favoring "social issue" dramas over genre filmmaking were already occurring during the era in which these films were made. African American film critic Loren Miller, writing for the journal *The Crisis* ("Hollywood's New Negro Films," June 1934, 8–9), complained explicitly about the reliance in race films on "lavish café or cabaret scenes," and thus asserting that these pictures fail to discuss black issues honestly and adequately.

25 Richard Dyer, *Only Entertainment* (London: Routledge, 1992), famously discusses this, with particular emphasis on the musical. Paula J. Massood, *Black City Cinema: African American Urban Experiences in Film* (Philadelphia: Temple University Press, 2003), while not discussing musical race movies in particular, does make a similar argument about genre films.

26 Reid, 18.

27 Perhaps reflecting that shift, Herb Jeffries in his African American singing cowboy movies sings jazz, not traditional cowboy songs.

28 Peter Stanfield, *Horse Opera: The Strange History of the 1930s Singing Cowboy* (Urbana: University of Illinois Press, 2002), 46–76, emphasizes these connections.

29 "Yeh-Heh-Heh-Hey, Baby," *Time* (June 18, 1956), 54.

30 March Hugunin, "ASCAP, BMI and the Democratization of American Popular Music," *Popular Music and Society* 7:1 (1979), 12.

31 Denisoff and Romanowski, 2, assert that "the LP … was especially conducive to symphonic and operatic music. Jazz, unsuited to the confines of the 78, was showcased. Broadway musicals and 'mood music' were strong sellers. All of these genres were aimed at adults."

32 Rick Kennedy and Randy McNutt, *Little Labels—Big Sound: Small Record Companies and the Rise of American Music* (Indiana University Press, 1999).

33 Denisoff and Romanowski, 3, cite that "c. 1955, LPs listed at $3.98 and 45 singles were priced at $.89."

34 Republic shifted focus away from theatrical production and towards the lucrative possibilities of television programming (using the same low-budget, quick production schedule strategies to churn out weekly episodes). Monogram reformatted itself as a new independent production company, Allied Artists, which did still produce exploitative horror films, but also invested in more ambitious and costlier productions as well.

35 Denisoff and Romanowski, 22.

36 "Z as in Zzzz, or Zowie," *Newsweek* (May 5, 1967), 61.

37 Denisoff and Romanowski, 116.

38 Dave Rogers, *Rock 'n' Roll* (London: Routledge and Kegan Paul, 1982), 16, mentions reports tied to screenings of *Rock Around the Clock*, for example.

39 "White Council vs. Rock and Roll," *Newsweek* (April 23, 1956), 32.

40 Denisoff and Romanowski, 33.

41 Mildren Hall, "Songwriters Blast BMI Before Senate Hearing," *Billboard* (March 24, 1958), 2, 12.

42 For example, Clive Hirshchorn, *The Hollywood Musical*, rev. ed. (New York: Portland House, 1991), 447, contains an addendum outside of the official main text to list "Miscellaneous Pop Musicals," but the citation for this list is *Rock Around the Clock* (1956), thus indicating that "pop" refers to rock music. Ethan Mordden, *The Hollywood Musical* (New York: St. Martin's Press, 1981), expends only 8 pages out of 242 on rock music, 209–216, and Gerald Mast, *Can't Help Singin': The American Musical on Stage and Screen* (Woodstock: Overlook Press, 1987), is so loathe to discuss rock music that one has to scan the index under "Rock music and video" to find the few quick mentions he gives it.

43 Denisoff and Romanowski, 18: "CBS's Mitch Miller dismissed the popularity of blues-derived material as a 'fad.'"

44 Denisoff and Romanowski, 33.

45 "Delinquency R & R, Deejays Get Into Act," *Billboard* (March 17, 1958), 6, 9.

46 See Keir Keightley, "Manufacturing Authenticity: Imagining the Music Industry in Anglo-American Cinema, 1955–62," in *Movie Music: The Film Reader*, ed. Kay Dickinson (New York: Routledge), 165–180.

47 The film emphasizes this by having it start out in Academy ratio and black-and-white, until Tom Ewell demands changes to color and widescreen. This is not a B film!

9

The Sound of Money: Musicals in the 1960s

As the past three chapters have emphasized, the 1950s were a major transitional period for the musical genre. Chapter 6 described the last glorious moment of original integrated musicals produced under a Hollywood studio system being forced to end due to the Supreme Court's "Paramount Decision." Chapter 7 detailed further problems for the genre due to competition from television, and the rise of blockbuster adaptations of Broadway musicals. Chapter 8 told of the rise of rock and roll and the perceived problems in trying to adapt this new sound to what had become the established parameters of the musical genre. Across these previous chapters has been an acknowledgment of a gradual fracturing of audiences—away from motion pictures, away from musicals, and even away from older forms of popular music.

These various factors would continue to interact with each other in the 1960s. The clash between rock music and typical showtunes would escalate, mirroring a larger social struggle in the United States over a growing list of issues: civil rights, freedom of speech (and protest), Vietnam, drug use, women's liberation, homosexuality, nuclear armament, the environment. The splintering of American society that had begun in the 1950s exploded in the mid-1960s across multiple axes (across generations, across political opinion, across race, across gender). As such, musicals celebrating unified communities seemed increasingly absurd to many viewers. The musical genre became one of many cultural battlegrounds during the period, ultimately to calamitous effect as the decade came to a close.

W(h)ither? Rock and Film, 1960–1965

As the 1960s started, rock-and-roll music was entering a new phase. The payola scandals discussed at the close of Chapter 8 had ended the careers of certain key figures. Other events had effectively removed others. Chuck Berry was convicted of transporting women across state lines for immoral purposes. Jerry Lee Lewis's career suffered greatly from the scandal of marrying a "child bride."

Free and Easy? A Defining History of the American Film Musical Genre, First Edition. Sean Griffin.
© 2018 Sean Griffin. Published 2018 by John Wiley & Sons Ltd.

Buddy Holly, Ritchie Valens, and the Big Bopper were killed in a plane crash. Elvis had been drafted into the Army.

With these early players missing, many in the record industry moved to rein in rock's dangerous, rebellious image. The major labels concertedly shifted rock from its rough-hewn rhythm-and-blues and hillbilly origins to a smoother, "pop" sound. The early 1960s then are remembered largely for the rise of various teen idols and girl groups singing soft pop ballads about dream dates and going to the prom. Under such circumstances, African American record producer Barry Gordy consciously sought to polish any sense of raw vocalizing out of the black artists on his Motown label, in order to appeal and crossover to the largely white pop music market.

Motion pictures aided and abetted this evolution in the early 1960s. The dance craze known as the Twist serves as a good example of the dynamic. An early version of the song "The Twist" was considered too raunchy to cross-over to the white pop charts. A new, cleaner version by Chubby Checker did well with young white audiences, becoming number one on the charts in the summer of 1960. It was when the Twist grew popular with *adults* in 1961 that it became regarded as a cultural phenomenon—with Checker's single reaching number one again in 1962.[1] Filmmaker Sam Katzman pulled out the script from *Rock Around the Clock* to produce a virtual remake, *Twist Around the Clock* (1961)—and a follow-up, *Don't Knock the Twist* (1962)—but not until the Twist had become accepted by grown-ups.

Filmmakers also put a number of the new teen idols into easily digestible musicals as well. Following in the footsteps of boy-next-door vocalist Pat Boone, the major studios promoted Tommy Sands, Bobby Rydell (both of whom could sing), and Fabian (who could not). After being a voice double in some early rock musicals, Connie Francis played a part on screen in MGM's *Where the Boys Are* (1960), performing two tunes in this ode to spring break in Fort Lauderdale, including the title song over the credits. The success of the picture led MGM to attempt to fashion her as a new version of young Judy Garland's talented-but-gawky persona. At the studio, she would star in *Follow the Boys* (1963), *Looking for Love* (1964), and *Where the Boys Meet the Girls* (1965), which was a loose remake of the Garland–Rooney film *Girl Crazy* (1943).

While MGM may have fashioned Francis in the Garland mold, the clearest heirs to Garland and Rooney in the early 1960s were making a series of pop musicals at independent company AIP (American International Pictures): Frankie Avalon and Annette Funicello. Their cycle of films, starting with *Beach Party* (1963), tapped into the emerging popularity of "surf music" from artists such as the Beach Boys and guitarist Dick Dale (who made an appearance in *Beach Party* and its follow-up *Muscle Beach Party* [1964]). Avalon and Funicello went on to a quick succession of films together: *Bikini Beach* (1964), *Beach Blanket Bingo* (1965), and *How to Stuff a Wild Bikini* (1965) (Figure 9.1). In addition, the studio featured them separately with others: *Pajama Party* (1964)

Figure 9.1 Annette Funicello and Frankie Avalon enjoy an endless summer with their young, white pals in *Beach Blanket Bingo* (1965). Snapshot taken from: Beach Blanket Bingo (1965).

for her; *Ski Party* (1964) for him. Surf music had its experimental aspects, particularly in expanding the possible uses of electric guitar, as well as in the Beach Boys' interest in multi-track recordings and in carefully constructed long-playing albums. Yet, surf music's focus on white, middle-class youth fit well with the larger pop music patterns of the early 1960s—and the "beach party" films emphasized the mainstream more than the edge.

Prior to these films, Avalon became a national star through the efforts of Dick Clark and his TV dance party *American Bandstand*, a touchstone in making rock music acceptable to white parents. Funicello was one of Walt Disney's original Mouseketeers on TV's *Mickey Mouse Club*, and was loaned to AIP by Disney for this cycle. For all of the lascivious looks at bikini-clad women shaking it up on the seashore, and a large amount of grade-school-level innuendo, no one ever actually has sex in these movies. The virginity of Funicello's recurring character Dee Dee is never seriously threatened, and (per instructions from Disney) she never even shows her navel. All of these pictures showed white middle-class teenagers enjoying an endless summer primarily (although, as *Ski Party* indicates, not solely) at the beach, engaging in random hijinks.

Frankie and Annette and their pals do not seem to have parents, but at times they encounter a few surly but inept adults (such as Don Rickles, Jesse White, and Paul Lynde) who try to impose on the vacation. The kids are remarkably resilient in resisting outside forces, and not just adult characters bemoaning "Where are the mothers of America?" One of the narrative strands in *Muscle Beach Party* has Frankie successfully resisting the lure of an Italian movie star. In *Bikini Beach*, the girls ultimately decide to stick with surf music and forsake the new singing sensation the Potato Bug (Frankie Avalon in a dual role, doing a blatant send-up of The Beatles). The most recurring nemesis was buffoon

Eric Von Zipper (Harvey Lembeck) and his inept biker gang called the Ratz. The ineffectual menace of Von Zipper and his cronies underscored just how non-threatening Frankie and Annette were to the status quo.

The music is also simple, upbeat, and unthreatening—and some of the songs that Frankie and Annette perform are hard-pressed to be categorized as rock at all. Even though surfing originated in the cultures of the Pacific Islands, the beach party films are incredibly white—made more apparent in the few times when people of color are acknowledged, such as the highly problematic nature of Buster Keaton playing an American Indian, or the sudden cameo performance of Little Stevie Wonder at the end of both *Muscle Beach Party* and *Bikini Beach*.

The record sales for surf music and the success of AIP's beach party cycle inevitably led to a slew of imitations by other film companies: *Surf Party* (1964), *Ride the Wild Surf* (1964), *For Those Who Think Young* (1964), *A Swingin' Summer* (1965), *The Girls on the Beach* (1965), *Wild on the Beach* (1965), and *Get Yourself a College Girl* (1965). Some of these films were made by small independent companies, some were produced for major studios like MGM and Fox. Regardless, all of these were low-budget affairs put together relatively quickly with a number of guest star acts surrounding (rather than part of) the plotline. Bobby Vinton, Jackie Del Shannon, The Righteous Brothers, The Four Seasons, and Lesley Gore, among others, made appearances to fill out the running times.

Beach party musicals were such the rage that even Elvis Presley made one: *Girl Happy* (1965). Copying someone else indicates just how different Presley was on screen after his return from Army service. While his pre-Army pictures had him playing dark, brooding characters, the post-Army musicals present sweet, charming fellows with, at most, a slight ne'er-do-well nature. His military stint won him greater respect and acceptance from those who previously considered him a harbinger of the downfall of Western society. The films he made upon returning furthered that trajectory—starting most obviously by having him play a soldier in his first post-Army film, *G.I. Blues* (1961). Through the early 1960s, Elvis musicals are less about tussling with the law and more about traveling to various glamorous vacation spots: *Blue Hawaii* (1962), *Fun in Acapulco* (1963), *It Happened at the World's Fair* (1963), *Viva Las Vegas* (1964), and the aforementioned *Girl Happy* (1965). In such environments, Presley's characters engage in various romantic entanglements while making music with their pals. Other films of his during this period are more prosaic in setting, but still retain the light comedic courtship plotlines. The typical conflict is that Presley's characters need to stop loafing around and having fun and finally become responsible adult males—and settle down with one girl. The audience is hardly in doubt on the outcome, because Presley's characters seem somewhat domesticated from the outset. While Presley gets paired with a number of beautiful co-stars (Juliet Prowse, Ursula

Andress, Ann-Margret), he is also regularly surrounded by children (*Follow That Dream* [1962], *Girls! Girls! Girls!* [1962], *It Happened at the World's Fair*, *Fun in Acapulco*).

The music he performs furthers this sense of domestication, for it has hardly any of the confrontational qualities of the songs in his pre-Army vehicles. Granted, even the early pictures included at least one ballad, but post-Army Elvis songs at times verge on "cutesy," including sharing tunes with the tykes under his charge. *G.I. Blues* has him warbling the lullaby "Big Boots" to put a little feller to sleep, and singing "Wooden Heart" to a troupe of marionettes as if he is Leslie Caron in *Lili* (1953). Other tunes threaten to turn Elvis into a travesty of his former self: "Rock-a-Hula Baby" in *Blue Hawaii*, "No Room to Rhumba in a Sports Car" in *Fun in Acapulco*, and "Do the Clam" in *Girl Happy*. Although starring in more musicals than anyone else during the 1960s, it seems as if Presley is not putting in much effort from picture to picture (except possibly in *Viva Las Vegas*, when he exhibits incredible chemistry with—and finds strong screen competition from—Ann-Margret).

Initially, Elvis's new mainstreamed image seemed to be working. The films were popular with audiences, and the soundtrack albums were smash hits. (It may stun readers to learn that "Wooden Heart" was a number one single for six weeks in Great Britain.) Yet, the dual decision to smooth out Presley's music *and* to focus more on his film career began to diminish his importance. To make matters worse, as producers realized that die-hard Elvis fans would pay to see him in anything, the budgets for his pictures started shrinking. *Blue Hawaii* is still trying to be a major motion picture; films in the late 1960s (*Harum Scarum* [1965], *Frankie and Johnny* [1966], *Spinout* [1966], *Clambake* [1967], *Speedway* [1968]) are strictly drive-in fodder. By 1966, the number of beach-related teen musicals began petering out as well—partly through overexposure, but also, as Frankie Avalon's "Potato Bug" role indicates, tastes in music were changing. Rock fans wanted something more intense than peppy beach party jingles or lukewarm Elvis.

In contrast to light and mindless pop tunes, folk music with connections to social protest gained a following in the early 1960s. Film and television both attempted to tap into this trend—but did so by attempting to dampen down folk's more radical aspects. Sam Katzman produced *Hootenanny Hoot* (1964) for MGM, and ABC televised a variety series called *Hootenanny* (1963–1964). *The Young Swingers* (1963), a low-budget independent film distributed by 20th Century-Fox, starts with a nightclub crowd twisting the night away, but it is revealed that the club is a co-op with weekly hootenanny events. Ultimately all three examples watered down their versions of the folk scene. Granted, *The Young Swingers* includes African American vocalist Gene McDaniels as part of the group of young adults running the co-op rather than a cameo. On the other hand, when the Sherwood Singers perform the classic "Greenback Dollar," they sing "hmm" instead of "damn." The ABC series blacklisted folk legends Pete

Seeger and the Weavers for suspicion of Communist-leanings—which led other artists (such as Joan Baez) to boycott the program.[2]

British youth had taken to rock music tremendously—and early rock musicals often led to greater theatre violence in the United Kingdom than in the United States.[3] Cultural forces there also attempted to shift rock music into safer territory in the early 1960s. Cliff Richard became a British version of a teen idol, starring in a series of musicals very similar in feel to the movies of Frankie and Annette: *The Young Ones* (1961), *Summer Holiday* (1963), and *Wonderful Life* (1964). A brief interest in traditional Dixieland jazz also surfaced, which led to the making of a British exploitation musical, *It's Trad, Dad!* (1962), directed by American expatriate Richard Lester. The "trad fad" faded, though, overwhelmed by a veritable explosion of new British rock groups. These bands openly announced their desire to "go back to the original sources," drawing inspiration from the early rhythm-and-blues and rock-and-roll performers.

Leading the way were a quartet from Liverpool named The Beatles. Their high-energy, driving sound practically steamrolled across two continents in 1964, drowning out the dreamy pop sound of the early 1960s. With such enormous popularity, United Artists approached The Beatles to make a film. The result, *A Hard Day's Night* (1964), was not only a huge hit (and a major hit album)—it was also hailed as a great piece of cinema.[4] No rock musical had ever gotten such critical acclaim before. Andrew Sarris in *Village Voice* even claimed it to be "the *Citizen Kane* of juke box musicals."[5] Staid reviewers known for refusing to even mention Elvis Presley by name because they were so revolted by his "caterwauling" admitted how much they enjoyed *A Hard Day's Night* as entertainment and as cinema. The film was even nominated for Academy Awards—including one for Best Original Screenplay.

Although made with a somewhat modest budget of $560,000,[6] there was no sense that this was a B film. Director Richard Lester instead was hailed for using ideas and techniques that critics associated with the French New Wave. The youthful, experimental outlook of the New Wave and the vibrant, unruly nature of rock music blended perfectly. As The Beatles went through a comic-book version of a day in their hectic lives, Lester used direct address, jump cuts, zoom lenses, slow and fast motion, and everything else he could think of to keep the energy high and the audience surprised and delighted. The slim plotline shows the forces of the music industry trying to keep the boys contained and obedient. The foursome, though, continually and gleefully go their own way—most memorably when they escape the confines of the BBC TV studios and find an open field to run and leap around in like children. "Can't Buy Me Love" pours out on the soundtrack as a helicopter-borne camera swirls around the boys to capture the sense of liberation (Figure 9.2).

A Hard Day's Night clearly heralded something big and new for rock on film. The beach party movies have charm, and do possess their own carnivalesque

Figure 9.2 A camera hovers over The Beatles to capture their joy and liberation, while "Can't Buy Me Love" blares joyously on the soundtrack in *A Hard Day's Night* (1964). Snapshot taken from: A Hard Day's Night (1964).

potential (with random jokes, out-of-the-blue cameos from actors like Vincent Price or Peter Lorre, and the chaos caused by the fringe-flying gyrations of dancer Candy Johnson). Presley too *does* perform his due share of raucous numbers, such as "Return to Sender" in *Girls! Girls! Girls!* and the title song in *Viva Las Vegas*. Nonetheless, *A Hard Day's Night* potentially opened the door for rock to move beyond low-budget drive-in musicals churned out in quick succession, to go further than Frankie and Annette, to stretch more than what Elvis seemed willing to do. Neither rock musicians nor their fans could be contained for long, it seemed, no matter how hard some tried to keep them under control. Yet, the "old school" was not ready to give up quietly. In fact, they were about to throw a lot of money into a last ditch effort to salvage the traditions of Tin Pan Alley and the Hit Parade.

Hello, Folly! Blockbuster Musicals, 1965–1970

As discussed in Chapter 7, the major Hollywood studios during the late 1950s began cutting down the actual number of films they produced annually, but invested very large amounts of money on one or two blockbuster pictures as a way to pull audiences away from their TV sets and back into theatres. Such elephantisis was most noticed in a number of Biblical and Greco-Roman epics, but this mindset impacted a number of genres, including the musical.

This strategy did pay off for the studios on certain pictures, particularly *The Ten Commandments* (1956) for Paramount and *Ben-Hur* (1959) for MGM. Yet, such economic bonanzas could be wiped out quickly if the next mammoth production failed at the box office—and, in the early 1960s, a number of such fiascos occurred. MGM, for example, sunk most of the profits it made with *Ben-Hur* into a costly remake of *Mutiny on the Bounty* (1962) starring Marlon Brando, which was released to lackluster reviews and even less enthusiastic ticket sales. Even more notorious was the troubled production of *Cleopatra* (1963), which took years to complete, going through multiple directors, and much scandal over star Elizabeth Taylor's love life.[7] The budget on the film had overrun so much that there was virtually no way for 20th Century-Fox to recoup its investment, and by 1964 the studio had cut its workforce and production schedule down to the bone. Both MGM and Fox were on the verge of closing down.

There was one major production that Fox kept moving forward during this time: a lavish film version of *The Sound of Music*. With a large amount of on-location work in Austria, the film took almost a year to shoot. Yet, the bankability of Rodgers and Hammerstein's last collaboration seems to have helped bolster the studio's faith in the project. Furthermore, while a number of gargantuan pictures were proving to be bad gambles for Hollywood, big-budget musicals were doing relatively well. In particular, 1964 had been a big year for the genre in many ways. While *A Hard Day's Night* reawakened the possibilities of rock musicals (not to mention Elvis and Ann-Margret in *Viva Las Vegas* and the various beach musicals), a good number of splashy and successful studio musicals also were released. Debbie Reynolds starred in MGM's *The Unsinkable Molly Brown*; Frank Sinatra and his "Rat Pack" gallivanted around in *Robin and the 7 Hoods*; and the two top grossers of the year were Disney's *Mary Poppins* and the Oscar-winning adaptation of *My Fair Lady*. So, while the industry was beginning to shy away from Biblical epics, musicals still seemed viable.

No one, though, figured just how viable *The Sound of Music* would be. It was released in 1965 to only moderate reviews, but audiences took to it like nothing anyone had witnessed. Certain customers went to the movie dozens of times (sometimes more). It quickly became the most successful movie of the decade— and before the original release was finished (in 1969!), it had even surpassed *Gone With the Wind* (1939) to become the biggest box-office grosser in history to that time. Overnight, Fox went from a virtual ghost town to a re-energized hive of activity. Such a juggernaut was impossible to ignore, and soon all the major studios were putting large-scale musicals on their production schedule.

Fox, unsurprisingly, led the charge, planning one major musical annually: *Doctor Dolittle* (1967), *Star!* (1968), and *Hello, Dolly!* (1969). Warner Bros. followed Lerner and Loewe's *My Fair Lady* with Lerner and Loewe's *Camelot* (1967), as well as a version of the 1947 Broadway hit *Finian's Rainbow* (1967). Paramount took another Lerner property, *Paint Your Wagon* (1969). Columbia released the Oscar-winning *Oliver!* (1968) and *Funny Girl* (1968). Universal produced *Thoroughly Modern Millie* (1967) and *Sweet Charity* (1969). MGM made the first musical obviously influenced by the success of *The Sound of Music*, *The Singing Nun* (1966), but this was relatively small scale compared with these other titles. Intriguingly, in lieu of its legacy, MGM lagged behind the other studios, not investing in anything too grand until its musical version of *Goodbye, Mr. Chips* in 1969. The trend even pulled in some well-financed independent productions released through United Artists, such as *How to Succeed in Business Without Really Trying* (1967) and *Chitty Chitty Bang Bang* (1968).

With the studios relying so heavily on these musicals to keep them afloat, the trend towards grander importance continued. Hollywood *needed* these musicals to be considered great filmmaking—*The Sound of Music* and *Oliver!* both won Best Picture Oscars, and *Doctor Dolittle*, *Funny Girl*, and *Hello, Dolly!* all got nominated for Best Picture. Highly regarded directors, whether they had experience working on musicals or not, still got tapped to helm these epics—including Richard Fleischer (*Doctor Dolittle*), George Roy Hill (*Thoroughly Modern Millie*), Carol Reed (*Oliver!*), and William Wyler (*Funny Girl*). It must be noted, though, that many with strong musical backgrounds were also involved. *Hello, Dolly!*, for example, has a large amount of old MGM Freed Unit talent behind the camera, including Roger Edens as producer and Gene Kelly as director. Perhaps taking from the success of *West Side Story*'s splitting of directing duties (between Robert Wise and Jerome Robbins), many of these productions had the director take charge of the book scenes, and an entire other crew and choreographer/director (such as Herbert Ross, Onna White, or Michael Kidd) helm the musical sequences. When it worked, there was a synthesis of everyone's artistic strengths; when it failed, there was an unwieldy collision of visions and styles.

This new round of musical roadshow productions differed from the 1955–1964 period in sheer scale. *Oklahoma!* and *West Side Story* are blockbusters; *Camelot*, *Hello, Dolly!*, and *Paint Your Wagon* are blockbusters on steroids. Huge sets, amazing locations, and thousands of extras (all in lavish costumes) create a sense of excess not seen since the most hyperbolic moments of the early talkie musicals. Almost every musical number is an overextended extravaganza. Small intimate moments are rare and fleeting. At times, these musicals feel like the filmic equivalent of watching a battleship maneuver into port—aweing you with its sheer size. George Roy Hill, the director of *Thoroughly Modern Millie*, actually claimed that producer Ross Hunter "put back 20 minutes of meaningless cream puff I had cut out of the picture," in order to turn it into a roadshow with intermission.[8] As *The New Yorker*'s Brendan Gill opined, Hunter (and implicitly other Hollywood studio executives at the time) thought that "twice as large is twice as good."[9]

The musical genre had always used spectacle, and certain moments in these late 1960s pictures have become iconic: the camera sweeping down on Julie

Figure 9.3 A camera hovers over Barbra Streisand to capture her ecstasy and determination in the iconic conclusion to "Don't Rain on My Parade" in *Funny Girl* (1968). Snapshot taken from: Funny Girl (1968).

Andrews twirling on an Austrian Alp at the opening of *The Sound of Music*; Barbra Streisand belting out "Don't Rain on My Parade" on a tugboat chugging past the Statue of Liberty in *Funny Girl* (Figure 9.3). There are many other examples, though. *Camelot* shows a royal wedding with every candle in medieval Europe lit, and presents Arthur's knights seated at a Round Table so big that it screams out for 70 mm.[10] Paramount built an entire western boom town for *Paint Your Wagon*, in order to utterly demolish it in the film's climax. The big production number in the first half of *Oliver!* is "Consider Yourself," with the camera tracking backward to show a mass of people in a bustling London marketplace marching in place to the final lines of the song. This number is matched at the start of the second half with the young title character looking out on an upper-middle-class key garden to watch the entire neighborhood perform "Who Will Buy?" (with a similar camera movement to take in the enormity of it all). Perhaps most spectacular is *Hello, Dolly!*'s "Before the Parade Passes By." An entire parade *does* pass by for six minutes, climaxing as Streisand bellows with all her might while the camera pulls back to the Los Angeles suburbs, revealing that Fox's entire Culver City studio (including the administrative buildings) has been redressed to present New York City's 14th Street circa 1890.[11]

Another key difference between the cycle of roadshow musicals that followed *Sound of Music* from those that preceded it is the (perhaps surprising) number of films that are *not* adaptations of Broadway hits. *Thoroughly Modern Millie, Doctor Dolittle, Star!, Chitty Chitty Bang Bang*, and *Goodbye Mr. Chips* were all original musicals given the blockbuster treatment. With so much money being gambled, one would think studio executives would stick with proven properties. The problem facing Hollywood, though, was that there was little left to grab. *The Sound of Music* was the last musical written by Rodgers and Hammerstein, and their era of influence was beginning to wane. A number of historians of musical theatre have regarded 1964 as the start of a change in Broadway musicals, with stage debuts of *Hello, Dolly!* and *Fiddler on the Roof* as the last examples of this style of integrated musical.[12] In the second half of the decade, Broadway musicals became more complicated in story structure, and the songwriting in them moved away from 32-bar tunes that could become hit records. Hollywood was thus increasingly left to fend for itself—creating new musicals or reaching back to older properties that had not yet been filmed (such as *Finian's Rainbow*, which debuted on stage in 1947, and *Paint Your Wagon*, which was first performed in 1951).

The problem was not just that Broadway "wasn't writing 'em like they used to." Popular music itself had become different. In the first few decades of the screen musical, the songs appearing in these films regularly became top-selling hits across the nation—musical tunes *were* America's popular music. By the mid-1960s, rock had come to completely dominate the popular music scene. Louis Armstrong's rendition of "Hello, Dolly!" became a number one single—but it stood alone, surrounded by a raft of Beatles records. When rock and roll first burst onto the national scene in the mid-1950s, it was largely the purview of 45s, with classical music, jazz, and showtunes dominating the long-playing album charts. During the late 1960s, though, album-oriented rock developed—and the US album charts are almost a pictorial record of the battle between two forms of music: musical soundtracks versus rock groups. By the end of the decade, rock had overtaken the charts, with showtunes becoming marginalized and for cult audiences.

As such, a growing disdain—and even outright antagonism—towards these blockbuster musical films began to develop. Audiences (and reviewers) increasingly saw these films as stubborn attempts to hang onto not only an outmoded form of popular songwriting, but also an old-fashioned style of filmmaking. While these epics heavily trumpeted state-of-the-art widescreen and audio technology, they also (by and large) followed the traditional Hollywood style. *A Hard Day's Night* found stylistic inspiration and energy from the French New Wave in its jump cuts and handheld camera; *The Sound of Music* is impeccable in its traditional three-point lighting, carefully balanced framing, and crisp continuity editing.[13] Throwing more and more money at these projects created a sense of desperately trying to hang onto the established way of doing things, resisting change at all costs.

Nonetheless, to paraphrase singer/songwriter Bob Dylan famously, the times *were* a-changin', and much faster than Hollywood executives seemed to be able to handle.[14] The African American civil rights movement had already become a major force by the early 1960s, and protests against US involvement in Vietnam and against nuclear proliferation had already begun during that period. The early part of the decade also saw the start of a renewed feminist movement, and even some fledgling gay rights activism. As the 1960s rolled forward, though, the volume and ferocity of discontent on all these fronts became accentuated. Many (particularly younger people) began "opting out" of mainstream society, moving to communes or living in public parks, experimenting with new drugs and new attitudes about sex. Simultaneously, rebellion against the established power structure (often referred to as the military-industrial complex) grew vociferous, at times calling for a full-out revolution. The establishment (and those who supported it) escalated their response, increasingly using clubs, police dogs, fire hoses, and tear gas to suppress dissent. Riots, assassinations, and police actions on college campuses were becoming regular occurrences by the end of the 1960s.

The mega-budget musicals from the major Hollywood studios, employing older styles of songwriting and filmmaking, exemplified "the establishment" and thus were prime targets for the counterculture to criticize. Many of the executives running the studios in the mid-1960s had been working in the industry since the 1930s. At the very least, detractors claimed that the escapist nature of these films kept the public distracted from the pressing issues of the day. The film version of *The Sound of Music* dropped two songs from the original Broadway production, songs that deepen and complicate the moral issues of trying to live and survive in Austria during the Nazi era. In removing these songs, the story becomes a much simpler conflict, with nuns on one side and Nazis on the other. The film masterfully manipulates its audience—particularly by showing the "good side" being able to make music, and anyone "not good" incapable (the Nazis, the Countess). Baron Von Trapp becomes likable when he joins in the singing; his daughter's beau Rolf loses his musicality as he is drawn into the Nazi Party. In its avowed nostalgia (with an opening title stating its time period as "the last Golden Years"), the movie invites viewers to revel in a hazy romantic past before everything exploded. No wonder so many people kept watching the film over and over again, attempting to hide from the growing chaos surrounding them in the streets and on their TVs.

Some critics often went further than accusations of escapism, asserting that these films were a form of propaganda, intentionally quelling dissent from the establishment.[15] The basic premise of these films—extravagant budgets to produce spectacle—were seen as problematic to the counterculture. While hippies and others were decrying corporate capitalism and the lack of attention to and exploitation of the poor and underprivileged in America, these films wallowed in material excess (even publicizing such excess to draw interest). Based on Dickens, *Oliver!* critiques workhouses for the poor, but it also plainly posits the young orphan's salvation in being adopted by a long-lost rich relative—moving from the grime and muck of lower-class London to the sunny ordered existence of a white-bricked home in Mayfair (all to the strains of "Who Will Buy?"). In a similar fashion, *Paint Your Wagon* presents a supposed satire on the pitfalls of capitalism, but does so in a quite disingenuous fashion—by spending millions of dollars in the hope of turning a hefty profit.[16] The last film personally overseen by Walt Disney before his death in 1967 almost sounds like a conscious attempt to rile the counterculture: the big budget musical *The Happiest Millionaire*.

Attitudes towards capital are only the tip of the proverbial establishment iceberg. Issues of race and ethnicity are also troublesome. Although often problematic, the first cycle of roadshow musicals in the late 1950s and early 1960s include many attempts to address racial prejudice. There are fewer examples of this dynamic in the second cycle. Instead, there is a marked emphasis on whiteness, with *Sound of Music* leading the way. When a person of color appears, it is notable amid the whiteness—Louis Armstrong making a token appearance to sing one chorus of "Hello, Dolly!" with Streisand; Sammy Davis, Jr dropping in to sing "The Rhythm of Life" in *Sweet Charity*;[17] an unseen multilingual chorus singing "I Am on My Way" over the opening credits to *Paint Your Wagon*.

One might be able to argue that these big-budget musicals were simply (and perhaps wisely) avoiding getting drawn into the heated racial tension in the country. Yet, other examples in these musicals seem to indicate that those in charge could not grasp the situation. The one film in this cycle that actively tries to discuss racial prejudice is *Finian's Rainbow*. Keenan Wynn's villainous Southern senator is turned black by an inadvertent magic wish to teach him the error of his prejudiced ways. *Finian's Rainbow* may have been progressive and liberal-leaning when it first played on Broadway in 1947—but having a white actor in blackface in 1967, even if the goal is to attack racial bias, is extremely out of step with the times. Similarly, *Thoroughly Modern Millie* includes in its parody of 1920s silent movies a white slavery ring run by the Chinese Mrs Meers (British actress Beatrice Lillie in an extreme geisha wig, heavy white powder, and slanted eye makeup). The aim is to make fun of the clichés, but such an intention seems to not recognize how volatile such images had become by the late 1960s.

Such attacks on these musicals have become standard in film histories, dismissing them as out of step and behind the times—and claiming moviegoers stayed away from them in droves.[18] Such assertions are themselves overly simplistic. Data indicates that actually a lot of people *did* go see these movies (particularly *Thoroughly Modern Millie*, *Chitty Chitty Bang Bang*, *Funny Girl*, *Oliver!*, and *Hello, Dolly!*).[19] Secondly, with the explicit need to appeal to as wide an audience as possible, these huge musicals often tried somehow to embrace traditional values *and* "go with the times." The film version of *Paint Your Wagon*, for example, rewrites the original book in order to tell a story about a *ménage a trois*. As mentioned, the film also attempts to be a satire of rampant capitalism. *Paint Your Wagon* was not alone in poking fun at materialism and conspicuous consumerism—other films include *How to Succeed in Business Without Really Trying*, *Finian's Rainbow*, and *A Funny Thing Happened on the Way to the Forum* (1966).

In a few of these instances, the studios tried to tap into the zeitgeist by hiring young directors with new ideas. *A Funny Thing on the Way to the Forum* is directed by Richard Lester, fresh from working with The Beatles. Warner Bros. chose Francis Ford Coppola, just out of UCLA's film school, to give some youthful energy to *Finian's Rainbow*. Bob Fosse, having left Hollywood in the mid-1950s to become a star director/choreographer on Broadway, was hired by Universal to shepherd *Sweet Charity*. The picture showcases his new and unique style of choreography in a tale of modern New York, complete with hippies, religious cults, and a visit to a Felliniesque discotheque. Unlike the majority of the late 1960s blockbuster musicals, these three films employ some New Wave techniques, including freeze-frames, handheld cameras, and jump cuts.

Another strategy was to tap into "swinging London." While not going so far as to put one of the "British Invasion" rock groups into a blockbuster, there is a strong British accent to this cycle. Julie Andrews and Rex Harrison are central figures, as well as British pop recording stars Petula Clark (*Finian's Rainbow, Goodbye, Mr. Chips*) and Tommy Steele (*Finian's Rainbow, The Happiest Millionaire* [1967], *Half a Sixpence* [1969]). *Oliver!* was a largely British production financed and distributed by Columbia. These films could make a glancing connection to the interest in London's "mod" culture, but without actually delving into the larger upheaval of traditional mores that "swinging London" heralded. These musicals also managed to be vaguely ethnic (Irish or Cockney) and yet still white—and to discuss class politics by safely placing the films in another country.

Where this cycle may have been most successful is in speaking to women—particularly through the new superstars most associated with this era: Julie Andrews and Barbra Streisand.[20] Andrews, hot from her Oscar-winning film debut in *Mary Poppins*, topped that success with *The Sound of Music* and became the reigning queen of the genre.[21] She would also star in *Thoroughly Modern Millie, Star!* and *Darling Lili* (1970). In 1968, Streisand made her first feature, recreating the role of Fanny Brice in *Funny Girl* that had brought her fame on Broadway. Her Oscar-winning performance officially declared her as yet another major star. From there, she would play the leads in *Hello, Dolly!* and *On a Clear Day You Can See Forever* (1970).

Andrews might not seem initially any feminist icon, her star image strongly associated with wholesome traditional family values (echoed in her clear, open soprano singing voice). *The Sound of Music* is arguably audacious in its sexism when the nuns sing a reprise of "How Do You Solve a Problem Like Maria?" as the female protagonist marches down the aisle in one of the most lavish weddings put on film. Yet, Andrews played feisty, strong-willed, and intelligent characters—often with a tomboyish air. These factors (wholesomeness, tomboy nature, intelligence) also work against attempts to regard her as a sexual object. The combination of sunny disposition and independent streak creates avenues for her films to negotiate gender during the rise of women's liberation.

As *Mary Poppins*, Andrews manages to assert her authority over every male character and not end up romantically entangled with any of them—but is able to do so via her mystical nature, flying off into the clouds as the film concludes. *Thoroughly Modern Millie* centrally focuses on women's liberation, but by having Andrews safely ensconced in the 1920s rather than the 1960s.[22]

Streisand, on the other hand, reaching film stardom four years after Andrews did, fashioned a star image that was much more explicitly and unapologetically independent and quirky. *Funny Girl*, *Hello, Dolly!*, and *On a Clear Day You Can See Forever* all show her characters longing for heterosexual bliss with a man— and the film version of *Funny Girl* ends with an interpolation of a Fanny Brice standard not performed in the Broadway play: "My Man." Yet, each of these films presents Streisand (and her characters) as sufficient unto themselves. Her Fanny Brice may desire Nicky Arnstein, but he is painfully aware that she does not *need* him. As the film wraps up, Brice/Streisand wails about her man, but she totally commands the screen by herself in a spotlight surrounded by darkness. She similarly overwhelms her partners in courtship in the other two films by her sheer force of presence. Walter Matthau in *Hello, Dolly!* and Yves Montand in *On a Clear Day* both wear the same slackjawed "what-just-happened" look on their faces. Her characters tend to steamroller their male suitors, and she herself quickly gained a similar reputation working with others on these films.[23] Such independence and uniqueness was furthered through a proud and unapologetic Jewish heritage—not changing her name, celebrating her profile.[24]

The strength and independence exhibited by Andrews and Streisand certainly seemed to draw women to these musical blockbusters. Yet, the one area where these films may have found some success in adapting to the times worked against them in another way: further driving away heterosexual adult males.[25] Both Streisand and Andrews tended to crowd their male romantic counterparts off the screen, and an actor of comparable musical stardom did not emerge during the era. Fred Astaire, gamely spry, made his last appearance in a musical film in *Finian's Rainbow*. Dick Van Dyke was an able co-star, but never came close to the box-office power of either Andrews or Streisand. Younger men, fresh from success on stage, made even less of an impression: Harve Presnell, Anthony Newley, Michael Crawford, Tommy Tune. Consequently, name actors with little singing ability star in a number of these opuses. A number of them attempted to follow the lead of Rex Harrison's portrayal of Henry Higgins in *My Fair Lady*: "talk-singing" in rhythm rather than attempting full-out vocalizing. Unsurprisingly, Harrison himself does so playing the title role in *Doctor Dolittle*. Actors in other Lerner and Loewe adaptations also adopt this strategy: Richard Harris in *Camelot* and Lee Marvin in *Paint Your Wagon*. Peter O'Toole also tries this method in *Goodbye, Mr. Chips*. A few fellows, though, attempt to legitimately sing. Walter Matthau gets by in *Hello, Dolly!*, but Clint Eastwood warbling "I Talk to the Trees" in *Paint Your Wagon* still has the power to leave viewers wide-eyed in disbelief.

The typical reaction to Eastwood in *Paint Your Wagon* highlights the problem—men in musicals were increasingly regarded as somehow emasculated. Even Elvis was losing his standing because of the innocuous musicals he agreed to make. Since at least the 1920s, the American film industry had conceptualized the most typical filmgoer to be female; in the late 1960s, that attitude changed and the focus shifted to young adult heterosexual males. This target group seemed actively resistant to strong non-objectified female performers. They also showed little interest in "family fare." Bowing to how much tastes had changed, the industry replaced the outmoded Production Code in 1967 with a Ratings System. Blockbuster musicals, trying to be available to all customers, were predominantly "G" rated for all audiences. Such a strategy, though, ended up driving away people looking for edgier fare.[26]

During the Depression and World War II, the musical had succeeded handsomely in managing to celebrate both individual liberty and communal bonds. Obviously, the major studios, encouraged by the success of *The Sound of Music*, thought the genre was the perfect method of attracting a mass audience in trying times. By the late 1960s, though, American society had become too fractured for such a strategy to work—and for certain parts of the population, even attempting to do so was seen as manipulative and offensive. The counterculture rebelled. People of color saw no connection to their lives. Straight young adult men considered it too girly or too gay. Producers and executives may have pictured themselves as Maria—winning over everyone's hearts with sincerity and a song. They discovered themselves to be more like King Arthur—straining to keep warring sides together and watching everything implode.

Furthermore, budgets ballooned beyond what it cost to make *The Sound of Music*. Those films then had to surpass *The Sound of Music* in revenues in order to match its success—and none of them did. While some did draw good crowds, the expenses necessitated *phenomenal* crowds. And some did rotten business. The most notorious of the flops was *Star!* Fox reuniting Julie Andrews with *Sound of Music* director Robert Wise obviously sounded like a wonderful idea. However, box office for this musical biopic of stage star Gertrude Lawrence was so tepid that the studio pulled the film, cut the picture down in running time and re-released it under the title *Those Were the Happy Times* with a new ad campaign, trying to pass it off to consumers as a totally different film. (It did not work.)[27]

1969 was a calamitous year for Hollywood, as the motion picture industry experienced a severe recession, the worst economic period since the peak of the Depression.[28] A number of executives were swept out, and the film companies became ripe pickings for conglomerates looking for cheap assets (particularly the real estate where the studios had their backlots, such as Fox's 14th Street set for *Hello, Dolly!*). Whether fairly or not, much of the blame for the financial woes was placed on the musical genre. Instead of saving the industry, the genre was now seen as causing its demise—and the age of the blockbuster musical came crashing down.

Born to Be Wild: Rock and Film, 1965–1970

While many college students and other counterculture types turned away from blockbuster musicals, that did not mean they had forsaken films altogether. Rather, they favored foreign "art cinema," guerilla documentaries, and experimental films—films that explored new ways of thinking—on what film was, what art was, what life was. Showings of "underground films" were often a mix of moviegoing, drug trip, and countercultural happening, and screenings sometimes got raided by the police. Rock (now without the "and roll") music was also a key component of the counterculture. Rock music was used as a form of protest. It was also used to celebrate a new radical lifestyle. And it could enhance the effects of different drugs. Valued for their similar liberating potential by the counterculture, motion pictures and rock music inevitably continued to interact.

In the wake of the success of *A Hard Day's Night*, there was no doubt that The Beatles would make a follow-up. Again directed by Richard Lester, *Help!* (1965) did well—although most considered it a step down from the first film (even The Beatles themselves). The Beatles helped usher in an entire "British Invasion" in American music—and some film producers tried out these other groups in the *Hard Day's Night* mold. Attempts to match the irreverence and energy of *A Hard Day's Night*, though, often feel muted and overly calculated. Many of these films are small-budget affairs distributed by the major studios, and thus follow the pattern of early 1960s rock musicals: trying to smooth the music out and pull the performers back into comfortable mainstream acceptance. Sweeter Brit pop groups (such as Herman's Hermits and the Dave Clark Five) were the usual choice rather than gritty, more confrontational bands (such as the Rolling Stones or The Who). By this period, though, neither side was buying the strategy—stuffy adults could no longer be convinced that rock was *not* dangerous, and wild youth distrusted any attempts to pre-package rock.

The counterculture wanted rock music to feel raw and real rather than slick and filtered through corporate suits. Because of this, fans of rock music started discovering ways to use rock music in film outside of the established parameters of the musical genre. For example, the documentary film seems the antithesis of the musical genre—actual versus performed; caught versus rehearsed; real versus stylized. Nonetheless, the second half of the 1960s saw a merging of the two as documentaries of rock concerts and music festivals became popular. D.A. Pennebaker's documentary *Don't Look Back* (1967) allows Bob Dylan the opportunity to resist efforts to "categorize, bowdlerize, sterilize, universalize or conventionalize" him and his music.[29] Pennebaker's next project, *Monterey Pop*

(1968), presents key performances by a stellar lineup of musicians, including Simon and Garfunkel, Jefferson Airplane, Janis Joplin, Jimi Hendrix, The Who, the Mamas & the Papas, and Otis Redding. Similarly, *Woodstock* (1970) is a "rockumentary" of the legendary music festival in upstate New York. The event quickly attained such mythic status that the film became a blockbuster road-show for the counterculture—a three-hour epic in widescreen, and an Oscar winner for Best Documentary.

Both *Monterey Pop* and *Woodstock* revel in the live performance of their musical artists, seeming to take pride when there is a small audio glitch or a vocal or instrumental imperfection. This is authentic—not some manufac-tured pre-recorded Hollywood musical. At the same time, both films contain a lot of stylized moments—even taking care to come up with different visual strategies from song to song. The split screens, mirrored images, and superim-positions of abstract colors and shapes connect with underground cinema and the counterculture, but are not that far removed from the excesses of Busby Berkeley either.

These films—and subsequent concert documentaries such as *Soul to Soul* (1971), *Wattstax* (1973), and *The Last Waltz* (1978)—refuse to bother with fitting the songs into some sort of narrative. Yet, they are more than a new generation's version of a revue. They capture a sense of the entire event by turn-ing the camera on the audience as well as the performers on stage, exploring the temporary communal environment created by the attendees.[30] In giving screen time to the audience along with the performers, these rockumentaries *do* invoke the celebration of community so common to the musical genre. *Monterey Pop* shows performers joining the audience to watch other acts play (including Mama Cass clearly mouthing an awe-struck "Wow" as Janis Jopin finishes wail-ing "Love Is Like a Ball and Chain"). Conversely, the audience members become performers—so caught up in the music that they rise up and start dancing. *Woodstock* shows this too. When the official performance has to stop for safety reasons during a rainstorm, the crowd takes over and starts making its own music with whatever objects are at hand. In the same film, Country Joe and the Fish encourages the concertgoers to sing "Fixin-to-Die Rag" with him. As he does so, the lyrics appear on the bottom of the film screen for an old-fashioned bouncing-ball sing-along (Figure 9.4). Thus, the audience in the movie theatre is invited to become part of the performance as well. These concert films create their own countercultural utopias in which the music invites everyone—the performers, the audience on screen, and the audience in the theatre—into a world of love and abundance. Woodstock is Oz. Brigadoon. Camelot.

Performers of color figured prominently in these rockumentaries—and without a narrative structure, all performers were potentially given equal opportunity to shine. Given that chance, a number of non-white artists took no prisoners. In *Monterey Pop*, Pete Townsend of The Who smashes his guitar while performing "My Generation," but Jimi Hendrix takes up the challenge

Figure 9.4 A bouncing ball encourages the film viewer to join with the swell of concert attendees who are singing along with Country Joe's "Fixin-to-Die Rag" in *Woodstock* (1970), exemplifying how the film blurs the distinction between performer and audience. Snapshot taken from: *Woodstock* (1970).

by dry humping his guitar, then squirting lighting fluid all over it, setting it on fire—and *then* smashing it into pieces. Hendrix also plays the final set in *Woodstock*, including a stunning deconstruction of "The Star-Spangled Banner" using his guitar to create the sounds of aerial bombing runs, machine gun fire, and ambulance sirens.[31] In *The T.A.M.I. Show* (1964), a very early version of a concert documentary, James Brown so thoroughly dominates the stage that the act after him—the Rolling Stones!—are obviously "gob-smacked," and lead singer Mick Jagger has a hard time figuring out what to do. The final quarter of *Monterey Pop* is given to Indian sitar master Ravi Shankar's awe-inspiring performance, followed by almost two minutes of standing ovation by the audience in the film (and often a form of "contact high" for film viewers). Granted, the footage of the festivalgoers in these films tends to be predominantly white (except for *Wattstax*, which was held near the predominantly African American area of Los Angeles). Still, the strong presence of and respect given to performers of color clearly adds to the utopian aims of these concert documentaries.

The Beatles attempted to invoke a "summer of love" utopia as well when they produced a musical event for television—inviting characters and the audience to join them on a *Magical Mystery Tour* (1967). Attempting to make the piece on their own (without Richard Lester) resulted in what was considered an incoherent final product, lambasted by British critics and never picked up for American broadcast. The psychedelic animated feature *Yellow Submarine* (1968) was much more successful (with critics and audiences) in presenting a magical other dimension where ultimately "All You Need Is Love." Their final film together was the documentary *Let It Be* (1970), covering the making of what would be their last album together. As such, it unwittingly exposed that countercultural rock was not always as utopian as *Monterey Pop* or *Woodstock* claimed.[32]

Magical Mystery Tour points out that television still had enormous impact on how people *watched* rock music. Most Americans saw The Beatles for the first time not in *A Hard Day's Night* but on *The Ed Sullivan Show*. Although consistently leery of impropriety, Sullivan invited a number of rock acts onto his program.[33] The variety hour hosted by folk singers and comedy duo the Smothers Brothers also showcased many notable rock groups, and aired a series of short video pieces produced by The Beatles. Elvis managed to resurrect his career not via filmmaking but through a legendary "comeback special" on NBC in 1968. Steve Binder, who directed this Elvis special, had previously worked on *The T.A.M.I. Show*. Television also had its imitation of *A Hard Day's Night*: *The Monkees* (1966–1968).[34] Even more so than the motion picture copies, *The Monkees* was an explicitly calculated attempt to duplicate The Beatles and their film image. Producers Bob Rafelson and Bert Schneider pitched the idea to NBC, and then went out and auditioned young men to create a group. Although the show only lasted two seasons, the band released a number of high-charting singles and top-selling albums.

Perhaps their reputation as the "Pre-Fab Four" began to work against them by 1968, when the show was cancelled, but a number of those involved in the making of the TV series had grown disenchanted as well. In the early going, not only were the bandmates not writing their songs—they also were not playing them either. Eventually, the foursome began complaining to the press about this, and they were allowed to play their own instruments. Producers Rafelson and Schneider were also becoming more radicalized as well. As such, they wanted to make something that spoke for the counterculture, to express the upheaval happening around the country. A similar shift had happened at American International Pictures. As rock music regained its aggressive edge, the fun poked at Eric Von Zipper and his motorcycle gang in the beach party musicals seemed out of step.[35] The studio thus moved from surf movies to a series of exploitation films about outlaw motorcycle gangs, starting with *The Wild Angels* (1966) starring Peter Fonda. Rafelson and Schneider teamed up with AIP veteran Jack Nicholson (as a screenwriter!) on a feature film with the Monkees. Expressing everyone's disenchantment, *Head* (1968) was too weird and "trippy" to appeal to the group's largely teenage audience.[36] Rafelson and Schneider then worked with Nicholson and Fonda on *Easy Rider* (1969). Released through Columbia, this modestly budgeted picture became a huge hit—possibly the only bright spot for the film industry during the 1969 recession—and helped usher in a new era of American filmmaking.

Hardly anyone considers *Easy Rider* to be a musical—Fonda himself has stated that part of the impetus to make *Easy Rider* was his disgust over the money spent on *Doctor Dolittle*.[37] Yet, music is a key aspect of the film. As Fonda and Dennis Hopper's characters jump on their bikes in search of America, the soundtrack blares with Steppenwolf's "Born to Be Wild." While the song plays, the film watches the duo ride their way across the country, editing shots together in tempo to create a sense that the bikes' movements are a form of choreography. The characters are longing to be free—and watching them freewheeling to this song creates the exhilarating sense that such independence is at hand. This moment also effectively liberates rock music from the structured expectations of a typical musical number. No one is singing or dancing on screen—it is not an integrated number, or even a show-making performance. "Born to Be Wild" simply "is" on the soundtrack.

Easy Rider was not the first film to use rock music this way. One can argue that some of the musical moments in *A Hard Day's Night* work this way. *The Graduate* (1967) introduces main character Ben (Dustin Hoffman) standing emotionless on an airport moving walkway, while Simon and Garfunkel fill the soundtrack with their lament about "The Sounds of Silence." *Easy Rider*'s use of "Born to Be Wild" is also strongly indebted to a landmark underground film, Kenneth Anger's *Scorpio Rising* (1963). Other than a few scattered sound effects (engines revving, tires squealing), the soundtrack to this short film is nothing but rock, helping to structure a dizzying array of images tied to motorcycle culture. Yet, this film is much more radical than *Easy Rider*. The film fetishizes the bikes and the men who ride them, bringing out the homoerotic nature of leather bikers and their all-male roughhousing with each other. The chosen tunes sing about biker worship ("Leader of the Pack," etc.), but also have women singing in low registers and men singing in high falsetto, so it is often difficult to judge the gender of the vocalists. *Easy Rider* has no desire to raise any connotations of queerness—and it is this version of straight masculine bravado in a new age that young adult males loved about the film.

Rock's rebelliousness had begun to defy the musical genre itself. While future years will see film musicals use rock music (in various evolutions), rock music itself no longer needs the genre to find a place in a film. As the 1960s ended, the increasingly bloated efforts to assert the primacy of the traditional musical had collapsed, and rock music began to abandon the genre in favor other formats (in concert documentaries, as background score). In a certain way, the sound of musicals was in deep danger of becoming the sound of silence.

Notes

1 R. Serge Denisoff and William D. Romanowski, *Risky Business: Rock in Film* (New Brunswick: Transaction Publishers, 1991), 111–112.
2 "Talent Boycott Threatened in Ban of Seeger, Weavers on 'Hootenanny'," *Variety* (March 20, 1963).

3 Denisoff and Romanowski, 26.

4 Denisoff and Romanowski report that eventual domestic rentals for the film totaled over $6 million (138), and that the soundtrack was the number one album in the United States for fourteen weeks (twenty-one weeks in Britain) (138).

5 Andrew Sarris, "Bravo Beatles!," *Village Voice*, August 27, 1964, 13.

6 Denisoff and Romanowski, 133.

7 For anyone who somehow does not know this history, Taylor (then married to singer Eddie Fisher) began an on-set affair with her co-star Richard Burton, leading to divorce and the first of two marriages to Burton.

8 Andrew Horton, *The Films of George Roy Hill* (New York: Columbia University Press, 1984), 63.

9 Brendan Gill, *The New Yorker* (April 1, 1967), 94.

10 The film was actually shot in 35 mm, but the image was "blown up" to 70 mm for roadshow distribution.

11 On the redressing of Fox's backlot for *Hello, Dolly!*, see Matthew Kennedy, *Roadshow! The Fall of Film Musicals in the 1960s* (Oxford: Oxford University Press, 2014), 139.

12 For example, Brooks Atkinson, *Broadway* (New York: Limelight Editions, 1974), 462; Ethan Mordden, *Open a New Window: The Broadway Musical in the 1960s* (New York: Palgrave, 2001), 69, sets the shift a bit earlier to 1960, considering the Broadway debut of *Camelot* as "the closing event of that era, the last major show of the Rodgers and Hammerstein kind."

13 If there is any analog to the influence of the French New Wave on *A Hard Day's Night* for *The Sound of Music*, it is the style and iconography of the German films starring Leni Reifenstahl—"mountain films" centered around a girl from the hills that promoted a strong sense of German national identity and pride. These films were so admired by Adolf Hitler that he chose her to direct two landmark non-fiction films, *Triumph of the Will* (1934) and *Olympia* (1938), which many consider to be some of the most accomplished examples of film propaganda ever created.

14 Abel Green, "Topheavy Film Studio Fade: Film Biz Ducks Overhead Load," *Variety* (October 29, 1969), 24, argued that the motion picture market "has changed faster than its shrewdest showmen could anticipate. Hence what was right two or three years ago just has been outpaced by the moods and mores of the times."

15 For example, Hollis Alpert, "Happy Producers Make Happy Movies," *Saturday Review* (April 15, 1967), 45, opines that *Thoroughly Modern Millie* "will not help in the slightest degree in alleviating poverty or ending the war in Vietnam."

16 CBS's Michael Campus reported that "young people are saying that it's a crime to spend $20 million on *Paint Your Wagon*. That amount could remake a city." (Quoted in Richard Stirling, *Julie Andrews: An Intimate Biography* [New York: St. Martin's, 2007], 329.)

17 Credit where it is due, the best friends of Charity (Shirley MacLaine) are played by Chita Rivera and Paula Kelly.

18 For example, Gerald Mast, *Can't Help Singin': The American Musical on Stage and Screen* (New York: Overlook Press, 1987), 218; Jon Lewis, *Hollywood v. Hard Core: How the Struggle over Censorship Saved the Modern Film Industry* (New York: New York University Press, 2001), 152; Barry Keith Grant, ed., *American Cinema of the 1960s: Themes and Variations* (New Brunswick: Rutgers University Press, 2008), 16.

19 Brett Farmer, "The Singing Sixties: Rethinking the Julie Andrews Roadshow Musical," in *The Sound of Musicals*, ed. Steven Cohan (London: British Film Institute, 2010), 114–127.

20 It is important to acknowledge that audiences were already familiar with both Andrews and Streisand before they made their feature film debuts. In addition to reaching stardom on Broadway first, both had done important work on television before going to Hollywood. Following Andrews' performance in Rodgers and Hammerstein's *Cinderella* (1957) for CBS, she was a guest star on a number of variety programs, and co-starred in a highly acclaimed TV special with comedian Carol Burnett, *Julie and Carol at Carnegie Hall* (1962). Streisand also made guest appearances years before her first film, including a memorable episode of *The Judy Garland Show* (1963), at one point singing with Garland *and* Ethel Merman. Streisand also starred in two major TV specials: *My Name Is Barbra* (1965) and *Color Me Barbra* (1966). Thus, by the time both made their feature debuts, they *had* been given training before the cameras. In fact, Streisand's performance of "My Man" in *My Name Is Barbra* would be almost duplicated in *Funny Girl*, when it was decided to add this song as the final number of the film.

21 After Jack Warner snubbed Andrews by giving her breakthrough part in *My Fair Lady* to Audrey Hepburn in the film version, it is doubtful he even bothered to approach Andrews about recreating the role of Guenevere for the adaptation of *Camelot*, knowing the response he would receive. Hence, Vanessa Redgrave.

22 See Farmer.

23 Kennedy, 134–136, for example, describes the growing animosity between Stresiand and co-star Walter Matthau on the set of *Hello, Dolly!*

24 Pamela Robertson Wojcik, "The Streisand Musical," in Cohan, 128–138.

25 Perhaps contributing to the box-office successes of *The Sound of Music* and *Oliver!* are "moments for the guys": *Sound of Music* turns into a Nazi escape thriller in its last section; *Oliver!* contains genuine menace in the villainous Bill Sykes (Oliver Reed)—plus he has a great dog.

26 *Oliver!*, the first picture to win an Academy Award under the new Ratings System, was rated G. Paramount exerted all of its influence to ensure that *Paint Your Wagon* got a G rating, even with its *ménage a trois*, requesting that the MPAA reconsider its decision to give it an M (for mature audiences) rating—and almost got it overturned (losing on a vote of 10 to 9). See Kennedy, 183.

27 Kennedy, 155–157, details the recutting and redistribution of *Star!*, and gives a thorough recounting of the late 1960s musical blockbuster era.

28 David A. Cook, *Lost Illusions: American Cinema in the Shadow of Watergate and Vietnam, 1970–1979* (Berkeley: University of California Press, 2000), 516, notes: "In 1969, United Artists lost $89 million, MGM lost $72 million, Fox lost $65 million, losing another $77.4 million in 1970, and Warners took a $25 million write-off on 1969 pictures in development." On page 8 of the book is a full-page picture of Julie Andrews as Maria in *The Sound of Music* in mid-Alp twirl, with a caption that the film "set Hollywood on an ill-fated Grail-quest for another blockbuster musical that ended in an industry-wide recession, 1969–1971." *Los Angeles Times* (March 17, 1971), 1, asserted: "If the country as a whole is in a recession, the motion picture business is in an out and out depression. More than half of the 30,000 local film union members are out of work. In some crafts joblessness is said to be running 85–90 percent."

29 The quoted material is taken from an August 21, 1967 review of the film in *Newsweek*.

30 David E. James, *Rock 'n' Film: Cinema's Dance with Popular Music* (Oxford: Oxford University Press, 2016), 231, argues that these particular rockumentaries create a new version of the dual-focus narrative in musicals theorized by Rick Altman, alternating between the artists and the audience.

31 Hendrix would get his own documentary tribute film after his death, *Jimi Hendrix* (1973).

32 To be fair, *Woodstock* does give some indication that all is not completely rosy—particularly when watching one female concertgoer having a paranoid crying fit, in what is assumed to be a "freak out" from some badly concocted LSD. ("Don't take the brown acid!" a stage manager memorably announces to the crowd.)

33 Some bands were just as contemptuous of him as he was leery of them. In 1967, the Rolling Stones agreed to Sullivan's demand that they change the lyrics of their song "Let's Spend the Night Together" to "Let's Spend Some Time Together"—but lead singer Mick Jagger performed the line repeatedly with rolling eyes and a pained look on his face. Later that year, Sullivan demanded that The Doors change the lyric "Girl, we couldn't get much higher" in their song "Light My Fire." On live television, lead singer Jim Morrison ignored the command and sang the original lyric, incensing Sullivan who banned them from further appearances.

34 *The Monkees* are not the only instance. A cartoon series of *The Beatles* (1965) also aired in the 1960s, and *The Banana Splits Adventure Hour* (1968) offered up a quartet of amusement-park-styled "big head" animals as a musical group doing skits and songs in between various cartoon shorts and live-action serial chapters.

35 One can watch the transition happening in *How to Stuff a Wild Bikini*. Suddenly, Annette's potential beau, played by Dwayne Hickman, is a motorcycle enthusiast—and teaches her how to ride. Thus, cycling is now a "good thing." To negotiate this, Eric Von Zipper (and his followers) are oddly transformed into corporate suits—complete with bowlers and ties—to keep them still "uncool."

36 See Paul B. Ramaeker, "'You Think They Call Us Plastic *Now* ...': The Monkees and *Head*," in *Soundtrack Available: Essays on Film and Popular Music*, ed. Pamela Robertson Wojcik and Arthur Knight (Durham: Duke University Press, 2001), 74–102.

37 Fonda claims that, while listening to MPAA head Jack Valenti plead for more family pictures like *Doctor Dolittle*, he realized "the time was right for a really good movie about motorcycles and drugs." Quoted in Seth Cagin and Philip Dray, *Hollywood Films of the Seventies: Sex, Drugs, Violence, Rock n' Roll, and Politics* (New York: Harper & Row, 1984), 47.

10

Whistling in the Dark: A Genre in Crisis

Darling Lili (1970), a mega-budget Paramount musical complete with intermission, opens with Julie Andrews alone in a small spotlight surrounded by darkness, as she sings "Often I feel my poor old heart is whistling in the dark ..." On one level, the wistful tune expresses the sense of despair much of the United States was feeling in the wake of multiple assassinations, riots, strikes, and ongoing fighting in Vietnam (even though the film's narrative takes place during World War I). This opening tune also describes the embattled nature of the musical genre itself by 1970. Musicals seemed out of place with the world in such a state. Most of the Hollywood film industry blamed its recession in 1969 on the box-office failure of many blockbuster musicals. Executives who had green lit these projects were swept out, and conglomerates with no previous experience in filmmaking took over many of the studios.

Although many critics and filmmakers claimed that the genre was dead, musicals did not disappear completely from theatre screens. Rather, the first half of the 1970s saw more experiments with what the genre could do than anytime since the early talkie era. Yet, such experimentation largely arose out of desperation and doubt in the established norms for the genre. Artists sought to discover what a musical should be for this new generation, questioning almost every tradition, cliché, and assumption associated with the musical. Such reappraisals also extended to employing a wide variety of forms of popular music, extending beyond the typical "showtune" in an effort to connect with contemporary audiences. What constituted a musical (and what did not) became increasingly hard to pinpoint. This chapter will explore the various ways the genre "whistled in the dark," groping in multiple directions, looking for a way to survive.

Free and Easy? A Defining History of the American Film Musical Genre, First Edition. Sean Griffin.
© 2018 Sean Griffin. Published 2018 by John Wiley & Sons Ltd.

The Conventional Integrated Musical in an Age of Not Believing

As the major studios financially reorganized in the 1970s, new executives undeniably reined in the emphasis on blockbuster musicals. 20th Century-Fox, for example, put an immediate end to its strategy of releasing one major musical spectacular every year—after three in a row failed to break even. Paramount similarly reassessed its commitment to musicals. It had two scheduled for 1970, but even having Julie Andrews or Barbra Streisand in them was no longer considered box-office insurance. The budget for Andrews' *Darling Lili* ballooned to nearly $25 million. Panicked executives eventually took control of the film away from noted and popular director Blake Edwards, re-editing it into what they hoped would turn the film into a profitable endeavor. Edwards was incensed, the film still ended up a box-office disaster (with just over $3 million in returns), and Julie Andrews did not make another film for four years.[1] Streisand's *On a Clear Day You Can See Forever* went through similar travails. Paramount accountants kept careful tabs on every expense that legendary Freed Unit director Vincente Minnelli proposed, and the studio decided *not* to release it as a roadshow, cutting fifteen minutes out in order to do so. For a reported final cost of $10 million, the picture brought in $14 million— just barely breaking even.[2]

While such examples indicate an industry actively abandoning the genre, the major studios actually *did* continue releasing musicals throughout the first part of the 1970s—and some were still clearly given large budgets. On average, two major musicals got distributed every year during this period. In addition to the two Paramount pictures just described, 1970 saw the release of *Scrooge!* by Columbia and *Song of Norway* in Cinerama. MGM's *The Boy Friend* and United Artists' *Fiddler on the Roof* came out in 1971. *Cabaret*, Columbia's *1776*, and United Artists' *Man of La Mancha* played on screens in 1972. Columbia's epic musical version of *Lost Horizon* came out in 1973, and Warner Bros's adaptation of *Mame* premiered in 1974. In 1975, 20th Century-Fox produced a high Art Deco original musical with Cole Porter tunes, *At Long Last Love*, and Streisand reprised the role of Fanny Brice for Columbia in *Funny Lady*.

"Family-oriented" musicals also proliferated during these years, becoming almost a subgenre unto themselves. Such projects were doubtless in reaction to the critical and box-office popularity of *Mary Poppins* (1964) and *Oliver!* (1968). Under the new Ratings System (unveiled in 1967), these G-rated musicals aimed at attracting and entertaining all ages, including *Willy Wonka and the Chocolate Factory* (1971), *Tom Sawyer* (1973), *Journey Back to Oz* (1974), *Bugsy Malone* (1976), and *The Slipper and the Rose* (1977). Producers of children's television contributed as well, with film versions of the TV series *Pufnstuf* (1970) and of the *Peanuts* animated TV specials (*A Boy Named Charlie Brown* [1970], *Snoopy Come Home* [1972]). TV animation powerhouse

Hanna-Barbera also stepped forward, making the theatrical feature *Charlotte's Web* (1973).[3] *The Blue Bird* (1976) was a big-budget US–Soviet co-production of the classic children's tale, with a number of Hollywood stars and notable Russian ballet dancers.

Unfortunately, few of these films did well with either critics or customers. Some became notorious box-office flops, such as *Mame* and *At Long Last Love*.[4] Industry wags supposedly referred to *Lost Horizon* as "Lost Investment," because Columbia took such a loss on the film.[5] *The Blue Bird* became infamous for its troubled production, and landed with a resounding thud upon its release.[6] Most of the other G-rated musicals did not fare as horrendously as *The Blue Bird*, but they were produced with much smaller budgets. Thus, much of the "family fare" simply came and went without much notice one way or the other.

These catastrophic failures are dismissed often with a knee-jerk accusation that they were badly made. A common cause for complaint lies in the casting of non-musical talent: Albert Finney in *Scrooge!*, Peter O'Toole and Sophia Loren in *Man of La Mancha*, Lucille Ball in *Mame*, everyone (except Bobby Van) in *Lost Horizon*, Cybill Shepard and Burt Reynolds in *At Long Last Love*. Such decisions followed trends set over the past decade. With the old studio system no longer in place to find and groom musical talent, film producers turned to stars regardless of their skill level at dancing or singing. As a result, performers either rasped their way through songs or had their singing voices replaced with doubles. Neither option seemed to work. Lucille Ball's rendering of the score to *Mame*, and Cybill Shepard and Burt Reynolds' on-set performances of classic Cole Porter tunes in *At Long Last Love* are embarrassing and often actively painful to the ear. On the other hand, switching from actual speaking voices to dubbed singing (for O'Toole in *La Mancha*, and for Peter Finch and Liv Ullmann in *Lost Horizon*) is often done clumsily. Arguably, the most jarring example of voice doubling occurs in *Bugsy Malone*, in which adult singing voices implausibly emerge out of the mouths of the pre-pubescent cast.[7]

Dancing fared no better, with the cast of *At Long Last Love* cavorting ineptly, or chorus boys in the title number of *Mame* simply lifting Lucille Ball around and planting her in various spots as a form of choreography. The largest dance sequence in *Lost Horizon*, intended as a ritual celebration of childbirth in Shangri-La, involves none of the leading players. The sequence was cut, though, when preview audiences erupted in laughter as a number of oiled-up male gymnasts and acrobats wearing nothing but what appear to be giant orange diapers suddenly appeared (perhaps reacting to the eruption of such obvious gay camp amid a supposed tribute to heterosexuality). Under such circumstances, it is perhaps not surprising that musicals during this era contain very few moments of dancing.

Ill-conceived creative decisions were often matched with outdated worldviews. Having white actors in "yellowface" to play the Asian inhabitants of

Lost Horizon's Shangri-La is stunningly behind the times.[8] While (thankfully) not including any stereotypical black servants on screen, the title number of *Mame* is still an elaborate celebration of clichéd Southern plantation life. Highlighting the felt need to support a conservative stance, producer Jack Warner acceded to President Nixon's personal request that the song "Cool Considerate Men" be cut from *1776* because it criticized the political right.[9]

As discussed in previous chapters, the genre has often been used to uphold traditional values. Yet, these early 1970s pictures exude an air of listlessness, as if no one working on them really has a passion for what they are creating, and the views being espoused are on their last legs.[10] *Lost Horizon* deals with a planeload of people escaping a society that has fallen into violent anarchy. *Man of La Mancha* introduces author Miguel de Cervantes awaiting interrogation by the Spanish Inquisition. Even the two films that did well critically and economically follow this pattern of despair. *Fiddler on the Roof* ends with the forced eviction of the inhabitants of a Russian Jewish shtetl, with the central family torn apart and possibly never to see each other again. *Cabaret* takes place in Berlin during the rise of the Nazi Party. (More on *Cabaret* later in this chapter.)

Whether intentionally or not, these musicals reflected a general national attitude that everything was collapsing. In reaction to President Nixon's decision to invade Vietnam's neighbor Cambodia, ROTC buildings at dozens of universities were bombed or torched. The National Guard was called out to quell student protesters, resulting in the use of clubs, tear gas, and gunfire—killing students at Jackson State in Mississippi and Kent State in Ohio. In 1973, the nation's military withdrew from Vietnam. Although Nixon referred to it as "peace with honor," the general consensus was that the United States had for the first time lost a war (a feeling reinforced by images of chaos when Saigon and the rest of South Vietnam "fell" to the North Vietnamese in 1975). At the same time, the Nixon administration was battling the growing Watergate scandal, exposing corruption of the democratic election process. Facing impeachment, Nixon resigned the office in disgrace.

Violence seemed everywhere. A standoff between members of the American Indian Movement and the FBI at the Wounded Knee reservation lasted for over two months, with machine gun fire and deaths on both sides. Radical underground protest groups continued to proliferate, such as the Weathermen, the FALN (Fuerzas Armadas de Liberación Nacional), and the Symbionese Liberation Army (most remembered for kidnapping heiress Patty Hearst in 1974). An assassination attempt was made on Governor Wallace of Alabama in 1972, and two were made on President Ford in one month in 1974. Airplane hijackings became a rampant new phenomenon, and a rash of serial killers emerged across the country.[11]

The Hollywood film industry's recession was soon matched by a general economic slump across the country. The Organization of Petroleum Exporting

Countries (OPEC) announced an oil embargo toward the United States in 1973, resulting in massive gasoline shortages (and a spike in prices). The United States also experienced a major period of "stagflation"—a sharp increase in inflation *and* in unemployment simultaneously.[12] Such economic woes were fed by the energy crisis, the collapse of the nation's steel industry, and the drying up of business investment in major urban areas. Across the country, urban decay became rampant, predominantly due to "white flight" to the suburbs, leaving underprivileged communities of color to live in declining city infrastructures.

With all of the studios facing tough times, much of the valuable real estate that held their vast backlots was sold off to housing developers, and warehouses full of furniture, costumes, and props were put on the auction block (including the iconic ruby slippers Judy Garland wore in *The Wizard of Oz* [1939]). Outside the studio gates, Hollywood Boulevard fell into seediness, with tattoo parlors, tacky gift shops, and dive bars standing alongside ornate but run-down movie palaces. The famed Hollywood sign itself was deteriorating, an overt symbol of the state of things. It is perhaps unsurprising then that musicals of the period increasingly show communities crumbling and characters losing faith.

Kelly Kessler's examination of musicals during this era argues that such alienation and doubt infects not only the storylines but also the stylistic choices.[13] When characters sing, for example, editing, shallow or rack focus, and sound design often work to isolate them from the people around them—as if they only feel able to sing by withdrawing into themselves. Song is no longer an outward expression shared with others. The one duet between Barbra Streisand and James Caan in *Funny Lady* is sung in their minds rather than openly. Similarly, when Ebenezer begins to sing in *Scrooge!*, the people around him cannot see or hear him. True, integrated musicals had been doing internal soliloquies for decades, often having the character framed by a window as a visual representation of looking into their soul. Yet, those instances happened at moments when the characters were left alone with their thoughts. In contrast, these 1970s musicals have characters retreat into themselves in the middle of a scene with other people. In *1776*, John Adams goes into imagined conversations with his wife while out on the busy streets of Philadelphia. *Fiddler's* protagonist Tevye (Topol) goes into musical moments of philosophical consideration in the middle of key conversations with each of his three oldest daughters. As he starts singing, Tevye is photographed in extreme close-up, off to the far side of the widescreen frame, with his daughters (and their beaus) out of focus and suddenly positioned far, far away from him (Figure 10.1). The decline of dance sequences in musicals also keeps people separated from interacting with each other.

The family-oriented musicals are not exempt from this dynamic. Like a number of other studios, the Walt Disney Company fell into artistic and economic doldrums during this period. Walt Disney's death in 1967 left the studio

Figure 10.1 Tevye (Topol) is suddenly far far away from his daughter and her prospective suitor as he goes into a musical reverie in *Fiddler on the Roof* (1971). Singing has now become an interiorized solitary thing rather than something that is shared with others. Snapshot taken from: Fiddler on the Roof (1971).

without a strong visionary. Songwriters Richard M. and Robert B. Sherman left the studio soon after Walt's death to work independently.[14] As a result, Disney was not at the forefront of the 1970s growth in family-oriented musicals. Its animated features included fewer and fewer songs, making it more difficult to classify films such as *Robin Hood* (1973) or *The Rescuers* (1977) as musicals. On the other hand, the Sherman Brothers became one of the most prolific teams writing for film musicals of this period, contributing songs for non-Disney films like *Snoopy Come Home, Charlotte's Web, Tom Sawyer*, and *The Slipper and the Rose*. Ironically, they would return to Disney to write the score for *Bedknobs and Broomsticks* (1971), one of the only two major musicals Disney produced during this period. (Both this film and *Pete's Dragon* [1977] modeled themselves on *Mary Poppins*: musicals combining live-action and animation.)

The dimming of the strength within the Disney studio indicates that G-rated musicals faced the same confusion other makers of musicals faced: not knowing exactly what worked anymore. The hope that G-rated musicals would bring in all audiences ultimately went unfulfilled. Rather, consumers started to regard anything G-rated as strictly for little kids, thus marginalizing the genre even further—creating the sense that only naive tots would still accept that people could break into song, or would still believe that people could live happily ever after in a harmonious community.

The sourness and doubt that invaded the genre during this period affected these productions too. The *Peanuts* films carry on the character neuroses for which the original comic strip is well known. The plot of *Snoopy Come Home* threatens to tear apart the circle of friends when Snoopy decides to leave Charlie Brown and live with his (now hospitalized) former owner. Further, while on his journey, Snoopy repeatedly deals with discrimination, announced with the ominously sung phrase: "No Dogs Allowed!" (Ironically, just such a prohibition resolves the core crisis: the apartment complex of Snoopy's first owner does not allow dogs.) *Willy Wonka* is almost gleefully sadistic in its display of children being punished in comically torturous ways, and a magical boat ride turns into a vivid, nightmarish, quasi-acid trip. Matching the felt need for isolation while singing, the love ballad written by the Sherman Brothers as the title "Waltz" for *The Slipper and the Rose* is sung by Cinderella and Prince Charming *after* the ball, when they are separated and expecting never to see each other again. Perhaps the prime example, though, is the central ballad for *Bedknobs and Broomsticks*, sung by Angela Lansbury's main character to the children under her care. When the Sherman Brothers write a song for a Disney musical titled "The Age of Not Believing," something definitely has changed.

Phantoms of Paradise: Rock and the Backstager

Intriguingly, while the film industry and much of the rest of the nation contracted economically, the music industry boomed in the early 1970s. Rock had become the *lingua franca* of American popular music. It was no longer the rowdy upstart, championed by small record labels churning out 45s to be played on tiny radio stations. As one music historian has put it, "in the previous decade, rock was the stuff of the counterculture; in the 1970s and on ..., this music *was* the culture."[15] In contrast, what had been regarded as mainstream popular music from the 1930s to the 1950s was rechristened as "easy listening" music, and ushered to the sidelines. Rock had become so widespread that, by the 1970s, a number of subgenres emerged, including reggae, glam, funk/soul, acid, singer/songwriter, and soft rock.[16] Rock even began seeping into the integrated musical. The theatrical musical *Hair* debuted in 1967 and opened with a celebration of the dawning of the "Age of Aquarius," a world of love, peace, and harmony. *Hair* and mega-concerts such as the Monterey Pop festival and Woodstock (and the movies of these events) offered rock music as something to believe in, something that could *and would* help create a new utopian society.

Unfortunately, such utopian dreams began to fall apart in somewhat rapid fashion. Rolling Stones member Brian Jones, who had been dealing with substance addiction, drowned in his own swimming pool. Both Janis Joplin and Jimi Hendrix would die by overdose in 1970, and Jim Morrison of the The Doors would pass away the following year. *Gimme Shelter* (1970), a concert documentary made by the Maysles Brothers, presents a polar opposite to the optimistic energy on display in *Woodstock* (1970), which had been released only nine months earlier. The film starts off with Stones frontman Mick Jagger, dressed as a mod Uncle Sam, telling a concert audience, "We're gonna have a look at you," and then singing "Jumping Jack Flash." Just as the song ends, the film cuts to the band glumly sitting in an editing room watching concert footage. A radio news report over this footage tells of the violence that erupted while they were performing at a mega-concert at the Altamont Speedway. Hell's Angels were hired as security, and a member of the motorcycle gang stabbed an audience member to death in front of the stage during the Stones' set. The climactic moment of the film is not some stunning musical performance, but "having a look" at footage of the incident with slow-motion replay and freeze-frames. Rather than a celebration of utopia, the film was entered as evidence in the subsequent murder trial.[17] Reports that concert organizers hired the Hell's Angels in order to lessen the budgetary needs for security added further outrage. The events at Altamont, like the numerous overdose deaths, reinforced the image of a music industry run by unscrupulous hucksters exploiting musicians and audiences, literally willing to kill for profits.

Dissention and division rather than brotherhood began to dominate the rock music scene. In 1970, The Beatles split up, Diana Ross left The Supremes for a solo career, and Simon and Garfunkel went their separate ways. The emergence of so many rock subgenres also indicated a lack of unity, with everyone going off into their own circles. To be fair, diversity in music tastes had existed for generations (as earlier chapters describe). Yet, in the first half of the twentieth century, there was a concerted effort to create a national consensus of "American" music, arguing American music's unique vibrancy was its ability to bring together diverse types of music into something new (a sonic embodiment of the "melting pot" mythos). In the aftermath of the 1960s counterculture and protest movements, much of the American populace no longer bought into that idea, and each musical taste somewhat defiantly resisted assimilation. During this period, various films tapped into each of the subgenres of rock: reggae (*The Harder They Come* [1972] with the legendary Jimmy Cliff); glam rock (the David Bowie concert film *Ziggy Stardust and the Spiders from Mars* [1973]); funk/soul (*Sparkle* [1976]); acid (the Led Zepplin concert film *The Song Remains the Same* [1976]).[18] Yet, none of these films found a mass audience, appealing only to one specific niche listener base. Those interested in seeing *The Harder They Come* generally were not interested in attending *The Song Remains the Same*. *Sparkle* was extremely popular in inner city theatres (particularly among African American women), but did not get bookings where most white audiences could see it. Importantly, industry strategists consciously fostered such separation, as evidenced by the development of radio station "formats" ("soft rock," "oldies," etc.), to compartmentalize and target audiences as potential customers.

The 1970s saw a subtle but important shift from a call for collective protest for social change to a championing of individual liberty (gay rights, a woman's rights over her body, etc.). "Self-empowerment" and "looking out for number one" became the mantras of the day. Cultural historians began to refer to 1970s America as "the Me Decade," and arguably a celebration of self-centeredness took hold. The rock music industry became an easy emblem of overindulgence and ruthless egotism, a reputation it had battled since its start. During the early years, artists and producers countered such accusations by presenting themselves as "little guys" with musical integrity fighting against attempts by "the Man" (the big record labels, the major Hollywood studios) to dilute or exploit their work. But, now the people involved in making rock music *were* the Man. Artists, agents, producers, and promoters who had identified as part of the counterculture were now taking business meetings and hiring lawyers. Rather than changing things, power and the lure of a lavish lifestyle seemed to have changed *them*.

Backstagers of the period express these sentiments strongly. Granted, backstagers of all decades commonly deal with the potential downside of working in the entertainment industries. In this era, though, it sometimes seems like no one makes it out alive. Death abounds in *Beyond the Valley of the Dolls* (1970), *Lady Sings the Blues* (1972), *Phantom of the Paradise* (1974), *Nashville* (1975), *Sparkle, A Star Is Born* (1976), *The Buddy Holly Story* (1978), and *The Rose* (1979). Previous backstagers also tended to present "one bad apple" (a scheming producer, a selfish diva) in an otherwise laudable environment. These new films find everyone at fault: the exploitative promoters and executives, the self-destructive artists, and even the ravenous fans.

The calumny heaped on unethical managers and agents goes to extremes never considered by Sam Katzman in the 1950s. Record producer "Z-Man" Barzell (John LaZar) goes completely berserk during a drug-fueled frenzy in the final moments of *Beyond the Valley of the Dolls*, revealing himself to be transsexual, then beheading one guest, and shooting a number of others.[19] *Phantom of the Paradise* goes even farther: industry tycoon Swan (Paul Williams) has signed a pact with Satan. Swan steals the work of meek composer Winslow Leach (William Finley), and when Leach tries to stand up for himself, the poor fellow's head gets smashed in a record press. Perhaps cutting too close to real life, Led Zepplin threatened a lawsuit for the film's use of the name of their label, Swan Song Records. Superimpositions of an alternate name were put in during post-production: Death Records.[20]

Untrustworthy managers, agents, and executives also appear in *A Star Is Born*, *The Buddy Holly Story*, and *The Rose*. Even punk rock, emerging from Great Britain as a revolt against the mainstream industry (and much, much more), gets denounced in the Sex Pistols' film *The Great Rock n' Roll Swindle* (1980). In that film, the band's manager, Malcolm McLaren, claims he concocted the Pistols (and punk rock itself) as a scam to make himself a fortune. The title character of *The Idolmaker* (1980), music promoter/producer Vincent Vacarri (Ray Sharkey), molds young men into rock stars, but has an obsessive need to control his protégés. The picture treats the lead character a bit more sympathetically, perhaps because the real-life inspiration, Bob Marucci (who helped start the careers of Frankie Avalon and Fabian), acted as technical advisor.

The Idolmaker makes the singers under Vincent's mentorship seem a bit ungrateful and self-serving—and this film was not alone in aiming criticism at the performers themselves. These movies often showed artists very open to exploitation by agents and producers in order to reach fame and fortune, and totally ruthless in their own right. While *Phantom of the Paradise* shows Leach desperately trying to protect his music from the evil Swan, other musicians are shown as petty and narcissistic. Singer Beef (Gerrit Graham) is "high-maintenance" but untalented. Ingénue Phoenix (Jessica Harper) abandons her moral integrity in favor of the excesses of stardom—ultimately stepping over the dead bodies of Winslow and Swan in her climb to higher glory. Other films link such egotism to excessive drug use (which usually leads to death): *A Star Is Born, Sparkle, The Rose*. Such films obviously allude to Hendrix and Joplin (and *The Rose* is a thinly veiled portrayal of Joplin by Bette Midler). Posthumous documentary tributes to both performers were made during this period. While neither specifically mentions or shows their drug habits, both *Jimi Hendrix* (1973) and *Janis* (1974) contain moments that undercut their iconic status (he is shown off stage as withdrawn and introverted, she is shown in a recording session obviously high, rambling, and at times verbally abusive to those around her).

The audience itself is often implicated as well, depicted as an unruly, fickle mob, easily swayed by crafty publicity, and always clamoring for more. Kris Kristofferson's rock idol James Norman Howard in *A Star Is Born* may be a jerk spiraling towards failure, but the audiences encountered by himself and star-in-utero Esther Hoffman (Barbra Streisand) are rude and obnoxious as well. Concert attendees in *Phantom of the Paradise* are presented as hysterical rabble akin to the masses that thronged to the Roman Coliseum, cheering madly as Beef gets electrocuted on stage, and breaking into an orgiastic riot in response to the carnage of the "rock wedding" that ends the film. Most bluntly, *The Great Rock n' Roll Swindle* used the tagline "The film that incriminates its audience" in some of its promotional material.

Although the backstagers of this period accuse the music industry of moral corrosion, the films themselves seem fascinated by the very things they profess to condemn, reveling in lurid moments of drug use, wild parties, and scandalous behavior in the recording studio or on stage. The concertgoers in *Phantom of the Paradise* may be grotesquely enjoying the sordidness on display ... but so is the supposed audience watching the film. In attempting to make the story more palatable for the "women's lib" era, the 1976 version of *A Star Is Born* exemplifies the slippery slope from self-empowerment to self-centeredness. Starring and co-produced by Barbra Streisand, the final sequence replaces the famous but problematic closing line "This is Mrs. Norman Maine" with an eight-minute-long close-up of Streisand singing, making the film feel less a feminist statement than a vanity project.

A number of backstagers during the 1970s acknowledge that such venality occurred in earlier times. *Bound for Glory* (1976), for example, does not shy away from showing Depression-era folk singer Woody Guthrie's inflated ego, abandoning his wife and kids, and enjoying his growing fame as a "man of the people."[21] *Lady Sings the Blues* covers all aforementioned tropes in telling the life story of jazz singer Billie Holliday (Diana Ross): a singer hooked on heroin, a number of malfeasant businessmen, and racist audiences (including a scene of Billie and her band driving past the remains of a lynching on their tour bus, followed by a performance of "Strange Fruit," a ballad about lynching which Holliday co-wrote). The film initially seems to end on the typical high-note of a backstager: the singer making a glorious triumph, defeating all the odds in concert. Yet, the film stays just a bit beyond the final ecstatic moments to superimpose a number of newspaper headlines acknowledging Holliday's impending (and quick) slide into despair and death.

The work of British director Ken Russell took things even farther back, covering famous classical composers such as Peter Tchaikovsky (*The Music Lovers* [1971]), Gustav Mahler (*Mahler* [1974]), and Franz Liszt (*Lisztomania* [1975]). Russell fashions each film as an expression of the style of the composer's work, but also consistently links these icons to the unscrupulous excesses of the current times. *Lisztomania* in particular largely abandons historical accuracy in favor of present-day orgiastic overload. The film's first few seconds, with Roger Daltrey (as Liszt) romping in bed with a woman to the tempo of a sequined metronome seems quite contemporary. When the woman's foppish husband bursts in, the ensuing melee is accompanied by country-and-western twanged narration. Liszt is depicted as the idol of 1800s teeny-boppers (who would rather hear him play "Chopsticks" than anything else), and his theatre dressing room (peopled with partygoers and hangers-on) looks little different from modern-day images of backstage at an arena rock concert ... but with powdered wigs. Liszt is an arrogant womanizer, but he himself gets exploited by a powerful Russian princess acting as his manager and publicist. The final portion of the film overtly connects music to power and corruption: Liszt figuratively battles rival composer Richard Wagner (Paul Nicholas) when Liszt's daughter and the teeny-boppers get lured by Wagner's music into becoming war-mongering fascists.

Glam rock heavily influenced the style of *Lisztomania* and other films of the era. Coming largely from Britain, glam pushed the fashion consciousness of 1960s "swinging London" to an extreme. Undercutting the "back-to-the-earth" sincerity and open emotion espoused by the anti-materialist hippie movement, glam artists such as David Bowie and Roxy Music intentionally accentuated stylization, irony, and Brechtian-alienation to convey that all musical performance involves calculated artificiality.[22] Thus, glam projected not only an aura of cynical self-absorption but also the importance of role-playing—not only within the music industry but also in life in general. Nowhere was this more acute than in glam's play with gender, which delighted some and disturbed others. The use of glamour to blur the boundaries between male and female (use of makeup, glitter, lamé, platform shoes) is used by a number of characters such as Z-Man in *Beyond the Valley of the Dolls*, Beef in *Phantom of the Paradise*, Frank in *The Rocky Horror Picture Show* (1975, to be discussed in the next section). Camp, yes, but consciously and overtly so—the gay connections to the musical genre in these instances are definitely *not* subtextual.[23]

Some musicals used glam to examine more than the music industry. The rock opera *Jesus Christ Superstar*, for example, turns the gospels into a different form of 1970s backstager, with Jesus (Ted Neely) buffeted between a fickle mob of groupies (Jesus' disciples) and various corrupt power figures (the Pharisees, Pilate). Furthermore, Judas (Carl Anderson) accuses Jesus of being a self-involved idol spiraling towards destruction. Herod (Josh Mostel) is perhaps the most directly glam figure, but the film version connects to glam's philosophy of distanciation by opening with the cast and crew driving into the desert in buses and trucks and showing them preparing to "put on a show."

Ken Russell's film version of *Tommy* (1975) takes the Who's rock opera and turns it into a thoroughly glam-filled allegory about the pitfalls of any form of idol worship. Tommy (Roger Daltrey) becomes worshipped for being a "Pinball Wizard," analogous to being a rock star *and* being a religious icon. He is surrounded by corrupted and corrupting figures (his parents, his sadistic cousin Kevin, his perverse Uncle Ernie, the Acid Queen). Youthful trauma happens when he witnesses his father being killed by his mother and stepfather. The pair stress to him that he didn't see or hear anything, which turns him blind, deaf, and mute for many years. Yet, the film takes time to go beyond Tommy's plight and shows a larger cycle of exploitation and trauma. For example, the first section of the film centers more on the tribulations of Tommy's mother (Ann-Margret), explaining (without justifying) the questionable choices she makes in raising her son. Her attempt to give herself and her son a better life results in her second marriage and in exploiting her son's celebrity as a "deaf, dumb, and blind" pinball wizard. In one of the film's most memorable moments, Mom symbolically revels in a sea of soap suds flowing out of a TV set—which then turns into a shitstorm of baked beans and chocolate (Figure 10.2).[24] On the other side, Tommy instigates the next generation of trauma: Sally Simpson, a young fan of the Pinball Wizard, gets caught in a melee at one of his "performances," physically scarring her for life. His followers are exploited by many of the people surrounding him, but the fans turn quickly on him, leaving a wasteland of destruction and death in their revolt. It becomes an unending circle of pain and retribution (reinforced by a motif of circles in the visual design—particularly the pinball itself being bounced around).

Possibly the most powerful depiction of the music industry as an allegory for the sorry state of contemporary society was Robert Altman's epic film *Nashville* (1975). Situated within the expanding country music industry rather than rock, and released just before the United States' Bicentennial year (the song "200 Years" is shown being recorded during the opening credits), the film

Figure 10.2 Ann-Margret wallows in soap suds and baked beans (and earns an Oscar nomination for Best Actress), metaphorically representing her vain attempts to overcome the guilt she feels about her "deaf, dumb, and blind" son in *Tommy* (1975). Snapshot taken from: Tommy (1975).

follows a cross-section of characters over a few days: groupies, agents, stars, aspirants, music reporters, and so on. Like the pinballs in *Tommy*, the individuals bounce off each other, but are too caught up in their own agendas to ever really make contact. An early set piece puts most of the cast in a traffic jam, unable to move forward. Altman's common technique of overlapping dialogue has no one listening to anyone else—including characters holding conversations while others perform rather than paying attention to the music. Power and profit motives dominate as people ready themselves to participate in a political rally.[25] The myopia climaxes at the rally, where one of the crowd shoots singing star Barbara Jean (Ronee Blakely). In the midst of the chaos, an aspiring singer grabs a microphone and starts singing the gospel-like tune "It Don't Worry Me." Eventually, the assembled not only calm down but join in the chorus: "You may say that I ain't free, but it don't worry me." As a helicoptered camera rises up to take in (or fly away from) the whole scene, it seems Americans only come together in a concerted effort to ignore life's harsh realities. *Nashville* itself was critically acclaimed but not widely viewed. While *Tommy* did do well at the box office, most of the films discussed in this section were financial failures, and some were actively despised.[26] Mick Jagger claimed he wanted to "get a look" in *Gimme Shelter*, but one song in *Tommy* advocates that we "Smash the Mirror," and the close of *Nashville* implies we all would rather simply turn away.

Life as a Cabaret: Deconstructing the Musical

Big-budget studio musicals and even family-oriented ones had a hard time mustering up faith in what the genre traditionally championed: individual freedom and communal harmony. Backstagers increasingly excoriated all aspects of the music industrial complex. A number of films went a step further, overtly dissecting merits of the musical genre itself. Deconstruction of other long-popular film genres began in late 1960s American cinema: the gangster film (*Bonnie and Clyde* [1967]), the horror film (*Targets* [1968]), the Western (*Little Big Man* [1970], *McCabe & Mrs. Miller* [1971]). Many film historians associate this trend with an era referred to as New American Cinema.[27] A new generation of filmmakers actively questioned traditions (in content and form), instead of following what had always been done. In so doing, such genre deconstruction usually reflected shifts in attitudes about society at large, and how genres had supported older belief systems. During the 1970s, this deconstructive impulse affected the musical both in Hollywood and on Broadway, but in slightly different ways.

Theatrical musicals faced many of the same problems that film musicals did: rock music, mushrooming budgets, and growing doubt and distrust in the genre's promise of utopia.[28] On stage, a new format emerged: the concept musical. Historian Ethan Mordden defines the concept musical as "a presentational rather than strictly narrative work that employs out-of-story elements to comment upon and at times take part in the action, utilizing avant-garde techniques to defy unities of place, time, and action."[29] Whereas classically integrated musicals aim to have all aspects (the songs, the dancing, the visual design) unite in a smoothly flowing storyline, concept musicals emphasize the contemplation of an issue or topic. Consequently, the narrative might be jumbled to help make a point, or be paused to evaluate the action, and the musical might finish without a clear story resolution. Musical numbers may drive the storyline forward (as in traditional integrated musicals), but sometimes the numbers act instead as *analysis* of the plot (a return of the Greek chorus, so to speak). Such moments seem to occur in a space outside the world the characters inhabit. Concept musicals are thus often associated with a multi-functional "unit set"—a vaguely abstract space designed to represent various locations by just shifting a few pieces. This complicated, jigsaw-like structure regularly gets used to represent a fractured society and a *dystopian* viewpoint.

A concept musical is also often very "meta" (to use a more current term), connecting the issue/concept under discussion to the show's own status *as a* musical. *Company* (first produced in 1970) uses the musical theatre term indicating the entire cast to announce its central concern: whether human company (romantic or otherwise) is desirable or ever truly achievable. The title of *Follies* (first produced in 1971) harkens back to Florenz Ziegfeld's legendary revues; it also refers to a theme of human foolishness and self-deception.

A Chorus Line (first produced in 1975) turns the spotlight on dancers conventionally hired to perform as anonymous identical cogs behind the star.

Many consider songwriter Stephen Sondheim the most important figure in musical theatre during this era. His concept musicals traverse a wide spectrum of subject matter: an adaption of an Ingmar Bergman film (*A Little Night Music*); a meta-history of economic relations between Japan and the West (*Pacific Overtures*); a tale of a grisly serial killer (*Sweeney Todd*); an examination of the purpose and value of art itself (*Sunday in the Park with George*).[30] His projects also self-reflexively explored the history of the musical genre. *Follies* pushes the splintered structure of the musical revue format to an extreme, until the show becomes some sort of nervous breakdown shared between the characters and the audience. *Merrily We Roll Along* literally upends the optimism of the typical Mickey Rooney–Judy Garland backstager by running the narrative backwards, thus undercutting the bright-eyed optimism of the young show-business hopefuls by introducing them as the jaded, angry middle-aged people they will become. *Into the Woods* invokes the traditional fairy-tale musical, but completely undermines the simple good/evil moral outlook typical of such "family-oriented" fare by showing what happens *after* "living happily ever after."

Sondheim's work was not immediately accepted and hailed. Critics and audiences had to *work* when listening to his songs, instead of sitting back and enjoying. The multi-faceted dimensions of his lyrics and the more complex composition of his melodies made Sondheim's work something appreciated more by a rarefied (verging on cult) audience than the general population.[31] This ambivalence towards Sondheim's shows is likely why Hollywood filmmakers did not rush to adapt them.[32] Harold Prince, who directed the original Broadway production of Sondheim's *A Little Night Music*, had to turn to European backers to make a film version in 1977. It died at the box office and disappeared quickly.[33] It would take thirty years until another Sondheim show was adapted into a motion picture.[34]

In general, only a few concept musicals appeared on movie screens in the 1970s. The British production of *Oh! What a Lovely War* (1969) depicts World War I in allegorical fashion, using the patriotic marches and novelty tunes of the period to indict jingoism then and now. *Jacques Brel Is Alive and Well and Living in Paris* (1975), an off-Broadway revue celebrating the French songwriter, was lensed for American Film Theatre (an independent company experimenting with limited distribution of cinematic versions of theatrical properties). On screen, people in a puppet theatre play various roles while performing songs that confront war, love, and death in an emotionally raw manner. Most film audiences considered the abstract and stark feel of the subject matter for both of these two films unappealing.

By and large, any attempts by Hollywood musicals to explore new forms were wedded to a relatively clear narrative. The film adaptation of *Godspell* (1973), for example, uses the life of Jesus to present a series of vaguely connected parables performed by a tribe of hippies wandering around Manhattan (although presenting the Son of God in circus clown makeup did not sit well with many audiences). *Jesus Christ Superstar* covers similar territory, a property first popularized as a "concept *album*" (a form that a number of groups turned towards by the end of the 1960s). *Tommy* was another "concept album" turned into a film that, while still highly surreal, provides a clearer storyline than the original recording offered.[35] Director Stanley Donen and songwriters Lerner and Loewe musicalized the popular book *The Little Prince* (1974), an already highly allegorical tale and possibly the one original "concept musical" to come from Hollywood. Its demise at the box office (and the lackluster response to *Godspell* and *Jesus Christ Superstar*) likely warned producers from further ventures into the concept musical.[36]

Although the concept musical *per se* may not have taken hold on screen, "meta" discussions about what it means to be a musical did become more pronounced. A number of films become self-reflexive by adding framing devices, showing the viewer that people are preparing to perform the musical entertainment we are about to see, as in *The Boy Friend* (1971), *Jesus Christ Superstar*, and *Man of La Mancha* (1972).[37] Many films of the period overtly invoke the traditions of the genre through the use of pastiche: a song consciously copying some older style of music, or an entire musical created as an imitation of a previous type of musical.[38] Pastiches of older movie musicals proliferated. *The Boy Friend*'s play within the movie is a pastiche of 1920s stage musicals, but the picture has characters imagining a more elaborate production echoing the work of Busby Berkeley in the 1930s, kaleidoscopic overhead patterns and all. (And, as an end joke, the big film producer watching the stage production announces that he has decided to make *Singin' in the Rain* [1952] instead.) *At Long Last Love*'s visual design is full Art Deco, and largely in shades of black, white, grey, and silver—thus invoking the feel of RKO Astaire and Rogers films. Among the elements of pastiche in *New York, New York* (1977) is a sequence entitled "Happy Endings," echoing such long-form musical numbers from the 1950s as "The Broadway Ballet" in *Singin' in the Rain* and "Born in a Trunk" in *A Star Is Born* (1954). Stanley Donen's *Movie Movie* (1978) is a pastiche of a 1930s double-feature, the second half—"Baxter's Beauties of 1933"—clearly modeled on *42nd Street* (1933). *Pennies from Heaven* (1981) is a compendium of 1930s musicals, including references to Busby Berkeley, Astaire and Rogers, the child performer craze, and even the vaudeville specialty act.

Pastiche likely proliferated because audiences were better able to recognize what was being referenced. Television aired older movie musicals at almost all hours of the day and night. Repertory houses showing classical Hollywood cinema sprang up in big cities and around college campuses during the 1960s. Film studies classes at universities increased during the 1960s and 1970s. MGM's most successful musical in the first half of the 1970s was a compilation of musical numbers from its glory days: *That's Entertainment!* (1974). Clearly reacting to the gloomy historical moment, the marketing tagline for this retrospective was "Boy. Do we need it now." The project did so much business that the studio quickly churned out *That's Entertainment, Part 2* in 1975.

The newest musical star to emerge during this era lent herself easily to such pastiche. As the daughter of Judy Garland and MGM musical auteur Vincente Minnelli, Liza Minnelli seemed a walking compendium of the genre's history. She pays tribute to her mother's work at MGM in *That's Entertainment!* In the animated musical *Journey Back to Oz*, she steps into Garland's ruby slippers by providing the voice of Dorothy. Minnelli's role and costumes in *New York, New York* are clearly designed to evoke the milieu of Garland's postwar MGM musicals.

Such descriptions sound as if this cycle of films glorified the history of the movie musical. Yet, the (sometimes highly produced) pastiches were inevitably undercut by the deconstructionist aims. If Minnelli raised the memory of her mother, for example, those memories were now colored by Garland's death by overdose in 1969. While *That's Entertainment!* canonized Kelly's performance of "Singin' in the Rain," *A Clockwork Orange* (1971) uses the song to accompany a rape/assault by a roving gang of thugs in futuristic Britain. A number of movies during this period can be described as "anti-musicals," films that seem actively antagonistic to the genre and everything it traditionally champions. Characters' faith in the philosophies traditionally espoused by musicals leads to tragedy rather than triumph. As with the films discussed in the previous section, "death by musical" becomes a common motif.

Examples of pastiche in "anti-musical" films (and theatrical concept musicals) consciously draw attention to the fact that they are imitations—a listener can somehow hear the quotation marks around the song, so to speak.[39] The obviousness in part occurs because these pastiches often undermine or challenge the attitudes of the old forms referenced. The songs of John Kander and Fred Ebb, major contributors to the concept musical, serve as case in point. The melodies initially sound like old-fashioned "razzmatazz" showtunes, yet include a few "wrong" notes or chords, creating a darker tinge than typical. Similarly, the lyrics on a surface level follow the typical clichés of vaudeville or Tin Pan Alley—but then include lines that suddenly and incisively expose the bias or hatred hiding within the clichés. For example, their Oscar-nominated tune "How Lucky Can You Get?" in *Funny Lady* sounds initially like a typical up-tempo Depression-era song—but it turns into a dark and bitter diatribe, expressing an inner turmoil underneath the glib surface.

Comparable to the manner in which 1970s backstagers often tear down the myths of fame, fortune, and collaborative effort, "anti-musicals" (like concept musicals) investigate the political uses of song and dance: to distract a population from reality and/or to maintain support for and belief in the status quo. The genre's support of community values, for example, is often undermined—presenting

Figure 10.3 Tim Curry as Dr. Frank N. Furter leads the rest of the cast of *The Rocky Horror Picture Show* in "Don't Dream It—Be It." A campy deconstruction of horror films and musicals, this number is obviously not the typical aquacade that starred Esther Williams. Snapshot taken from: The Rocky Horror Picture Show (1975).

those values as stringent and a hindrance to individual liberty. On the other hand, the genre's celebration of freedom becomes suspect too, potentially leading to either isolation or total chaos. Exposing the nightmarish implications behind the sunny dreams of the musical is central to blending the genre with the horror film in *Phantom of the Paradise* and *The Rocky Horror Picture Show* (1975). The central character of *The Rocky Horror Picture Show*, Dr. Frank N. Furter (Tim Curry), functions as the "mad scientist" of a horror film but also envisions himself as the star of a musical extravaganza. What the musical genre would read as his attempt to "put on a show," the horror genre would read as "his evil plan." The culmination of his efforts is an aquacade to the song "Don't Dream It—Be It"—but it happens only through him controlling the minds and bodies of others (Figure 10.3). Frank is ultimately vanquished, killed by his hunchbacked assistant.

Conventional attitudes about romance and desire also got torn down. *At Long Last Love* employs the romantic farce typical of Astaire and Rogers' films but presents a quartet of shallow, soulless people constantly changing partners. Francis Ford Coppola's *One from the Heart* (1981) shows an average couple (Frederic Forrest, Teri Garr) bored with their relationship and yearning for the romantic excitement found in traditional musicals, resulting in both being lured by exotic alternatives (Raul Julia, Natassia Kinski) in a completely studio-fabricated Las Vegas. It seems that the protagonists are so trapped in their fantasies that the songs are sung in their heads (and with the professional voices of Tom Waits and Crystal Gayle). Their relationship is saved when he finally sings "You Are My Sunshine" to her in his imperfect voice. In a similar fashion, *Pennies from Heaven*'s Arthur (Steve Martin) yearns for the transcendent love that people sing about, often imagining himself in musical production numbers and lip-syncing to original 1930s recordings. Unfortunately, that belief causes him to abandon his wife, to lead a small-town schoolteacher into big-city prostitution, and to implicate himself in the murder of a blind girl.[40]

Rocky Horror also presents conventional heterosexual romance as bland and boring, but takes Brad and Janet (Barry Bostwick, Susan Sarandon) down a very different path than the above films.[41] They are the horror-cliché couple that need to be saved from the monstrous Frank N. Furter when they become stranded at his castle in a rainstorm. Yet, Frank and his cohort are like the inhabitants of Oz: a glamorous, exciting alternative to heteronormative marriage, as Frank exclaims in his introductory number, "I'm a Sweet Transvestite." Frank seduces both of them, luring them into exploring a range of sexual pleasures, and everyone ends up in the pool in bustiers, boas, fishnet stockings, and stiletto heels. (This is not your typical Esther Williams water ballet!)

Rocky Horror was not the only film to exploit the greater freedom that the Ratings System offered to depict onscreen sex. For a brief moment in the mid-1970s, fueled by the unexpected crossover success of *Deep Throat* (1974), mainstream audiences began openly attending explicit X-rated films. As such, pornographic films with slightly higher budgets and ambitions were produced for a few years, including a number of musicals. *Alice in Wonderland: An X-Rated Musical Fantasy* (1976) and a pornographic musical version of *Cinderella* (1977) overtly exposed the sexuality hidden within the fairy-tale musicals, just as family-friendly musicals were growing in number. *The First Nudie Musical* (1976) uses the backstager structure to lampoon both the porn industry and the musical genre, including a hilarious low-budget production number with chorus boys dressed up as Dancing Dildos.[42]

New York, New York tears apart the traditional genre notion that success in show business and in romance are co-related. Aspiring saxophone player Jimmy (Robert de Niro) and aspiring singer Francine (Liza Minnelli) spark professionally and romantically, and he describes to her a utopian concept perfectly suited for a classic Hollywood musical: searching for "a major chord" of fame, fortune, and romance. Yet, the film demonstrates that achieving *his* "major chord" is at the expense of *hers*, and vice versa. His need to be in charge and more successful than her leads him to affairs and violent outbursts. The film ends with them divorced and pursuing separate careers. Her big Hollywood movie (the "Happy Endings" sequence) serves as ironic juxtaposition: Jimmy sits by himself in a theatre watching his former wife become a star in a musical about finding fulfillment in both show business and love. The title song also underscores their incompatibility: his version is a slow jazz instrumental, hers is a brassy showtune anthem.

The endings of these films are, without exception, depressing. Boy does not reunite with girl at the end of *New York, New York.* Dr. Frank N. Furter is dead and Brad and Janet are left like detritus after their experiences in *Rocky Horror. Pennies from Heaven* might seem to counter this trend when Arthur somehow magically steps away from being hung for murder to reunite with the school-teacher in the final moments of the film, telling her that "songs don't end that way." Yet, the film seems to indicate this moment (and the ensuing lines of chorus girls strutting to "The Glory of Love") is simply his (and our) final attempt to escape the reality of what is about to happen.

The most important artist involved in "anti-musicals" (and a key figure in the rise of the theatrical concept musical) was Bob Fosse. Like Liza Minnelli, Fosse had ties to the MGM musical, having danced in *Kiss Me, Kate* (1953) and *Give a Girl a Break* (1953). He left Hollywood for Broadway to become a choreographer and director. Perhaps the Freed Unit's grooming of choreographers to be directors acted as a model for Fosse (and Gower Champion, who also left MGM to become a very successful director/choreographer). While song-writers in the Rodgers & Hammerstein era gained greater creative authority by also becoming producers, choreographers asserted control by becoming directors.[43] Fosse's unique vision is immediately evident in his choreographic style. Dancers get put into jagged patterns, with deadpan expressions and odd contortions, like soulless machines or puppets. Often only one part moves (one finger snapping, or one shoulder rolling), as if the pieces of the body are alienated from each other. The dancer's body is itself, in a sense, deconstructed (Figure 10.4).

Figure 10.4 Liza Minnelli performs "Mein Herr" in *Cabaret* (1972). This pose epitomizes the way director/choreographer Bob Fosse isolates body parts to express a sense of alienation: Minnelli's extended left foot seems totally disassociated from the rest of her. Snapshot taken from: Cabaret (1972).

Fosse's musical films express a fascination with the glitz and tinsel of show business, but also expose it as tacky, grubby, and filled with manipulation. *All That Jazz* (1979) has obvious autobiographical overtones, based on his own heart attack in the mid-1970s (and predicting his death in 1987). In it, Joe Gideon (Roy Schneider) is an A-list choreographer/director who pops pills, chain smokes, and sleeps with almost every woman he encounters, all supposedly for the sake of his craft. As a consequence, he experiences a massive coronary, undergoes open heart surgery, and has a terminal relapse while still in recovery. Like Arthur in *Pennies from Heaven*, Joe chooses to live his last moments in the fantasy of a massive musical performance. "Bye Bye Love" is interrupted before its conclusion by a cut to him being zipped up into a body bag, followed by Ethel Merman erupting on the soundtrack with "There's No Business Like Show Business."

Fosse directed what many consider to be the best and most important musical of this period—*Cabaret*, based on the Kander and Ebb stage hit, starring Liza Minnelli (Fosse and Minnelli both won Academy Awards). In eliminating the integrated numbers in the original 1966 stage incarnation, the film version becomes *more* of a concept musical. All but one of the songs are performed at the titular cabaret and provide commentary on the storyline. For example, Fosse cross-cuts between an onstage slap-clap lederhosen folk dance led by the cabaret's Master of Ceremonies (Joel Grey, also an Oscar winner) and two Nazis beating up a gentleman in a back alley. Later, when lead character Sally Bowles sees that a man she just met owns a limousine, the film cuts immediately from her wide-eyed reaction to "The Money Song," a new song written for the film.[44]

The cabaret acts as a metaphor for how people try to shut out what they do not want to see or hear. Performers and clientele blithely revel in decadence while the Nazi party comes to power, driven onward in their blindness by the unnerving and slightly demonic MC. As such, the film vaguely indicts the phenomenal popularity of the film version of *The Sound of Music*. Both films take place in the same time period and deal with the rise of the Nazi Germany, and *Cabaret*'s "Tomorrow Belongs to Me" echoes "Edelweiss" in *The Sound of Music*. In Fosse's film, a fresh-scrubbed young man in a rural setting begins to sing a pastiche of a folk song, rhapsodizing about nature and home—and the enchanted population enthusiastically joins in the singing. The camera eventually tilts slightly downward, though, to show that he is wearing a Nazi swastika armband, and the orchestration moves from a pastoral idyll into an aggressively insistent march. Just as Sally Bowles and other characters ignore what is happening by ensconcing themselves at the cabaret, scads of contemporary audiences tried to escape the upheaval of the late 1960s by going over and over again to watch *The Sound of Music*. (The parallels to teeny-boppers lured to Wagnerian fascism in *Lisztomania*, or the crowd singing "It Don't Worry Me" in *Nashville* should also be noted.)

Changes to the original book of the stage musical further deconstruct the romantic conventions of the genre. The film replaces the subplot of a middle-aged couple with Fritz (Fritz Wepper), who has successfully hidden his Jewish heritage, falling in love with Jewish heiress Natalia (Marisa Berenson). Fosse juxtaposes their relationship with the MC singing "If You Could See Her Through My Eyes" … to a gorilla. In case the movie-goer misses the connection, Kander and Ebb end the song with "She wouldn't look Jewish at all," a line that still has power to shock and discomfort audiences. Their story concludes with a wedding—but there is every indication that this couple is doomed by the impending Holocaust. "Boy does get girl," but this is a happy ending?

The film also reworks the relationship between Sally Bowles and the male protagonist. Both versions show their romance ultimately failing. The film goes farther, though, in explaining why. Scenarist Jay Allen not only has Brian admit to Sally that he doesn't sleep with girls, but also creates Max (Helmut Griem), a character who has sex with both of them.[45] After Max departs suddenly, Sally finds herself pregnant and Brian offers to marry her. Sally eventually realizes that a conventional marriage with a child would end up a disaster for everyone: she would resent giving up her career, he would still be attracted to men, and the baby would be caught in the middle. Boy getting girl would be an *unhappy* ending, so Sally ends the pregnancy.

It is her one moment of clarity, though—and it is partly motivated by a desire to keep following a different form of delusion: becoming a star. Minnelli's final number is the title song, sung like a celebration of life, but equally readable as symbolic of Sally's return to fantasy. The film concludes as the cabaret finishes its presentation. The MC asserts that all troubles have been forgotten, bows stiffly and exits, and the camera pans across a warped mirror on the stage reflecting the audience of the cabaret (including some in Nazi uniforms) and, implicitly, the audience in the movie theatre—yes, another 1970s musical turning a mirror on its audience.

The production of deconstructionist musicals may have seemed like a smart business strategy in the 1970s. If audiences were turning away from traditional musicals—then perhaps musicals that criticized traditional musicals might attract customers! *Cabaret* and *All That Jazz* were the only two of this trend to do well critically and at the box office, though. The others did horribly. *At Long Last Love* severely weakened director Peter Bogdanovich's career, and *New York, New York*'s poor performance tarnished director Martin Scorcese's reputation. Perhaps pushing the concept of pastiche to a new level, *New York, New York* paralleled the fate of the Judy Garland version of *A Star Is Born*. United Artists pulled the film after its initial premiere to edit it down to a shorter running time, the "Happy Endings" sequence being among the cuts. No one, neither fans nor haters of the genre, wanted to see anti-musicals. To some, such films (and the reaction to them) appeared to be nailing the coffin on the genre rather than resuscitating it.

Conclusion

If the general memory of this era is that the musical died, it is not necessarily because films that centered around performed song and dance disappeared. Rather, that memory exists because critics and audiences by this time would only regard a film that contained integrated numbers as a musical. Many of the films discussed in this chapter are still not largely regarded as musicals. Pictures about musicians or composers are now usually considered biographies with some music, rather than backstage musicals, for example. *Nashville* is rarely thought of as a musical but more as a study *of* the music industry (and of America itself). People even argued whether *Cabaret* was a musical or not, *The New York Times* describing it "not so much a movie musical as it is a movie with a lot of music in it."[46]

The crisis that the genre faced was figuring out how to break out of the constrictions of conventional integrated showtunes. As a consequence, the era can be regarded as an exciting one, filled with rampant experimentation. True, despair hung over quite a number of the films, and quite a number of ideas fell flat. Nonetheless, the unique appeal of the Dancing Dildo number in *The First Nudie Musical* (1976), Tim Curry strutting as Frank N. Furter in *The Rocky Horror Picture Show*, or Valerie Harper doing some sort of unique rendition of the Funky Chicken in *Phantom of the Paradise* is not to be missed. Any era that includes *Cabaret*, *Tommy*, and *Nashville* is an important one.

Notes

1 Furthermore, that film—*The Tamarind Seed* (1974)—was not a musical. For an extended discussion of the production of *Darling Lili*, see Matthew Kennedy, *Roadshow! The Fall of Film Musicals in the 1960s* (Oxford: Oxford University Press, 2014), 174–178.

2 Purportedly, when Minnelli yelled "Cut!" after shooting a lavish banquet sequence, the production designer shouted out "Don't eat any more!" *Los Angeles Times* (May 29, 1969); Stephen Harvey, *Directed by Vincente Minnelli* (New York: Harper & Row, 1989), 288, describes the cutting down of the film by Paramount executives.

3 William Hanna and Joseph Barbera moved into television in the late 1950s when MGM closed up its shorts division. At MGM, the duo produced the popular Tom & Jerry cartoons, and thus did the animation used in a number of that studio's memorable musicals (*Anchors Aweigh* [1945], *Dangerous When Wet* [1953], *Invitation to the Dance* [1956]). In the mid-1960s, their company produced a couple of theatrical features spun off from their most successful TV series: *Hey There, It's Yogi Bear* (1964) and *A Man Called Flintstone* (1966).

4 In reaction to the trouncing the film received in the press, *At Long Last Love*'s director Peter Bogdanovich wrote an open letter rant, which was published in various newspapers. To read the letter, see http://www.lettersofnote. com/2011/06/i-await-you-hollywood-feverishly.html

5 A lot of writing on the film mentions the "Lost Investment" nickname, such as Harry and Michael Medved, *The Hollywood Hall of Shame: The Most Expensive Flops in Movie History* (New York: Perigee, 1984), 216.

6 On the incredibly troubled production of *The Blue Bird*, see Patrick McGilligan, *George Cukor: A Double Life* (New York: St. Martin's Press, 1991), 315–317.

7 Lee Gambin, *We Can Be Who We Are: Movie Musicals from the 1970s* (Albany: BearManor Media, 2015), 329, contains an interview with Archie Hahn, one of the voice doubles for the young actors, admitting, "we didn't know who was going to play what parts at the time, so it was a guess as to what they were going to sound like." In the booklet accompanying the DVD release in 2003, director Alan Parker describes how songwriter Paul Williams was "on tour at the time, and as he stopped in each new city, they would find a recording studio and send us the resultant tapes … I told Paul that I didn't want squeaky kids voices and he interpreted this in his own way. Anyway, as the tapes arrived, scarcely weeks away from filming, we had no choice but to go along with it!"

8 Pauline Kael's review in *The New Yorker* (March 17, 1973), 119–121, pointed out that "the Orientals are kept in their places, and no blacks … are among the residents."

9 To be fair to *1776*, the film still contains the stunning "Molasses to Rum to Slaves" number excoriating both North and South for maintaining slavery.

10 Reports about the strained atmosphere during production of a number of these films repeatedly got leaked to the public. For example, see Rex Reed, "Elizabeth Taylor Sees Red in 'The Blue Bird,'" *Ladies' Home Journal* (October 1975), and Frank Pierson, "My Battles with Barbra and Jon," *New West* (November 11, 1976), 27–43 (on *A Star Is Born*).

11 Brendan I. Koerner, *The Skies Belong to Us: Love and Terror in the Golden Age of Hijacking* (New York: Crown Publishers, 2013), 8, asserts that hijackings during this period happened "often at a clip of one or more per week … [and] many days when two planes were hijacked simultaneously." (In 1972 alone, 40 hijackings occurred.)

12 Things were even worse in the United Kingdom, with unemployment reaching close to 20 percent.

13 Kelly Kessler, *Destabilizing the Hollywood Musical: Music, Masculinity, and Mayhem* (New York: Palgrave Macmillan, 2010), 60–69.

14 The two claim that various studio employees were jealous of Walt's fondness for them, and that they experienced a backlash after his death, in *The Boys: The Sherman Brothers' Story* (2009). They also describe the growing stress that collaborating with each other caused during the 1970s.

15 Ken Tucker, *Rock of Ages: The Rolling Stone History of Rock & Roll* (New York: Summit Books, 1986), 468.

16 Tucker, 467: "The growing size of the rock audience and the industry that had grown up to accommodate it encouraged fragmentation."

17 Tucker, 495: "One of the primary pieces of evidence employed by the prosecution [of the Hell's Angels] was the climactic footage of a documentary film …: the Maysles Brothers' *Gimme Shelter*."

18 While *Sparkle* is structured like a typical backstage musical, the most famous examples of funk/soul in 1970s American film are found not in musicals but in blaxploitation action films, particularly *Shaft* (1971) and *Superfly* (1973). Curtis Mayfield, composer of the score for *Sparkle*, had a much greater success with his soundtrack album to *Superfly*.

19 The representation of "Z-Man"/"Super Woman" in the film is so confused (and ill-informed) that attempts to find a more politically correct term than "transsexual" seem pointless.

20 Led Zepplin's lawsuit is mentioned on the extra materials on the home video release of *Phantom of the Paradise*, but see also Stephen Jones, *The Essential Monster Movie Guide* (New York: Billboard Books, 2000), 299.

21 Judith Sims, "Tim Buckley Dead at 28," *Rolling Stone* 193 (August 14, 1975), reported that singer Tim Buckley was supposedly "seriously considered" for the title role but died of a drug overdose just before production was scheduled to begin.

22 See Tucker, 487–493.

23 Although not overtly employing a "glam aesthetic" (as he did in many other films of the period), Russell's *The Music Lovers* effectively outs Tchaikovsky as homosexual, and the plot pivots around attempts to put him back in the closet. In addition to the transsexual music producer, one member of the female rock band in *Beyond the Valley of the Dolls* (1970) falls in love with another woman.

24 Adding to the sense of exploitation and suffering, the press reported how a shard of the exploding TV screen badly sliced Ann-Margret's hand when this sequence was filmed. (At least she got an Oscar nomination in compensation.) Russell saw this sequence as retribution for how much he hated making TV commercials selling laundry detergent and baked beans at the start of his career.

25 The film's opening declares the importance of commerce: a faux TV ad "hard-selling" the movie soundtrack as a method of announcing the stars of the film. The campaign that holds the rally is for a never-seen candidate, but we hear his words blaring out of loudspeakers consistently, vague platitudes inciting people's fears and emotions rather than confronting actual issues.

26 For example, Charles Champlin, "Sexploiteer Hitchhikes on Dolls' Title," *Los Angeles Times* (June 18, 1970), G1, declares that 20th Century-Fox had "fouled its own nest" by releasing *Beyond the Valley of the Dolls*.

27 The term "New American Cinema" is a slippery one, and has been used by various people to describe *different* eras or filmmakers. For example, a group of experimental filmmakers in the early 1960s (such as Jonas Mekas, Jack Smith, and Ron Rice) put out a manifesto referring to themselves as the "New American Cinema Group" (http://film-makerscoop.com/about/history accessed on February 12, 2016). Jon Lewis, in his Introduction to *The New American Cinema* (Durham: Duke University Press, 1998), 1, mentions his use of the term in regard to "the so-called auteur renaissance that took shape after the studios adopted the MPAA Ratings System in 1968," but acknowledges "the emergence, around 1980, of another new American cinema that seemed largely a consequence of a new conglomerate, multinational Hollywood." To differentiate the two movements that Lewis describes here, I am using "New American Cinema" as a term for the former group (which is also how Criterion uses it to group certain films in its home video collection), and the term "New Hollywood" in Chapter 11 to designate the latter.

28 Ethan Mordden, *One More Kiss: The Broadway Musical in the 1970s* (New York: Palgrave, 2003), 6, describes how "the capitalization and maintenance of a good-sized show ... [had] grown out of all proportion to the potential gross" for a musical on Broadway. While such budget-to-profit disparities had been growing during the 1960s, the inflation of the 1970s exacerbated the situation.

29 Mordden, 127.

30 *Company*, with a Sondheim score, is considered the turning point for the advent of the concept musical. It is not regarded as the "first" concept musical, just as *Oklahoma!* was not the first integrated musical. Intriguingly, many cite a lesser-known Rodgers and Hammerstein property, *Allegro* (first produced in 1947, and never adapted to film), as the first concept musical (including Sondheim himself).

31 Mordden, 33, opines that "when the form's composer-in-chief is nationally popular, he and Broadway are in sync with a public. When he is controversial, however much eventually accepted, Broadway is losing its public."

32 As will be discussed in Chapter 12, some Sondheim properties have eventually been turned into movies—but, as of 2014, *Company*, *Follies*, and *Sunday in the Park with George* still have not been adapted to the big screen.

33 *A Little Night Music* and a number of other musicals discussed in this chapter are notoriously unavailable (or very hard to find) on home video or DVD.

34 *Sweeney Todd* (2007), to be discussed in Chapter 12. On the other hand, televised performances of Sondheim's work happened regularly during this time span, almost always on American public television via tapings of the original productions or "concert readings." More on this in Chapter 12 as well.

35 The eventual Broadway production, *The Who's Tommy* (first staged in 1993), is even more focused on narrative than concept.

36 Budget and box-office numbers for *The Little Prince* are hard to come by, but director Stanley Donen candidly refers to the film as a "financial fiasco," in Joseph Andrew Casper, *Stanley Donen* (Metuchen: Scarecrow Press, 1983), 213. Costing reportedly $1.3 million, *Godspell* brought in $1.2 million in domestic rentals. *Jesus Christ Superstar* did the best of this trio: from a projected budget of $3.5 million (R. Serge Denisoff and William D. Romanowski, *Risky Business: Rock in Film* [New Brunswick: Transaction Publishers, 1991], 211), it earned $10.8 million in rentals in its initial release ("Big Rentals of 1973," *Variety* [January 9, 1974], 19, 60), Yet, Denisoff and Romanowski, 212–213, relate the amount of political, religious, and aesthetic calumny heaped on the film version of *Jesus Christ Superstar* upon its release.

37 The framing device is part of the original stage version of *Man of La Mancha*, but was added to *The Boy Friend* and *Jesus Christ Superstar* in their adaptation to film.

38 Use of pastiche goes back decades. Integrated musicals relied on them often to create the proper setting. For example, something set on a *Show Boat* in the 1880s includes an imitation of a "coon song" ("Can't Help Lovin' Dat Man").

39 This is in contrast to the pastiches that appeared in musicals prior to this era. Two songs in *Meet Me in St. Louis* (1944) are original compositions meant to sound like they were actually written around 1906: "You and I" and "Over the Bannister." "Edelweiss" in *The Sound of Music* is such an effective pastiche of an Austrian folk song that some people actually think it *is* an Austrian folk song.

40 *Pennies from Heaven* is arguably the last of the "anti-musical" film cycle, but while the film came out in 1981, it originated as a 1978 British TV miniseries, so still within the time period discussed in this chapter.

41 Similarly, the "Liebestraum" sequence in the glam-influenced *Lisztomania* depicts Liszt's relationship with Marie (Fiona Lewis) as a silent-movie parody, presenting heterosexual romance as theatrical and artificial.

42 For more on all three of these films, see Gambin, 344–347, 405–407, 333–344 respectively. *The First Nudie Musical* was not the first musical of the 1970s to include a giant dildo. *Lisztomania* includes a huge phallus in an extravagant castration dream ballet (yes, you read that correctly).

43 So much so that Fosse either got credit for the books of the stage musicals he directed (such as *Big Deal* in 1986, and [with Fred Ebb] *Chicago* in 1975), or unique billing indicating the depth of his involvement (such as *Sweet Charity* in 1966 being "Conceived by Bob Fosse"). Importantly, when Rodgers & Hammerstein produced their concept musical *Allegro*, they hired Agnes de Mille (who had choreographed *Oklahoma!* and *Carousel*) to direct.

44 The original Broadway score also contained a tune titled "The Money Song," but Fosse requested an entirely new one be written to fit the rest of the revisions being made for the film version. Stage revivals of *Cabaret* invariably elect to use the second version.

45 Isherwood's stories *do* have the characters visit gay clubs, but do not explicitly "out" the male protagonist. The influence of the film version has led to stage revivals inserting much more queerness into their productions than had been present in 1966. The extremely popular Broadway revival in the mid-1990s even rewrote portions of the original dialogue.

46 Roger Greenspan, "Liza Minnelli Stirs a Lively 'Cabaret,'" *New York Times* (February 14, 1972): 22.

11

Can't Stop the Music: Musicals and the New Hollywood

A number of key histories of the film musical genre peter out around the end of the 1970s. Ethan Mordden's *The Hollywood Musical* was published in 1982, and Rick Altman's *The American Film Musical* came out in 1987, and neither have been updated.[1] Jane Feuer did write a new chapter in the second edition of her seminal work *The Hollywood Musical* to include discussion of some of the films in this chapter, but that was done in 1993.[2] A critical consensus began to build that the genre had reached its nadir in mainstream popularity and in its ability to evolve with the times. According to this framework, some brave filmmakers ventured forth occasionally to attempt to revive the musical film, but greater interest was not spurred. The film musical was effectively dead.

Certainly, examples of what had become the predominant definition of a musical film—that is, integrated song and dance—were few and far between. Adaptations of Broadway musicals dwindled significantly by the 1980s, and original integrated film musicals were even harder to find. Yet, sounding the genre's death knell was only appropriate if one kept solely to that one standard definition. Musical performance on film did not disappear. The emphasis during the late 1970s and through the 1980s was not so much on Broadway but on how the recorded music industry used film and the musical genre. As such, this era (roughly 1977–1987) gives rise to new forms and new ways of defining what might constitute a musical film.

Such a shift reflects the development of new business patterns within the motion picture industry. The growth of conglomerate cross-promotion of entertainment, a strategy termed "synergy," helped revive Hollywood's fortunes. The second half of the 1970s witnessed the box-office explosion of films such as *Jaws* (1975), *Rocky* (1976), and *Star Wars* (1977). Writers soon began referring to this emerging moment as a "New Hollywood" to reflect this era's return to the type of traditional escapist entertainment that the major Hollywood studios had produced in the classical era of the 1930s, 1940s, and 1950s. Such movies negotiated through the parameters of contemporary attitudes, but ultimately reinvested in the myths and beliefs of an earlier generation: upholding the idea that old-fashioned virtue and a strong work

Free and Easy? A Defining History of the American Film Musical Genre, First Edition. Sean Griffin.
© 2018 Sean Griffin. Published 2018 by John Wiley & Sons Ltd.

ethic would lead to success, and that good could triumph over evil (and that one could tell easily which was which).

A number of books and articles have been devoted to the rise of this New Hollywood.[3] Few have examined the importance of the musical genre, even though a number of the major hits of the period were musicals. The industry's growing focus on young adult straight male customers led to dismissing musicals as a "feminine" genre. Discussions of synergy in New Hollywood also usually focus on the burgeoning interest in merchandising, which favored fantasy and science-fiction pictures. Yet, two flurries of film musical production (one in the late 1970s, and another in the mid-1980s) occurred within the New Hollywood era, both strongly tied to synergistic collaboration with the music industry.

Stayin' Alive: The Music Industry and the Film Musical in the Late 1970s

As noted in the previous chapter, a severe slump at the box office in the early 1970s led to various conglomerates buying up a number of major Hollywood studios. A number of non-entertainment corporations were involved (such as Gulf + Western and Transamerica), but the recorded music industry participated as well. Record sales grew throughout the decade, reaching $2.4 billion in 1975 (equaling motion picture box-office receipts for that year), and approaching $4 billion by 1979.[4] Thus, record companies had the capital to start buying up the holdings that the film companies were shedding.[5] A basic example would be Phonogram buying up MGM Records in 1972,[6] but record executives stepped into film production too. Barry Gordy's Motown Productions transitioned Diana Ross into movie stardom with *Lady Sings the Blues* (1972), which Paramount released. EMI Records entered into an agreement in 1976 with Columbia Pictures to jointly produce four films.[7] Casablanca Records merged with producer Peter Guber's Filmworks, Inc. in 1976, and entered into an ambitious slate of movie projects.[8]

The music companies' interest in motion picture production was clearly connected to the possibilities of selling a text across multiple "platforms." Traditionally, historians point to *Star Wars* as the wake-up call to the profits to be gained from "horizontal integration," after 20th Century-Fox signed away the merchandising rights to producer/director George Lucas. Yet, the Hollywood studios had done cross-promotion with the recording industry for decades, in the release of soundtrack albums. By the latter half of the 1960s, though, rock music dominated album sales, except for the phenomenal success of the soundtrack to *The Sound of Music* (1965). As a result, most producers of film musicals in the early 1970s did not focus too heavily on the revenue potential from album tie-ins.[9]

Nonetheless, certain soundtrack albums did extremely well during this period. Blaxploitation films such as *Shaft* (1971) and *SuperFly* (1972) spawned a number of popular albums.[10] The Woodstock concert was a cultural phenomenon, becoming a very successful Oscar-winning documentary, and a huge-selling album. Motown's soundtrack to *Lady Sings the Blues* went to number one on the Billboard charts, selling over two million copies. *American Graffiti* (1973) spun off a hugely popular nostalgia-fest album filled with late 1950s/early 1960s pop music.[11] Furthermore, these three examples were multiple sides: *Lady Sings the Blues* and *American Graffiti* filled two long-playing discs, and *Woodstock* was a triple-LP album. The artistic and commercial success of such double-LPs as The Beatles' *White Album* and The Who's *Tommy* seemed to have spurred such expansion during the 1970s (including Stevie Wonder's *Songs in the Key of Life*, Neil Diamond's *Hot August Nights*, Elton John's *Goodbye Yellow Brick Road*, and Peter Frampton's *Frampton Comes Alive*).

Where things shifted was that, rather than studios using records to help sell the pictures, the music industry entered into film production in order to move records. *A Hard Day's Night* (1964) presaged this development, with United Artists reportedly being more interested in releasing a soundtrack of Beatles' music than they were in making the movie.[12] By the mid-1970s, such an outlook was becoming the norm. When Frank Pierson met with Warner Bros. executives about directing the Barbra Streisand version of *A Star Is Born* (1976), they told him: "It would be nice if the picture was good, but the bottom line is to ... shoot her singing six numbers, and we'll make $60 million."[13] The film and the soundtrack were both released during the Christmas season, and the album had sold over three million copies by the following summer.[14]

Perhaps the most insightful of these record executives was Robert Stigwood. An Australian who had worked at one time with Beatles manager Brian Epstein, Stigwood incorporated himself into RSO (Robert Stigwood Organization) in 1968. In addition to managing various recording artists, he supported the early career of composer Andrew Lloyd Webber, producing the stage versions of *Joseph and the Amazing Technicolor Dreamcoat* and *Jesus Christ Superstar*. The latter property gained an initial popularity as a two-disc concept album before getting financial backing for stage productions in London's West End and then on Broadway ... followed by a film version. Thus, multiple double-LP versions were generated from one score in relatively quick succession: the concept album, the original cast albums, and the soundtrack album. Stigwood began working with the philosophy that one "built on a musical vehicle so that it got better known than the play or movie of which it was part."[15] RSO was incorporated into PolyGram Records in 1970, putting Stigwood on its Board of Directors. In 1975, Stigwood produced not only the film version of *Jesus Christ Superstar* but also the cinematic adaptation of The Who's *Tommy*, thus creating another re-envisioning of a hit double-LP, this time with contributions from a number of A-list recording stars, including Elton John and Tina Turner. Thus, Stigwood had begun implementing horizontal integration ahead of *Star Wars*.

PolyGram agreed to put substantial investment into film production under Stigwood's supervision, and he began partnering with agent/producer Allan Carr.[16] Their first project starred one of Carr's clients, actor John Travolta, with soundtrack music provided by one of Stigwood's clients, the Bee Gees: *Saturday Night Fever* (1977). Selling the music was always at the forefront. Four months before the film's Christmas release, a teaser trailer for the film began screening in 1500 theatres, blaring the Bee Gees tune "Stayin' Alive," which had just been released as a single. Four different songs would be released before the film opened—and snippets of all four played over a second trailer released over Thanksgiving. The album was "shipped gold," meaning that a half million copies were distributed all at once, and 850,000 units were sold before the film had premiered.[17] By February 1977, all four singles were in the US *Billboard* Top Ten, and 15 million albums eventually sold in the United States. Oh, and the film did well too. A tagline on posters asked "Where do you go when the record is over ..." Released through Paramount, *Saturday Night Fever* made Travolta an Oscar-nominated star, and it became one of the top-grossing films of the decade.

Stigwood followed the same business pattern with his next production, again with Carr and Travolta: *Grease* (1978). Singles were released in advance of the film and double-LP, and the music featured prominently in trailers. The soundtrack was another smash hit, selling 22 million copies globally.[18] Two new strategies enhanced the film's popularity. First, *Grease* was rated PG, in order to broaden the potential consumer base. (*Saturday Night Fever* was rated R, and demands by teenage fans of the album led to a recut PG version.) Second, the film was Paramount's big summer release, as Hollywood began regarding summer as prime blockbuster season, when the kids got out from school. As a result, while *Saturday Night Fever* sold more records, *Grease* did better at the box office, becoming the fourth most successful film of the decade (after *Star Wars*, *Jaws*, and *The Exorcist* [1973]).

A surge of music-oriented films emerged in the late 1970s as a consequence. Stigwood and Carr would work together on *Sgt. Pepper's Lonely Hearts Club Band* (1978) for Universal, and Carr on his own would produce *Can't Stop the Music* (1980) through EMI Films. Motown Productions partnered with Casablanca Filmworks in making *Thank God, It's Friday* (1978) (which was distributed by Columbia), and solely produced *The Wiz* (1978) (which was released by Universal). The low-budget *Roller Boogie* (1979) and *Skatetown, U.S.A.* (1979) jumped on a new trend of disco roller-skating. A number of actual or fictionalized biographies of musical performers were also developed to capitalize on potential soundtrack profits: *The Buddy Holly Story* (1978), *The Rose* (1979), *One Trick Pony* (1980), *Honeysuckle Rose* (1980), and *Coal Miner's Daughter* (1980).

In spearheading more musical film production, the recording industry was taking quite a hefty amount of the rewards. Both *Saturday Night Fever* and *Grease* did very well for Paramount, but the studio was somewhat aggravated watching so much profit going to Stigwood and PolyGram. As such, the studios started trying to get a larger slice. Paramount, for example, began discussing a possible merger with EMI. Universal developed *Xanadu* (1980) in house, with the soundtrack released through its own MCA Records label. MGM was sole producer of *Fame* (1980), contracting with RSO Records simply to release the soundtrack album.

In addition to leading the move to horizontal integration, *Saturday Night Fever* and *Grease* exemplify another key characteristic of New Hollywood: a return to escapist entertainment and reviving a belief in the American Dream of success, wealth, and happiness. This new cycle of films marks a shift away from the dour, doubtful, and deconstructive attitude that dominates musical films made during the first half of the 1970s. Stigwood had been part of that early 1970s trend with *Jesus Christ Superstar* and *Tommy*. *Saturday Night Fever* exhibits the shadow of this frame of mind as well. Tony Manero (Travolta) is a working-class young man who escapes from the bleak future before him at the local discotheque where he gets treated like a star. Towards the end of the film, though, Tony's bubble is burst on two fronts. First, although he and his partner win the big dance contest, he realizes that another couple have outshone him. Later that night, one of Tony's friends makes explicit how trapped they all feel in their dead-end existence, and falls to his death from the Verrazano Bridge. At the film's close, Tony realizes he needs to wake up and grow up—but his lack of education and training still leave him few options. The film is shot mostly on location, showing the grimy nature of mid-1970s New York and Brooklyn, echoing the "kitchen sink realism" of early 1960s British cinema.

Nonetheless, audiences seemed to disregard the downbeat nature of the narrative. Moviegoers were just as fascinated as Tony was with the fantasy of success—everyone came to watch Travolta explode on the dance floor, the sound design shifting from raw on-location dialogue recording to multilayered disco music in Dolby Stereo (Figure 11.1).[19] Such enjoyment was encouraged by a marketing campaign that emphasized the music, and the poster presenting what would become an iconic image for the era: a triumphant Tony in his white leisure suit signaling victory on the dance floor. Viewers wanted the dream, the spectacle, and the excess rather than criticism of it—a point reinforced by the major box-office failure of the deconstructive *New York, New York*, which came out the same year. While a few more of the "anti-musicals" discussed in Chapter 10 got made during the late 1970s and very early 1980s, they were overshadowed by films that expressed this new form of optimism and escapism.

Some of these films follow *Saturday Night Fever*'s pattern: acknowledging some of the hard realities of life, but ultimately glorifying dreams fulfilled.

Figure 11.1 John Travolta's working-class Brooklynite finds release and success on the disco dance floor in *Saturday Night Fever* (1977). Snapshot taken from: Saturday Night Fever (1977).

Fame, for example, shows the ups and downs of various students at the New York Academy for the Performing Arts—but what viewers seem to remember most is the exuberance of the entire school dancing in the street to the Oscar-winning title tune ("I wanna live forever!") and not the misfortunes some of the characters encounter. *The Buddy Holly Story* (1978, Columbia, soundtrack through Epic Records), a biopic of the 1950s rock vocalist, also acknowledges a variety of potentially dour topics. Racial tensions arise repeatedly, for example. Holly (Gary Busey) slugs a white record producer over refusing to record his version of "nigger music." He also encounters hurdles in attempting to marry a Mexican American. The film also mirrors the final moments of *Lady Sings the Blues*: a climactic performance followed by graphics announcing the subsequent death of the performer. Yet, the film feels very unlike *Lady Sings the Blues* because it remains resolutely upbeat. Holly consistently overcomes any hardships. Somewhat disingenuously, the main person blocking Holly's interracial romance is the woman's mother, whom he easily charms. Booked to play at the famous Apollo Theater, he wins over the hostile African American audience by the time he finishes ripping through "Oh Boy!" The film's finale of Holly joyously rocking out before the scroll describing his death by plane crash feels more like "going out on a high note" rather than the sense of doom that pervades the end of *Lady Sings the Blues*. In so doing, the film works to turn Holly into a rock legend rather than use him to demonize show business. *Coal Miner's Daughter* (1980) would tell the tale of country star Loretta Lynn (with Oscar-winning Sissy Spacek) in a similar fashion: acknowledging her meager economic background, as well as her battle with drug dependence, but ultimately reaffirming the American Dream rather than dissecting it.

J.P. Telotte argues that the need to inject at least a bit more realism into these musicals, a "more sober though still affirmative feeling," can also be seen in their lack of integrated song and dance.[20] Contemporary film audiences seemed to regard breaking out into song or dance with incredulity, so these films eschew the practice. Regarding *Saturday Night Fever* as a musical poses problems for some because, even though there is plenty of music, none of the characters sing a note. The songs are either played on the radio, at the disco, or simply act as background score. Yet, the film centers around dancing, and it had a huge impact on popular dance in America. A new sub-category of the musical genre begins to emerge here: the "dance film." Director Herbert Ross's *The Turning Point* (1978) came out a year after *Saturday Night Fever*. Although focused on the world of ballet, featuring reigning superstar Mikhail Baryshnikov, it follows the same guidelines: (1) protagonists who work—or aspire to work—as dancers; (2) tons of choreography, but (3) no characters singing.[21] The dance film works easily for soundtrack album producers. There is no need to "write for the characters," figuring out integrated songs that might also work as breakout singles. Rather, the characters simply dance to whatever potential hit songs get chosen.

That said, *Grease* (1978), in adapting a Broadway hit with integrated song and dance, falls more squarely into the accepted definition of a musical, and offers an alternative to the strategy posed by *Saturday Night Fever*. Instead of offering a more realistic environment that includes a believable space to indulge in song and dance, *Grease* seems to agree with contemporary audiences that this is all ridiculous ... and then revels in its artificiality. This sense of cynical escapism became more prominent across mainstream American filmmaking by the end of the 1970s. New Hollywood filmmaking drew on elements of classical Hollywood but, instead of dissecting the assumptions of classic genres, used pastiche to revive and celebrate them. Thus, a large number of New Hollywood films take on the feel of comic books in their style and outlook. *Grease* has none of the "kitchen sink realism" of *Saturday Night Fever*. While the original stage property was gritty and raunchy, Stigwood, Carr, director Randall Kleiser, and choreographer Patricia Birch turned it into a comic-book confection (including an animated cartoon credit sequence). Stigwood's adaptation of The Beatles' classic rock album *Sgt. Pepper's Lonely Hearts Club Band* has none of the social critique found in his version of the Who's classic rock album *Tommy*. Instead, it has the visual design and outlook of an amusement park (most spectacularly in a rendition of a giant gooey cheeseburger in the town's public square). *Xanadu* turns late 1970s Venice Beach into a fantasyland, and includes a cartoon sequence as well. The exploitation roller-disco movies are similarly populated with two-dimensional archetypes for comedic enjoyment. Everything was aimed for a simple uncomplicated atmosphere of fun.

Disco music fit easily into this optimism. Its emphasis on glitter and spectacle and sexual abandon parallels glam rock, but without glam's sense of emotional remove or critical distanciation. Disco tends to revel in the excess without complication. Disco was about feeling good, about liberation from restraint. Disco also took elements from soul, particularly in emphasizing danceable music. *Saturday Night Fever* and subsequent films made use of the theatrical aspects of 1970s discotheques: flashing lights, mirrored globes, and dry ice effects to match the lush layers of orchestration. Neil Bogart, president of Casablanca Records, observed that club patrons were like Tony Manero – "they wanted to be the star" – and such spectacle helped them feel that way.[22] In its glorification of excess (as one popular song put it, "More, more, more!"), disco shifted away from the anti-capitalist communal aims of the 1960s counterculture. Disco wasn't about going to free concerts, it was about getting past the velvet rope in front of Studio 54, New York's most famous club. Such a consumer ethic played easily into the objectives of conglomerate media cross-promotion.

Disco also had the potential to bring multiple consumer groups together in a way that funk, glam, and other rock subgenres did not do, because it originally appealed to a variety of communities. Disco developed throughout the early 1970s in clubs that catered to black and Latino clientele.[23] It is perhaps not accidental that the couple Tony Manero feels outperformed him and his partner are coded as Latino. Motown co-produced *Thank God, It's Friday* with Casablanca, giving African American disco superstar Donna Summer her first film, singing the Oscar-winning "The Last Dance." Quincy Jones's orchestrations in the film version of *The Wiz* highlight the link between soul/funk and disco, a connection also made in the blaxploitation picture *Disco Godfather* (1979).

Disco also came to prominence in gay nightclubs, feeding into the burgeoning gay liberation movement. A number of people involved in making these films were (or were rumored to be) gay, including Carr, Stigwood, and songwriter Paul Jabara (who penned "The Last Dance"). Disco's excess lends itself quite easily to the pleasure of camp. The cartoonish feel of *Grease* has camp value, such as the "Beauty School Dropout" number with male greasers as angels and chorus girls parading in giant pyramids of silver hair rollers. *Can't Stop the Music* easily reads as a chaotic gay male camp extravaganza, complete with an all-male Berkeleyesque presentation of "Y.M.C.A." The climactic production number in *Xanadu* is also appreciable as camp, with Olivia Newton-John and her entourage roller-skating around the flashy titular nightclub in a constantly changing array of outfits.

Disco also appealed to women, with Donna Summer and other female vocalists asserting their strength and independence in a number of disco "anthems." It is notable that, of the top five box-office champions of the 1970s, *Grease* is both the only musical and the only picture marketed to female consumers.[24] Young women seemed to enjoy Sandy (Olivia Newton-John) moving from sweet girl-next-door to tight-leather sexpot more as an expression of rebellion against social norms than as a lesson in sexually objectifying one's self. In *Xanadu*, Newton-John plays a Greek semi-deity, coming to the rescue of various mortal men rather than needing rescue herself.

Saturday Night Fever helped disco become a full-fledged mainstream craze, as white heterosexual men (represented by Tony Manero) finally took an interest in it. In this manner, disco traveled a similar path that ragtime, jazz, and rock and roll had done. The resultant surge of musical film production did not last, though. One key factor for the downturn was the focus on the soundtrack albums above the films themselves. The excitement of having the Bee Gees and Peter Frampton join with various guest stars to create a double-LP tribute to The Beatles with *Sgt. Pepper's Lonely Hearts Club Band* was not accompanied by any strong thought as to how to turn this project into a viable motion picture (and the final homage to the original album cover is largely a sad collection of B-list TV game show celebrities). *Xanadu* seemed more interested in creating an LP that had one side of Olivia Newton-John songs and one side of cuts from the Electric Light Orchestra than in creating a film. The soundtrack to the remake of *The Jazz Singer* (1980) may have gotten Neil Diamond three hit singles, but the film was immediately regarded as a major embarrassment.

The lack of cinematic forethought was not the only factor, though. Disco's roots within marginalized cultures soon worked against its mainstream popularity. For example, although critics tore apart Sidney Lumet's lackluster direction of *The Wiz*, other industry wags saw its spectacular box-office failure as a sign that white audiences were not interested in black films. Many have blamed *The Wiz* for ending studio interest in films about African Americans that had grown during the 1970s, and Motown largely stopped its forays into motion picture production. The gradual realization of disco's connection to gay culture also made it anathema to many young straight men. Perhaps surprising to people today, many straight listeners did not instantly recognize the gay connotations to the songs sung by the Village People ("Macho Man," "Y.M.C.A.," "In the Navy") (Figure 11.2). Once they did, though, straight men began running away from disco in droves. Homosexual rumors (rightly or wrongly) got attached to Travolta, causing major problems for his career as the 1980s began. Even though Carr changed the title of his Village People opus from *Discoland* to *Can't Stop the Music* because he recognized the growing backlash, the film still did horrible business. "Disco sucks" became a mantra, and when a Chicago radio DJ decided to blow up a pile of disco records between the first and second games of a baseball double-header, the attendees turned the moment into a "Disco Riot."

While disco connected with American society's interest in uplift rather than criticism, and in New Hollywood's optimistic outlook, it ultimately ran counter to the last major aspect of this culture shift. In returning to old forms and old values, New Hollywood and mainstream America were embracing a

Figure 11.2 Nothing homosexual happening here. The Village People fling their assorted silvery spangles with maximum flair while doing "The Milkshake" in *Can't Stop the Music* (1980). Snapshot taken from: Can't Stop the Music (1980).

more conservative social attitude. Disco's association with sexual liberation, particularly (but not exclusively) with homosexuality ran counter to this shift. As such, disco and the films that embraced it were quickly quashed, and what had seemed like a resurgence of the genre ended up being only a blip on the radar.

If the early 1970s parallel the talkie revolution for the genre (in terms of the amount of experimentation as to what constituted a musical), then the early 1980s resemble in many ways what genre historians have referred to as "the slump" of the early 1930s. Yet, just as musicals still got made during the early 1930s, musicals continued to appear in spite of the sudden flame-out of disco. Certain filmmakers thought that other kinds of music might still draw an audience. A few more films based on "album-oriented" rock or concept albums were produced in this period, such as The Who's *Quadrophenia* (1979) and *Pink Floyd—The Wall* (1982). Paramount tried out *Grease 2* (1982). Adaptations of a few theatrical musicals got made: *Hair* (1979), *The Best Little Whorehouse in Texas* (1982), and *Annie* (1982). Somewhat anachronistically, a successful 1981 Broadway revival of the Gilbert and Sullivan operetta *The Pirates of Penzance* engendered not only a film version in 1983, but also a knock-off, *The Pirate Movie* (1982). Intriguingly, MGM attempted to resuscitate its heritage by investing in musicals. In the wake of *Fame* and *Pennies from Heaven* came *Yes, Giorgio!* (1982), *Victor/Victoria* (1982), and *Yentl* (1983).[25] *Yes, Giorgio!* sought to turn operatic superstar Luciano Pavarotti into the next Mario Lanza. *Victor/Victoria* and *Yentl* starred Julie Andrews and Barbra Streisand respectively in their first musicals of the decade. Although some of these films attracted an audience, none did landmark business either in ticket or in soundtrack sales.

On the opposite side of the spectrum from "showtunes" was the emergence of punk rock in New York and Great Britain. Punk actively resisted attempts at commercialization, and the form arose precisely because its performers and fans rebelled against the corporate mentality. Punk was loud, angry, messy, and violent. As Stacy Thompson writes, punk culture emphasizes "shows over recordings, and raw over clean production."[26] Hence, punk was of little help to the music or film industries. A few motion pictures attempted to capture the punk aesthetic. Yet, as historian David Laderman describes, such films are largely "spurned by punk purists as too commercial and passed over by mainstream film histories as too trashy."[27] The amount of money, power, and coordination needed to produce even a low-budget exploitation film stands as a perfect example of what punk rebels against. *Rock and Roll High School* (1979) is gleefully rebellious and features The Ramones, but takes place in a completely non-punk suburban high school filled with preppies and jocks. Stigwood's attempt to cash in on punk, *Times Square* (1980), was a blatant exploitative gesture, but even director Derek Jarman's avant-garde punk extravaganza, *Jubilee* (1978), was excoriated by those within the subculture for selling out.[28] Punk in various fashions would continue beyond the late 1970s and early 1980s, but it consciously thrives on the fringes of the marketplace—a position that motion picture producers have little interest in pursuing.

Perhaps unsurprisingly, the most popular musical released during this period was the one most directly aimed at young adult straight (and largely white) males. *The Blues Brothers* (1981) showcases some of the legends of African American jazz/blues/funk/soul (James Brown, Ray Charles, Aretha Franklin, Cab Calloway) but centers on two white guys co-opting the music for their own. While containing a plethora of numbers (even integrating Franklin's rendition of "Respect" into the narrative), the film appealed to its target market by promoting itself as a comedy rather than as a musical. Based on characters created by Dan Ackroyd and John Belushi for the TV sketch comedy show *Saturday Night Live, The Blues Brothers* inadvertently indicated the importance that video would very soon have on reviving the fortunes of the film genre and of the music industry as a whole.

Cinematic Boogaloo: The Impact of Music Video

The downfall of disco signaled a larger and more thorough collapse of the entire music industry at the start of the 1980s. Soon, it wasn't just disco-related albums like the soundtrack to *Sgt. Pepper's Lonely Hearts Club Band* that were doing disastrously.[29] In the course of two years, total sales dropped 20 percent.[30] "From a high point in 1978 of 726.2 million album sales, the number dropped to 575.6 million units in 1982."[31] By February of 1982, *Time* was announcing "Rock Hits the Hard Place."[32] The sudden staggering drop in business led to huge employee layoffs at the record companies. Such measures paralleled what was occurring all across the United States as a new recession took hold. By 1982, nationwide unemployment had passed 10 percent, the highest since the Depression.

The music industry laid major blame for its woes on the growth of home recording, consumers using now-readily-available blank cassette tapes to record music off the radio or from borrowed records rather than paying for singles or albums. With the cost of albums increasing and many citizens worried about their own economic stability, the growth of home recorded music made sense. The high-concept escapist entertainment coming out of Hollywood kept the major studios relatively flush during this period, but they too feared the impact of home recording. Home video and cable television became widely available across the country as the 1980s began, leading Disney and Universal to sue Sony (unsuccessfully) in order to keep their Betamax system off the market. Yet, rather than siphoning off profits, cable TV and home video would lead to a new phase of expanded profits for both industries.

A new cable station debuted in the summer of 1981. MTV filled its programming with short video clips of songs, with either the performers on camera or some other form of visual accompaniment. These "music videos" were produced by the record companies and offered free of charge as promotional material to encourage sales.[33] The music video format had various predecessors. Soundies during the 1940s and Scopitones in the 1960s were 16 mm performances of music to be shown via a visual jukebox in public settings. Pre-filmed or pre-taped performances to be aired on television variety programs or "dance party" shows, often produced by the artists or their record labels, became common in the 1950s and 1960s, most particularly on the British programme *Top of the Pops* (1964–2006). Two Beatles videos played on *The Smothers Brothers Comedy Hour* (1967–1969), and many have pointed to the style of the numbers in The Beatles' films *A Hard Day's Night* (1964) and *Help!* (1965) as major influences on the aesthetics of music video.[34] During the 1970s, rock and pop artists increasingly dominated TV variety shows, not just as weekly guests but as hosts of their own hours (such as Sonny and Cher, Donny and Marie Osmond, and Tony Orlando and Dawn). By the definition of the term, variety shows had no narrative requiring integration of the music performances, and pre-produced pieces similarly stood alone. Again, audiences interested in pop music (i.e., newer generations) were not being acclimated to the rhetoric of transitioning from story to song.

The potential of MTV was not immediately evident to the music industry, but soon budding consumers all over the nation were chanting its highly successful slogan "I Want My MTV!" By 1982, the impact of MTV was becoming apparent. A *Billboard* survey found that "new acts who made their bow on MTV enjoyed an immediate 10 to 15 percent increase in sales."[35] While only three albums sold more than two million units in 1982, by the end of the first quarter of 1983, four were poised to do so or more, and each had substantial play on MTV.[36] By 1984, the entire record industry had not only rebounded, it had surpassed its all-time peak in 1978 at the height of the disco phenomenon.[37] The industry began to realize the videos they were giving away were valuable material, so MTV in 1984 signed contracts, paying for the exclusive rights (for a predetermined period) to air videos produced by three of the major labels. Exclusive rights had become prized because a number of other channels and programs began showcasing music videos as well.[38] The music video format became so dominant on television that it effectively spelled the demise of *American Bandstand* (after three decades) and other dance-party shows, as well as the collapse of the variety show genre. The importance of sound quality to music videos also helped spur the rapid changeover to stereo television in the United States in 1984.[39]

The avalanche of music videos in the 1980s emphasized certain visual aesthetics. Most noticed was the quick pace of editing, exhilarating and possibly overwhelming viewers.[40] In addition to shorter shot lengths, the editing strategies often link random images to each other rather than following classic continuity patterns—thus accentuating the potential incomprehensibility. The images themselves tend to loud colors and other forms of lavish stylization, perhaps attempting to register in the viewer's mind quickly before the video suddenly cuts to something else. Performers, musical instruments, or other props thrust aggressively out toward the camera. Inadvertent explosions occur frequently. All manner of special effects get employed, and videos often act as testing ground for new advances in computer-generated imagery.

While finding certain recurrent stylistic decisions across a number of 1980s videos, though, one *exclusive* aesthetic pattern did not actually exist. The rapid, disjunctive editing and flashy visuals are used to draw viewer attention, in recognition of the distracted nature of television watching (at home, in a bar/club, etc.). Yet, if *every* video has the same fast editing pace and bold *mise-en-scene*, then they all begin to blur together. Thus, music video makers consistently aim to present something different to make their work stand out from the crowd—including videos done in one take rather than with fast cutting, or in black-and-white rather than brash colors.

As interest in music videos exploded, the hunt for new concepts to grab viewer attention led to the dusting off of *older* concepts. A number of music videos turn to the history of musical films for inspiration.[41] Perhaps the most notable instance of this occurs in Madonna's "Material Girl" video (1985), where she performs a pastiche of Marilyn Monroe's rendition of "Diamonds Are a Girl's Best Friend" in *Gentlemen Prefer Blondes* (1953). Yet, this one video is just the tip of the proverbial iceberg. People noted the influence of *West Side Story* (1961) on Michael Jackson's breakthrough video "Beat It" (1983), for example.[42] Paula Abdul's dance with the animated MC Skat Kat in "Opposites Attract" (1990) was inspired by Gene Kelly dancing with Jerry the Mouse in

Anchors Aweigh (1945), and her video for "Cold Hearted Snake" (1990) reworked Bob Fosse's "Take Off with Us" in *All That Jazz* (1979).[43] While not quoting specifically, the visual design of Janet Jackson's videos to "When I Think of You" (1986) and "Alright" (1990) evoke the feel of a 1950s MGM Freed Unit production—likely due to the fact that choreographer Michael Kidd participated in their creation (with Cyd Charisse, the Nicholas Brothers, and Cab Calloway appearing in "Alright").

Such pastiches of older musicals frame the music video format as a type of musical number. A number of videos include some semblance of storyline, situating the song performed in the context of a narrative situation. As such, some videos started including brief scripted scenes before the music would begin, indicating how music video aesthetics might fit into the larger structure of a musical. Arguably, the most well-known example of a narrative wraparound occurs in *Michael Jackson's Thriller* (1983), a fourteen-minute blend of horror film and dance sequence that played in theatres as well as television. The zombie choreography has since become iconic, and in 2009 the video would be the first (and, to this date, only) music video to ever be selected for the National Film Registry by the US Library of Congress. *Thriller* became a best-selling home video as well, and was soon followed by the release of a number of collections of videos by individual artists.[44]

Such popularity and potential was not lost on filmmakers, and the summer of 1983 saw the first major instance of a film musical incorporating the look and feel of music videos. *Flashdance* (1983), which *Variety* described as "pretty much like looking at MTV for 96 minutes," was a box-office smash for Paramount and a top-selling album. On the heels of that success, Paramount released *Footloose* (1984) the following spring, another hit which critic Roger Ebert recognized as having "at least three segments ... that can be used as TV music videos."[45] Just as with the cycle of films in the late 1970s, the movies and the soundtrack albums for both of these properties worked in synergistic tandem, each hyping sales of the other. This time, though, music video was added to the mix. Paramount used footage from the film to create a series of videos for cuts from the *Flashdance* soundtrack—thus not only acting as promotion for the singles and album, but also as trailers for the film ... which Paramount got to run for free repeatedly on MTV and other music video programs.[46] *Footloose* followed the same pattern, releasing three singles and accompanying videos in advance of the film's premiere. The videos were in such heavy rotation that there were reports of the film's star Kevin Bacon being "mobbed by teenage girls at *sneak previews*."[47]

In the wake of such back-to-back success, "1984 saw film producers, feature directors, and music video makers between the sheets for a near orgiastic display of financial backing."[48] An onslaught of music video-influenced musicals appeared in theatres in the mid-1980s. Only a few were financed by the major studios, though—such as Universal's "rock-and-roll fable" *Streets of Fire* (1984) and Columbia's *Fast Forward* (1985). Perhaps still smarting from the fallout of their investment in disco musicals, the major studios decided to cash in quickly and get out. For example, although deciding to revisit *Saturday Night Fever's* Tony Manero in *Staying Alive* (1983), Paramount withdrew from further musical productions after release of *Footloose.*

Much as they did in the 1950s and early 1960s, smaller independent studios rushed in where the major studios feared to tread. Independent production companies proliferated during the 1980s in response to the explosive demand for product created by the new home video market and cable television. The major studios could not turn out titles fast enough to meet the rapid turnover at video rental stores and the programming needs of cable channels, so small companies quickly formed to fill that gap. As long as budgets were kept low, a sale to cable and a release to home video after a brief theatrical run would invariably generate profit. Cannon Films, led by Menahem Golan and Yoran Globus, became well known in the industry for following this strategy throughout the decade. Its first venture into producing a musical film occurred in 1980. *The Apple* was a low-budget disco-tinged retelling of the story of Adam and Eve that still has the power to stun audiences with its oddness. Sensing the ripeness of the music video moment, Golan–Globus quickly churned out a series of cheaply made pictures. *Breakin'* and *Breakin' 2: Electric Boogaloo* both made it into theatres in 1984, followed by *Rappin'* (1985). Their output competed with exploitation films from other small companies, including *Body Rock* (1984), *Beat Street* (1984), and *Krush Groove* (1985).

While borrowing many of the aesthetic stylistics of music video, these films also tapped into subcultures spreading across inner cities across the nation that emphasized creative expression through graffiti, rap music, and breakdancing. *Flashdance* brought breakdancing to white mainstream audiences. Protagonist Alex (Jennifer Beals) is shown with a crowd watching a troupe performing out on a street corner, and wows the panel at her dance school audition by copying some of their moves, including the signature move of spinning around on one's back like a top. While acknowledging breakdancing's origins, though, *Flashdance* largely removes the form from its environment and focuses on how one individual can use it to accomplish her own dreams. *Footloose* is even further removed from the city streets, taking place in a fictional Midwestern farm town, as Chicago-raised protagonist Ren (Kevin Bacon) teaches other white kids a stripped-down version of popping and locking.

On the other hand, the low-budgeted independent musicals that flooded the market in the wake of *Flashdance's* success tend to have protagonists of color, and include the trio of tagging, rapping, and breaking. While Wayne "Frosty Freeze" Frost and the Rock Steady Crew got their brief moment in *Flashdance* performing for Alex, Frost features much more prominently in *Beat Street* (1985). The first small company film to cover the scene even predates *Flashdance* by a few months. *Wild Style* (1983) more directly focuses on graffiti artists, but includes rapping and breaking, recognizing the need to depict the overall milieu. Two of the main characters in the *Breakin'* pictures are played by hip-hop dance

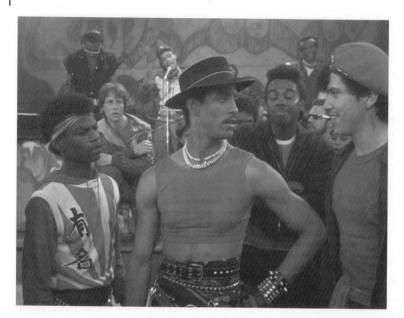

Figure 11.3 Performers of color, like Michael "Boogaloo Shrimp" Chambers (left), Adolfo "Shabba-Doo" Quinones (center) and rapper Ice t (in the far back), had greater onscreen opportunities in musicals produced by smaller film companies, such as Cannon Films' *Breakin'* (1984). Snapshot taken from: Breakin' (1984).

pioneers Adolfo "Shabba-Doo" Quinones and Michael "Boogaloo Shrimp" Chambers, and rapper Ice T is featured in both films (Figure 11.3). *Krush Groove* is a fictionalized version of Russell Simmons' foundation of Mos Def Records, with Blair Underwood as Russell. The film features Run DMC, Sheila E., the Fat Boys, New Edition, and Kurtis Blow, as well as a young LL Cool J in a brief audition scene. The one white rap group to perform (the Beastie Boys prior to their own career breakthrough) gets roundly booed by the audience at the club. The antagonists in all these films tend to be privileged white male outsiders.

Furthermore, the films produced by independent studios tend to emphasize the importance of community, particularly in stressing loyalty to one's "crew." Unlike Alex in *Flashdance*, pursuing one's own dream is seen as selfish and ultimately causes heartache for everyone. Perhaps the most well-remembered plot contrivance of these movies occurs in *Breakin' 2: Electric Boogaloo*: trying to save an East Los Angeles community recreation center from being bulldozed by a greedy developer. (The film's end credits express thanks to the citizens of East Los Angeles as well.) Although Russell, as the head of fledgling record company, functions as the central character in *Krush Groove*, the film alternates among the narratives of a variety of people in the neighborhood—and conflict arises when individuals start looking out for their own interests instead of acting as part of a team. It is only when they learn to stand together that all is resolved. As such, the conclusion has all the star performers collaborate, each contributing a verse to the title song.

The focus on performers of color in these theatrical films stands in contrast to the very vocal protests against MTV occurring at the same time, accusing the channel of suppressing videos by black artists. In attempting to draw a young white audience with greater spending power, MTV consciously shied away from musicians of color in favor of white performers doing heavy metal or New Wave music. In late 1982, for example, although seven of the top thirty-five albums on *Billboard*'s charts were by black artists, there was little airplay of videos from them on MTV.[49] Over a year later, a survey showed that still none of the twenty-one artists in regular circulation on MTV was black.[50] In response, music video programs on other stations, including the major networks, began airing more African American artists.[51] A key moment in television music history occurred in 1983 when NBC aired a special commemorating the 25th anniversary of Motown Records, and Michael Jackson introduced the moonwalk to millions of amazed white viewers. Eventually, MTV began including more videos by black performers, leading to the introduction of *Yo! MTV Raps* in 1988.

It is important to acknowledge that the showcasing of performers of color in these low-budget musicals contains its own problems—they are not called exploitation films for no reason. Although many people in front of the camera were black and Latino, most of the creative personnel behind the camera were not. As such, the films have a tendency to present a shallow and simplistic version of urban street life. Most of these films are brightly lit using lots of primary and day-glo colors, to create the environment of a comic book. The use of this type of visual design in *Breakin'*, matched with many of the sequences filmed on the strand along Venice Beach, makes the picture feel much like a Frankie-and-Annette beach party musical. (It should be noted that Avalon and Funicello were reunited on screen during this era in *Back to the Beach* [1987].) In other words, these movies fall more into the path suggested by *Grease* than the more somber tones of *Saturday Night Fever*. Adolfo Quinones later expressed regret for participating in *Breakin' 2* because of its artificiality, which is perhaps most obvious in the incongruous inclusion of a mime and two blond-haired, blue-eyed tykes as members of the East LA rec center community. The *Breakin'* films and others added such Anglos hoping to appeal to white audiences. Quinones and Chambers both disliked working with the white female lead Lucinda Dickey, because her training was in gymnastics rather than in hip-hop. It is perhaps ironic that *Flashdance*'s star, Jennifer Beals, is of mixed racial heritage—but reviews of the film indicate that most white audiences did not seem to recognize her as such.[52]

Such choices arguably detach these films from their cultural roots, even as the plotlines stress the importance of community. The emphasis on jump cuts and close-ups in music video also emphasize separation and isolation. For example, floor-level close-ups of one person's feet in movement are recurrent in all of these movies, emphasizing one part of the body rather than showing the entire person.[53] The musical moments are also consciously dissociated from the other parts of these films. Those involved in making *Flashdance* acknowledged that the film was designed so that sequences could easily be moved around during the editing process. As music and film scholar Jeff Smith points out, "such modularity is significant in that it lays bare the film's structure as a series of discrete set pieces, any of which might be adapted to a music video format."[54] While music videos might contain some narrative aspect to them, Carol Vernalis points out that narrative is decentered in importance, and can suddenly be jettisoned in favor of some other structural element within a video (and then, just as suddenly, return).[55] The detachable nature of music-video-inspired musical numbers works against integrating number and narrative. Thus, many of these films fit into the developing category of the dance film, where characters dance to records or their boom-box but do not break into song. Concert films, which contain no plot at all, also saw a brief resurgence: *Stop Making Sense* (1984), *U2: Rattle and Hum* (1988), *Madonna: Truth or Dare* (1991).

Isolating scenes, songs, and performers into discrete segments removes the opportunity to build a strong sense of connection and feeling, and that absence is often replaced with increased surface spectacle (fast editing, explosions, bright colors). Such lack of depth is enhanced by the increased artificiality in the visual design, ultimately threatening to flatten the performer into as much of a commodity as the record being promoted. In adopting the music video style, then, filmmakers arguably succeed in exploiting and commodifying the performers better than the villains in the storylines.

Previous chapters have discussed the dichotomy in the history of rock music, "always seen as a cyclical movement between high (authentic) and low (co-opted) points."[56] Rock musicals often dealt with this concern in their narratives—evil managers or corrupted stars versus the raw honesty of a young composer or artist. In the period covered in this chapter, punk functioned as some form of protest against the corporatization of rock (most epitomized in the high production values of disco). The narratives of punk musicals usually center on fears of "selling out" (and the films themselves were often regarded as "sell-outs"). Yet, the "punker-than-thou" in-fighting vaguely indicated that punk was just as much a manufactured pose as anything else. The emerging New Wave music of the 1980s emphasized synthesizers and rhythm machines, underlining a sense of robotic manufacture of music. The rampant use of pastiche in music videos also suggests that everyone is copying someone else (as would the growth of music "sampling"). Hence, while 1980s music videos highlighted the artificiality of popular music, there was no longer any sense of shock, outrage, or condemnation at such exposure. Rather, the videos showed a cynical acceptance of the situation, if not an outright celebration of the plastic two-dimensionality of things.[57]

Critics often complained about the lack of actual musical talent of certain vocalists or groups, claiming that their popularity was solely due to slick, eye-catching videos. Perhaps the best example of celebrating a manufactured group is the reaction to *This Is Spinal Tap* (1984). As a parody of a rock documentary, following the travails of a fictional heavy metal band, the film highlights the growing sense that everything (even documentary) is simply a pose or style that can be imitated. Yet, the film gained such a following that the actors playing the band members eventually did go on tour and release albums. "The reaction to Spinal Tap's videos ... was so strong that the line between reality and parody was nearly erased."[58]

The cynical and exploitative viewpoint synced with the larger cultural outlook of the United States by the mid-1980s. Under the presidency of Ronald Reagan, the country believed that it could spend its way out of the recession that started the decade. Conspicuous consumerism ran rampant, as greed was considered good, and "the person who dies with the most toys wins." The revolution hoped for by the 1960s counterculture had failed to happen, replaced with an awareness that everything is corrupt, but nothing can be changed, so one might as well try to sit on the top of the pyramid. The cynical escapism of New Hollywood matched the larger mindset perfectly. Music videos also spoke for this age not only by presenting artists as manufactured commodities, but also as expressions of ego, of the star detached from everyone else, but whom everyone else wants to imitate. This shift in attitude might explain the critical and box-office failure of *A Chorus Line* (1985), one of the very few Broadway musicals to be adapted into a movie in during this time. The original play exposes the shared hardships of those dancers who stand out of the spotlight rather than the star—an outlook alien to the "win-at-any-cost" zeitgeist of the Reagan era, resulting in an awkward movie that tries to turn the property into a group version of *Flashdance*.

In *Body Rock*, Chilly D (Lorenzo Lamas) abandons his family and friends for quick fame. While initially seduced by the glamour and attention, he discovers that he is being exploited and his career comes crashing down when he refuses to go along. He eventually makes things right by getting his "Body Rock" Crew their big break at the "Rap-stravaganza" being held at a high-end club. The problem with the film is that Chilly D has no sense of music or dance in his soul—he simply wants to get rich and famous. Such an attitude is accentuated by the fact that Lamas himself has no skills as either a breaker or a rapper.[59] Hence, his anger at being exploited seems disingenuous because he himself is a white guy stepping on the backs of others to get ahead. The only difference between him and the "evil" investor is that the rich guy turns out to be homosexual—which is revealed when he takes Chilly D to a gay leather bar and kisses him on the dance floor.[60]

The acceptance and celebration of such commodification had particular implications for female artists. As a backlash against the feminist movement gained momentum in the 1980s, a number of music videos seemed to present women as sexual objects for young men to ogle (or for young women to imitate). (Intriguingly, a number of the "disowned" punk films, such as *Breaking Glass* [1980], *Times Square*, and *Ladies and Gentlemen, The Fabulous Stains* [1982], center around aspiring female performers attempting to keep from being turned into commodities.)[61] Yet, certain female performers complicated that viewpoint, presenting their sexuality as a form of empowerment. Madonna became one of the key artists of the decade, presenting herself consistently in her videos as a sexualized but assertive figure. Further, she consistently altered her image from video to video—from her thrift shop mélange in "Like a Virgin" to imitation Marilyn Monroe in "Material Girl" to vaguely Jean Seberg-gamin in "Papa Don't Preach" to German Expressionist diva in "Express Yourself" to Spanish senorita in "Take a Bow." Her ever-changing look indicated that each of these personae were equally fabricated, and that no one could know or own whomever Madonna Ciccone actually was.[62] Nonetheless, many feminist critics expressed ambivalence that positive progress was being made by being in charge of one's own exploitation.

If anything, *Flashdance* creates greater problems than Madonna's video *oeuvre*. The plot seems to celebrate the achievements of an active female. Alex supports herself working two jobs, one of them as a welder, and shows her ultimately accomplishing her goal to pursue a career as a dancer. Her style of dance is aggressive and athletic. She also constantly asserts her control over her sexual relationship with her beau (Michael Nouri). The problem is that her beau is also her boss at the factory, and he is the one who uses his power to get her an audition at the dance academy. Further, Alex's body is constantly on display. She may be owning her sexual desire by staring straight at her partner (and the camera) while taking off her bra inside her droopy sweatshirt, but she is also performing a form of strip tease. The music video style of the film enhances the treatment of Alex as an object. The movie follows many of the elements found in *Saturday Night Fever*, but instead of photographing the rundown shabbiness of an inner city, everything looks like a fashion magazine photo layout (even when she is welding).[63] The use of quick editing in her dance sequences breaks her body up into pieces for the consumer to put together. It also allowed the filmmakers to present pieces from different bodies: Marine Jahan acts as a body double for Jennifer Beals in many of the shots, and in the final audition, gymnast Sharon Shapiro is substituted to do various flips, while *male* dancer Richard "Crazy Legs" Colón performs the climatic back spinning (Figure 11.4).[64] Claims of female empowerment are therefore highly compromised when men behind the camera are manipulating the woman's body to such a degree.

A few artists used the growth of independent filmmaking to gain greater agency over their image and their music. Prince maintained almost total control over the production of *Purple Rain* (1984), with his managers acting as producers, filming in his hometown Minneapolis with a small budget, and hiring a first-time director fresh out of film school. Against all expectations of

Figure 11.4 This freeze-frame from the climactic dance audition of *Flashdance* (1983) reveals that it is not Jennifer Beals spinning, but male dancer Richard "Crazy Legs" Colón (note the moustache). Snapshot taken from: Flashdance (1983).

distributor Warner Bros., the film was a sensation and won Prince an Oscar for Best Original Song Score.[65] Similarly, the Talking Heads put together the financing of their concert film *Stop Making Sense* largely on their own in order to maintain control over the project, including the use of smooth, gliding, long takes and long shots rather than the typical rapid editing and close-ups of music videos, and the use of new digital audio recording techniques.[66] Band member David Byrne leveraged the picture's critical and box-office success to get almost complete creative control from Warner Bros. in directing *True Stories* (1986). Other performance artists followed in the wake of Byrne and the Talking Heads in transferring their staged pieces onto film, such as Laurie Anderson (*Home of the Brave* [1986]) and Sandra Bernhard (*Without You I'm Nothing* [1990]).

Ultimately, though, while the advent of music videos has had a lasting impact on the American motion picture industry, it did not successfully revive the musical genre. A number of directors who achieved notice for their work in music videos transitioned into helming theatrical features, such as David Fincher, Michael Bay, and Spike Jonze. Julian Temple was the only one of these directors who showed an interest in making musical films: the British produced *Absolute Beginners* (1986) and *Earth Girls Are Easy* (1989). The majority of the other directors focused more on action or suspense movies, where they could use their experience in music video aesthetics to put together stylish projects that lent themselves to rapidly edited set pieces. Following the pattern that rock in film took in the late 1960s, music video style left the musical genre behind and became employed more commonly for montage sequences in otherwise dramatic or comedic movies, such as *Beverly Hills Cop* (1984), *Against All Odds* (1984), *The Breakfast Club* (1985), and *Top Gun* (1986). Perhaps the most influential film in adopting the feel of music video was not *Flashdance* but the original *Rocky*. That picture's training sequence set to the song "Gonna Fly Now" became a template copied by a number of other films throughout the 1980s—including even some of the musicals just discussed (*Breakin'*, *Footloose*, and *Body Rock* all include training montages where white characters are taught to how to dance). Using video style to depict sports training or aerial dogfights rather than dancing was likely seen as having more appeal to straight young men, who by this time had become the key target of Hollywood filmmakers.

The precarious nature of independent production companies also made it difficult to maintain momentum or to build strong synergy. Russell Simmons and his Mos Def Records were the impetus behind *Krush Groove*, but his focus has remained primarily with the recording industry rather than film production. *Purple Rain* was a smash film and album, but Prince's follow-ups, *Behind the Cherry Moon* (1986) and *Graffiti Bridge* (1990), died quickly. *Breakin'* was Golan–Globus's most successful film, but attempts to find and exploit the next hot music trend (*Rappin'*, *Salsa* [1988]) ended in failure. By the end of the decade, the two producers had split up, competing by each putting out a film hyping a supposed new dance craze: Globus's *Lambada* (1990) and Golan's *The Forbidden Dance* (1990). The lambada and both films went nowhere with US audiences. An example that flowed in a different direction than these others was the history of *Eddie and the Cruisers* (1983). The film did very poorly in its initial release, but the need for programming on cable television led to its rediscovery, and eventually a hit soundtrack album. Attempts to capitalize on this fluke success, though, foundered. Fans were attracted to the star Michael Paré as Eddie, so the actual band that played the songs in this muddled rock version of *Citizen Kane* were not able to take advantage of the album's success, and the sequel, *Eddie and the Cruisers II: Eddie Lives!* (1989), disappeared quickly.

Dirty Dancing (1987) acts as a bookmark signaling the end of this cycle. It was a major success, but also epitomizes the issues that brought this moment to its end. The film was produced by Vestron, an independent company that had begun as a home video distributor before expanding into feature production. The film focuses on another active female character—Baby (Jennifer Grey)—who learns to "dirty dance" (complete with training montage) during the summer of 1963 at a vacation resort in the Poconos. The emphasis is on dancing, not singing—a variation on the backstager rather than an integrated musical.[67] "Dirty dancing" is vaguely associated with black and Latino cultures, but actual characters of color are largely absent. In their place, this culture is associated with the white working class, represented by Johnny (Patrick Swayze) who works as a dance instructor at the resort. As the nickname "Baby" may indicate, the film is not beyond the gender issues of other musicals in this cycle. The narrative does show her yearning for Johnny and having "daddy issues," but she is always the one who takes action and solves the problems of the others.[68] While showing her becoming more feminine in her presentation as she learns to dance, Swayze's shirtless body is on display much more than Grey's is. In the climactic final performance, it is Baby's decision and accomplishment to run down the aisle, throw herself into the air, and maintain her balance as Johnny holds her aloft.

The film's success surprised the industry, but Vestron proved incapable of building on its windfall. Although the soundtrack album sold well, Vestron had no experience in the music industry. The profits from the film were put into a slate of projects that failed at the box office, and Vestron itself was bankrupt within a few years. Such a state of affairs put the rights to the property in legal limbo, problematizing any efforts to create spinoff projects. Eventually, a quickly cancelled TV series in 1988 and a pseudo-sequel (*Dirty Dancing: Havana Nights* [2004]) were produced. Without the financial strength and broad expertise of an entertainment conglomerate, *Dirty Dancing* was unable to generate any major synergy.[69]

One final problem threads through the entire time span covered in this chapter: lack of faith by filmmakers in the musical genre. In the wake of the collapse of the blockbuster musicals of the late 1960s, and the number of failures during the early 1970s, almost all of the films of the late 1970s and through the 1980s hedge their bets. As discussed, integration is largely abandoned—audiences would no longer suspend disbelief. The rise of the dance film practically removes on-camera singing. In returning to a form of backstager, though, there is still a sense of resistance. There are often fewer moments identifiable as numbers in these films, and the pictures usually cut away from them quickly, almost as if embarrassed. For example, Francis Ford Coppola's *The Cotton Club* (1984), about the famous 1930s Harlem nightclub, looks and feels exactly like a classic Hollywood musical—but seems afraid to actually be one because it shies away from a full presentation of any performance.[70] With all of these factors, it is no wonder that so many have issues with considering a number of the films in this chapter as musicals. The recorded music industry helped keep the genre going during this period, but the musical seemed to need a major film studio to assert both its confidence in the genre and its ability to generate synergy. Luckily, one was poised to do so.

Notes

1 Ethan Mordden, *The Hollywood Musical* (New York: St. Martin's Press, 1982); Rick Altman, *The American Film Musical* (Bloomington: Indiana University Press, 1987).

2   Jane Feuer, *The Hollywood Musical*, 2nd ed. (Bloomington: Indiana University Press, 1982, 1993).

3   For example, Thomas Schatz, "The New Hollywood," in *Film Theory Goes to the Movies*, ed. Jim Collins, Hilary Radner, and Ava Preacher Collins (New York: Routledge, 1993), 8–36; J.P. Telotte, "The New Hollywood Musical: From *Saturday Night Fever* to *Footloose*," in *Genre and Contemporary Hollywood*, ed. Steve Neale (London: British Film Institute, 2002), 48–61. The term "New Hollywood" is slippery. For example, Stefan Kanfer, "The Shock of Freedom in Films," *Time* (December 6, 1967), was a cover story that used the "New Hollywood" designation to describe the era *preceding* the shift to a ultra-commercialized "high concept" cinema of nostalgia.

4   Russell Sanjek and David Sanjek, *Pennies from Heaven: The American Popular Music Business in the Twentieth Century* (New York: De Capo Press, 1996), 594, on 1975 figures; 586 on 1979 figures, quoting from federal government's 1979 Copyright Royalty Tribunal 1979.

5   The first major instance of the music industry buying into motion picture production occurred in 1952, when Decca Records bought Universal and created the conglomerate MCA.

6   Sanjek and Sanjek, 534.

7   Sanjek and Sanjek, 601.

8   Among its non-music-related productions were hit films such as *The Deep* (1977) and *Midnight Express* (1978).

9   Jeff Smith, *The Sounds of Commerce: Marketing Popular Film Music* (New York: Columbia University Press, 1998), describes the efforts of the major studios to enter into the recorded music industry in the late 1950s and during the 1960s, either buying established labels or founding their own from scratch. By the 1970s, most of the studios' music divisions had been bought up by more powerful record companies. Only Warners' division survived and thrived, due to aggressive expansion beyond being an ancillary to the motion picture division.

10 See David E. James, *Rock 'n' Film: Cinema's Dance with Popular Music* (Oxford: Oxford University Press, 2016), 313–328.

11 Filmmaker George Lucas purportedly emphasized the importance of the songs when pitching *American Graffiti* to various studios by referring to it as a type of musical (Smith, 174; see also Michael Pye and Lynda Myles, *The Movie Brats* [New York: Harmony Books, 1983]).

12 Peter Brown and Steven Gaines, *The Love You Make: An Insider's Story of The Beatles* (New York: McGraw-Hill, 1983), 133: "Even if the movie was a flop, United Artists was almost certain to make a profit from record sales."

13 Frank Pierson, "My Battles with Barbra and Jon," *New York* 9:46 (November 15, 1976), 50.

14 Sanjek and Sanjek, 532.

15 "Supermogul in the Land of Opportunity," *Forbes* (July 10, 1978), 42.

16 Sanjek and Sanjek, 596, state that PolyGram would invest "five million dollars in each of the following five years for acquisition and development of screen properties."

17 Smith, 197.

18 Sanjek and Sanjek, 599.

19 While films before *Saturday Night Fever* had been done in Dolby Stereo, it and *Star Wars* were the breakthrough films that encouraged theatres to invest in the technology. See Mark Kerins, *Beyond Dolby (Stereo): Cinema in the Digital Sound Age* (Bloomington: Indiana University Press, 2011), 31–32.

20 Telotte, 48.

21 *The Turning Point* was and is less considered a musical than *Saturday Night Fever*, most likely because of how each film was marketed. The most widely used poster for *The Turning Point* featured close-ups of its two stars (Anne Bancroft and Shirley Maclaine) rather than an image of dancing, emphasizing it as a woman's melodrama. *The Turning Point* also did not heavily promote its soundtrack album (consisting of classical music selections).

22 Sanjek and Sanjek, 558.

23 See Richard Dyer, "In Defense of Disco," in *On Record: Rock, Pop & the Written Word*, ed. Simon Frith and Andrew Goodwin (New York: Pantheon, 1990), 410–418, for a discussion of disco's connection to these marginalized communities.

24 Of the others, *Star Wars*, *Jaws*, and *The Godfather* (1972) exemplify the shift towards aiming product at young men. *The Exorcist* (1973) is not as obviously directed at a male audience, but the presentation of young girl as demon certainly seems to express the anxiety that women's liberation had on American men at the time.

25 One could add to that list *Fame* and *Pennies from Heaven*. Both have connections to old-fashioned musicals (*Fame* feels like an updated Garland–Rooney backstager; *Pennies from Heaven* explicitly pastiches classical Hollywood musicals), but have key components that keep them from being completely traditional (*Fame*'s use of contemporary rock/funk; *Pennies from Heaven*'s deconstructionist aims).

26 Stacy Thompson, *Punk Productions: Unfinished Business* (Albany: State University of New York Press, 2004), 123.

27 David Laderman, *Punk Slash! Musicals: Tracking Slip-Sync on Film* (Austin: University of Texas Press, 2010), 2.

28 Laderman, 43, describes how "several of the punk musicians involved in the film walked out in apparent disgust" and that punk fashion designer Vivienne Westwood designed a t-shirt that "was covered by a long handwritten screen explaining her disgust at the film as an exploitive work that did not understand punk."

29 Sanjek and Sanjek, 634, describe the "shipment to dealers of four million *Sgt. Pepper* LPs featuring the Bee Gees, Frampton, and other Stigwood clients and the necessity to take back half of them on the old 100 percent return basis."

30 Sanjek and Sanjek, 610: "A CBS study of home tapes in 1980 indicated that they were responsible for an annual [recorded music] industry loss of $700 to $800 million, or 20 percent."

31 Ken Tucker, *Rock of Ages: The Rolling Stone History of Rock & Roll* (New York: Summit Books, 1986), 574.

32 Jay Cocks, "Rock Hits the Hard Place," *Time* 119:7 (February 2, 1982), 74–76.

33 PolyGram was the only one that charged MTV for use of the videos it produced in the initial rollout of the channel (Tucker, 592).

34 Such as Ken Dancyger, *The Technique of Film and Video Editing: History, Theory, and Practice* (New York: Focal Press, 2011), 134; and Scott Witmer, *History of Rock Bands* (Edina: ABDO, 2010), 15.

35 Sanjek and Sanjek, 640.

36 Sanjek and Sanjek, 644.

37 Sanjek and Sanjek, 653.

38 Outside of MTV itself, by 1983, the BET Network included fifteen hours a week of *Video Soul*, ABC and NBC were airing late night programs (*New York Hot Tracks* and *Friday Night Videos*, respectively), and *MV3* was a syndicated music video program. See R. Serge Denisoff, *Inside MTV* (New Brunswick: Transaction Publishers, 1988).

39 The NBC police drama *Miami Vice* also helped popularize stereo TV, partially because its style was heavily influenced by the aesthetics of music video.

40 See Kay Dickinson, "Pop, Speed, Teenagers and the 'MTV Aesthetic,'" in *Movie Music: The Film Reader*, ed. Kay Dickinson (London: Routledge, 2003), 143–152.

41 E. Ann Kaplan, *Rocking Around the Clock: Music Television, Postmodernism, and Consumer Culture* (New York: Routledge, 1987), 33–34, notes "what one first notices about rock videos, namely their frequent reliance on classical Hollywood film genres, whether it be incorporation, parody, pastiche, or ridicule of representations from mainstream cinema that is going on."

42 Carole J. Clover, "Dancin' in the Rain," *Critical Inquiry* 21 (Summer 1995), 722–747, also reads Jackson's extended solo dance sequence in the video for "Black and White" as a reworking of Gene Kelly's iconic performance to the title song in *Singin' in the Rain* (1952).

43 Bob Fosse's influence on music video goes far beyond this one instance. Many have pointed out the similarities between Fosse's performance as the Snake in *The Little Prince* (1974) and Michael Jackson's style of choreography. Beyoncé's video for "Get Me Bodied" overtly pastiches the discotheque sequence in *Sweet Charity* (1969), and her "Single Ladies" video borrows heavily from the choreography he created for Gwen Verdon's dance to "Mexican Divorce" on *The Ed Sullivan Show* in 1969.

44 Within three months of the release of the *Thriller* video, 300,000 VHS copies had been sold at $29.98 each (Sanjek and Sanjek, 647). Other top-selling home video anthologies include Madonna's *Immaculate Collection*, and collections of pieces by Wham!, Billy Idol, Bruce Springsteen, and Janet Jackson.

45 "Flashdance," *Variety* (December 31, 1982); Roger Ebert, "Footloose," *Chicago Sun-Times* (January 1, 1984).

46 With none of the album artists actually appearing in the film, the videos for *Flashdance* did not show the performers. Smith, 201, points out that "MTV became sensitive to charges that it offered free advertising time to Hollywood and thereafter stipulated that future film-inspired videos would have to include the recording artists in at least 50 percent of the video's footage."

47 Marianne Meyer, "The Rock Movideo," in *Rolling Stone Review*, ed. Ira Robbins (New York: Charles Scribners Sons, 1985), 168.

48 Meyer, 168.

49 Sanjek and Sanjek, 640.

50 Sanjek and Sanjek, 650. See also, Denisoff, 98–116.

51 In addition to BET's fifteen hours a week of videos, ABC's after-prime-time *New York Hot Tracks* was "black-oriented," and NBC's *Friday Night Videos* was more inclusive of black artists than MTV at the time.

52 For example, Janet Maslin, "*Flashdance*: Pittsburgh and Dance," *New York Times* (April 15, 1983) refers to Alex as "the world's only proficient teen-age girl" in this form of street dancing. Kathryn Kalinak, "*Flashdance*: The Dead End Kid," *Jump Cut* 29 (February 1984), 3–5, focuses mainly on gender issues in the film, but when the article delves briefly into issues of race, no mention indicates that Alex may be of mixed racial heritage.

53 Examples include "Maniac" in *Flashdance*; the title credits in *Footloose* and *Breakin'*, and various dance breaks in *Body Rock*.

54 Smith, 201.

55 Carol Vernalis, *Experiencing Music Video: Aesthetics and Cultural Context* (New York: Columbia University Press, 2004), xi, argues that narrative is simply one element within the structure of a music video and "no single element is allowed to dominate."

56 Lawrence Grossberg, "Cinema, Postmodernity, and Authenticity," in Dickinson, 93.

57 "Authentic inauthenticity says that authenticity is itself a construction, an image, which no better and no worse than any other … The only authenticity is to know and even admit that you are not being authentic, to fake it without faking the fact that you are faking it … The logic of authentic inauthenticity is the obverse of ideology: people know what they are doing but they do it anyway, even if they claim not to believe in the values implied by what they are consciously doing" (Grossberg, 95).

58 Meyer, 170.

59 The film mimics *Flashdance*'s use of body doubles and close-ups when trying to show Lamas's character dancing, including a "Maniac"-style dance workout montage.

60 A number of queer artists were part of 1980s New Wave music, and *Breakin'* includes a black character who can be read as gay (the female lead's best friend who introduces her to the breakdance scene and goes by the handle "Cupcakes"). Yet, as *Body Rock* exemplifies, a number of other films in this cycle are not as welcoming.

61 Laderman.

62 See Pamela Robertson, *Guilty Pleasures: Feminist Camp from Mae West to Madonna* (Durham: Duke University Press, 1996), 115–138.

63 The mismatch between the style and outlook of these two films may help explain why *Staying Alive*, a sequel to *Saturday Night Fever* but attempting to match the feel of *Flashdance*, failed so miserably.

64 Deborah Caulfield, "OK, Jennifer, Who Did the Dancing?" *Los Angeles Times* (May 22, 1983), Sec. 6, p. 1, quotes Jennifer Beals admitting, "Marine did ALL the dancing in the sequences they finally used on the screen … I mean they used my face for close-ups, and a few other times, but when I watched closely I could easily tell the difference between the two of us." On Shapiro and Colón: "'Flashdance,' 30 Years Later: B-Boy Recalls Girling Up for Final Scene," Yahoo! Movietalk, April 15, 2013 (https://www.yahoo.com/movies/bp/flashdance-30-years-later-b-boy-recalls-girling-170107851.html).

65 Of course, gaining agency for one's self is often at the expense of others. Prince's relationship with his band, the Revolution, as well as his friendship with co-stars Morris Day and The Time, dissolved soon after the film's release. Further, while championing the artistic vision of a man of mixed-race heritage, critics accused the film of sexism. Female lead Apollonia was required to strip to her underwear and jump into an ice-cold river for one memorable scene, and she gets slapped hard by Prince later in the film.

66 Meyer, 171.

67 Jane Feuer, "Is *Dirty Dancing* a Musical, and Why Should It Matter?," in *The Time of Our Lives: "Dirty Dancing" and Popular Culture*, ed. Yannis Tzioumakis and Sian Lincoln (Detroit: Wayne University Press, 2013), 59–72.

68 One of the crises involves a single woman discovering she's pregnant. Baby helps arrange for her to get an abortion, which was still illegal in 1963. The film raises the dangers of such unregulated procedures, but the movie never invites the viewer to judge the woman as immoral for deciding to end the pregnancy.

69 An entire anthology covers this film from multiple viewpoints: *The Time of Our Lives: "Dirty Dancing" and Popular Culture*, ed. Yannis Tzioumakis and Sian Lincoln (Detroit: Wayne University Press, 2013).

70 Coppola's *One from the Heart* (1981), discussed in Chapter 10, follows a similar pattern of evoking the classic Hollywood musical but never going "full out" in presenting a complete musical number.

12

Just Like Scheherezade: Reviving the Musical Film Genre

During the 1970s and 1980s, the musical genre on film was repeatedly written off for dead. Those films that did include music were often not regarded *as* musicals, but rather movies that happened to have music in them. Those pictures that critics, audiences, and even the filmmakers *did* accept as part of the genre—that is, with integrated song and dance—were extremely few in number and did poorly. Then, in the 1990s, a resurgence in the integrated musical occurred. Much like MGM in the post-World War II era, the Walt Disney Company led the way, keeping the genre alive by continually spinning out musical tales like the mythical Scheherezade. Disney championed the musical in multiple ways: in reviving its animated features; in supporting live-action musical film production; in helping resurrect musicals on television; and in its investment in live theatrical musicals. The company also invested in projects that featured music heavily but did not necessarily fit within the narrow precepts of integration.

Disney was not alone. A number of other people reinvested in the genre, particularly artists of color, as well as female and queer filmmakers. In attempting to speak from their own viewpoints, these artists at times also stepped outside the parameters of integration. Thus, the Scheherezade metaphor applies here too, with artists creating musical entertainment as a form of empowerment. Disney's musicals reflect the multiculturalism that spread across the United States during the 1990s. Such optimism and celebration, though, was followed by widespread fear and concern after the events of September 11, 2001 and a Great Recession that began in 2008. Negotiating the genre's balance between individual liberty and the bonds of the community took on a greater sense of urgency under such seismic cultural shifts. Intriguingly, musical entertainment still found audiences yearning for the utopia the genre traditionally promised, but refashioned for a different social climate—as well as for newer media platforms. This final chapter examines how Disney and others kept the musical alive in multiple ways—and why.

Free and Easy? A Defining History of the American Film Musical Genre, First Edition. Sean Griffin.
© 2018 Sean Griffin. Published 2018 by John Wiley & Sons Ltd.

A Whole New World: The New Disney Animated Musical

Disney's commitment to the musical genre developed as it dug itself out of the tribulations of the 1970s and 1980s, a period when it produced fewer films that did less and less business. The board of directors approved a major shakeup in 1985, hiring a new slate of executives including Frank Wells from Warner Bros., and Michael Eisner and Jeffrey Katzenberg from Paramount. Under the nickname "Team Disney," this trio (and the number of new people they brought with them) revitalized Disney's image and profit margin.[1] Musicals, though, were not initially part of that business strategy. Rather, one of the first moves was to emphasize the studio's newly created Touchstone Pictures subsidiary, in order to make pictures that could compete with other Hollywood studios, unhampered by the "family-friendly" expectations that came with the Disney label. Touchstone did well with a number of comedies such as *Down and Out in Beverly Hills* (1986) and *Three Men and a Baby* (1987). A key performer in a number of these farces was Bette Midler, who appeared in *Down and Out*, as well as *Ruthless People* (1986), *Outrageous Fortune* (1987), and *Big Business* (1988). Using Midler as a comedienne rather than as a songstress indicates Team Disney's lack of initial interest in the musical genre.

Three movies in 1986, though, heralded a sea change for Disney and for the musical genre. Disney itself released a new animated feature, *The Great Mouse Detective*, hoping to reassert its dominance in this area. The film was the studio's first use of computer-generated imagery, or CGI (in a climactic chase through the gears of London's Big Ben), and included a few songs. Although the film did relatively well, it was eclipsed by another animated feature *not produced at Disney*. *An American Tail* was released by Universal, produced by Steven Spielberg, and directed by Don Bluth (an animator who had left Disney to create his own animation studio). While also containing only a smattering of songs, one of them—"Somewhere Out There"—earned an Oscar nomination and became a moderately successful single. The gauntlet had been thrown, and Team Disney vowed to not let this challenge go unmet.

The third 1986 film *was* a traditional integrated musical. *Little Shop of Horrors* adapted an off-Broadway musical based on a famous low-budget 1960 horror film. A young songwriting team had written the score: lyricist Howard Ashman and composer Alan Menken. The property takes the original black-and-white movie and gives it a bright comic-book look and attitude, much like the feel of the comedies that Touchstone was releasing at the time. Ashman and Menken's score balances between camp pastiches of early 1960s pop tunes and earnest ballads expressing the despairs and hope of the characters. "Somewhere That's Green" exemplifies this balance in one song—satirizing the artificiality of the Scotchguarded utopia the character longs for, and yet empathizing with her desire for a better life nonetheless. The two had written a somewhat similar "wish song" for another show, *Smile*, in which a character sings of her childhood dreams about Disneyland. Perhaps, then, it was inevitable that Disney would eventually hire the duo to write for their animated features.

Their initial effort for the company was *The Little Mermaid* (1989), a return to the fairy-tale format for which Disney was famous. The film was quickly hailed by critics and audiences, and successfully overshadowed Spielberg/ Bluth's second collaboration, *The Land Before Time* (1989). Their second collaboration with Disney, *Beauty and the Beast* (1991), became the first musical to earn a Best Picture Oscar nomination since *All That Jazz* in 1979, and the first animated film to *ever* earn such a nomination. Ashman and Menken's third collaboration, *Aladdin* (1992), helped confirm the general opinion that Disney had entered a second Golden Age in animation (the first being the 1930s and Disney's first five animated features). *Aladdin* was followed by *The Lion King* (1993), with songs by Elton John and Tim Rice, which earned more at the box office than any animated film had ever done. Every year through the rest of the decade, a new Disney animated musical played in theatres: *Pocahontas* (1995), *The Hunchback of Notre Dame* (1996), *Hercules* (1997), *Mulan* (1998), and *Tarzan* (1999). The studio opened a second animation studio in Florida, and also produced two musicals done in stop-motion animation (*The Nightmare Before Christmas* [1993], *James and the Giant Peach* [1996]). Disney music came to dominate the Academy Award category for Best Song, winning eight times from 1989 to 1999.[2]

Disney recognized the multiple opportunities for synergy that animated musicals created. The company had been at the forefront of cross-promotion since the 1930s, long before the age of New Hollywood, as the cartoons sold merchandise and vice versa, TV series could promote new movies and the theme parks, and so on. In this new era, a successful animated musical not only brought in box-office receipts but generated content that could be repackaged and sold through multiple platforms: home video sales, afternoon TV series spinoffs, merchandise, theme park attractions, and soundtrack albums. Disney also began creating straight-to-video musical sequels of their theatrical animated features, such as *Aladdin II: The Return of Jafar* (1994) and *Beauty and the Beast: The Enchanted Christmas* (1997).

Seeing the success of Disney, a number of other studios formed their own animation units or entered into partnerships with various animation companies. For example, Warner Bros. worked with Don Bluth's company on *Thumbelina* (1994), and with Rankin/Bass (famous for their animated Christmas specials on TV, beginning with *Rudolph the Red-Nosed Reindeer* [1964]) on a reworking of Rodgers and Hammerstein's *The King and I* (1999). Its own new animation division produced *Quest for Camelot* (1998).[3] 20th Century-Fox took a play it had filmed in 1956 and refashioned it into the animated musical *Anastasia* (1997) (also overseen by Don Bluth). Jeffrey Katzenberg left Disney in the mid-1990s to form his own company, and one of its first releases was an animated musical version of the tale of Moses, *The Prince of Egypt* (1998). By the end of the decade, the influence of the Disney musical was so apparent that it was parodied in the animated musical *South Park: Bigger, Longer, Uncut* (1999). The Devil's "wish song," "Up There," is modeled on *The Little Mermaid*'s "Part of Your World," for example, and "Kyle's Mom's a Bitch" includes a section satirizing the "It's a Small World" attraction at the Disney theme parks.

Disney's revival followed a strategy common across Hollywood at the time: reviving formulas that had succeeded in the past. Choosing well-known fairy tales made these films pre-sold projects and a welcome return to form for the studio. Yet, conventional wisdom held that 20–35 year olds were not interested in musicals, and these films are unashamed in their embrace of the integrated musical format.[4] A number of reviews of *Beauty and the Beast*, such as Janet Maslin's for the *New York Times*, commended the film for "combining ... animation techniques with the best of Broadway."[5] After a brief prologue, the film opens with an elaborate number introducing the entire village, and setting up a number of key traits for the main characters. "The Circle of Life," the opening number for *The Lion King*, which shows the entire animal kingdom witnessing and honoring the birth of the new lion cub, was considered so effective that it was used complete and on its own as a trailer for the film. Both of these examples indicate that Disney not only made these as musicals, but was *proudly asserting* their genre status.

Nonetheless, young adult customers flocked to Disney's animated musicals in the 1990s. While maintaining cuddly characters and a lot of slapstick humor that kids would appreciate, the main characters were given deeper psychological motivations for their actions, and some jokes were aimed at older viewers. For example, when asked what a girl might like as a romantic gesture, a character in *Beauty and the Beast* lists off flowers, or candy, or promises you don't intend to keep. Similarly, while the manic energy of the Genie in *Aladdin*, voiced by Robin Williams, delights many children, the rapid-fire cultural references he makes are for the grown-ups. The inclusion of more sophisticated humor is also reflected in the musical numbers. Ashman and Menken's songs add enough self-awareness to keep older audiences alert and amused. The production number excess of songs like "Under the Sea" (from *Little Mermaid*) and "Be Our Guest" (from *Beauty and the Beast*) consciously evoke the feel of Busby Berkeley, and one fish in the first number is shown dressed up like Carmen Miranda. "You've Never Had a Friend Like Me," the Genie's introductory number in *Aladdin*, has the design of a Las Vegas extravaganza (and ends with him turning on a neon "Applause" sign).

Animation itself as well as the use of fantasy made audiences a bit more comfortable with characters breaking into song out of nowhere. The return to fairy-tale musicals also appealed to adult nostalgia for the Disney animation of their own childhood. Invoking nostalgia is done lightly, though, to keep the

Figure 12.1 The music swells in the penultimate moments of *Beauty and the Beast* (1991) as the two main characters admit their love for each other. The resurrection of Disney animation in the 1990s also helped revive interest in the musical genre. Snapshot taken from: Beauty and the Beast (1991).

films from feeling too old-fashioned or sentimental. In its place is the ironic humor and campy pastiche found in the songs of Ashman and Menken. Such "winking" to an audience too "hip" for musicals seems to express that the film-makers think breaking into song is amusingly weird too, and strategically softens the defenses of viewers who tend to squirm at the unguarded emotionality typical of integrated musicals. Slowly, though, the films increase the audience's emotional investment and willing suspension of disbelief. Thus, by the time Belle is weeping over the dying Beast (to use a prime example), most viewers have completely succumbed to the romanticism of the piece (Figure 12.1).

By the late 1990s, though, it seemed as if audiences had once again had their fill of animated musicals. After continually ratcheting up higher box-office numbers with each successive feature up through *The Lion King*, Disney saw a bit of a drop-off with *Pocahontas*, and an even greater dip in ticket sales for *The Hunchback of Notre Dame*. The musical sequences in Disney animated features were scaled back in the early 2000s—but this gambit did not bring audiences back.[6] By this time, Disney's traditional cel animation was losing ground to computer-generated imagery. Granted, the Second Golden Age is partly indebted to advances in computer software. For example, the most iconic moment in *Beauty and the Beast*, the camera sweeping down through the ballroom as Belle and her beau dance to the title tune, is a combination of CGI and computer-assisted animation to help keep the characters in correct perspective during the movement. By the end of the 1990s, though, computer animation's three-dimensional rendering and amount of detail was eclipsing cel animation. Disney still reaped profits from the rise of computer animation, having entered into a partnership with Pixar. Yet, Pixar's output began over-shadowing the work done by Disney's own animation division, leading the studio to let go much of its staff at the end of the 1990s. Pixar films during this period contain songs (often from the pen of Randy Newman), but for background score or for montage sequences, and were less regarded as musicals.

Still, the opportunities for synergy kept Disney interested in the musical genre, leading it to expand into a new realm for the company. Walt Disney Theatrical was established in 1993, and began converting the cartoons that critics were claiming were just like Broadway shows *into* actual Broadway shows. Its first production was an adaptation of *Beauty and the Beast* (opening in 1994), which was followed by an extremely successful version of *The Lion King* (opening in 1997), as well as *Mary Poppins* (opening in London in 2004), *Tarzan* (opening in 2006), *The Little Mermaid* (opening in 2008), and *Aladdin* (opening in 2014). To house these productions, Disney bought and renovated Broadway's historic New Amsterdam Theater, and became a major participant in the revitalization of the Times Square area.

A number of New Yorkers grumbled about the "Disneyfication" of the area and of Broadway musicals in general, but musical theatre had begun mirroring the strategies of New Hollywood long before Disney Theatricals was formed.[7] Broadway musicals shifted in the 1980s to elaborate spectacles dubbed "mega-musicals" that, like Hollywood franchises, could be marketed heavily with the use of an easily recognized graphic: two feline eyes for *Cats*, a portrait of a French waif for *Les Miserables*.[8] (Most of these mega-musicals also dealt with the worry that audiences no longer accepted people shifting out of dialogue and into song by eliminating such transitions and being entirely sung-through.) By the turn of the millennium, the number of mega-musicals lessened, supplanted by theatrical versions of movies and by "jukebox musicals" that used hit songs from the past. Such productions refashioned pre-sold music or movies to fit the now-sacrosanct expectation for integrated numbers. Thus, stand-alone pop songs were squeezed into a narrative. A number of movies with musical elements were reworked in order to turn them into *integrated* musicals. The first majorly successful instance of such reworking was the 1979 Broadway production of the 1933 Busby Berkeley backstager *42nd Street*. By the 2000s, an onslaught of examples lit up signs down Broadway, including a number of titles discussed in previous chapters, such as *Footloose* (opening in 1998), *Saturday Night Fever* (opening in London in 1998), and *Dirty Dancing* (opening in Australia in 2004). Thus, the influence of motion pictures on Broadway had been going on long before Disney threw itself into theatrical productions, and has continued apace.

By the mid-2000s, Disney found renewed success in producing animated musicals. A live-action/animation hybrid, *Enchanted* (2007), showed the studio mildly sending up its own princess formula. Yet, Disney marketing embarked on a major campaign promoting its line of princesses, which then resulted in a number of new musical princesses being introduced: *The Princess and the Frog* (2009), *Tangled* (2010), and *Frozen* (2013). The last two titles also successfully transitioned the traditional Disney fairy-tale environment into total computer animation. With each new feature, audiences grew more enamored, and *Frozen* unexpectedly became the most successful film in the company's history to date.

God Help the Outcasts: Musicals in a Multicultural Era

Disney's animated features (and their imitators at other studios) revived the musical genre, but they did not spark a concomitant rise in live-action theatrical film musicals during the 1990s. While Broadway and London's West End turned increasingly to musical adaptations of motion pictures, the drought of movie versions of hit theatrical musicals continued. Well-known concept musicals of the 1970s and early 1980s, such as those penned by Stephen Sondheim, still seemed risky to try to translate into film. Mega-musicals of the 1980s and 1990s, such as those penned by Andrew Lloyd Webber, provided potential for cinematic spectacle, but they were sung-through and thus seemed too close to opera, a perceived hard sell to young adults (male or female). Disney *did* attempt to extend its musical output to live-action, including the one major adaptation of a Broadway show during the 1990s: *Evita* (1996), starring Madonna. Reaction was middling, and was not followed by other adaptations through the decade.

Live-action integrated film musicals written directly for the screen were also scarce. Again, Disney ventured, but *Newsies* (1992) dropped like a thud at the box office.[9] Director James Brooks convinced Columbia to bankroll *I'll Do Anything* (1994), with integrated numbers written by Prince, Carole King, and others, and choreography by Twyla Tharp—but executives were so unnerved by preview audience reaction that all of the numbers were eliminated before general release.[10] Yet, there were consistent instances suggesting that filmmakers (and audiences) still found some charm and delight in the musical format. Certain motion pictures would suddenly and surprisingly erupt into an integrated musical number. *Muriel's Wedding* (1994), for example, includes a pastiche of 1970s Swedish pop group ABBA music videos. That film's director, Australian P.J. Hogan, would also guide Rupert Everett and the rest of the cast of *My Best Friend's Wedding* (1997) in a glorious unexpected rendition of "I Say a Little Prayer." *Wayne's World* (1992), based on a *Saturday Night Live* skit, famously opens with a full lip-synced performance of Queen's "Bohemian Rhapsody." P.T. Anderson's film *Magnolia* (1999) was inspired by the songs of Aimee Mann and, at one particular juncture, characters in the multiple plot strands join together (through editing) to sing Mann's "Wise Up."

Other films contained a number of musical moments, such as *Sister Act* (1992) and *Swing Kids* (1993), again both produced by Disney—but were not promoted as musicals. At times, columnists would point out how much these films seemed to want to be musicals.[11]

A number of these "sort-of" musicals were being made outside the major Hollywood studios. As described in Chapter 11, independent filmmaking had grown significantly during the 1980s in reaction to the boom in home video. As long as costs were kept manageable, independent films aimed at a particular niche market could make a profit in home video sales after a brief theatrical run. The limited budgets of independent filmmaking seem antithetical to the lavish production values associated with the musical genre, but such was not the case. Much like those making B films during the classical Hollywood era, independent films that focused on musical performance were numerous. Examples from the 1980s, such as those from Golan-Globus, leaned more towards exploitation of the latest subcultural trends (breakdancing, rap, salsa dancing, etc.). By the start of the 1990s, though, minoritized artists began making their own independent films, speaking from and to their own communities with their own viewpoints, their own concerns ... and often their own musical heritage.

The first noticeable trend was the number of African American directors emerging from independent cinema, led by the success of Spike Lee. Lee's films spoke frankly about the lives and attitudes of African American society. As his father, Bill Lee, is an accomplished jazz musician, it is unsurprising that music would be prominent in Spike's pictures (and Bill wrote the scores for a number of them). A full-fledged integrated musical moment occurs in Lee's second feature-length film, *School Daze* (1988), a confrontation in a black beauty parlor done in song and dance between the "Wanna-be" light-skinned sorority sisters with straightened hair, and the "Jigaboo" female college students advocating the beauty of the natural kink in their hair. The entire set piece invokes black heritage, using the style of swing jazz for the melody to musical-ize a cultural tradition of "doing the dozens" between the two sides. The number also fits a common trait in Lee's films: raising difficult issues about race to provoke discussion rather than to provide clear answers. Yet, as the only such moment in the entire film, it seems to erupt out of nowhere. Thus, this film (and other music-heavy Spike Lee "joints," such as *Do the Right Thing* [1989] and *Mo' Better Blues* [1990]) is similar to others during the period: "musical-ish" to many viewers, but perhaps not officially "musicals." Independent film-makers during the 1990s used music the way they wanted, thus challenging and potentially reshaping the parameters of the genre.

Other African American directors also focused on music. Robert Townsend directed *The Five Heartbeats* (1989), about a fictional 1950s rhythm-and-blues group, and would later direct Beyoncé in MTV's *Carmen: A Hip Hopera* (2001). Reginald Hudlin directed *House Party* (1990) with the rap duo Kid n' Play, which spawned two sequels. The growth of hip-hop during the 1990s led to a number of rap artists on the big screen—such as Ice Cube in the series of *Friday* films (starting in 1995) and the *Barbershop* franchise (beginning in 2002), and Tupac Shakur in *Juice* (1992). Parodies of the hip-hop industry also appeared: *CB4* (1993), *Fear of a Black Hat* (1994). Again, while few people regarded these pictures definitively as "musicals," these films displayed the importance of music within American black culture: how it gave voice to their lives, how it bonded people together as a community, and how it could offer black artists (including the filmmakers themselves) opportunities for success.

Latino filmmakers also acknowledged music's ability to express individuality (from the dominant white culture) and a communal heritage. For example, director Gregory Nava directed the musical biopic *Selena* (1997), helping launch Jennifer Lopez to stardom as the famous Tejano singer. Luis Valdez, who founded El Teatro Campesino, and a key figure in the Chicano movement, used music prominently in both *Zoot Suit* (1981, based on his 1978 play) and *La Bamba* (1987). *Zoot Suit* uses swing music and jitterbug choreography to create a sense of "magical realism" (a hallmark of Latin American literature) in depicting the oppression of Mexican Americans in Los Angeles during the 1940s (including the "Sleepy Lagoon" murders and the "Zoot Suit" riots).[12] *La Bamba* is a musical biography of Ritchie Valens, an early rock-and-roll singer (played by Lou Diamond Phillips). In many ways, Valens epitomizes an assimilationist philosophy: gaining success by adapting to mainstream white society (maintaining a squeaky-clean boy-next-door image, and even agreeing to change his last name from Valenzuela to a less-ethnic-sounding Valens). On the other side, his hot-headed half-brother Bob (Esai Morales) is the rebel, entering the film on a motorcycle, after a stint in jail. Yet, Bob keeps his little brother rooted in Mexican heritage, including a sojourn to Tijuana. During this trip, Ritchie hears "La Bamba" for the first time and decides to record his own rock version (performed on the soundtrack by Los Lobos). The movie ultimately supports both strategies: working within the system as well as fighting against it. "La Bamba" is the B side for Valens' "Donna," a smooth love ballad for his white girlfriend. The final image of the film shows Ritchie and Bob chasing each other to the top of a hill, each prodding the other to go farther (Figure 12.2).

Female directors had been largely denied opportunities within mainstream Hollywood cinema for decades. During the 1970s and 1980s, a number of women turned to documentary filmmaking, including Penelope Spheeris, who directed a series of films capturing evolving trends in rock music, including punk and heavy metal. The success of *The Decline of Western Civilization* (1981) and its sequel (1988) helped her move to fictional filmmaking, such as the aforementioned *Wayne's World*. Spheeris's documentaries focus on male-dominated (and often sexist) subcultures, but other female directors working in independent cinema focused on the relationship music has had in women's lives. Allison Anders directed a veiled biography of singer/songwriter Carole

Figure 12.2 Ritchie Valens (Lou Diamond Phillips) and his brother Bob (Esai Morales) chase each other up the hill to success in the musical biopic *La Bamba* (1988), directed by El Teatro Campesino founder Luis Valdez. Snapshot taken from: La Bamba (1988).

King, titled *Grace of My Heart* (1996). Using pastiches of 1960s tunes newly written by female artists such as Joni Mitchell, Lesley Gore, and Carole Bayer Sager, the film shows how female songwriters survived in a man's world. Maggie Greenwald's *Songcatcher* (2000) reaches even farther back to reclaim women ignored or erased from music history. It fictionally tells of early 1900s musicologist Olive Dame Campbell's discovery that Appalachian folk music preserved the thought-lost ballads of medieval Britain—and how credit for this work was stolen by her male mentor. The film emphasizes the centrality of Appalachian women in passing the songs from generation to generation, and a number of female country artists (Dolly Parton, Emmylou Harris, Rosanne Cash) assisted in the film's making.

The early 1990s also saw a new independent film movement referred to as New Queer Cinema. Connected to the protests and activism over the AIDS crisis, these filmmakers were open and unapologetic in depicting lesbian, gay, or otherwise non-heteronormative sexual desire, often using camp in a confrontational manner to speak out about issues of sexuality. A number of the films employ music—such as the incongruous appearance of Annie Lennox singing Cole Porter's "Every Time We Say Goodbye" during a key moment in Derek Jarman's film version of the Elizabethan play *Edward II* (1991) or Todd Haynes' queer depiction of the glam rock era, *Velvet Goldmine* (1998). Since the musical as a whole had become so socially attached to gay culture, it is perhaps inevitable that a few of these films *are* recognized as full-fledged musicals rather than being "musical-ish." Canadian director John Greyson created a musical about AIDS, *Zero Patience* (1996), for example, and John Cameron Mitchell adapted his off-Broadway show about a transgender rock star, *Hedwig and the Angry Inch* (2001). These films use singing, dancing, and various other common tropes of the genre (overly stylized visual design, accentuated emotions, the use of fantasy) to depict all of life as a type of performance. If "all the world's a stage," then nothing can claim to be natural or normal—and all forms of gender identity or sexual desire are equally viable. *Hedwig* particularly stresses the unclassifiable: someone born with a male body who undergoes a botched sex-change operation, and thus no longer fits easily into the category of male or female—which then complicates the viability of labels such as "homosexual" or "heterosexual."

Hedwig links its blurring of male/female and of homo/hetero with the concept of national identity. *Hedwig*'s first line of dialogue is "I'm the Berlin Wall, baby!"—as a citizen of a bifurcated Cold War Germany, he identifies with the limbo area in between. The interaction between narrative and number makes the genre ideal for dealing with such fuzzy boundaries, and *Hedwig* was not alone in making musical connections across race, gender, and sexuality. A very early example is *Illusions* (1982), a short film directed by Julie Dash, about a light-skinned African American woman (Lonette McKee) passing for white as an assistant to the head of a major Hollywood studio during World War II. During the film, she supervises the recording of a black singer dubbing for a white female star, exposing how the artifice endemic to the genre can be both a source of exploitation and advancement for people of color as well as for women of all backgrounds. John Waters' *Hairspray* (1988) centers on Tracy, a full-figured teenage Baltimore girl (Ricki Lake) whose optimism and determination win her a place on the local TV dance party program. She then uses her neighborhood stardom in a fight to racially integrate the show. While there is no specifically gay or lesbian character in the film, gay director Waters infuses the film with his particular outrageous queer sensibility, and female impersonator Divine plays both Tracy's mother and a racist male TV station owner. A later example, *Colma* (2006), is an integrated musical about a new generation in the sleepy San Francisco suburb (famous for its cemeteries!), focusing on a gay Filipino boy (H.P. Mendoza, who wrote the screenplay and score), his straight Filipino gal pal (L.A. Renigen), and his straight Latino buddy (Jake Moreno).

The breadth of viewpoints in independent cinema during this moment reflected a growing emphasis on multiculturalism across much of US culture during the 1990s. Ongoing growth in the national economy created jobs and raised incomes for most of the population, and President Bill Clinton celebrated inclusivity and diversity as one of the country's great strengths. Diane Negra points out that multiculturalism became so valued during this era that celebrations of ethnic heritage within otherwise "white" culture (Irish, Italian, etc.) grew more pronounced.[13] A famous line of dialogue from the British backstager about the life of a fictional Irish rhythm-and-blues band, *The Commitments* (1991), encapsulates such a sentiment (albeit in a problematized fashion). Attempting to forge a bond between the bandmates by connecting being working-class Irish to African American soul music, the band's manager instructs them to chant, "Say it once and say it loud—I'm black and I'm proud!"[14]

Even Disney's animated musicals began to show the effects of multiculturalism. *Aladdin* contains the studio's first Arabian princess, Jasmine—followed by the Native American *Pocahontas* and the Chinese *Mulan*. The legend of Mulan—a woman who disguises herself as a man in order to become a soldier—also plays with gender complexity in ways familiar to New Queer Cinema. A number of queer artists—composers, animators, voice talent—contributed to Disney animation during this period, most importantly lyricist/producer Howard Ashman, who died from complications tied to AIDS in 1991. The camp quotient and other slightly veiled queer elements in Disney animation became part of the formula for attracting adult audiences to these films.

One of the recurring themes in Disney animation since the 1930s worked well for the multicultural 1990s: championing the outsider. *Dumbo* (1941) functions as one of a number of examples: the little elephant who is made fun of for his oversized ears, until he and everyone else learns that those ears make him able to fly. This new cycle more often emphasizes the outsider status of the protagonists (often showing the characters wishing they could be someone else), and the villains are those who judge them as inferior, odd, or monstrous. The films Ashman wrote (*The Little Mermaid, Beauty and the Beast, Aladdin*) often show the lead characters closeting their true selves, trying to be someone else rather than taking pride in who they are. Happy endings occur when the main character stands up for his or her uniqueness, with the community coming to recognize and celebrate the value of individual difference. The central ballad of *The Hunchback of Notre Dame* proclaims this tenet overtly: "God Help the Outcasts."[15]

Audiences of color, who felt their histories and cultures were being exploited and incorrectly portrayed by the studio, did not always welcome Disney's efforts, though. A strong protest by Arab Americans, for example, led to one minor revision of a song lyric in *Aladdin* when it was released on home video.[16] The studio attempted to forestall further complaints by publicizing heavily its consultation with members of minoritized communities in preparation for various projects.[17] Women also criticized Disney's traditional depiction of sweet, pretty, young damsels longing for nothing more than marriage to a prince. Likely in reaction, screenwriter Linda Woolverton created a more assertive female lead character for *Beauty and the Beast*, and female protagonists such as Pocahontas and Mulan became more athletic and in pursuit of more than a husband.

Such celebration of multiculturalism gradually encouraged the major studios to take chances on films with non-white protagonists. Whitney Houston starred in *The Bodyguard* (1992), a property originally conceived for Barbra Streisand. Warner Bros. introduced many in the United States to Spanish film star Antonio Banderas in *The Mambo Kings* (1993), a backstager about Cuban musician brothers immigrating to the United States in the 1950s. Disney's Touchstone Pictures released a biopic of rock legends Ike and Tina Turner, *What's Love Got to Do with It* (1993), the first film to garner nominations for African Americans in both Best Actor (Laurence Fishburne) and Best Actress (Angela Bassett).

American audiences also began to get opportunities to see how motion pictures from other parts of the globe used music and dance during the 1990s. "Bollywood" film, India's popular cinema, began making inroads in US markets, giving Indian communities access to such films and exposing non-Indian customers to the elaborate spectacular musicals sequences that occurred in almost every film, whether it be a romantic comedy, an action adventure, a historical epic, or anything else. The previously mentioned *The Commitments* presaged a trend in British filmmaking showing down-and-out members of the working class using music and dance as a way to overcome their circumstances: *Brassed Off* (1996), *The Full Monty* (1997), *Billy Elliott* (2000). Often these British films focused on the reclaiming of a new form of masculine pride in a new "service economy," but *Little Voice* (1998) centered on a shy and disparaged young woman finding fulfillment and empowerment through her singing abilities. Australia also seemed to be exploding with musical energy with films like *Strictly Ballroom* (1992) and *The Adventures of Priscilla, Queen of the Desert* (1994).

As the millennium came to a close, a number of highly regarded directors took on the challenge of making a musical: Woody Allen's *Everyone Says I Love You* (1996), Lars von Trier's *Dancer in the Dark* (2000), Kenneth Branagh's *Love's Labour's Lost* (2000). Baz Luhrmann, the director of *Strictly Ballroom*, worked with 20th Century-Fox to bring his own vision for a full-throttle live-action musical to the screen. The resultant *Moulin Rouge!* (2001) is absolutely unashamed and unapologetic in being a musical, almost confronting the audience with its stylization and outbursts of song and dance—beginning with a conductor appearing at the bottom of the screen to conduct an unseen orchestra (supposedly "in the pit") in the Fox fanfare as the curtains open, and then segueing into a flourish of "The Sound of Music." Like the Disney animation renaissance, the first half of the film uses over-the-top spectacle and camp humor, thus approving of and inviting incredulous laughter from the viewer. Interviews with the cast and crew indicate that they themselves had trouble keeping from laughing while filming Jim Broadbent and Richard Roxburgh's hilarious rendition of Madonna's "Like a Virgin."[18] The second half then moves into very operatic melodrama, including a climactic performance referencing Bollywood cinema (including the song "Chamma Chamma" from *China Gate* [1998]) (Figure 12.3). The film was Fox's big summer release, and

Figure 12.3 Ewan McGregor and Nicole Kidman declare their love amid the spectacle of a Bollywood-influence production number in *Moulin Rouge!* (2001), spurring renewed live-action musical film production. Snapshot taken from: Moulin Rouge! (2001).

became the first live-action musical to be nominated for the Best Picture Oscar since *All That Jazz* (1979).

In the wake of Luhrmann's success, Miramax (an independent company that Disney acquired in 1993) gave the go-ahead to adapt the 1975 Broadway hit *Chicago*. Its successful release in the Christmas season of 2002 and Oscar for Best Picture indicated to many that a corner had been turned.[19] Soon, a large backlog of Broadway musicals were finally turned into motion pictures: *Phantom of the Opera* (2004), *The Producers* (2005), *Rent* (2005), *Dreamgirls* (2006), *Hairspray* (2007), *Sweeney Todd* (2007), *Mamma Mia!* (2008), *Nine* (2009), *Rock of Ages* (2012), *Les Misérables* (2012), *Jersey Boys* (2014), *Into the Woods* (2014), and *The Last 5 Years* (2014). Biographies of musicians also started appearing: *De-Lovely* (2004, about Cole Porter), as well as *Beyond the Sea* (2004, about Bobby Darrin), *Ray* (2004, about Ray Charles), *Walk the Line* (2005, about Johnny Cash), *La Vie en Rose* (2007, about Edith Piaf), and (more recently) *Get On Up* (2014, about James Brown), *I Saw the Light* (2016, about Hank Williams), and *Miles Ahead* (2016, about Miles Davis). Many of these films won or were nominated for major awards, particularly for the performers. Contrary to common belief within Hollywood that musicals rarely did well in foreign markets, a number of these titles (*Moulin Rouge!*, *Mamma Mia!*, *Dreamgirls*, *Sweeney Todd*) actually did better overseas than in the United States.[20]

Alongside these prestige projects came a spate of smaller-budgeted dance films. *Save the Last Dance* (2001) actually hit theatres before *Moulin Rouge!*, and its success spurred a flurry of others aimed at youth audiences: *Honey* (2003), *You Got Served* (2004), *Take the Lead* (2006), *How She Move* (2007), *Stomp the Yard* (2007), *StreetDance* (2010), *Go for It!* (2011), *StreetDance 2*

(2012), and *Make Your Move* (2013). As might be expected, Disney put its hand into this development too, taking the success of *Step Up* (2006) and turning it into a reliably profitable franchise (with further entries in 2008, 2010, 2012 and 2014).[21] Other films moved them into other areas of music or choreography, such as marching bands (*Drumline* [2002]), and university *a capella* singing (*Pitch Perfect* [2012] and its sequel [2015]). An early, largely forgotten entry, *Get Over It* (2001), dealt with a varsity basketball jock deciding to audition for the high school musical to be near the girl who just broke up with him. Films about rap, either fictional or biographical, got produced as well. *8 Mile* (2002), *Hustle & Flow* (2005), *Get Rich or Die Tryin'* (2005), *Notorious* (2009), and *Straight Outta Compton* (2015) may not have felt like musicals to most audiences, but all of them (perhaps surprisingly) follow the well-worn patterns of the backstager.

Parodies of these subgenres indicated the growing strength of the musical. *Walk Hard: The Dewey Cox Story* (2007) poked fun at the new rash of musical biopics, while the Wayans Brothers consortium took aim at *Dance Flick* (2009). An Oscar category for Best Musical was even discussed. In 2000, the Academy created rules for the category, and that an award would be presented if five or more films qualified. Yet, in doing so, the Academy entered into the fray about what was considered to be a musical film. The bylaws for the category assert that films must contain at least five original songs by the same songwriting team, and that they be not only "substantively rendered, clearly audible (and) intelligible" but also "further the storyline."[22] Under this definition, only films with integrated numbers would be considered, leaving backstagers and biopics automatically out of the running. The emphasis on songs also severely limited the chances for dance films to be considered. Lastly, in titling the category as Best *Original* Musical, all adaptations of theatrical musicals were also eliminated from consideration. Even with all of these hurdles, four films managed to fit the prescriptions in 2004: the Disney animated film *Home on the Range*; *Team America: World Police* from *South Park* creators Trey Parker and Matt Stone; the French film *The Chorus*; and a low-budget independent film about real estate called *Open House*. When Dan Mirvish, the director of *Open House* (and one of the founders of the Slamdance Film Festival), learned about the nascent Oscar category, he hustled funds to put together a second musical film titled *Big in Germany*, and got it screened in the Los Angeles area just under the wire in order to achieve the five needed contenders. The Academy's Board of Governors ultimately decided against holding the category that year, and revised the rules so that currently nine or more films need to be eligible before the category can be opened.[23]

This growth of live-action musical (or "musical-ish") motion pictures during this period might seem to fly in the face of larger historical events. While *Moulin Rouge!* was still playing in theatres, the horrific events of September 11, 2001 substantially shifted the consciousness of the United States and the rest of the world. Many of the musicals that have followed express a bleak outlook. Even *Moulin Rouge!*, for all of its campy outrageousness, ends on a somber, elegiac note. *Chicago* examines celebrity murderers with black humor. A sizeable amount of the adapted Broadway properties have dark elements, such as *Phantom of the Opera, Dreamgirls, Rent, Nine,* and the overtly titled *Les Misérables.* It is perhaps unsurprising that, in this zeitgeist, Stephen Sondheim's *Sweeney Todd* and *Into the Woods* finally made it to the big screen. A number of the musical biopics also wallow in despair and trauma. One could find such darkness in many of the musicals of the 1970s (as discussed in Chapter 10), but the post-9/11 musicals are usually not as self-reflexive as those earlier films. Although some of the more recent films do deal with show business, they do not prod the viewer to reflect on the traditions of the genre itself as much as films like *New York, New York* (1977), *All That Jazz* (1979), and *Pennies from Heaven* (1981) do. Director Rob Marshall, for example, convinced producers to make a film version of *Chicago* by describing how he would turn all of the self-reflexive aspects that are in the original stage version into fantasy sequences in the minds of the characters.[24]

Adding to the somberness, several musicals offer sympathy or greater understanding for characters that would otherwise be considered evil or villainous. The Phantom of the Opera and Sweeney Todd are both crazed murderers, for example. One can see a version of this even in the Disney animated musicals. The Beast in *Beauty and the Beast,* Quasimodo in *The Hunchback of Notre Dame,* and Elsa in *Frozen* are regarded as monsters by other characters, but the audience is invited to care for them. Even outright villains get to have their own numbers in these cartoons, moments for them to express *their* dreams and longings. On one hand, this trend can be seen as an attempt to encourage understanding across cultures rather than mindless hatred and fear of others in a post-9/11 world. On the other hand, arguing that a person's violent or vindictive behavior needs to be understood in context approximates the rationalizations and justification of actions taken by the United States (imprisonment without charge; "enhanced-interrogation" techniques; massive surveillance strategies) in the wake of 9/11.

Granted, not every single post-9/11 musical is filled with melancholy and cynicism. Films such as *Hairspray* and *Mamma Mia!* are bright and buoyant, for example. Also, perhaps surprisingly in the face of a rise in xenophobia in the United States in the years since 9/11, a number of these films still celebrate a multiculturalist outlook. Supporting cultural diversity remains a smart box-office strategy in attracting multiple consumer groups to the box office. A number of dance films, for example, have the central boy and girl come from different cultural identities, and thus different styles of music and dance—usually one having classical dance training, and one learning moves from the street. *Save the Last Dance* (2001) helped popularize this strain—with Julia Stiles as the white ballet dancer and Sean Patrick Thomas as the black hip-hop

Figure 12.4 Julia Stiles' ballet students learns some street moves from Sean Patrick Thomas in *Save the Last Dance* (2001), presaging a slew of similar "dance movies." Snapshot taken from: Save the Last Dance (2001).

dancer (Figure 12.4). They come together as partners in dance and in romance when they share and appreciate each other's talents. The tagline for the film's marketing was "The only person you need to be is yourself." While not *always* depicting racial or ethnic antagonism, the need to simultaneously support unique abilities and yet blend as a team remains constant in these pictures.

A key group that is still thought to not be attracted to musicals, though, is straight white males, and so various means have been used to draw their interest. A number of the larger productions, for example, still offer a straight white male at the center of their narratives, including *Moulin Rouge!* Many of the films featuring ambitious and independent female lead characters also manage to show off their bodies in sexually suggestive clothing and choreography, including *Chicago* and most dance films.[25] On the other hand, during the 2010s, some in the industry began to focus more on female consumers. Musicals remained strongly associated with female audiences, and dance flicks or star vehicles like Christina Aguilera's *Burlesque* (2010) were strongly marketed towards them. Disney hired Linda Woolverton and the Latino husband-and-wife songwriting team Robert Lopez and Kristen Anderson-Lopez to craft *Frozen*, an adaptation of queer fairy-tale author Hans Christian Andersen's "The Snow Queen," into a story about the bond between sisters rather than the traditional tale of a princess longing for her Prince Charming. The story is, by design, filled with dread of an approaching endless winter, but offers hope and happiness nonetheless, and became the most successful film of 2013. Perhaps precisely because of the trauma caused by 9/11 and the new era of global terror, (some) audiences seem to find solace and escape in musicals—much as the genre did for audiences during the Depression and World War II.

Don't Stop Believin': The Musical on Television and Beyond

One of the reasons why industry pundits have considered abandoning pursuit of the 18–25 year old straight male demographic recently has been because that audience segment increasingly prefers video gaming over theatrical motion pictures. The rise of video games and other forms of media entertainment in recent years has impacted the musical genre in a number of other ways as well, and I conclude this history with an examination of some of these, and their implications for the future.

While live-action big-screen musicals sputtered to find their way during the 1990s, such was not the case on the small screen. Filmed versions of live performances of Sondheim's work were aired on PBS during the 1980s and 1990s, for example. *Great Performances* presented *Follies in Concert* (1985), and *American Playhouse* showed *Sunday in the Park with George* (1986) and *Into the Woods* (1991). The 1990s saw a resurgence of musicals on the major networks in an attempt to deal with the continued growing competition of original programming on cable stations. CBS broadcast a new production of *Gypsy*, starring Bette Midler, during the Christmas season of 1993. Its success led to other TV versions of Broadway classics, including *Bye Bye Birdie* (1995) and *South Pacific* (2001). Songwriter Jerry Herman even wrote a new musical for television, *Mrs. Santa Claus* (1995), starring Angela Lansbury. Disney stuck its hand in here as well, programming a remake of Rodgers and Hammerstein's *Cinderella* as part of its weekly *Wonderful World of Disney* anthology program in 1996. Disney followed up the popularity of *Cinderella* with a new production of *Annie* the following year, and *The Music Man* in 2003. *Cinderella* and *Annie* both exemplified the multicultural moment in their casting. *Cinderella* was a pet project of Whitney Houston, who plays the Fairy Godmother, with Brandy as Cinderella, Filipino Paolo Montalban as the Prince, and "color-blind" casting in all of the other parts. Girls of various racial/ethnic identities play orphans in *Annie*, which also presents a multiracial romance between Daddy Warbucks (Victor Garber) and his assistant (Audra McDonald).

The participation of people like Lansbury, Garber, and McDonald indicates how these projects tapped Broadway's talent pool. In addition, these television productions became a training ground for talent interested in reviving the film musical. Neil Meron and Craig Zadan, arguably the Arthur Freeds of this period, produced many of these programs: *Gypsy*; *Cinderella*; *Annie*; *The Music Man*; as well as a two-part biopic, *Life with Judy Garland: Me and My Shadows* (2001), which included re-creations of some of Garland's most iconic numbers.

They used television (and the support from Disney) to re-create the conservatory atmosphere of the classical studio system, training young talent on how to choreograph, direct, and shoot musicals for the camera, most prominently Rob Marshall. Marshall garnered attention choreographing *Mrs. Santa Claus* and *Cinderella*, and moved into directing as well as choreographing *Annie*. These efforts laid the groundwork for *Chicago*, which Meron and Zadan produced and Marshall directed. Meron and Zadan then produced the big-screen version of the Broadway musical *Hairspray*, and a remake of *Footloose* (the original being Zadan's first credit as producer back in 1984). Marshall is the closest thing to a film musical auteur since Bob Fosse, going on to direct *Nine* and *Into the Woods*. Meron and Zadan also had a hand in the career of Bill Condon, who wrote the screenplay for *Chicago*, before directing *Dreamgirls*.

The interest in producing TV-movie musicals ebbed in the mid-2000s, possibly as these artists moved to the big screen, but the musical genre continued to loom over American television. Musical numbers started proliferating within ongoing television series during this period. Early examples of this trend can be found in a number of animated TV shows. Perhaps following the belief that audiences felt more comfortable with cartoon characters breaking into song, programs like *The Simpsons* (1989–), *South Park* (1997–), and *Family Guy* (1999–2003; 2005–) regularly included musical sequences. Unlike Disney's animated features, though, these series were aimed more squarely at adult viewers, as reflected in musical numbers rhapsodizing about outrageous topics, such as *Family Guy* rewriting the lyrics to "Me Ol' Bamboo" from *Chitty Chitty Bang Bang* (1968) into "Everything Goes Better with a Bag of Weed." These series also poked fun at the surreal nature of the musical genre itself, such as *The Simpsons'* musical version of *A Streetcar Named Desire*. Sometimes both things are accomplished at the same time, such as *South Park*'s sendup of Christmas musical TV specials: "Mr. Hanky's Christmas Classics," hosted by a magical talking (and singing) piece of excrement.

As the 2000s began, live-action series started including musical numbers as well. "Musical episodes" were produced for *Scrubs* (2001–2010), *House M.D.* (2004–2012), *Grey's Anatomy* (2005–), *Bones* (2005–), *Psych* (2006–2014), and others. The characters from these series are put into an integrated musical format for one special (and usually highly promoted) episode. Thus, these shows take advantage of the structure of episodic television to create but isolate a "musical moment" similar to the spate of motion pictures that erupt into one number but are otherwise non-musical. These shows also share the cynical humor towards the genre that runs through this era—regarding the eruption into song and dance as amusing. The proliferation of musical episodes implies that both the artists and the audiences find delight in the form, but such pleasure is disavowed through isolation and dismissive laughter. Perhaps the musical episode "Once More, with Feeling" from *Buffy the Vampire Slayer* (1997–2003) is the most famous of these episodes because it breaks this pattern to a degree. As a series dealing with the supernatural, a demon's spell causes the characters to break into musical numbers. While the episode does find humor in everyone suddenly singing (with extras in the background rhapsodizing about getting out laundry stains or trying to get out of a traffic ticket), ultimately the musical sequences gain in dramatic force as the characters are compelled to express deep emotions they have been repressing.[26]

Song and dance also found its way into "reality programming," a format which exploded as the new millennium began. Reality TV producers reworked the "dance party" and variety show formats popular in the pre-music video era of American television by adding a competitive element. Performers are now contestants, as judges and viewers rate each individual's musical talent, ultimately to crown a champion. Examples of such programming include *American Idol* (2002–2016), *Dancing with the Stars* (2005–), *So You Think You Can Dance* (2005–), *America's Got Talent* (2006–), *The X Factor* (2011–2013), and *The Voice* (2011–). In inviting audiences to watch (and vote), these competitions may reflect the less congenial atmosphere of post-9/11 society. Rather than bringing people together, performers (and their supporters) vie against each other. The programs often display a variety of types of song or dance (hip-hop dance and ballet; country and western and rhythm and blues), but in opposition to each other. The enormous impact of *American Idol* suggested that each season was a contest to decide which vocalist (and the style of music they sang) would win as the "most" or "best" version of American music. (Ironically, many of these shows are US versions of British franchises.)

On the other hand, some detractors to these talent contests accused the programs of forcing participants into one particular style of performing—to follow the rigid demands of competitive ballroom dancing on *Dancing with the Stars*, for example, or fit into the confines of contemporary pop vocals on *American Idol*. Many of these programs *do* emphasize a mainstream version of pop music which, by definition, potentially attracts the largest audience. Contemporary pop (a smoothed out blend of electronica, hip-hop, and rhythm and blues, with maybe a bit of folk or grunge added) also appeals strongly to teenagers and young adults, who are regarded as the most desirable viewers to television advertisers.

In the mid-1990s, as boy bands and young female pop divas prepared to overtake the independent grunge scene, Disney had the potential to lead the way again. The Disney Channel aired *The All New Mickey Mouse Club* (1989–1994) featuring a number of young performers who would soon become major pop stars, including Britney Spears, Christina Aguilera, and Justin Timberlake. While Disney cast them for the series, the company did not put them under exclusive contract, as it had done with talent like Annette Funicello in the late 1950s. Thus, Disney had no participation (and no profit) from the hugely successful careers that each of them had after the show ended. In the ensuing years, Disney actively searched for, groomed, and *held onto* young performers with breakout potential as pop music idols: Miley Cyrus, Demi Lovato, Selena Gomez, the Jonas Brothers. Television programs helped build their stardom, which translated into hit records (through Disney's Hollywood Records), sold-out concert tours, and tons of merchandising. A relatively reliable formula developed of always having a new promotable youngster in the pipeline ready to step in when the current star grew too old (and usually ready to break out of the squeaky-clean demands of the Disney brand). In addition to developing individual teen idols, Disney's pop factory created the phenomenally successful *High School Musical* franchise. The initial made-for-TV film aired on the Disney Channel in 2006, to astounding ratings, heavy DVD sales, and a top-selling soundtrack album. Such success led to a TV-movie sequel in 2007, and a theatrical release of a third chapter in 2008, as well as DVD sing-along versions, a concert tour, an ice show, a video game, and a stage play for actual high school drama clubs to produce.[27]

Whether consciously or not, *High School Musical* borrows much of its premise from *Get Over It*: a "jock" and a "braniac" bond over their love of singing, particularly singing together. *High School Musical* adds more of the clique in-fighting common to American high school life, with the athletes, the smart students, and the theatre kids antagonizing each other. Typical of this era, the ethnically and culturally diverse teens each struggle with feeling like outsiders. Typical of Disney, though, subcultural difference is smoothed out and kept "family-friendly"—no deep discussion of racial prejudice happens, and there are only hints that any characters may be queer.[28] Resolution occurs when everyone accepts everyone else's individuality. "Stick to the Status Quo," from the first movie, shows the rest of the student body reacting to the two leads openly auditioning for the school musical by admitting their secret passions: the athlete who loves to bake; the smart girl who loves to pop and lock; the stoner who plays the cello. Steven Cohan's points out how the franchise celebrates "embracing one's difference through musical theatre to achieve a much fuller, more truthful expression of identity and desire."[29] At the end, everyone is in the gym celebrating their uniqueness *as a group* (and the cast faces out at the audience while dancing, so that viewers at home can learn the steps and join in): "We're All in This Together."

Other Disney Channel original movie musicals tried to recapture the "lightning-in-a-bottle" success of *High School Musical*, including *Camp Rock* (2008, a somewhat updated version of Rooney-and-Garland backstagers) and *Teen Beach Movie* (2013, a conscious pastiche of the beach party movies that starred Annette Funicello). The most obvious heir to *High School Musical*, though, was the non-Disney series *Glee* (2009–2015), a fanciful look at high school glee club competitions. In its first season, *Glee* was a cultural phenomenon, producing multiple hit soundtracks as each weekly episode added more recordings to release. *Glee* is a fictional narrative musical series, rather than a reality TV show competition, a variety program, or a series with a "one-off" musical

Figure 12.5 Chris Colfer, Amber Riley, Jenna Ushkowitz, Lea Michele, and Cory Monteith (left to right) proudly power through "Don't Stop Believin'" in the pilot episode of the TV series *Glee* (2009). Snapshot taken from: Glee (2009).

episode. In its wake have come a number of others: *Nashville* (2012–), *Smash* (2012–2013, produced by Meron and Zadan), *Empire* (2015–), *Galavant* (2015–2016, produced by Disney, with songs by Alan Menken), *Crazy Ex-Girlfriend* (2015–). Many of these programs are backstagers—characters working in the music industry or in theatre—and the songs performed are done within a (relatively) realistic context. While often flaunting believability in the amount of production design and rehearsal needed for the level of performances presented, *Glee* offers its numbers usually as part of the glee club's rehearsals or competitions (Figure 12.5). Yet, on some occasions, *Glee* includes integrated musical sequences, and *Galavant* and *Crazy Ex-Girlfriend* both predominantly integrate their numbers. *Smash* is a backstager, but the Broadway show being assembled in the series is presented as an integrated musical about Marilyn Monroe.[30] The ongoing narratives of all of these programs leads to greater character complexity. Like other texts mentioned above, characters once considered villains get their own numbers, and empathy gets spread across multiple levels.

The remarkable growth of musical series on television was joined in the mid-2010s by a return to large-scale TV-event adaptations of classic Broadway musicals. NBC has led the way, beginning with a version of *The Sound of Music* during the Christmas season of 2013, produced by Meron and Zadan. Its huge ratings began a new holiday tradition of such productions, with Meron and Zadan working with NBC to put on *Peter Pan* in 2014 and *The Wiz* in 2015. Fox entered into the race as well with a production of *Grease* (2016). Unlike the TV musicals of the mid-1990s, this new cycle of adaptations are performed live. The decision to return to live broadcast programming is not simply nostalgia for television's Golden Age, but also a strategy to lure people away from other media. While *Gypsy* and *Cinderella* tried to compete with cable television, *The Sound of Music* was done to compete with the growing popularity of the internet and social media.

By the 2010s, internet transfer speeds had increased, making it possible to send and receive audio and video files, and to stream media wirelessly through laptop computers, smart phones, and digital tablets. People increasingly watched media via these devices rather than at movie theatres or on conventional television. At first, only small amounts of data could be handled, so the first versions of music-oriented media distributed on the web were either music videos or skits that included some form of musical performance (like "Sunday Afternoon" and "Dick in a Box," which were originally made for NBC's *Saturday Night Live*). Soon, though, it became possible to present full TV episodes or feature films ... or make them! Steven Cohan surmised in the wake of the success of the *High School Musical* franchise and *Glee* that "today's world of convergent electronic media home video—whether cablecast, streamed via the Internet, or played back on DVD—will be crucial in grounding the exhibition of film musicals for a contemporary audience whose relation to the cinema multiplex is not their only means of accessing entertainment forms."[31] What he did not realize (writing in 2010) was that social and streaming media would not only become increasingly the mode of exhibiting musicals, but also a growing space for production of musicals.

The television industry inadvertently created a situation that led to the creation of the first notable musical made specifically for the web. During a television writers' strike in 2008 over residuals for cable and home video, Joss Whedon (creator of *Buffy the Vampire Slayer*) got together with other idling artists to create *Dr. Horrible's Sing-Along Blog*. Spanning three fifteen-minute episodes, *Dr. Horrible* takes advantage of the internet's traditional short format to tell its story. Following patterns already discussed above, the title character (Neil Patrick Harris) aspires to super-villain status, yet the viewer is encouraged to sympathize with him. Also similar is how the opening episode plays the situation and the use of musical numbers for laughs, but the end of the final episode is remarkably dramatic and downbeat, as he achieves his goal via the death of the woman he secretly loves. *Dr. Horrible* was distributed free for a certain time, but then made available only through purchase by download or through conventional DVD (and the soundtrack was also made available on iTunes). Neither television nor theatrical film were involved.

In having the lead character consistently speak towards the camera, *Dr. Horrible* creates a fictional version of an internet video-blog, a format that proliferated online because the average person increasingly had access to equipment and software to create and distribute his or her own content. If the dividing line between villain and hero was getting muddied, so was the boundary between creator and audience. A number of websites became popular by providing the means to share content with others. Artists did not need to sign contracts with a Hollywood film studio, or get their program picked up by a major television network. MySpace, which had originally been an all-purpose social media site, transformed into a place for musicians to share their original music. YouTube caused even more impact as a space for sharing video content, with individuals creating their own "channels" to which others could subscribe. Other social media sites and applications (Facebook, Instagram, Twitter, Pinterest, Vine) have become platforms for individuals all over the world to produce and exhibit their own material (albeit shaped by the contours of the site or app). Inevitably, a number use the opportunity to promote themselves as budding artists, resulting in a variety of viral videos of original songs/songwriters, and helping make stars out of Justin Bieber, Ariana Grande, and Darren Criss.

Before getting cast in *Glee*, Criss not only had his own YouTube channel but was also involved in Team StarKid, a group from the University of Michigan that created their own original stage musicals. Their first major production, the parodic *A Very Potter Musical* (2009), was filmed and became a viral online sensation. Two "Harry Potter" sequels were produced and also made available, as well as musical parodies of Batman and *Star Wars*, and musicals based on original material. In 2013, they produced *Twisted*, a satiric retelling of Disney's *Aladdin* from the point of view of the evil wazir, Jafar. Team StarKid successfully used the internet fundraising site Kickstarter to solicit funds for this production, raising the requested amount within two hours.[32]

The above examples aim at professional quality in order to build careers in the various entertainment industries. On the other hand, a number of people have created musical content for the sheer enjoyment of putting stuff out there for others to see. Reflecting the love of cynical humor in this era, the internet is awash with amateur parodies of professionally produced music videos. Other videos show groups of people doing choreography to the latest overplayed hit pop tune, such as Katy Perry's "California Gurls," Carly Rae Jepsen's "Call Me Maybe," or Mark Ronson and Bruno Mars' "Uptown Funk."

These amateur video performances often seem to show the average person not trying to make it in show business but trying to turn their life (and the lives of others) into a musical—if even for a moment. People with access to Auto-Tune software (which can alter vocal and instrumental pitch) remix local news interviews into musical numbers (albeit usually exploiting the speech patterns of lower-income or racially marginalized people). Videos of flash mob choreography or of elaborate proposals of marriage turn public spaces and real world situations into a realm of musical fantasy not only for the people performing but for those present who were not in on the planning. Other videos simply show people singing in the car or dancing in the living room—recording the feeling of letting go, singing out, or "dancing like no one's looking" ... and then connecting with others by sharing that sense of freedom. Even certain video games allow the average person to become a musical performer: "Dance Dance Revolution" or "Guitar Hero."

Are such instances musicals? They certainly hark back to what have been traditionally considered musicals, still negotiating the same balance between liberation and structure, between the individual and the community, but refashioned for new needs, new technologies, and new forms of entertainment. Some may continue to say the musical is dying or dead. Such critics continue to complain that modern-day audiences are not willing to suspend disbelief when characters break out into spontaneous song. Yet, those critics are themselves unwilling to accept anything that does *not* have characters breaking into spontaneous song as a musical. In certain ways, the musical is flourishing— and the future awaits. All one has to do is open up to the possibilities in all their forms. As it is written in the final moments of *Sweet Charity* (1969): "And they lived *hopefully* ever after ..."

Notes

1 Among those covering this era, see Ron Grover, *The Disney Touch: How a Daring Management Team Revived an Entertainment Empire* (Homewood: Business One Irwin, 1991); Joe Flower, *Prince of the Magic Kingdom: Michael Eisner and the Re-Making of Disney* (New York: John Wiley & Sons, 1991); and James B. Stewart, *Disney War* (New York: Simon & Schuster, 2005).

2 "Under the Sea" from *The Little Mermaid*; "Beauty and the Beast" from *Beauty and the Beast*; "A Whole New World" from *Aladdin*; "Can You Feel the Love Tonight?" from *The Lion King*; "Colors of the Wind" from *Pocahontas*; "I'll Be in Your Heart" from *Tarzan*; plus, from live-action musicals that Disney released, "Sooner or Later" from *Dick Tracy* (1990) and "You Must Love Me" from *Evita* (1996).

3 Of course, Warner Bros. had had a renowned animation department in the past, the home of Bugs Bunny and his menagerie of friends. Yet, the studio had closed down that department in the mid-1960s. Its re-entry into animation *was* tied to its history, with Bugs, Daffy, and the rest of the crew cavorting with basketball legend Michael Jordan in *Space Jam* (1996), a non-musical film.

4 For example, David Rooney and Jonathan Bing, "Can Hollywood Carry a Tune? Despite Success of 'Chicago', Studios Still Leery of Musicals," *Variety* (March 10–16, 2003), 51, quotes producer Harvey Weinstein that it is "conventional wisdom" that teenage boys in particular "would watch volleyball on TV before they'd see musicals for free."

5   Janet Maslin, "'Beauty and the Beast' Updated in Form and Content," *New York Times* (November 13, 1991).

6   Such failures include *Atlantis: The Lost Empire* (2001), *Treasure Planet* (2002), and *Home on the Range* (2004). The last of these did include songs by Alan Menken and Glenn Slater.

7   For example, Steve Nelson, "Broadway and the Beast: Disney Comes to Times Square," *Drama Review* 39:2 (1995), 71–85; Maurya Wickstrom, "Commodities, Mimesis, and *The Lion King*: Retail Theatre for the 1990s," *Theatre Journal* 51 (1999), 287–298.

8   See Elizabeth L. Wollman, *The Theater Will Rock: A History of the Rock Musical, from Hair to Hedwig* (Ann Arbor: University of Michigan Press, 2009), 120–129, for a rundown of the era of the mega-musical.

9   The film did gain a cult following from pre-teen audiences (particularly girls) through home video, and eventually became an unexpected hit stage musical produced by Disney in 2011. More on musicals and TV and other media in the final section of this chapter.

10 Robert W. Butler, "Anything to Save the Movie: James L. Brooks Dumped the Music, Rewrote the Scenes and Did More Filming for 'I'll Do Anything,'" *Kansas City Star* (February 3, 1994), E1.

11 For example, Joe Neumaier, "The Songs of 'My Best Friend's Wedding,'" *Entertainment Weekly* (July 18, 1997): "The summer's hit date movie is at heart a classic movie musical." Rita Kempley, *Washington Post* (December 10, 1993), refers to *Sister Act 2: Back in the Habit* (1993) and its predecessor as a "comedy-cum-musical."

12 For more analysis on *Zoot Suit*, see Desirée J. Garcia, *The Migration of the Musical Film: From Ethnic Margins to American Mainstream* (New Brunswick: Rutgers University Press, 2014), 170–184.

13 Diane Negra, *The Irish in Us: Irishness, Performativity, and Popular Culture* (Durham: Duke University Press, 2006), 1–19.

14 For a deeper analysis of the implications of this line of dialogue, see Catherine M. Eagan, "Still 'Black' and 'Proud': Irish America and the Racial Politics of Hibernophilia," in Negra, 20–63.

15 For more on this, see Sean Griffin, *Tinker Belles and Evil Queens: The Walt Disney from the Inside Out* (New York: New York University Press, 1999), 143–152.

16 See Jack G. Sheehan, "Arab Caricatures Deface Disney's *Aladdin*," *Los Angeles Times* (December 21, 1992), F5; Casey Kasem and Jay Goldworthy, "No Magic in *Aladdin*'s Offensive Lyrics," *Los Angeles Times* (April 19, 1993), F3; and David J. Fox, "Disney Will Alter Song in *Aladdin*," *Los Angeles Times* (July 19, 1993), F1.

17 Carrie Ricky, "Disney's 'Pocahontas': Is It Fact or Fiction? What Did She Wear? Did She Style Her Hair? Were She and John Smith a Pair?," *Philadelphia*

Inquirer (June 18, 1995), describes the number of Native American consultants that Disney worked with on *Pocahontas*. Stephen Schaefer, "Disney's Newest Heroine Fights Her Own Battles in 'Mulan,'" *Boston Herald* (June 15, 1998), discusses the search for Asian voice actors to play the various roles in *Mulan*, and Jeff Kurtti, *The Art of Mulan* (New York: Hyperion Books, 1998), describes the project's creative team taking a research trip to Beijing.

18 This is in the DVD extras.

19 For example, Rooney and Bing, 1, while still reporting some reticence (as indicated by the article's title), declared that "Hollywood has expressed excitement that the long-dormant musical is ready for a comeback."

20 Steven Cohan, "Introduction: How Do You Solve a Problem Like the Film Musical?," *The Sound of Musicals*, ed. Steven Cohan (London: BFI, 2010), 1.

21 To be fair, Disney's Touchstone picked up the first three films for distribution from Summit Entertainment. The fourth and fifth entries (*Step Up Revolution* [2012] and *Step Up All In* [2014]) have been released without Disney's involvement.

22 Justin Chang, "Tuner Hopefuls Cue Indie Chorus," *Variety* (January 19, 2005), 5, 59.

23 On the 2004 decision, see Timothy M. Gray, "Original Musical Not Playing Oscar's Tune," *Daily Variety* (December 16, 2004), 5. On the current rules for the Original Musical category, see http://www.oscars.org/sites/oscars/files/89aa_rules.pdf

24 Christopher Rawson, "The Starry Cast of 'Chicago' Follows Rob Marshall's Lead in His Big-screen Directing Debut," *Pittsburgh Post-Gazette* (April 21, 2002), describes how Marshall worked with screenwriter Bill Condon to turn the bulk of the musical numbers into the fantasies of protagonist Roxie Hart.

25 Granted, on the other side, men's bodies have become more objectified in dance films as well. Channing Tatum starred in the first *Step Up* film, and has reworked his early career as an exotic dancer into *Magic Mike* (2012) and *Magic Mike XXL* (2015).

26 For more on the ways in which the ongoing narrative design of contemporary American television has impacted its use of the tropes of the film musical genre, see Christopher Culp, "'This Isn't Real, but I Just Wanna Feel': Musicals, Television, and the Queer Ineffable Passage of Time," presented at Society for Cinema and Media Studies Conference, Montreal, 2015.

27 Cohan, "Introduction," 5. Quotes are from Denise Martin, "Smoke & Mirrors: TV Tuner Trills Teens," *Variety* (January 30–February 5, 2006), 9; and Steve Clarke, "'High School Musical' Is New Kid on Europe Block," *Variety* (September 18–24, 2006), 25.

28 Sharpay's brother Ryan (Lucas Gabreel) and nerdy composer Kelsi (Olesya Rulin) ... who are vaguely paired up with each other in *High School Musical* 3.

29 Cohan, "Introduction," 8.

30 During the second season, a competing integrated musical production was shown being workshopped, with lyrics written by different songwriters.

31 Cohan, "Introduction," 12.

32 Natalie Fisher, "StarKid's 'Twisted' Launches Kickstarter, Hits Goal in 2 hours," *hypable* (March 23, 2013) (http://www.hypable.com/starkid-launches-twisted-kickstarter-fans-meet-goal-in-2-hours/). *Holy Musical, B@man!* was produced in 2012, and the *Star Wars* parody, *Ani*, was produced in 2014.

Index

Free and Easy? A Defining History of the American Film Musical Genre, First Edition. Sean Griffin.
© 2018 Sean Griffin. Published 2018 by John Wiley & Sons Ltd.